PASSENGER ARRIVALS

1819-1820

PASSENGER ARRIVALS

1819 — 1820

A Transcript of the List of Passengers
Who Arrived in the United States
from the 1st October, 1819,
to the 30th September,
1820

WITH AN ADDED INDEX

CLEARFIELD

Originally Published As
*Letter from the Secretary of State, with a Transcript
of the List of Passengers Who Arrived in the United States
from the 1st October, 1819, to the 30th September, 1820*
Washington, 1821

Reprinted with added Title-page and Index
Genealogical Publishing Company
Baltimore, 1967

Reprinted with added Half-title, Title-page, and Index
Genealogical Publishing Company
Baltimore, 1971

Reprinted for
Clearfield Company, Inc. by
Genealogical Publishing Co., Inc.
Baltimore, Maryland
1991, 2000

Library of Congress Catalogue Card Number 67-28025
International Standard Book Number: 0-8063-0347-6

Made in the United States of America

LETTER

FROM THE

SECRETARY OF STATE,

WITH A TRANSCRIPT OF

THE LIST OF PASSENGERS

Who arrived in the United States from the 1st October, 1819, to the 30th
September, 1820.

FEBRUARY 18, 1821.
Printed by order of the Senate of the United States.

WASHINGTON:

PRINTED BY GALES & SEATON.

1821.

DEPARTMENT OF STATE,
Washington, 17*th* *February,* 1821.

SIR: I have the honor to transmit to the Senate a transcript of all the Lists of Passengers taken on board ships and vessels in foreign ports and places, which arrived in the United States from the first of October, 1819, to the 30th September, 1820, inclusive, that have been returned to this office by the Collectors of the Customs, in pursuance of the 5th section of the act of 2d March, 1819, "regulating passenger ships and vessels;" by which it appears, that the number of persons of all descriptions, so taken on board ships and vessels arriving in the United States during the period referred to, viz. for the last quarter of 1819, and the three first quarters of 1820, amounts to 10,247.

I have the honor to be, with very great respect,

Sir, your obedt. and very humble servant,

JOHN QUINCY ADAMS.

The President pro tempore of the Senate.

A Register of Passengers arriving in the United States, from the 1st Oct. 1819, to 30th Sept. 1820.

QUARTER ENDING DECEMBER 31, 1819.

Custom House, with the name of the Collector.	Names of Passengers.	Age.	Sex.	Occupation.	Country to which they belong	Country of which they intend to become inhab's	Ship or Vessel, with the name of the Master or Commander.
WISCASSET, Francis Cook	William Galon	41	male	Schoolmaster	G. Britain	Wiscasset	Brig Belisarius from Dublin, I. D. Gove.
	Robert Cooper	22	do	Cabinet maker	do	do	
	Francis Stensford	22	do	Weaver	do	do	
PETERSBURG, Va. Joseph Jones	Thomas Colquhoun	45	do	Merchant	Scotland	Petersburg	The vessel and commander not mentioned.
	Frs. Ann Colquhoun	36	female		Virginia	do	
	Ann Jane Colquhoun	14	do		do	do	
	Mary Colquhoun	12	do		London	do	
	Frs. A. Colquhoun, jr.	11	do		do	do	
	Thos. R. Colquhoun	6	male		do	do	
	Barbary Colquhoun	2	female		do	do	
	Eleanor Ralph	36	do	Spinster			
	Abbey Leeds	17	do	do	Boston	Boston	
	Roderick Colquhoun	16	male	Clerk	Petersburg	Petersburg	
	William S. Simpson	25	do	do	London	do	
	John Lee	19	do	do	do	do	
	Mary Ledrick	22	female	Spinster	do	do	
	Jane M'Kenzie	36	do	do	do.	Richmond	
BEAUFORT, S. C. William Joiner,							No arrival of passengers for the quarter.
DIGHTON, Nath'l Williams	John Ford	unknown	male	Seaman	Spain	Spain	Sloop Golden Age, William C. Greene.
	Pedro Labron	do	do	do	do	do	N. B. The seamen who arrived in the sloop Golden Age were taken from the wreck of the Spanish brig Antony from Matanzas, cast away on the island of Bermudas.
	Martin Bland	do	do	do	do	do	
	Antone Blake	do	do	do	do	do	
	Antone Gariere	do	do	dc	do	do	
	Salvado Fenner	do	do	do	do	do	
	Felix Roberts	do	do	do	do.	do	

LIST of Passengers, &c.—Quarter ending 30th December, 1819.

Custom House with the name of the Collector.	Names of Passengers.	Age.	Sex.	Occupation.	Country to which they belong.	Country of which they intend to become inhab's	Ship or Vessel, with the name of the Master or Commander.
Dighton, Nath'l Williams,	Felix Loret	unknown	male	Seaman	Spain	Spain	
	Gabriel Valloe	do	do	do	do	do	
	Pedro Joon	do	do	do	do	do	
	Christon	do	do	do	do	do	
	Felix Villivar						
Oxford, Jno. Willis,							No arrival of passengers for the quarter.

LIST of Passengers, &c.—Quarter ending March 31, 1820.

Custom House with the name of the Collector.	Names of Passengers.	Age.		Sex.	Occupation.	Country, to which they belong.	Country of which they intend to become inhab's	Ship or Vessel, with the name of the Master or Commander.
New-York, David Gelston,	I. M. Meert	38		male	Merchant	Holland		Brig Hippomenes, Lemuel Bourne.
	Stillman Rinford	24		do	Mariner	Boston, U.S.	Boston, U.S.	Brig Mary, William Maxwell.
	Samuel Hazard	29		do	Merchant	U. States	U. States	Ship Hector, James Gillender.
	Gilbert Fowley	40	4	do	Ship master	do	do	
	Samuel Wright	25	2	do	Merchant	G. Britain	do	
	Thomas Lewis	51	8	do	do	U. States	do	
	John Lyman	19	6	do	Servant	France	do	
	George Codman	27	3	do	Gentleman	U. States	do	
	Luis P. De Luze	26	9	do	Merchant	Neufchatel	do	
	Jer. Van Reanselear	26	5	do	Gentleman	U. States	do	
	Felix Henry	38	3	do	Laborer	G. Britain	G. Britain	
	John Jackson	40	7	do	Merchant	do	U. States	Brig Greyhound, Thomas Beason.
	James Johnson	35		do	do	do	New-York	Brig Chauncy, George W. Grice.
	John Madden	36	5	do	do	U. States	Hayti	
	Lewis Themassen	36		do	Unknown	America	G. Britain	Brig Hamet, Charles Little.
	Charles Larochel	22		do	Merchant	Hayti	do	
	S. I. Seymore	24		do	Servant	G. Britain	U. States	Ship So. Carolina Packet, A. J. Cartwright
	Samuel Baily	17		do	Servant	do	do	
	Charlotte Eastburn	40		female	Lady	U. States	New York	Ship Gleaner, John O. Znill.
	Menton Eastburn	19		male	Gentleman	do	do	
	A. Moulet	28		female	Mechanic	France	do	
	Mrs. Moulet	32		do		do	do	
	Miss Moulet	7		do		do	do	
	Moulet	6				do	do	Brig New Bean, John Cushing
	Moulet	5				do		
	Thomas Hockley	23		male	Merchant	U. States	U. States	
	George Schuverer	18		do	do	do	dc	

LIST of Passengers, &c.—Quarter ending 31st March, 1820.

Custom House, with the name of the Collector.	Names of Passengers.	Age.	Sex.	Occupation.	Country to which they belong.	Country of which they intend to become inhb's.	Ship or Vessel, with the name of the Master or Commander.
	Hugh Chambers	29 5	male	Supercargo	U. States	U. States	Brig New Bean, John Cushing
	Thomas M. Rogers	47 4	do	do	do	do	
	Abraham Sylva	18 2	do	Servant boy	Bengal	do	
	Servant boy					do	
	G. S. M'Nutt	29	do	Mariner	U. States	do	Schooner William, Allen Hullet
	Henry Guthree	32	do	Currier	do	do	
	Lucy Guthree	26	female	None	Scotland	do	
	Eliza Guthree	1 6	do	do	do	do	
	H. Guthree	0 8	do	do	U. States	do	
	John O'Brien, jr.	21	male	Merchant	Spain	do	Brig Hope, Gilbert B. Smith
	Joaquin A. Canes	16	do	do	France	do	
	P. Willero	30	do	do	America	do	Schooner Sisters, Charles Winslow
	J. D. Corey	28	do	do	France	do	
	Bayaud	35	do	do	Spain	do	
	C. Orybeade	25	do	do	England	do	
	Hugh Flachety, Esq.	38	do	do	England	England	Scbr. Charlotte Corday, J. G. Russell
	John Gorman	26		None	U. States	U. States	
	Phebe Hammond	11	female	do	England	do	Ship Hercules, N. Cobb
	Hannah Holland	22	do		do	do	
	Thomas Holland	3	male	Storekeeper	do	do	
	James Burnes	34	do		G. Britain	do	
	Hannah Burnes	33	female		do	do	
	Thomas Burnes	11	male		do	do	
	Deborah Burnes	9	female		do	do	
	Joseph Burnes	6	male		do	do	
	Ann Maria Burnes	4	female		do	do	
	Alfred Burnes	1 6	male		do	do	

Name	Age	No.	Sex	Occupation	Country	Destination	Vessel
Thomas Stukney	28		male	Merchant	G. Britain	U. States	Brig Juliana, Elgit Samson
John Dear	29		do	do	do	do	
Richard Dear	22		do	do	do	do	
John Billing	32		do	do	do	do	
Raphael Romeo	34		do	Merchant	Spain	do	
Vicente Davilo	30		do	Servant	do	do	
Fernando	29		do	Merchant	Denmark	do	
Daniel Crookshank		2	do	Merchant	Martinique	Martinique	Danish sloop Frederick, Samuel Chant
Bagard, Supercargo				do	Ireland	America	Brig La Gratitude, L. Depensier
Rose Dealey	27		female	do	America	do	Schooner Nancy, Ruben Crowly
Peggy Hager	24		do		do	do	
George Dowsee	20	1	male		America	do	
Christian Dowsee	12	1	do		do	do	
	9	3	do		do	do	
John Dennison	64		do	Falconer	Canada	Canada	Ship Ann, R. R. Crocker
John F. Taylor	18		do	do	do	do	
William Corcoran	26		do	Gentleman	Ireland	U. States	
Samuel Meis	60		do	Laborer	England	do	
Mary Ann Bessell	10		female	Spinstress	do	do	
Sarah Bessell	8		do	do	do	do	
William Macoly	25		male	Printer	do	do	
Betsy Campbell	18		female	Spinstress	do	do	
David Curry	29		male	Merchant	U. States	do	Brig Orion, Enoch Wheeler
G. Barter	23		do	do	do	do	
H. I. Revinason	38		do	do	do	do	
Lemuel De Forest	30		do	Stonecutter	do	do	Brig Laura Ann, Robert A. Hubbell
Charles Wallace	26		do	Merchant	do	do	
J. Postrigus	30		do	Shoemaker	Spain	do	
Daniel Donly	26		do	Supercargo	U. States	do	
Samuel Clark	47		do	Stonecutter	do	do	
James Crichton	39		do	Merchant	do	do	Schooner William, Allen Dexter
Geo. Wetherspoon	23		do	do	Scotland	G. Britain	Ship Albion, Jno. Williams
William Lewis	34		do	do	England	do	
Eliza Lewis	35		female	do	do	do	
Thomas Lewis	13		male	Farmer	do	do	
George Brown	42		do	do	do	do	
Abm. Wardel	26		do	do	do	U. States	
James Johnson	27		do	do	do	do	
Robert Hyslop	24		do	do	America	do	Schooner Buffalo, John Ham

LIST of Passengers, &c.—Quarter ending March 31, 1820.

Custom House, with the name of the Collector.	Names of Passengers.	Age.	Sex.	Occupation.	Country to which they belong.	Country of which they intend to become inh'bts.	Ship or Vessel, with the Name of the Master or Commander.
New York. David Gelston	Osias Goodwin, jr.	26	male	Merchant	U. States	U. States	Ship Maria, J. C. Raby.
	Wm. Wallace	33	do	Attorney	G. Britain		Brig Andromache, Elias Fornham.
	Alexander H. Shaw	21	do	Gentleman	do		
	William Duncan	28	do	Merchant	do		
	Morris H. Tache	22	do	do	U. States		
	Cornelius Agnew	21	do	do	Connecticut	do	Brig Helen, William Gold.
	F. C. Bassett	35	do	Mariner	New York.	do	Brig Hammond, James Gifford.
	Samuel Read	47	do	Merchant	France	do	
	M. Roth	40	do	Sec. Legation	do	do	French ship St. Martin, C. De Joly.
	M. Delarue	21	do	Merchant	do		
	M. Chappelle	41	do	Blacksmith	U. States		Brig Helicon, Seth C. Macy.
	Jeremiah Mullony	31	do	Merchant	do	Havana	
	Michael Vincent	42	do		do	Boston	* Died January 29, 1820.
	Hannah Reddins*	20	female				
	Louisa Reddins	7	do				
	John Andrews	23	male	Mariner	America	America	Brig Two Marys, Elisha King.
	Lewis Chatto	22	do	do	Germany	do	
	William Wells	26	do	do	do	do	
	H. K. Smith	47	do	Mechanic	do	do	
	Elizabeth Smith	50	female	Spinstress	do	do	
	Aleda Smith	25	do		do	do	
	Catherine Smith	22	do		do	do	
	Anna Smith	17	do		do	do	
	William Smith	13	male	Mechanic	do	do	
	G. Schultz	52	do	do	do	do	
	Gustavus Schultz	20	do		do	do	
	John L. Buchanan	15	do		do	do	

Name	Age	Sex	Occupation	Country belonging	Country intended	Ship
B. D. Hugo	29	male	Farmer	Germany	America	Ship Hesperus, Archibald M'Corkell.
Solomon Dean	50	do	Laborer	America	do	
James M'Mullen	30	do	do	Ireland	do	
George W. Nealy	30	female	Spinster	do	do	
Mary Hamilton	23	male	Laborer	do	do	
Arch. M'Conoughy	25	do	Trader	do	do	
John M. Dormer	27	female	Milliner	do	do	Ship Telegraph, Hector Coffin.
Mrs. Dormer	24	do	None	do	do	
Margaret Graham	26	male	do	do	do	
James Graham	5	do		Bermuda	do	
Thomas Butterfield	40	do	Mariner	do	Bermuda	Ship Eclipse, David Price.
William Bayman	36	do	do	Ireland	do	
John Gratton	21		Merchant	do	U. States	Ship Erin, William Newcomb.
Steerage						
Briget Manly	40	female	Woman	do	do	
Helen Manly	17	do		do	do	
Jane Manly	15	do		do	do	
Leonora Manly	10	do		do	do	
James Walsh	32	male	Clerk	do	do	
Thomas Higgs	23	do		do	do	
Betsey Hart	42	female	Woman	do	do	
Jno. Boyd	27	male	Baker	Greenock	do	Schooner Rambler, Thomas Hamilton.
Robert Rhodes	26	do	Weaver	G. Britain	do	Ship Richmond, William Rugan.
Charlotte Rhodes	23	female	None	do	do	
Frances Rhodes	1	do	do	do	do	
Joseph Greaves	43	male	Farmer	do	do	
Betsey Greaves	47	female	None	do	do	
Martha Greaves	9	female	do	do	do	
John Greaves	4	male		do	do	
Curtis Burgan	40	do	Farmer	do	do	
David Miller	31	do	do	do	do	
Richard Burk	28	do	Butcher	do	do	
Thomas Beer	35	do	Farmer	do	do	
Hannah Beer	36	female	None	do	do	
Richard Beer	10	male	do	do	do	
Mary Beer	8	female	do	do	do	
Eliza Beer	4	female	do	do	do	
Robert Foss	34	male	Butcher	do	do	

LIST of Passengers, &c.—Quarter ending March 31, 1820.

Custom House with the name of the Collector.	Names of Passengers.	Age.	Sex.	Occupation.	Country to which they belong.	Country of which they intend to become inhab's	Ship or Vessel, with the name of the Master or Commander.
New-York, David Gelston,	Lydia Foss	34	female	None	G. Britain	U. States	Ship Richmond, William Rugan.
	Jno. Foss	7	male	do	do	do	
	Ellen Foss	4	female	do	do	do	
	Joseph Blunt	40	male	Farmer	do	do	
	Sarah Blunt	40	female	None	do	do	
	Sarah Blunt, jr.	19	do	do	do	do	
	Mary Blunt	10	do	do	do	do	
	William Blunt	15	male	do	do	do	
	Phœbe Blunt	13	female	do	do	do	
	Samuel Blunt	12	male	do	do	do	
	Melliant Blunt	11	female	do	do	do	
	Hannah Blunt	10	do	do	do	do	
	Samuel Greves	29	male	Farmer	do	do	
	Sarah Greves	25	female	None	do	do	
	Mary Greves	4	do	do	do	do	
	Mary Beer	60	do	Unknown	do	do	
	Christian Erickson	40	male	Ship master	Philadelphia	do	
	Owen Jones	20	do	Tailor	G. Britain	do	
	Benjamin Blount	1	do	None	do	do	
	Job Blount	2	do	do	do	do	
	Ann Blount	6	female	do	do	do	
	Eliza Blount	4	do	do	do	do	
	Sarah Foss	3	do	do	do	do	
	Elizabeth Foss	1 6	male	do	do	do	
	Henry Beer	3	do	do	do	do	
	Thomas Beer	1 6	do	do	do	do	
	John Greves	1	do	do	do	do	

Name	Age	Sex	Occupation			Ship / Notes
Walter Thompson	36	male	Gentleman	U. States	U. States	Ship Importer, William Lee, jr.
Joseph Warey	30	do	Merchant	do	do	Schooner Cordelia, Reuben Asgur.
Wm. Boardnave	40	do	do	do	do	Schooner Mercator, Jno. R. Taber.
Joseph Pescatora	25	do	Gentleman	Prussia	Prussia	
Daniel Macorer	36	do	Mechanic	Switzerland	U. States	Brig Anna Maria, B. Barenda.
Michael Reiss	26	do	do	do	do	
Thomas Fowler	23	do	Gentleman	U. States	do	Sloop Liberty, Joseph Tyler.
Philies	36	do	do	do	do	
Benjamin Clapp	26	do	do	do	do	Ship Elias Benger, Ozias Ansley.
Wm. D. Thompson	22	do	do	do	do	
Thos. W. Castoley		do	do	G. Britain	do	
Peter Jarnon	55	do	Merchant	France	U. States	Brig Friendship, Nathaniel Gadding.
M. A. Reynolds	35	do	do	America	Denmark	Brig Booer, Thomas Humphries.
F. C. Wermmbrenus	30	do	do	Denmark	New York	
Elijah Farrington	27	do	Chairmaker	America	Havana	
Simon Martines	20	do	Merchant	Havana		
Benith Fernandz	20	do	do	U. States	U. States	Brig Mary, Greenman Geer.
Ichabod Allen	30	do	Mariner	do	do	
Holback	18	do	do	do		
Joseph Lament	36	do	Merchant	do		Ship Parnassor, J. Hitch.
John Ward	26	do	do	do		Brig Margaret, Andrew Hussey.
Edmund Dirluz	22	do	do	do		
John Murley	26	do	do	England		
Samuel Church*	40	do	Cooper	U. States	U. States	Brig Silkworm, Nathaniel Rogers.
James M'Ellie	24	do	Gentleman	G. Britain		Schooner Charlotte Corday, J. C, Russell.
Nathaniel Richey	26	do	do	do		
Robert Welch	25	do	do	do		
Jane Small	24	female	Lady	U. States	U. States	
Sarah Hampton	28	do	do	do		
John Worden	26	male	Gentleman	do		Schooner Andrew Jackson, Nathan Gillet.
Nathaniel Dery	20	do	do	do		Ship Ann Maria, Isaac Waite.
Samuel Rider	40	do	Shoemaker	New York	dc	
Mathew Troop	12	female	None	U. States	do	
Jane Pollard	6	male	do	G. Britain	do	
Marsden Haddock	61	do	do	U. States	do	
Edward Haddock	39	do	do	do	do	
Edward Whitely	21	do	Laborer	do	do	
Obadiah Parritt	24	do	Farmer	do	do	

*Died 6th February.

LIST of Passengers, &c.—Quarter ending March 31, 1820.

Custom House, with the name of the Collector.	Names of Passengers.	Age.	Sex.	Occupation.	Country to which they belong.	Country of which they intend to be-come inhab's	Ship or Vessel, with the Name of the Master or Commander.
New-York, David Gelston	Theodosia Parritt	23	female	None	G. Britain	U. States	
	William Wilson	7	male	Merchant	do	do	
	Thomas Monilaus	40	do	Shop keeper	do	do	
	Mary Monilaus	40	female	None	do	do	
	James Park	17	male	do	do	do	
	Laurence Kcefe	42	do	Farmer	do	do	
	John Cornwall	25	do	Seaman	do	do	
	Gorton Ornborns	42	do	Merchant	do	do	
	William Ridgeway	33	do	Manufacturer	do	do	Ship Courier, Jonathan Eldridge.
	John Wolson	32	do	Merchant	do	do	
	John W. Clarke	30	do	Musician	do	do	
	Cuthbert Landreth	32	do	Laborer	do	do	
	James Robb	34	do	Carpenter	do	do	
	Walter Kitchen	50	do	Weaver	do	do	
	Robert Williams	28	do	Merchant	do	do	
	Andrew Ure	55	do	Gardener	do	do	
	Thomas Wood	18	do	Carpenter	do	do	
	John Wood, jr.	30	do	do	do	do	
	Henry A. Launey	30	do	Laborer	do	do	
	Samuel Grundy	45	do	Gentleman	Not known	do	
	George Keates	28	do	Merchant	G. Britain	do	
	Molly Clark	25	female	do	do	do	
	William Clark	1 6	male	Spinstress	do	do	
	Charles Clark	3	do	None	do	do	
	Andrew Kitchen	34	do	do	do	do	
	Alexander Philips	32	do	Weaver	Germany	Baltimore	Ship Stephania, Miles R. Burkee.
				Merchant			

Name	Age	Sex	Occupation	Native	Destination	Ship
T. Krozer	24	male	Clerk	Germany	Baltimore	
Dauberey Farrel	25	do	Planter	U. States	Kentucky	
Nicholas A. Fromont	42	do	Officer	France	N. Carolina	
William Jones	60	do	Farmer	U. States	New York	British Brig Hibernia, Jno. S. Wattling.
I. Butler	22	do	Pastry cook	England	Albany	
John Brittle	28	do	do	do	do	
Mrs. Hunt	60	female	Spinster	Ireland	New York	
Edward Croswaith	24	male	do	do	W. country	
James Croswaith	22	do	Clerk	do	do	
Wm. H. Clark	34	do	Gentleman	do	do	
T. Daily	27	do	do	do	do	Brig Wilmot, Wm. Hathaway.
Gattike	32	do	Distiller	Holland		
John Naeff	28	do	do	do		Schooner Fanny, Nathaniel Davis.
Nathaniel Mitchell	22	do	Merchant	U. States	U. States	
Felix Bossex	25	do	do	do	do	Ship Chauncy, Donald M'Kay.
Peter W. Snoco	40	do	do	do	do	Brig Ambuscade, Robert Skidmore.
F. Salman	23	do	do	do	do	
S. Marsland	28	do	Mariner	do	do	
D. Penoria	40	do	Merchant	do	do	
Fox Garate	25	do	Mariner	do	do	
L. Arzeno	40	do	Mariner	do	do	
A. Maitine	14	do	Merchant	do	do	
I. Thomas	30	do	Farmer	do	do	
Wm. Rankin	39	dc	Mariner	do	do	
Peter Joseph	30	dc	do	do	do	
Joseph Anthony	30	do	do	do	do	
Francis Sands	28	do	do	do	do	Brig Planter, Samuel Sanderson.
H. N. Manson	30	do	Merchant	Sweden	St. Barts	Brig Seneca, James Clark.
Geo. Chuinger	26	do	do	U. States	U. States	Sloop Olive Branch, Ebenezer Haws.
John Butler	54	do	Seaman	Norfolk	Norfolk	
Henry Wedley	30	do	do	Dartmouth	Dartmouth	
Benjamin Barnard	40	do	Mariner	U. States	New York	Schooner Dime, Oliver Arnsburgh.
John Barbour	35	do	Merchant	do	Groton	
Parker Smith	22	do	Butcher	England	N. London	
James Welsh	40	do	Mariner	do	U. States	
William Lorimer	28	do	Draper	do	do	
John Kirk	26	do	Baker	do	do	Ship Nancy, Joseph Brooke.
Joseph Young	22	do	Servant	U. States	db	

LIST of Passengers, &c.—Quarter ending March 31, 1820.

Custom House, with the name of the Collector.	Names of Passengers.	Age.	Sex.	Occupation.	Country to which they belong.	Country of which they intend to become inhab's	Ship or Vessel, with the name of the Master or Commander.
New-York, David Gelston,	Morris Lee	30	male	Cooper	England	U. States	Ship Nancy, Joseph Brooke.
	Thomas Smytherman	25	do	Farmer	do	do	
	Thomas Cotton	23	do	Laborer	do	do	
	Thomas Hibler	23	do	do	do	do	
	John Cross	29	do	Watchmaker	do	do	
	Rachel Cross	20	female	Spinstress	do	do	
	Julia Cross	10	do	None	do	do	
	James Glasson	25	male	Farmer	Ireland	do	Brig Abeona, James Dryburg.
	Hiram Taylor	19	do	Supercargo	U. States	New-York	Brig Reindeer, James Wibray.
	James Innes	22	do	Silversmith	New-York	U. States	Brig Mary, John M. Noyes.
	John Haeff	25	do	Gentleman	U. States	do	Brig Actress, Benjamin Noyes.
	William P. Dickson	28	do	Merchant	do	do	
	Elisha Huntington	21	do	do	do	do	
	Jacob Booie	24	do	Mechanic	Ireland	do	Brig Decatur, Mayer Brownel.
	David Ryan	33	do	Farmer	do	do	Ship Manhattan, David Tan, jr.
	John Leaureau	13	do	Bootmaker	England	do	
	John Rogers	42	do	None	do	do	
	Sophia Dashwood	8	female	do	do	do	
	Thos. Dashwood, jr.	10	male	do	do	do	
	Thomas Dashwood	5	do	do	do	do	
	Robert Dashwood	2	do	do	do	do	
	Sophia Dashwood, jr.	12	female	do	do	do	
	Mary Dashwood	19	do	do	do	do	
	George Stanfield	45	male	Farmer	do	do	
	Margaret Hughes	15	female	None	do	do	
	Eliza Hughes	13	do	do	do	do	
	Jane Hughes		do	do	do	do	

Name	Age	Sex	Occupation	From	To	Vessel
William Hughes	9	male	Farmer	England	U. States	
Mary Hughes	6	female	do	do	do	
Martha Robinson	30	male	do	do	do	
Allen Orr	40	male	Laborer	do	do	
Catharine Orr	38	female	None	do	do	
Catharine Orr, jr.	33	do	do	do	do	
Mary Orr	1	do	do	do	do	
Hugh Goodwin	30	male	Laborer	Ireland	do	
Eliza Goodwin	28	female	None	do	do	
John Brown	26	male	Farmer	do	do	
John Smith	21	do	Bootmaker	England	do	
Robert Cullum	28	do	Farmer	do	do	
Eliza Cullum	28	female	None	do	do	
Eliza Cullum, jr.	3	do	do	do	do	
George Cullum	1	male	do	do	do	
Thomas Burrill	21	do	Laborer	do	do	
John M'Kee	32	do	do	do	do	
Thomas Keigh	27	do	do	Ireland	do	
Mr. Averel	36	do	Mariner	New-York	New-York	Ship Fanny, ' Griffith.
Joharm Kempmeyer	18	do	Merchant	Hamburgh	U. States	Ship Zwey (..reder, Christian Haims.
Johannas Matthau	22	do	do	do	do	
Lamon	26	do	Tallowchandl'r	France	Not known	
George W. Granie	21	do	Gentleman	New-York	Not known	Brig Greyhound, Thomas Bedson.
James M'Keil	22	do	Merchant	Halifax	Halifax	
John Mitter	42	do	Carpenter	U. States	U. States	
M. A. Liberty	40	do	Merchant	G. Britain	G. Britain	Schooner Nancy, Reuben Crowell.
Thomas Read	30	do	Gentleman	England	U. States	Ship Martha, William Sketchley.
William Fletcher	26	do	Merchant	do	do	
F. W. Sperry	34	do	do	U. States	do	
William H. Mayer	28	do	Pin & needle maker			
Elizabeth Mayer	30	female	None	Germany	do	Ship Belfast, Elijah Bunker.
Augustine Fontain	32	male	Soldier	do	do.	
William Gotobea	21	do	Accountant	France	Uncertain	
Francis Williams	46	do	Mechanic	G. Britain	U. States	Ship Washington, F. M. Mount.
Robert Williams	18	do	None	do	do	
Thomas Jennings	26	do	Mechanic	do	do	
Amelia Jennings	31	female	Seamstress	do	do	

LIST of Passengers, &c.—Quarter ending March 31, 1820.

Custom House, with the name of the Collector.	Names of Passengers.	Age.	Sex.	Occupation.	Country to which they belong.	Country of which they intend to become inhab's	Ship or Vessel with the name of the Master or Commander.
New-York, David Gelston,	Mathew R. Lewis	21	male	Merchant	G. Britain	U. States	Ship Washington, F. M. Mount.
	Mary Ann Mount	17	female	Lady	do	do	
	Sarah	20	male	Servant	do	do	
	John James Hinley	24	do	Merchant	U. State	do	Brig Active, Arnold Clark.
	James Hector	31	do	Farmer	Scotland	do	Ship Euphrates, Stoddard.
	Thomas Henderson	30	do	do	do	do	
	Hellin Henderson	25	do	do	do	do	
	James Henderson	2	do	do	do	do	
	Robert Henderson	6	do	do	do	do	
	Benjamin Jones	31	do	do	do	do	
	Jeoffry Mills	42	do	do	do	do	
	George Claucy	30	do	Gentleman	Ireland	do	Ship S. Carolina Packet, A. I. Cartwright.
	Ann Claucy	24	female	Lady	do	do	
	Eliza Claucy	2	do	Child	do	do	
	Cinthy Pierce (mulat)	3	do	Servant	U. States	do	
	Michael Gorman	35	male	Gentleman	Ireland	do	
	B. F. Bourne	24	do	U. S. Navy	U. States	do	Ship Henry, Stephen Devall.
	Benjamin Brown	30	do	do	do	do	
	Nathaniel Strong	13	do	Merchant	do	do	Schooner Eliza Pigott, Robert Waterman:
	William Frazer	40	do	do	do	do	
	D. Moncreiff	45	do	do	do	do	
	Edward H. Horton	28	do	Mariner	Montreal	do	Brig Superb, Daniel Aymer.
	Benjamin Hager	27	do	Clerk	do	do	Schooner Buffalo, John Ham.
	Hugh Makay	43	do	Mariner	U. States	do	
	John Green	37	do	None	do	do	Schooner Britannia, Jno. Geather.
	Mary Green	31	female		do	do	
	Antonio Zañones	40	male	Grocer	France	do	

	Name	Age	Sex	Occupation	Country	U. States	Remarks
RICHMOND. J. Gibbons.	Grac. Laynagamano	35	male	Grocer	France	do	Schooner Sally Ann, Charles Redin.
	John Desby	23	do	Merchant	U. States	do	Brig Portland, John Lawyer.
	Edward Lowry	26	do	Butcher	do	do	
	Victor Le Brun	49	do	Tobacconist	do	do	A return from the port of Richmond, but no vessel arriving for the Quarter.
PHILADELPHIA. John Steele.	Joseph Broadbent	19	do.	Merchant	G. Britain	do	Ship Lancaster, Isaac Burkhart.
	Alex. M'Gowan	27	do	Draper	do	do	
	B. Albroyd	25	do	Farmer	do	do	
	James Curran	40	do	Laborer	do	do	
	John Curran	11	do	do	do	do	
	Richard Curran	10	do	do	do	do	
	Thomas Curran	7	do	do	do	do	
	John Marden	23	do	do	do	do	
	James Delany	24	do	Merchant	do	do	
	William Henrey	27	do	do	do	do	
	John Henrey	26	do	do	do	do	
	James Hillis	26	do	Farmer	do	do	
	Eve Graham	50	female	Spinster	do	do	Brig Ceres, William Patterson.
	Mary Ann Graham	17	do	do	do	do	
	Sarah Graham	15	do	do	do	do	
	John Graham	10	male	None	do	do	
	Matty Graham	8	female	do	do	do	
	Eve Graham, jr.	6	do	do	do	do	
	Thomas Graham	2	male	do	do	do	
	Jane Drummond	25	female	Spinster	do	do	
	Samuel Drummond	4	male	None	do	do	
	Ann Drummond	2	female	do	do	do	
	John Richards	18	male	Laborer	do	do	
	Mary O'Neill	28	female	Spinster	do	do	
	Margaret Owens	10	do	None	do	do	
	Michael Kirwan	25	male	Clerk	do	do	
	Maria Kirwan	22	female	Wife	do	do	
	Eliza Kirwan	2	do	None	do	do	
	Samuel Dobbia	22	male	Farmer	do	do	
	H. G. Good	25	do	Merchant	do	do	
	Maria Kennedy	8	female	None	do	do	
	John F. Moracin	26	male	Planter	St. J. de Cuba	do	Schr. Little George Eyre, Alex. Moore.

LIST of Passengers, &c.—Quarter ending March 31, 1820.

Custom House, with the Name of the Collector.	Names of Passengers.	Age.	Sex.	Occupation.	Country to which they belong.	Country of which they intend to become inhab's.	Ship or Vessel, with the name of the Master or Commander.
Philadelphia. John Steele.	Godfrey Deabette	40	male	Sardinian Con.	Sardinia	U. States	Ship Hunter, Andrew Davis.
	Deabette	30	female	Wife	do	do	
	Deabette	13	do	Daughter	do	do	
	Deabette	6	male	Son	do	do	
	Peterluga	35	do	Secretary	France	do	
	Francour	40	do	None	do	do	
	Francour	12	do	do	U. States	do	
	Rasilly	45	do	Farmer	G. Britain	do	
	Williams	30	female	Wife	do	do	
	Williams	35	male	Military	Poland	do	
	Gregory Vandusky	18	do	Clerk	France	do	
	Gossis	32	do	Military service U. S.		St. Thomas	Sloop Young Man's Companion, of Balt.
	F. M. Hormand		do			U. States	
Baltimore, s. H. M'Culloch.	William Gallup	32	do	Supercargo	Germany	U. States	Schooner Good Return, of Baltimore.
	Frederick Berthaud	27	do	Merchant	U. States	New-York	
	A. Gorton	45	do	Master mariner	France	U. States	
	John Cook	29	do	do	U. States	do	
	Mr. Price	24	do	Merchant	do	do	Schooner Maria, of Baltimore.
	I. Shackleford	24	do	Mariner	do	do	
	G. Wilson	29	do	Merchant	do	do	Brig Fame, of Salem.
	P. Durkey	54	do	Mariner	do	do	
	H. Rhodewald	23	do	Merchant	Germany	do	
	I. Rich	24	do	do	U. States	do	
	Thomas Rosendale	25	do	Watchman	Germany	Illinois Ter.	Brig Robert, of Baltimore.
	I. H. Smith	35	do	Farmer	U. States	do	Ship Commerce, of Salem.
	Mrs. Smith	23	female	Spinster	do	do	

Name	Age	Sex	Occupation	Country	Destination	Vessel
R. W. Folger	25	male	merchant	U. States	Peru, Spain.	Schooner Wasp, of Salem.
Matius de la Fueate	45	do	do	Lima	Baltimore	Ship Balloon, of Baltimore.
A. M. Anderson	27	do	do	U. States	do	
William R. Leeds	19	do	Accountant	do	U. States	Brig Edward, of Baltimore.
John Young	20	do	Farmer	dc	do	Schooner Maria, packet of Salem.
S. M'Dermot	32	do	Clerk	Germany	Baltimore	Schooner Sampson, of Baltimore.
H. Myers	23	do	Supercargo	U. States	U. States	Schooner Luminary, of Baltimore.
A. Compte	23	do	Mariner	do	do	
F. Snow	38	do	Merchant	do	do	
Francis Adams	27	do	Supercargo	G. Britain	do	Schooner Dart, of Baltimore.
G. Goddard	35	do	Merchant	U. States	do	Ship Amazon, of do
Wm. G. Bolgianc	20	do	Supercargo	do	do	Schooner Philenia, of do
A. Farro	45	do	Supercargo	do	do	
William Baker	30	do	Mariner	do	do	Ship Amazon, of do
G. Gillingham	26	do	Supercargo	do	do	Brig William and Thomas of Portsmouth.
F. Arcambae	25	do	Merchant	do	do	Schooner Col. G. Armistead, of Baltimore.
Joseph Goulson	22	do	Surgeon	G. Britain	do	Ship Hope, of Philadelphia.
Alexander Adams	50	do	Shopkeeper	do	do	
James Johnson	20	do	Clerk	do	do	
Richard Veal	42	do	Farmer	do	do	
Temperance Veal	36	female	None	do	do	
Richard Veal, jr.	13	male	do	do	do	
William Veal	10	do	do	do	do	
Mary Veal	7	female	do	do	do	
Isaac Veal	1	male	do	do	do	
Catharine Tumblin	24	female	do	do	do	
Flora Tumblin	1	do	do	do	do	
Samuel Wheatcroft	40	male	Labore.	do	do	
Eliza Wheatcroft	40	female	None	do	do	
William M. Smith	20	male	Laborer	do	do	
Rebecca Smith	19	female	None	do	do	
T. Smith	2	male	do	do	do	
Jane Shepherd	28	female	do	do	do	
Jane Bayles	50	do	do	do	do	
E. Donavan	14	do	do	do	do	
S. Veron*	24	male	Mariner	U. States	do	* Died on the voyage.
I. M. Sewell	30	do	Merchant	do	do	Schooner Independence, of Baltimore.
I. W. Shirwood	19	do	do	do	do	Schooner President, of Fairhaven.

LIST of Passengers, &c.—Quarter ending March 31, 1820.

Custom House, with the Name of the Collector.	Names of Passengers.	Age.	Sex.	Occupation.	Country to which they belong.	Country of which they intend to become inhab's	Ship or Vessel, with the Name of the Master or Commander.
BALTIMORE, James H. M'Culloch.	Armstrong	28	male	Seaman	U. States	U. States	Schooner Maria, of Baltimore.
	P. Kammerdeemer	39	do	Tailor & Farm'r	Berne	do	Brig Temperance, of Baltimore.
	G. Kammerdeemer	40	female	None	do	do	
	J. Kammerdeemer	6	male	do	do	do	
	Johan. Philip	36	do	do	do	do	
	F. Karl Wondel	28	do	Farmer	do	do	
	Henry S. Ellfiring	22	do	Merchant	Hanover	do	
	Philip Bocker	34	do	Saddler	Nassau	do	
	Thaddeus Brudon	41	do	Gilder	Baden	do	
	Henry Eckardt	34	do	Butcher	Wirtemberg	do	
	Theodore Eckardt	22	female	None	do	do	
	Alina Eckardt	1	do	do	do	do	
	Catarina Froderick	2	do	do	do	do	
	Joseph Gorring	23	male	Distiller	Baden	do	
	Frederick Wild	22	do	Baker	Prussia	do	
	J. W. Schade	21	female	None	Hossia	do	
	C. Magnues	19	male	Butcher	France	do	
	F. Meurserson	40	do	do	Waldeck	do	
	F. Meurserson, jr.	16	do	do	do	do	
	J. B. Boungor	21	do	do	Baden	do	
	C. Konselor	21	do	do	do	do	
	G. P. Fiescior	18	do	Tailor	Waldeck	do	
	J. G. Slotterbeck	30	do	Baker	Wirtemberg	do	
	P. Sorrison	25	do	Farmer	Holland	do	
	C. Raunterhorry	25	do	Baker	Hosia	do	
	S. Eockhardt	23	do	do	do	do	
	J. F. Dautel	45	do	Farmer	Wirtemberg	do	

Name	Age	Sex	Occupation	Wirtemberg	U. States
Gottlevid Dautel	19	female	None	do	do
John Dautel	13	male	do	do	do
Elizabeth Dautel	10	female	do	do	do
J. A. Schaefer	44	male	Farmer	do	do
Catharina Schaefer	19	female	None	do	do
Rosina Schaefer	18	do	do	do	do
Christina Schaefer	16	do	do	do	do
Sobpina Schaefer, jr.	14	do	do	do	do
Barbara Schaefer	13	do	do	do	do
Jacob Schaefer	11	male	do	do	do
J. Eugoldhart	32	do	Cooper	do	do
Christiana do	29	female	None	do	do
John Eugoldhart	8	male	do	do	do
Maria Eugoldhart	6	female	do	do	do
J. A. Augustin	20	male	Farmer	do	do
J. S. Morger	22	do	Baker	do	do
F. Stuiber	30	do	Farmer	do	do
Catharine Stuiber	34	female	None	do	do
Jno. Mathaus Forb	33	male	Baker	do	do
Gottlick Scheudler	26	male	do	do	do
Sopbina Schaefer	47	female	None	do	do
Joanna Schaefer	20	female	do	do	do
I. Carl Wies.	47	male	Merchant	do	do
I. I. Keerl	18	do	Shoemaker	do	do
I. F. Grogel	40	do	Farmer	do	do
Dorothou Gogel	46	female	None	do	do
John Gogel	14	male	do	do	do
Gottlick Gogel	10	do	do	do	do
Carl Gogel	8	female	do	do	do
Maria Gogel	6	male	do	do	do
I. Northdurf	35	male	Farmer	do	do
Fred. Northdurf	36	do	None	do	do
Augusta Northdurf	8	female	do	do	do
Christiana Northdurf	5	do	do	do	do
Johanna Northdurf	2	female	do	do	do
F. Mitchell	26	male	Merchant	Baden	no
M. Dominick	23	do	Doctor	France	do
Christina Hauger	21	female	None	Wirtemberg	do

LIST of Passengers, &c.—Quarter ending March 31, 1820.

Custom House, with the name of Collector.	Names of Passengers.	Age.	Sex.	Occupation.	Country to which they belong.	Country of which they intend to become inhab's	Ship or Vessel, with the name of the Master or Commander.
BALTIMORE, James H. M'Culloch.	Frederick Hauger	19	male	None	Wirtemberg	U. States	Brig Temperance, of Baltimore.
	Audrous Hauger	17	do	do	do	do	
	F. Reichlor	24	do	Baker	do	do	
	G. Carpenter	27	do	Merchant	U. States	do	Schooner Chase, of Baltimore.
	John Larnier	36	do	Seaman	England	do	Schooner Dandy, of Baltimore.
	Daniel Schutte	23	do	Merchant	U. States	do	Brig Alabama, of Baltimore.
	I. B. Budd	22	do	do	do	do	
	Thomas Westley	30	do	Cabinetmaker	do	do	
	S. Percival	40	do	Lieut. U. S.	do	do	Brig Canada, of Baltimore.
	P. Zapulona	30	do	Storekeeper	Italy	do	Brig Harriet, of Baltimore.
	R. Rogers	27	do	Merchant	U. States	do	
	A S. Dangan	26	do	Mariner	do	do	
	R. Henry	35	do	Merchant	do	do	Schooner Thomas Tenant, of Baltimore.
	Boyd	33	do	do.	do	do	
	M. U. Pringle	40	do	do	do	do	Brig Savage, of Baltimore.
	Wm. Hunt	31	female	Sup. glassworks	England	do	Ship Belvidere, of Baltimore.
	H. Moore	14	male	None	do	do	
	F. Moore	21	do	Mechanic	do	do	
	Wn. Moore	13	do	None	do	do	
	Ann Moore	11	female	do	do	do	
	Elizabeth Pearson	45	do	do	do	do	
	Richard Pearson	18	male	Farmer	do	do	Ship Ea, of Baltimore.
	Julius Conte	38	do	Merchant	U. States	do	Schooner P. S. of Baltimore.
	Samuel C. Child	30	do	Mariner	do	do	Schooner Azariah, of Baltimore.
	J. G. Banks	34	do	Merchant	do	do	Schooner Congress, of Baltimore.
	F. Woodward	24	do	do	do	do	Schooner Young Haley, of Baltimore.
	William P. Mathews	24	do	do	do	do	

	Name	Age	Sex	Occupation	Country	Destination	Vessel
New Port, William Ellery, acting collector.	O. Jones	36	male	Minister	England	Temporay	Schooner Eclipse, of Baltimore.
	J. W. Doran	21	do	Gentleman	Ireland	do	Ship Robert Burns, of N. Y.
	Robert M. Cascadden	30		Merchant	U. States	U. States	
	Margaret Cascadden	22	female	Wife	Ireland	do	
	James Cascadden	19	male	Merchant		do	
	Anna Patterson	28	female	Spinster	U. States	do	
	Patrick Patterson	1	male	None	do,	do	
	William Boyle	25	do	Farmer	Ireland	do	
	Robert Underwood	14	do	do	do	do	
	Barney Fitzgerald	28	do	do	do	do	
	Nancy Fitzgerald	28	female	Wife	do	do	
	Anna Fitzgerald	1	do	None	do	do	
	Betsey Glass	20	do	Servant	do	do	
	Nancy Campbell	20	do	do.	do	do	
	Nancy Lenox	16	do	do	do	do	
	Catharine Campbell	15	do	do	do	do	
	Theop's Lesslace, jr.	42	male	Merchant	France	France	Schooner Telegraph, of N. Y.
	Moses Greenwood	34	do	do	Massachus'ts	U. States	Schooner Maria, of Providence, M. Foy.
	Benjamin Shaw	70	do	Seaman	U. States	do	
	John Allen	25	do	do	do	do	
	Charles Colesworthy	25	do	de	do	do	
	Peter J. Menville	25	do	Merchant	Barbadoes	Barbadoes	Indian Hunter, of N. Y. Jno. Brown.
	Daniel Somerscales	33	do	Shipmaster	England	England	
	Hugh M'Kay	19	do	Merchant	Tobago	Tobago	
	Francis Tiley	34	do	do	England	Philadelphia	
	Manuel Viera	26	do	do	West Isles	West Isles	Brig Eliza Haley, of Plymouth, Jos. Cooper.
	Antonio Viera	23	do	None	do	do.	
	Domingo Viera	5	do	do	do	do	
Savannah, A. S. Bullock	Mrs. Riley	30	female	Lady	U. States	U. States	Schooner Mary Rose, Horace Treat.
	James Riley	16	male	Boy	do	do	
	J. Van Harlin	35	do	Merchant	Cuba	Cuba	
	A. Gareer	35	do	do	Ireland	U. States	
	B. Miller	30	do	Mechanic	do	do	
	John Sirmitt	25	do	do	do	do	
	J. P. Wheeler	27	do	Merchant	G. Britain	Charleston	Ship Hercules, Robert Kereal,
	S. Hothan	40	do	Farmer	do	To return	
	R. R. Bradshaw	24	do	Merchant	do	do	
	John H. Rawlings*	33	do	do	Virginia	do	* Died 17th November, 1819.

4

LIST of Passengers, &c.—Quarter ending March 31, 1820.

Custom House, with the name of the Collector.	Names of Passengers.	Age.	Sex.	Occupation.	Country to which they belong.	Country of which they intend to become inhab's	Ship or Vessel, with the name of the Master or Commander.
SAVANNAH, A. S. Bullock	Joseph Adolphe	19	male	Merchant	Nantz,France	Charleston	American Schooner Phanton, J. Bruchet.
	Jean L. Blanc	20	do	Seaman	Havre, do	do	
	Henry Hunt	35	do	Shipmaster	U. States		Sall & Hope, of Providence, Jas. M. Blinn.
	George Wm. Gleystem	22	do	Merchant	Germany	Germany	Brig Anton, Frederick Bahle.
	Thomas C. Haywood	45	do	Chairmaker	Charlestown	Charlestown	Ship Romeo, Wm. P. Foot.
	John Partrick	19	do	Merchant	Maryland	Baltimore	Schooner Decatur, Wm. F. Bleah.
	Geo. B. Shirg	20	do	do	Havana	Havana	
	Joseph Carpenter	25	do	do	Matanzas	Matanzas	
	Wm. A. Slocum	20	do	do	Virginia	Virginia	Ship Juliet, Samuel Swanton.
	James Smith	22	do	Mariner	Savannah	Savannah	
	Adam Selbzer	27	do	Merchant	Baltimore	Baltimore	
	Daniel Coil	26	do	Carpenter	Savannah	Savannah	
	John Cinon	38	do	Artificer	do	U. States	Schooner Katy, Peter Douville.
	Louis Merault	62	do	Tailor	do	do	
	Louis Benart	32	do	do	do	do	
	Francis Dousset	32	female	Carpenter	do	do	
	Maria Jeanne Serapine	35	male	None	Philadelphia		Brig Sarah, of Sackett's, Stephen E. Cole.
	Felix & three children	21	do	do	New York		
	John S. Smith, jr.	25	do	Merchant	U. States	U. States	Sloop James, of St. Mary's, Samuel Flood.
	Isaac U. Horton	24	do	do	do	do	
	John Clendenning	33	do	do	do	do	
	Samuel Snow	34	do	do	do	do	
	Philip Duel	29	do	Sailmaker	England	England	Brig Alexander, of Boston, Henry Kemp.
	William Shaw	22	do	Merchant	America		
	Joseph Walker	32	do		Martinique		
	Lebrin Gardner	23	do	Merchant	Sheffield		Brig Carolina, D. E. Brown.
	Auguste Dufruce	30	do	Merchant		Augusta,Geo.	
	George Oats						

District / Collector	Name	Age	Sex	Occupation	Country to which belonging	Country of destination	Vessel
	—— Cook	25	male	do	Portugal	U. States	Ship Nancy, Elkanah Bray.
	Claude Francois Vouriot	45	do	Gentleman	do	do	
	Alexander Martin	33	do		do	do	Brig Isabelle, of Philadelphia, Lucas Moliere;
	Servant Paul	14	do	Servant	do	do	
	John Henschele	45	do	Farmer	do	do	
	Christian Henschele	37	female		do	do	
	Helena Henschele	17	male		do	do	
	George Henschele	15	do		do	do	
	Jacob Henschele	10	do		do	do	
	Hanrick Henschele	13	do		do	do	
	Frederick Henschele	8	do		do	do	
	Philip Henschele	6	do		do	do	
	Christiana Henschele	37	female		do	do	
	Christiana Henschele	9	do		do	do	
	John Michael Ultz	18	male		do	do	
	Jacob Helnger	35	do		do	do	
	Sottleib Schiek	22	do		do	do	
	Lathea Helnger	30	female		do	do	
	John Geo. Henschele	19	male		do	do	
	Louisa Helnger	5	female		do	do	
PROVIDENCE, Thomas Coles.	John Parker	25	male	Merchant	America	Philadelphia	Schooner Mary Rose, Horace Treat.
	Sarah Luzette	18	female	Lady	do	do	
	Maria Smith		do	do	U. States		
	James M. Brown	22	male	Jeweller	do	New-York	Schooner Experiment, Daniel Paine.
DIS. COLUMBIA, Jno. Barnes.	Samuel Harper	46	do	Carpenter	U. States	U. States	Schooner Farmer's Friend, Alex. Simmes.
	John Dowling	32	do	Laborer	do	Dis. Columb.	
	David Farrall	23	do	Shoemaker	Ireland	do	
PITTSBURG, Va. Joseph Jones.	-	-	-	-	-	-	No passenger arriving for the quarter ending 31st March, 1820.
DIS. NANTUCKET, M. T. Morton.	-	-	-	-	-	-	No passenger arriving for the quarter ending 31st March 1820.
PORTSMOUTH, Timothy Upham.	Usher Parsons	35	male	Surg. U. S. navy	U. States	U. States	Ship Harmony, Woodward,
CHARLESTON, James R. Pringle.	Joseph Coppinger	18	do	Merchant	Spain	Charleston	Schooner Margaret.
	Joseph Guadarama	18	do	do	do	do	
	Manuel Guere	30	do	do	do	do	
	Michael Maslerson	30	do	do	U. States	New York	Sloop Connecticut.
	Thomas Herbert	25	do	Carpenter	do	Salisbury	

LIST of Passengers, &c.—Quarter ending 31st March, 1820.

Custom House, with the name of the Collector.	Passengers.	Age.	Sex.	Occupation.	Country to which they belong.	Country of which they intend to become inhab's	Ship or Vessel, with the name of the Master or Commander.
CHARLESTON, James R. Pringle.	Mary Anne Eagan	25	female	Lady	Britain	Baltimore	Brig Columbia.
	Margaret Eagan	under 9 years	do	None	do	do	
	John Eagan		male	do	do	do	
	William Eagan		do	do	do	do	
	Theresa Eagan		female	do	do	do	
	Eliza Eagan		do		do	do	
	Mary Moss		do		do	do	
	Thomas Moorhead	23	male	Farmer	do	do	
	Eliza English	36	female	Note	do	do	
	John English	32	male		do	do	
	John English, jr.	12	do		do	do	
	Lawrence English	3	do		do	do	
	Andrew English	3	do		do	do	
	Ellen M'Carran	7	female		do	do	
	Margaret Woods	55	do		do	do	
	James Emery	27	male	Merchant	U. States	New-York	Sloop Ann.
	Patrick Dillon	28	do	do	Charleston	Charleston	
	Thomas M'Gowan	30	do	Mariner	do	do	Schooner Adventure.
	Gilbert	28	do	do	do	do	
	Thomas Barnard	35	do	do	do	do	
	William Parkham	43	do	Carpenter	do	do	
	Issadore Grognel	23	do	Merchant	France	France	Brig Edward, D. Douglas.
	Charlotte F. Grognel	18	female	Lady,	do	do	
	Emel Marc Mandet	25	male	Merchant	do	do	Sloop Jay.
	Joane Antoenie	20	do	do	do	do	
	Edward E. Bungon	13	do	do	do	do	
	William Miller	25	do	do	U. States	Charleston	Schooner Mary Ann.

Name	Age	Sex	Occupation	Country	Port	Ship
George Crombelholm	30	male	Merchant	U. States	Charleston	Brig Columbia.
Samuel Mitchell	51	do	do	do	New York	Schooner Comet
John F. Fortune	23	do	Merchant	do	Charleston,	
Ann Charties	20	female	None	do	do	
Anthony Moore	30	male	Mariner	Spain	Havana	
Garrer	25	do	Engineer	do	do	
Thomas Barnet	25	do	Mariner	Britain	Liverpool	
John Dies	21	do	do	Spain	Havana	
Granades	35	do	Merchant	do	do	
Anthony Trial	30	do	do	do	St. Augustine	Schooner Jane.
John Pelica	21	do	do	do	do	
John Warton	30	do	Mariner	U. States	U. States	Schooner Ann.
Andrew Gay	45	do	Merchant	do	do	
William Melly	22	do	do	Spain	St. Augustine	
Manuel Giano Bly	21	do	do	do	do	
John Kean	47	do	Laborer	G. Britain	S. Carolina	Brig Mary.
Patrick Dempsey	20	do	do	do	do	
Ann Burke	50	female	Spinster	do	do	
Mary Keary	22	do	Mantuamaker	U. States	do	
Thomas Bourke	17	male	Laborer	do	do	
Mary Thompson	5	female	None	do	do	
Eliza Fraizer	23	do	Spinster	do	do	
William Peacock	50	male	Dancing Mast.	do	do	
George Weir	22	do	Farmer	Britain	do	Brig Angelina.
Martha Weir	21	female		do	do	
John Weir	1	male		do	do	
Thomas Smith	31	do	Farmer	do	do	
Mary Smith	26	female		do	do	
Rebecca Smith	4	do		do	do	
Bess Smith	2	do		do	do	
Isabella Smith	4	do		do	do	
Hugh Moore	16	male		do	do	
William Fox	21	do		do	do	
Margaret Fox	19	female		do	do	
Mary Fox	50	do		do	do	
Joseph Sanchez	20	male	Merchant	Spain	Charleston	Schooner Eudora.
Samuel Yates	36	do	do	U. States	do	Brig Catharine.
Jane Yates	32	female	Lady	do	do	

LIST of Passengers, &c.—Quarter ending March 31, 1820.

Custom House, with the name of the Collector.	Names of Passengers.	Age.	Sex.	Occupation.	Country to which they belong.	Country of which they intend to become inhb's.	Ship or Vessel, with the name of the Master or Commander.
CHARLESTON. James R. Pringle.	E. Farley	26	female	Lady	U. States	Charleston	Brig Catharine.
	Thomas Frink	22	male		do	do	
	Bazil Gonzales	35	do	Merchant	do	do	
	Fontaine	36	do	do	France	France	
	L. H. G. Schutt	32	do	do	U. States	Charleston	Ship Java.
	Isaac Laures	31	do	Servant	do	do	
	Lucifer	48	do	Merchant	France	France	
	William Arnott	30	do	Mason	U. States	U. States	Schooner Sally.
	Prudence Hibbert	22	female	Lady	U. States	Boston	Schooner Mary.
	John P. Lavinciendier	45	male	Merchant	St. Domingo	Charleston	
	Jacques Biecies	30	do	Cabinetmaker	do	do	Sloop Lawrence.
	Chapman Levy	35	do	Lawyer	U. States	do	
	Alex. M'Gilvery	40	do	Auctioneer	do	do	
	Stephen Lancaster	32	do	Merchant	do	do	Ship Elizabeth.
	Angulo Sante	40	do	do	do	do	
	Thomas Hindley	38	do		Britain	Britain	
	John Hall	28	do		do	do	
	William Mitchell	31	do		do	do	Ship Mars.
	William Barber	28	do		do	do	Schooner Mary Ann.
	Niel M'Niel	18	do		U. States	Charleston	
	James M'Namy	40	do	do	do	do	
	James Hatch	33	do	Mariner	do	do	
	John Helfred	21	do	do	do	do	
	Lorenzo Henry	34	do	Merchant	do	do	Schooner Margaret.
	Alexander England	15	do		do	do	
	Samuel Porter	22	do	Planter	do	do	
	James Matthews	42	do	Trader	do	do	Brig Perseverance

Name	Age	Sex	Occupation	Country	Port	Vessel
Manuel Fernandes	38	male	Trader	U. States	Charleston	Brig Perseverance.
Joseph Squeber	25	do	Mariner	do	New-York	Schooner Echo.
Anthony Gray	48	do	do	do	do	
Luther Whiting	30	do	Merchant	do	do	
Jacobas	25	do	do	do	Charleston	
Francis Bourke	25	do	do	do	do	Schooner Charleston Packet.
Thompson	23	female	Merchant	do	do	
James Flemming	45	male	do	do	do	
James P. Ripley	25	do	do	do	Boston	
Joseph M. Mayhle	32	do	do	do	New-York	Ship Montgomery
Pasquil Mascalette	45	do	Mariner	do	Charleston	
Sextus Gaillard	19	do	do	do	do	
Samuel Gaillard	18	do	do	do	do	
James Sligman	30	do	Soap boiler	Germany	N. Orleans	Brig Eliza.
Anthony Yallick	50	do	Mariner	U. States	do	
Jose Frara	39	do	Merchant	G. Britain	Charleston	
William Brown	21	do	Shoemaker	do	do	
George Burne	19	do	do	do	Charleston	
Anthony Marra	25	do	Merchant	Spain	Cadiz	
Francis Perez	26	do	do	do.	St. Croix	
John Linet	25	do	do	G. Britain	Charleston	
John Patterson	24	do	Mariner	do	do	Schooner Mercury.
John Morisson	35	do	Merchant	do	do	
Peter Coffin	45	do	Spinster	do	do	Brig Harriet.
Catharine Duncan	27	female	Farmer	do	do	
John Hedley	55	male	Merchant	G. Britain	do	
James Mager	24	do	do	do	do	
John Owen Johnson	24	do	Farmer	do	do	
John M'Kelvey	47	do	do	do	do	
Robert Harper	45	do	do	do	do	
John Malcolm	36	do	do	do	do	
Peter Cad	18	do	do	do	do	
John Young	63	female	None	do	do	
Sarah Young	64	do	do	do	do	
Jane Young	24	do	do	do	do	
Ann Young	22	do	do	do	do	
Margaret Young	20	do.	do	do	do	
John Wilson	25	male	do	do	do	

LIST of Passengers, &c.—Quarter ending 31st March, 1820.

Custom House with the name of the Collector.	Names of Passengers.	Age.	Sex.	Occupation.	Country to which they belong.	Country of which they intend to become inhab's	Ship or Vessel, with the name of the Master or Commander.
CHARLESTON, James R. Pringle.	Jane Hare	20	female	None	G. Britain	Charleston	Ship Harriet.
	Margaret Hare	20	do	do	do	do	
	Alexander Hare	13	male	do	do	do	
	Samuel Aikin	21	do	do	do	do	
	Nancy Aikin	65	female	do	do	do	
	Margaret Aikin	30	do	do	do	do	
	Eliza Aikin	25	do	do	do	do	
	Nancy Aikin	23	do	do	do	do	
	John Aikin	5	male	do	do	do	
	Matilda Crawford	9	female	do	do	do	
	Alexander Rogers	17	male	do	do	do	
	John Richardson	23	do	do	do	do	
	Robert Lynn	35	do	do	do	do	
	Daniel M'Canty	24	do	do	do	do	
	John Henry	32	do	do	do	do	
	William Shegog	20	do.	do	do	do	
	Jane Wilson	21	female	do	do	do	
	Joseph Fernandez	40	male	Mariner	U. States	Philadelphia	Schooner Comet.
	Hugh Rogers	41	do	Merchant	do.	Charleston	
	John Lopez	35	do	do	Spain	do	
	John Dias	44	do	do	Spain	do	
	John Shoulbread	25	do	Surgeon	U. States	do	Ship Octavia.
	Peter Neilson	23	do	Merchant	Britain	do	
	John Tudor	20	do	do	do	do	
	Frisbee	35	do	Mariner	U. States	New-Haven	
	Hon. Patrick Brown	60	do	Judge	Britain	Nassau	Brig Adeline.
	Sir Charles Saxton	50	do	Gentleman	do	London	

Mississippi.
Beverly Chew.

Name	Age	Sex	Occupation	Country	Destination	Ship
Francois	40	male	Servant	France	London	Schooner Margaret.
Vincent Gonsales	25	do	Mariner	Portugal	Havanna	Ship South Carolina Packet.
William Ward	27	do	Merchant	Britain	Charleston	
Joseph Hodgson	34	do	Mechanic	do	do	
William Hodgson	11	do	do	do	do	
Richard C. Codman	21	do	Merchant	U. States	Boston	Brig Joseph.
James Dean	30	do	do	do	Charleston	Schooner Susan.
E. M. Pollack	28	do	Laborer	Holland	N. Orleans	Brig Planter.
Francis Dollman	31	do	Farmer	Germany	do	
Sophia M. Hongerkamp	26	female	House serv't	Holland	do	
A. P. Ysserman	45	male	Blacksmith	do	do	
Johanna M. Debot	26	female	None	do	do	
Hendrick Klonne	47	male	Merchant	Germany	do	
L. M. Rondenburg	35	do	Laborer	Holland	do	
Harsog M. Voltyn	21	do	Matress mak'r	do	do	
Moriac	30	do	Merchant	France	do	Ship Alexandre.
Wallestein	25	do	Clerk	do	do	
Richard	36	do	Doctor	do	do	
Legross	45	do.	Merchant	do	do	
Legross, fille	15	do	None	do	do	
Molly and sister	17	females	None	do	do	
Mrs. Cheret dau'r & child	55	do.	Baker	Genoa	do	
Brignon and family	34	male	None	do	do	
Charles and wife	55	do	Architect	do.	do	
Hulm and Family	40	do	Planter	Kentucky	do	
Caron	45	do	Tailor	Switzerland	do	
Janin	36	do	Schoolmaster	France	do	
Lacroix	30	do	do	do	do	
Bachent	34	do	Mariner	do	do	
Le Boucher	28	do	Laborer	do	do	
Jean Lutez	20	do	Mariner	do	do	
I. Chastang	38	do	Cabinetmaker	do	do	
John Boraigne	32	do	Clerk	N. Orleans	do	
I. Ditch	50	do	Carpenter	France	do	
Jos. Canovas and wife	34	do	Merchant	Germany	Havana	Brig Hero.
Antonio Herez	30	do	do	Mahon.	N. Orleans	
Gouffier	50	do	Priest	France	do	
		do	Tailor	N. Orleans	do	
I. Killburn	50	do	Seaman	Connecticut	Connecticut	Brig Forest.

LIST of Passengers, &c.—Quarter ending March 31, 1820.

Custom House, with the name of the Collector.	Names of Passengers.	Age.	Sex.	Occupation.	Country to which they belong.	Country of which they intend to become inh'bts.	Ship or Vessel, with the Name of the Master or Commander.
Mississippi. Beverly Chew.	Alfred Spooner	32	male	Farmer	Vermont	Vermont	Brig Forest.
	D. M'Call	33	do	Merchant	N. Carolina	Natchez	
	J. Felts	30	do	do	do	N: Carolina	
	John Wyer	23	do	Laborer	Holland	N. Orleans	
	Joseph L. Adams	19	do	Seaman	N. Hampsh.		
	James Jones	32	do	do	Baltimore		
	J. B. Recouïe	20	do	Schoolmaster	France	Louisiana	Ship L'Esperance.
	Honore Jaum	23	do	Merchant	do	do	
	Claude Mauberret	40	do	Blacksmith	do	do	
	Sebastian Brulard	15	do	Clerk	do	do	
	Claude Busquit	22	do	Baker	do	do	
	Jean Languone	40	do	Schoolmaster	do	do	
	Jean Guimbellot	22	do	Merchant	do	do	
	Jean Francis Baget	20	do	do	do		
	Pedro Reggier	40	do	Spanish officer	Spain	Spain	Schooner Athenian.
	Parks	22	do	Merchant	U. States	U. States	
	Antonio Cara Vergue	40	do	Tailor	N. Orleans	Louisiana	
	Alexaidro	50	do	Mariner	Spain	Spain	
	Juan Portugues	44	do	do	do	Pensacola	
	Dacres	45	do	Rigger	Germany	N. Orleans	Ship Thomas Gordon
	M. Dacres	30	female	Wife	do	do	
	Jeremiah Wolden	21	male	Cooper	U. States	Louisiana	Schooner Junius.
	Francis Ricaud, wife and two children	46	do	Merchant	France	do	Ship Atalanta.
	Emile Manauton	17	do	Clerk	do	do	
	John Francis Lafon	37	do	Military	do	do	
	Lt, Tirtrou	22	do	Manufacturer	do	do	

Name	Age	Sex	Occupation			Vessel
		male		France	Louisiana	
Vaquelair, wife and child	28		Engineer	France	Louisiana	Ship Atalanta.
J. A. Destrehan	66	do	Planter	Louisiana	do	
H. Baw	49	do	Merchant	France	do	
N. B. Le Breton	22	do		Louisiana	France	
Martin Hasle	19	do	Cutler	France	Louisiana	
Roumage and wife	34	do	Merchant	do	do	
John Marie Gaubert	37	do	Mariner	de	do	
Moulinier Desplanchet	48	do	do	do	do	
Alexander Coutard	9	do		do	do	
Sauriat Dufossat	28	do	Planter	Louisiana	do	
Francis Solomon	29	do	Merchant	Switzerland	do	
Jn. Jn. Villouet	35	do	Cooper	France	do	
Jos. Turpin	18	do	Bricklayer	St. Domingo	do	
Francois Chazot	30	do	Baker	France	do	
Bartholeme	28	do		do	do	
Francois Roir	40	do	Doctor	do	do	
James M'Kinley	35	do	Mariner	U. States	do	
Archibald B. Bate	40	do	do	do	do	
Francois Pernicò	21	do	do	Spain	do	
Bocachitte	21	do	do	do	do	
George Dihlmar	22	do	Cabinetmaker	Germany	U. States	Schooner William and John.
Andrew Weimar and two children	38	do	Shoemaker	do	do	
Johannas Klie and two children	49	do	Farmer	do	do	
Carpar Notman	36	do	do	do	do	
Elizabeth Lippers and four children	40	female	do	do	do	
John Smith, wife and three children	36	male	do	do	do	Brig Johanna Catharine.
Jacob Gluk	17	do	do	do	do	
Jacob Schray	20	do	do	do	do	
John C. Klingling	24	do	Plumber	do	do	
John M. Tiffer	23	do	Cooper	do	U. States	
J. Bontuck and wife	37	do	Farmer	do	do	
E. Vanseigoth	15	do		do	do	
John Walker		do	Coppersmith	do	do	

LIST of Passengers, &c.—Quarter ending March 31, 1820.

Custom House, with the name of the Collector.	Names of Passengers.	Age.	Sex.	Occupation.	Country to which they belong.	Country of which they intend to become inhab's	Ship or Vessel, with the Name of the Master or Commander.
Mississippi. Beverly Chew.	Jos. Gerhard Stien	25	male	Blacksmith	Germany	U. States	Brig Johanna Catharine.
	C. L. Wolfengering	24	female	Baker	do	do	
	Doltage Bussink	21	do	do	do	do	
	Marin E. Whilinges	19	do	Pastry Cook	do	do	
	Marin Doudrick	20	do	Workmaid	do	do	
	Jos. Lampert and wife	33	male	Cabinetmaker	do	do	
	Fred. Reper and wife	43	do	Carver	do	do	
	Adam Noble	36	do	Farmer	do	do	
	Philip Martin Sprains	35	do	do	do	do	
	Anter Dounen, Verger	25	do	Gardener	do	do	
	Christian Manser	33	do	Cooper	do	do	
	Cornelius Cattenlagen	19	da	Shoemaker	do	do	
	Thomas Knipper	16	do	Farmer	do	do	
	Francis Houthouser	23	do	Weaver	do	do	
	Henry Conrad	19	do	Tailor	do	do	
	Cd. Snidler and wife	30	do	Schoolmaster	do	do	
	Frederick Deig	52	do	Tailor	do	do	
	Wilhelmina	24	female	Seamstress	do	do	
	H. Wm. Parker	20	male	Baker	do	do	
	H. Osterdorf and wife	52	do	Mason	do	do	
	Henry Hopkins	19	do	Silversmith	do	do	
	Dick Garret Mirson	15	do		do	do	
	John C. Ludenk	18	do	Tailor	do	do	
	Chrn. G. Valkouniver	19	do	Butcher	do	do	
	Bernlear Engle	20	do	Weaver	do	do	
	Antonio Balstrins	34	do	Hatter	do	do	
	Henry Meyer	20	do	Doctor	do	do	

Name	Age	Sex	Occupation	Germany	U. States	Ship
G. Seybert	21	female	Seamstress	Germany	U. States	
Jno. Gohrung, wife and 4 children	40	male	Shoemaker	do	do	
J. Michael Skunkraft and 2 children	40	do	Miller	do	do	
J. Dederick Rikker	30	do	Farmer	do	do	
Jno. Gotlein Mauser	38	do	Butcher	do	do	
Betsy Levy Hokernot and son	30	female	Work girl	do	do	
Elizabeth de Bock	21	do	do	do	do	
John Wisketchel	20	male	wagon maker	do	do	
Joseph Winkler	27	do	do	do	do	
A. Solomon Kerkhan	20	do	wax maker	do	do	
C. Hy. Peterson & wife	30	do	Shoemaker	do	do	
Jacobus Miller	19	do	Clerk	do	do	
Wolf Isaac Engender	20	do	Farmer	do	do	
Ann Maria Frederstoff	50	female	Cook	do	do	
Hernest Weil	26	male	Clerk	do	do	
H. Hermanus Harnock	15	do	Farmer	do	do	
Chris'e Grenleit & wife	22	do	do	do	do	
Johannah Michelvild	40	female	Tailoress	do	do	
Frederick Simon	36	male	Tailor	do	do	
Aaron Levi de Haan, wife and 3 children	21	do	Merchant	do	do	
Ann Maria Bussink	20	female	None	do	do	
Johannes H. Lehman	22	male	Carpenter	do	do	
Henrick Erdman	15	do		do	do	
Justin Van Luden	24	do	Watchmaker	do	do	
Frederick Carson		do	Hatter	do	do	
Hermanus Kocke		do	Carpenter	do	do	
Henry Smith		do	Merchant	do	do	
Sam. Levy Dehain		do	do	do	do	
Hastor Corns		do	do	do	do	
N. Solomon Vendeberg	26	do	do	do	do	
Hugh Tuill	32	do	do	England	England	Brig Isabella.
Wm. Cook	19	do		Ireland	N. Orleans	Brig Alexander.
James Gleney	86	do		do	do	
Peter Gicho		do	Merchant	America	America	Schooner Cadmus.

LIST of Passengers, &c.—Quarter ending March 34, 1820.

Custom House, with the name of the Collector.	Names of Passengers.	Age.	Sex.	Occupation.	Country to which they belong.	Country of which they intend to become inhab's	Ship or Vessel, with the name of the Master or Commander.
Mississippi. Beverly Chew.	Francis Zanette	46	male	Hairdresser	Tyrol	Tyrol	Schooner Cadmus.
	Demlap	23	do	Merchant	France	Louisiana	Brig Mentor.
	Pierre Lafanlanghe	47	female		do	N. Orleans	Schooner Dart.
	M. L. Jas. Laufaulunghe	36	male		do	do	
	Charles Leslie	26	do		Pittsburg	Pittsburg	Schooner Mary and Sally.
	William Brown	30	do	Mariner, and man of color		N. Orleans	
	F. B. Blanchard	21	do	Merchant	Louisiana	Louisiana	Schooner Brisk.
	F. Soubereaze	35	do	do	do	do	
	Salvador Perez	40	do	do	do	do	
	Juan de Kaquedlana	45	do	do	do	do	
	Jos. Domingues	30	do	Carpenter	Campeachy	Campeachy	Schooner Thorn.
	M. Domingues	17	do	Boy	do	do	
	Joachim Berron	7	do	Shoemaker			
	Wm. Snead	35	do	Merchant	England	Boston	Brig Mary Ann.
	Wm. Prollet	55	do	Servant	do	England	Brig Commerce
	Harry	26	do		N. Orleans	N. Orleans	Ship Jane Ann.
	Pierre Fouga	29	female	Doctor	France	do	
	Mrs. Roucher	33	male	None	do	Louisiana	Brig Gustave.
	Francis Belliard	39	do	Goldsmith	do	do	
	Joseph A. B. Ville	29	do	Clerk	do	do	
	James C. Carvin	22	do	Engraver	do	do	
	Benjamin Kimnath	40	do	Clerk	do	do	
	J. B. Laforia	26	do	Merchant	do	do	
	Louis Laporte	25	do	Clerk	do	do	
	H. Clalerette	56	do	Merchant	do	do	Ship Missouri.
	S. Bernard			Planter			

Name	Age	Sex	Occupation	Country	Country	Vessel
Henry Pechard	22	male	Merchant	France	Louisiana	Schooner Brutus.
Louis F. Herbert	24	do	Priest	do	do	Ship L' Angle.
Charles F. Aneelin	25	do	Clerk	do	St. Louis	
B. M. Burdet	20	do	Clerk	do	N. Orleans	
Levet	20	do	Planter	do	do	
Mathieu Quinon	37	do	Clerk	do	France	Schooner Ceres.
Casnard	19	do	Merchant	do	do	Brig Sumatra.
Brutus Lacoul	26	do	do	do	Louisiana	
Jn. St. Marc	58	do	Physician	do	do	
Bd. Lafon	35	do	Merchant	England	England	Schooner Victory
George Salkeld	48	do	Merchant	do	do	
George Robinson	24	do	do	do	do	
Charles Chorly	23	do	do	do	Spain	
P. Alba	33	do	do	do	do	
M. Palao	27	do	do	U. States		
C. Miflin	28	do	do	Spain		
J. Bar	38	do	Seaman	do		
M. Auvas	40	female	Seaman	France	Louisiana	Ship Artherien.
M. Pao	50	male	Planter	France	do	
Brand	21	do	Merchant	do	do	
Julien Dufard	24	do	Clerk	do	do	
Jean Jeaornon	23	do	Physician	do	do	
Jarras	28	do	Printer	do		
Fourcan	50	do	Clerk	St. Domingo	N. Orleans	Brig Despatch.
Planton	40	do		do	do	
Miss Louise	23	female		de	do	
Fleury	14	male	Merchant	Germany	Louisiana	Brig Wilhelmine Charlotte.
H. Mobins	30	female	Merchant	do	do	
Mrs. Mobins	20	male	None	do	do	
Mrs. Blackmann	26	female	Merchant	do	do	
Mrs. Blackmann	30	do		do	do	
Miss Meyer	18	male	Planter	do	do	
Nieman	60	female		do	do	
Mrs. Nieman	40		Planter	do	do	
Miss Nieman	22	male	do	do	do	
George Nieman	20	do	do	do	do	
Anton Frederick	28	do		do	do	
C. Kluberger	22			do	do	

LIST of Passengers, &c.—Quarter ending March 31, 1820.

Custom House, with the name of the Collector.	Names of Passengers.	Age.	Sex.	Occupation.	Country to which they belong.	Country of which they intend to become inhab's	Ship or Vessel, with the name of the Master or Commander.
MISSISSIPPI. Beverly Chew.	George C. Meyer	18	male	Planter	Germany	Louisiana	Brig Wilhelmine Charlotte.
	H. B. Munderloh	24	do	Merchant	do	do	
	G. Schneider	25	female		do	do	
	Mrs. Schneider	40	do	Planter	do	do	
	F. Maack	15	male	Baker	do	do	
	H. Bushmann	21	do	Distiller	do	do	
	Fk. Kammilmann	28	do	Servant	do	do	
	L. Hartneit	48	do	Joiner	do	do	
	E. F. Obemdeick	19	do	Baker	do	do	
	I. F. Stinholf	24	do	Tailor	do	do	
	I. Vondamm	20	do	Baker	do	do	
	E. Matharin	26	do	do	do	do	
	P. F. Minzenmier	18	do	Tailor	do	do	
	E. B. J. Heydekamp	36	do	Cooper	do	do	
	Alexander Fricke	30	do	Painter	do	do	
	I. D. Graper	21	do	Tailor	do	do	
	P. Metzinger	21	do	Baker	do	do	
	L. Begmann	22	do	Joiner	do	do	
	H. Bossie	42	do	Baker	do	do	
	C. Schwenattfeyer	22	do	Shoemaker	do	do	
	H. Blanke	37	do	Tailor	do	do	
	F. N. Selle	30	do	Engraver	do	do	
	I. G. Kruger	27	do	Gardener	do	do	
	I. I. Sabbo	24	do	Laborer	do	do	
	I. Hamann	27	do	do	do	do	
	C. Pfeffer	30	do	Butcher	do	do	
	D. Kundsen	12	do	Joiner	do	do	

Name	Age	Sex	Occupation	Country	Whither bound	Remarks
C. Wagener	17	do	Gardener	Germany	Louisiana	Brig Wilhelmine Charlotte.
I. Stuhn	25	do	Baker	do	do	
I. Kamann	23	do	Planter	do	do	
H. Miller	23	do	Merchant	do	do	
C. Luders	34	do	Baker	do	do	
Miss Medefinton	34	female	None	do	do	
G. Schneider	2 6	male	do	do	do	
James Stewart	24	do	Clerk	England	do	Ship Barclay.
David Henderson	21	do	Farmer	do	do	
I. P. Kingston	37	do	Merchant	do	do	
Pro. Lanoix	50	do	Merchant	U. States	do	Brig Georgiana.
Simon Dubeau	26	do	Cooper	France	do	Ship Grand Corneille.
Turton.	22	do	do	do	do	
Dutestre	25	do	Mariner	do	do	
Mrs. Caen	28	female		do	do	
Angeligine Guignolet	19	do		do	do	Put on board at sea, by an Insurgent privateer.
Grau	30	male	Mariner			
Grau	28	do	do-do			
Carlos	20	do				
I. W. Rivarde	23	do	Merchant	U. States	Louisiana	Barque Richmond.
Alexander Hasle	22	do	Mariner	do	U. States	Brig L'Adele.
Charles Tessinden	36	do	Merchant	do	do	Schooner Adeline.
Lindon Crooker		do	do	do	de	
Simon Morrill		do	Mariner	do	do	
Joseph Alan Sylvest		do	do	G. Britain	do	
Benjamin Michard		do	Trader	England	do	
John Scott	28	do	Merchant	do	Transient	Ship Alexander.
Mrs. Scott	19	female	None	do	do	
Ger. Robertson	19	male	Clerk	Germany	Louisiana	
Henry Long	50	do	Mariner	England	Transient	Ship Catharine.
John Shearon	30	do	Servant	France	Louisiana	
Jean Mallet	23	do	Refiner	Ireland	do	
Dennis O'Keife	24	do	Carpenter	do	db	
Jeremiah Dempsey	23	do	Farmer]	do	do	
John O'Neil	25	do	do	da	do	
David O'Neil	23	do	do	de	do	
Michael Muleaky	24	do	do	Germany	do	
Charles Heach	42	do	Mariner	Germany	do	Brig Lyon.

LIST of Passengers, &c.—Quarter ending March 31, 1820.

Custom House, with the Name of the Collector.	Names of Passengers.	Age.	Sex.	Occupation.	Country to which they belong.	Country of which they intend to become inhab's	Ship or Vessel, with the Name of the Master or Commander.
MISSISSIPPI, B. Chew.	John Lague	40	male	Mariner	France	Transient	Brig Lyon.
	Thomas Shields	40	do	Navy U. S.	N. Orleans	N. Orleans	Sloop Commodore Patterson.
	I. Brandegu	30	do	Merchant	U. States		
	Harris	22	do	do	Jamaica		
	Wm. C. J. Jerome	32	do	Planter	France	Kentucky	Brig Eugene.
	Peter Whiteside	58	do	Merchant	U. States		
	Edmund Le Lardeaux	34	do	Planter	France	Ken. or Ohio	
	Charles Julius Masias	18	do	do	do	do	
	Eugene Perrault	29	do	do	do	do	
	Achile St. Aulaire	18	do	do	do	do	
	John B. Waldman	22	do	do	Germany	do	
	Frederick Schorch	32	do	Physician	do	do	
	John Emmerath	49	do	Merchant	do	do	
	Charles Traub	33	do	Clerk	do	do	
	Auguste Traub	2	do		do	do	
	Mary Traub	23	female		France	do	
	Peter L. Lousette	49	male	Servant	Germany	do	
	William Durrick	28	do	Architect	do	do	
	Christopher A. Seitz	33	do	Planter	do	do	
	Catharine Seitz	32	female		do	do	
	Michael C. Seitz	7	male		do	do	
	John Seitz	5	do		do	do	
	Catharine Seitz, jr.	2 6	female		do	do	
	Adolphus Seitz	6	male		do	do	
	Mary	24	female	Servant	do	do	
	John Ebert Ruff	34	male	Planter	do	do	
	Mary M. Ruff	28	female		do	do	

Name	Age	Sex	Occupation		
Magdalene M. Ruff	3	female		do	do
Jeremy Ruff	3	male		do	do
Jno. Ebert Ruff, jr.	1	do		do	do
Geo. Harry Walter	51		Planter	do	do
Christina Walter	35	female		do	do
John E. Hanselmann	57	male	Pinmake.	do	do
Frederica Hanselmann	36	female		do	do
Earnest F. Hanselmann	27	male	Painter	do	do
Catharine Hanselmann	16	female		do	do
Louisa Hanselmann	6	do		do	do
Wilhelm. Hanselmann	5	do		do	do
Charles Hanselmann	8	male		do	do
Earnest Hanselmann, jr.	2	do		do	do
Gustave Hanselmann	0 6	female	Planter	do	do
John Adam Killer	53	male	Planter	do	do
Elizabeth Killer	41	female		do	do
Elizabeth Killer, jr.	19	do		do	do
Chas. Frederick Killer	15	male		do	do
John Adam Killer, jr.	14	do		do	do
John Lewis Killer	10	do.		do	do
Ann Elizabeth Killer	5	female		do	do
Margaret Killer	2	do		do	do
Eugene M. Killer*	6			do	Kentucky
John Giegner	42	male	Planter	do	do
Wilhelmina Giegner	38	female		do	do
Christian Giegner	15	male		do	do
Barbara Giegner	14	female		do	do
Mary Giegner	11	do		do	do
Adam Giegner	6	male		do	do
John Giegner	2	do		do	do
Adam Muller	34	do	Planter	do	do
Catharine Muller	31	female		do	do
James Muller	7	male		do	do
John Muller	5	do		do	do
Catharine Muller, jr.	3	female		do	do
Barbara Muller	2	do		do	do
Frederick Muller	53	male	Planter	do	do
Gothara Muller	16	female		do	do

* Born and died on the voyage.

LIST of Passengers, &c.—Quarter ending March 31, 1820.

Custom House, with the name of Collector.	Names of Passengers.	Age.	Sex.	Occupation.	Country to which they belong.	Country of which they intend to become inhab's	Ship or Vessel, with the name of the Master or Commander.
MISSISSIPPI, B. Chew.	Catharine Muller	14	female		Germany	Kentucky	Brig Eugene.
	Ann Mary Muller	11	do		do	do	
	George F. Muller	26	male	Planter	do	do	
	Rose Muller	19	female		do	do	
	Ann Muller	1	do		do	do	
	Conrad Stark	60	male	Baker	do	do	
	Margaret Stark	32	female	Planter	do	do	
	Margaret Stark, jr.	28	do		do	do	
	Magdalene Stark	8	do		do	do	
	Dorothea Stark	6	do		no	do	
	Christiana Stark	3	do		do	do	
	Conrad Stark	1	male		Born on board	do	
	Eugenia Virginia Stark		female		Germany	do	
	John George Diegel	56	male	Planter	do	do	
	J. G. Diegel	19	do	do	do	do	
	Joseph Diegel	30	do	do	do	do	
	Barbara Diegel	34	female		do	do	
	John Diegel	1 6	male		do	do	
	Martin Gruner	36	do	Planter	do	do	
	Catharine Gruner	28	female		do	do	
	John George Gruner	2 6	male		do	do	
	John Gruner	9	do		do	do	
	Charles S. Muller	43	do	Planter	do	do	
	Christiana Muller	41	female		do	do	
	John Muller	15	male		do	do	
	Sigismond Muller	13	do		do	do	
	John George Muller	10	do		do	do	

Name		Sex	Occupation	Native of	Destination	Remarks
Matthew Muller	8	male		Germany	Kentucky	
Jane Muller	6	female		do	do	
Christiana Muller	5	do		do	do	
Frederick Muller	2	male		do	do	
Caroline Muller*	3	female		do	do	* Died on the voyage.
Chr. Fred. Humann	40	male	Planter	do	do	
Ann Mary Humann	42	female		do	do	
Catharine Humann	13	do		do	do	
Theophilus Humann	10	male		do	do	
Christopher Humann	7	do		do	do	
James Humann	3	do		do	do	
John L. Wacker	48	female	Schoolmaster	do	do	
Magdalen Wacker	28	male		do	do	
Frederick Wacker	7	do		do	do	
James T. Kan	27	female	Planter	do	do	
Widow Rose Wittell	62	do	Wash. woman	do	do	
Caroline Wittell	23	do	do	do	do	
Rose Wittell	20	do	do	do	do	
John Geo. Yauch	39	male	Planter	do	do	
Ann Mary Yauch	34	female		do	do	
John Geo. Yauch, jr.	14	male		do	do	
James Yauch	12	do		do	do	
Ann Yauch	7	female		do	do	
Mary Yauch	3	do		do	do	
Christiana Yauch*	6 3	do		do	do	* Died on board.
Samuel F. Kies	28	male	Planter	do	do	
James Wittell	28	do	do	do	do	
Ann Mary Wittell	24	female		do	do	
Ann Barbara Wittell	6	do		do	do	
James Wittell	2	male		do	do	
Charles Julius Wittell	3	do	Planter	Born on board Germany	do	
Daniel Ruff	40	female		do	do	
Mary Ruff	24	male		do	do	
Joseph Ruff	15	female		do	do	
Victoria Ruff	10	male		do	do	
Peter Ruff	5	female		do	do	
Magdalene Ruff	3	male		do	do	
Godfrey Schenerle	51			do	do	

LIST of Passengers, &c.—Quarter ending March 31, 1820.

Custom House, with the name of the Collector.	Names of Passengers.	Age.	Sex.	Occupation.	Country to which they belong.	Country of which they intend to become inhab's	Ship or Vessel with the name of the Master or Commander.
MISSISSIPPI, B. Chew.	Catharine Shenerle	42	female		Germany	Kentucky	Brig Eugene.
	Catharine do jr.	19	do		do	do	
	Elizabeth do	15	do		do	do	
	Frederica do	10	do		do	do	
	Christiana do	9	do		do	do	
	Dorothea do	8	do		do	do	
	Margaret do	7	do		do	do	
	Christopher do	6	male		do	do	
	Theophilus do	2	do		do	do	
	John Geo. Ruff	28	do	Planter	do	do	
	David Baltz	21	do	Physician	do	do	
	John Elssaesser	46	do	Planter	do	do	
	Christiana do	45	female		do	do	
	Ann Mary	21	do		do	do	
	Christiana do jr.	18	do		do	do	
	Catharine do	15	do		do	do	
	Ann Elizabeth do	12	do		do	do	
	Barbara do	8	do		do	do	
	John do	4	male		do	do	
	Margaret do	2	female		do	do	
	Joseph Fred. Schaeffer	47	male	Planter	do	do	
	Catharine do	46	female		do	do	
	Joseph Fk. do jr.	19	male		do	do	
	John do	15	do		do	do	
	Theophilus do	12	do		do	do	
	Elizabeth do	8	female		do	do	
	David do	4	male		do	do	

Name	Age		Sex	Occupation			Vessel
James Hummel	40		male		Germany	Kentucky	
Margaret Hummel do	42		female		do	do	
James do	13	6	male		do	do	
Barbara do	9		female		do	do	
Philip Adam do	3	6	male		do	do	
Magdalene M. do			female		born on board		
John L. Ehninger	48		male	Planter	Germany	do	
Mary Magdalene do	45		female		do	do	
Mary do jr.	19		do		do	do	
Lewis Harry do	17		male		do	do	
Rose Magdalene do	12		female		do	do	
Theophilus Fred. do	11		male		do	do	
William Worst	39		male	Cook	do	Louisiana	Brig Calypso.
Augustine Ducoes	25		do	Merchant	Spain	Transient	
Etienne Bordier	26		do	do	France	Louisiana	
J. Breton	32		do	do	U. States	do	
Alexander Harang	45		do	Planter	do	do	Brig Elk.
Leon Bacas	35		do	Carpenter	do		
William Bass	40		do	Merchant	do		
J. B. Labranche	41		do	Planter	France	Louisiana	Ship Warrington.
Octave Labranche	23		do	do	do	do	
Jean Jaquet	20		do	Clerk	do	do	
Jaques Carleron	21		do	do	do	do	
Birabin	22		do	do	do	do	
Darose	33		do	do	do	do	
J. H. Fayset	20		do	Farmer	do	do	
E. Pacquet	28		do	Planter	do	do	
J. Bouson	28		do	Clerk	do	do	
Mrs. Bouson & 2 child	24		female	do	do	do	
J. Mirle	16		male	do	do	do	
Borasson	13		do	do	do	do	
Viviur	17		do	do	do	do	
Bernard	18		do	do	do	do	
Lacoste	24		do	do	do	do	
P. Greu	20		do	do	do	do	
J. Dignac	17		do	do	do	do	
G. Leonard	16		do	do	do	do	
J. Odichon	18		do	do	do	do	

LIST *of Passengers, &c.—Quarter ending 31st March, 1820.*

Custom House, with the name of the Collector.	Passengers.	Age.	Sex.	Occupation.	Country to which they belong.	Country of which they intend to become inhab's	Ship or Vessel, with the name of the Master or Commander.
MISSISSIPPI, B. Chew.	J. Pages	40	male	Mason	France	Louisiana	Ship Warrington.
	F. L. Lafontaine	22	do	Mariner	do	do	
	Chas. M'Louan	25	do	Soldier	Ireland	do	
	John Gharnau	22	do	Servant	do	do	
	Nicholas Chierrin	45	do	Physician	France	France	Ship North America.
	John Hamegos	40	do	Farmer	Louisiana	Louisiana	
	Mrs. Hamegos & 3 child.	35	female		do	do	
	M. Delvaille	40	male	Merchant	France	Transient	Ship Schuylkill.
	J. Seymour	42	do	Seaman	U. States	U. States	Schooner San Antonio.
	E. Govins	19	do	Farmer	do	do	
	M. F. M'Cala	50	female		do	do	
	Cognard	50	male	Planter	France	Louisiana	Ship Caroline.
	Le Mignon	44	do	Surgeon	do	do	
	Roth	45	do	Painter	do	do	
	Roth, jr.	8	do		do	do	
	Boudin	25	do	Clerk	U. States		
	Burnel	25	do	Mariner	France		
	Felix Levillion	17	do		do	do	
	Louis Lefevre	28	do	Mariner	do	do	
	Louis Laporte	30	do	do	U. States		
	Charles Jones	20	do	do	G. Britain		
	James Gordon	26	do	Merchant	Spain	G. Britain	Barque Waterloo.
	Michael Orb	44	do	do	U. States	Spain	Schooner Henry.
	John Avril	25	do	do	Ireland	U. States	
	John Martin	30	do	Gunsmith	France		Ship Balize.
	Thomas	30	do	Servant		Mobile	

Name	Age	Sex	Occupation	Country	Destination	Vessel
Manuel Garcia, jr.	30	male	Farmer	Spain		Schooner Victory.
Parker	26	do	Merchant	U. States		
Rosalie	30	female	do	do		
Le Blank and child	50	do	do	do		
Franchette	28	do	do	do		
Rachael and 2 children	40	do	do			
Peter Lafitte	50	male	Mariner	France	U. States	Schooner Pegasus.
Perige	34	do	do	Italy		
Bamon	22	do	do	France		
Antonio	55	do	Merchant	Spain		
Benjamin Wolf	29	do	do	England	U. States	Schooner George Pickett, S. Harney.
George	27	do	do	Italy		
Mathieu	50	do	do	France		
Wm. Forest	44	do	do	U. States		
Violier	47	do	do	France		
Frederick Trey	25	do	Wax bleacher	Germany	Louisiana	Galliot Fortuna.
Francis Andres	18	do	Shoemaker	do	do	
M. A. Azle	31	do	do	Russia	do	
Henriette Batzmyer	18	female	Farmer	Germany	do	
C. Bentheim	42	male		do	do	
Mary Elizabeth do	18	female	do	do	do	
Rudolph Bernstein	42	male	do	do	do	
Frederick	10	do.		do	do	
C. Mary Englis	28	female	Servant	do	do	
Anna M. Dorothea	72	do		do	do	
A. H. Peter Blucher	32	male	Carpenter	do	do	
George Blucher	31	do	Tailor	do	do	
Elizabeth do	24	female		do	do	
Jacob do	1	male		do	do	
John Bruning	31	do	Joiner & carp.	do	do	
Charles Haenmrick	26	do	Butcher	do	do	
Philip Franz	24	do	Brewer	do	do	
John H. Fricke	37	do	Joiner	do	do	
Louisa do and 2 child.	27	female		do	do	
J. Albert Gartleman	44	male	Carpenter	do	do	
Ann Eliza do	38	female		do	do	
John do	14	male		do	do	
Mary Gerlach	28	female		do	do	

Dis. Edenton, Saml. Treadwell.

7

LIST of Passengers, &c.—Quarter ending March 31, 1820.

Custom House, with the Name of the Collector.	Names of Passengers.	Age.	Sex.	Occupation.	Country to which they belong.	Country of which they intend to become inhab's	Ship or Vessel, with the name of the Master or Commander.
EDENTON. Saml. Treadwell.	Randolph C. Gorner	21	male	Tailor	Germany	Louisiana	Galliot Fortuna.
	John Griebsch	20	do	Blacksmith	do	do	
	Christ. Hahn	26	do	Barber	do	do	
	John C. Hempeecht	26	do	Shoemaker	do	do	
	John Hinkel	39	do	Farmer	do	do	
	Ann M. Hinkel	31	female		do	do	
	Jacob Hinkel	5	male		do	do	
	Henry Hinkel	3	do		do	do	
	John Hinkel, jr.	1	do		do	do	
	Gotlieb Jonchin	36	do	Tailor	do	do	
	Anthony Kahle	32	do	Carpenter	do	do	
	John C. Kern	23	do	Blacksmith	do	do	
	C. C. Klein	23	do	Shoemaker	do	do	
	James Kleiber	23	do	do	do	do	
	J. F. Kritznier	25	do	Joiner	do	do	
	Ludivig Kuch	23	do	Painter	do	do	
	John Lange	42	do	Butcher	do	do	
	John C. Larehen	38	do	Tailor	do	do	
	Henry Lenike	19	do	Laborer	do	do	
	D. T. F. Mathussan	25	do	Barber	do	do	
	G. H. Meyer	34	do	Farmer	do	do	
	F. W. Muller	27	do	Joiner	do	do	
	John Muller	29	do	Carpenter	do	do	
	Ann E. Muller	24	female		do	do	
	John Muller	4	male		do	do	
	Elizabeth Muller	2	female		do	do	
	John Jost Muller	8	male		do	do	

Name	Age	Sex	Occupation	Country	Destination	Ship
Elizabeth Muller	10	female	Laborer	Germany	Louisiana	Galliot Fortuna.
Conrad Neidle	19	male	Butcher	do	do	
Nathaniel Petri	18	do	Shoemaker	do	do	
Charles L. Pieper	25	do	Butcher	do	do	
George M. Petri	25	do	Shoemaker	do	do	
Charles L. Pieper	25	do	Tailor	do	do	
George N. Pinkenille	23	do	Shoemaker	do	do	
I. Rossler	23	do	Tailor	do	do	
William Sanders	19	do	do	do	do	
Henry Sandmann	22	do	Shoemaker	do	do	
Charles Scheffler	26	do	Brewer	do	do	
Andrew Schmidt	29	do	Farmer	do	do	
Jacob Schuler	20	do	do	do	do	
John Schulenberg	53	female		do	do	
Gretz Schulenberg	40	male		do	do	
Frederick Schulenberg	11	do	Farmer	do	do	
William Schulenberg	9	do		do	do	
John M. Seifert	29	female	Farmer	do	do	
Josephina Seifert	28	male		do	do	
Charles J. Seigmund	33	do	Ropemaker	do	do	
Francis M. Sievers	32	do	Mason	do	do	
H. C. Stange	21	do	Shoemaker	do	do	
Christ. Hechell	45	do	Painter & joiner	do	do	
George Struthoff	28	do	Shoemaker	do	do	
Henry Tutt	20	do	Laborer	do	do	
Jno. H. Wahrenberg	26	do	Carpenter	do	do	
Charles Washman	17	do	Mason	do	do	
F. C. Westermann	32	do	Carpenter	do	do	
F. Wilkins	37	do	Shoemaker	do	do	
Johanna Wilkins	32	female		do	do	
G. F. Windeller	28	male	do	do	do	
Ann M. Windeller	26	female		do	do	
Albert F. Windeller	2	male		do	do	
John Thomas	20	do	Farmer	France	do	Brig Aleine.
L. Delachaux	20	do	Merchant	U. States	do	Sloop Gold Huntress.
Benjamin W. Basden	27	do	do	do	do	
Caleb Fellows	50	do	do	do	do	
Francois Ls. Bruisere	47	do	do	do	do	

LIST of Passengers, &c.—Quarter ending 31st March, 1820.

Custom House, with the name of the Collector.	Names of Passengers.	Age.	Sex.	Occupation.	Country to which they belong.	Country of which they intend to become inhab's	Ship or Vessel, with the name of the Master or Commander.
	Thomas Harrison	30	male	Merchant	U. States	Loüisiana	Sloop Gold Huntress.
	Delasige	53	do	Plant. r	do		
	Walker	50	do	merchant	England		
	Graves	35	do	do	do		
	Boyden	22	do	Mechanic	U. States		
	Losado	35	do	Priest	do	do	Schooner Deus Soeurs.
	Pre. Riens Leroy	32	do	Baker	do	do	Schooner Dos Amigos.
	Zamy Aubry	20	do	Shoemaker	do	do	Ship Resolution.
	A. Baker	40	female	Merchant	do	Guadaloupe	Schooner Hope.
	Mrs. Fagus	43	male	Merchant	Guadaloupe	Louisiana	
	Juan Rodon	35	do	Carpenter	Spain	do	
	Charles Brown	37	do	do	U. States	do	Sloop Lewis.
	Guillerno Estevan	32	do	do	do	do	
	Domingo Caymares	35	do	Merchant	do	do	
	John Carlisle	23	female		do	do	
	Mrs. Carlisle & child		male	Carpenter	do	do	Schooner Favorite.
	E. Kent	25	do	Mariner	do	do	
	William Gardner	20	do	Merchant	do	do	
	James Watson	23	do	Mariner	do	do	
	Thomas Dennis	35	do	Carpenter	England	N. Orleans	
	Laurence Boyle	40	do	Merchant	Ireland	do	
	R. Currell	26	do	Clerk	U. States		
	D. H. Dorsey	22	do	Gunsmith	St. Domingo		
	J. I. Barbaret	28	do				
	Mrs. Duvall	65	do				
Boston and Charlestown, H. A. S. Dearborn.	James Savage	20	do	Mariner	U. States	U. States	Brig Caspian, Stephen Standley.
	Benjamin Howard	20	do				

Name	Age	Sex	Occupation			Vessel
Benjamin Gordon	40	male	Mariner	U. States	U. States	Brig Margaret, E. Davenport.
William Chewer	27	do	Merchant	Nova Scotia	do	Schooner Cherub, William Athearn.
Charlotte Chewer	24	female	Merchantess	do	do	
Alexander Frazier	25	male	Merchant	N. Brunsw'k	N. Brunswick	
Alfred Tupper	22	do	Accountant	U. States	U. States	
James Matthews	29	do	Stonecutter	Scotland	Nova Scotia	
Michael O'Brien	22	do	Sailor	Nova Scotia	do	
James M. Groath	30	do	Trader	Ireland	do	
John Dorrell	23	do	do	do	do	
Robert Dawson	30	do	Fair trader	Scotland	do	Schooner Victory, Samuel Barker.
John Fairbanks	29	do	Merchant	Nova Scotia	do	
Flavan Duhamel	28	do	Mariner	do	do	
John Homer	38	do	do	do	do	
John Butters	27	do	Merchant	do	do	
Richard Lewis	26	do	Mariner	New York	New-York	
Philip Brasher	29	do	do	U. States	U. States	
John Dowling	29	do	Trader	N.Brunswick	N. Brunswick	
Johanna C. Diehl	40	do	Butcher	Germany	U. States	Brig Telemachus, W. Wood.
Francis Moreau	27	do	Military officer	France	France	
Robert Dodd	40	do	Farmer	England	U. States	
I. S. Newton	39	do	Artist	do	do	
Christopher Thompson	45	do	Trader	do	do	Brig Horace, Jno. Collyer.
Chas. Henry Titius	43	do	do	France	Undecided	
Mrs. Rowe, wife of mate	52	female			U. States	
Thomas Myrick	28	male	Mariner	U. States	U. States	Schooner Cherub, William Athearn.
Sargent Ingersol	23	do	do	do	do	
Daniel Muno	19	do	Carpenter	G. Britain	G. Britain	
William C. Sears	45	do	Merchant	St.Johns,NB	on a visit U.S.	Schooner Jefferson, Joseph Howard.
Nathaniel Scott	20	do	Farmer	U. States	U. States	
Allen Munroe, 2d	13	do	Mariner	do	do	
John Cornell	26	do	do	do	do	Brig Charity, Caleb U. Grozer.
James Sargent, jr.	27	do	Merchant	do	do	
Peter Henry Wilt	18	do	do	Hamburg	do	
Peter Noleine		do	Carpenter	Moscow	do	
Benjamin Robinson	40	do		U. States	U. States	Brig Resolution, Carl. F. Gaedig.
Mary Thaxter	40	female	Baker	do	do	Schooner America, D. Stover.
Joshua Thaxter	17	male	do	do	do	Schooner Victory, Samuel Barker.
John Thanter	7	do		do		

LIST of Passengers, &c.—Quarter ending March 31, 1820.

Custom House, with the name of the Collector.	Names of Passengers.	Age.	Sex.	Occupation.	Country to which they belong.	Country of which they intend to become inhb's.	Ship or Vessel, with the name of the Master or Commander.
BOSTON AND CHARLESTOWN, H. A. S. Dearborn.	William Thaxter	1	male		U. States	U. States	Schooner Victory, Samuel Barker.
	Mary Thaxter	10	female		do	Portland	
	Emeline Thaxter	3	do		do	do	
	Mary Rowl	21	male		Nova Scotia	U. States	
	Grace Dunlop	31	female		do	do	
	Jane Dunlop	6	do		do	do	
	Rachel Dunlop	1	do		do	do	
	Samuel Baker	44	male	Butcner	U. States	do	
	Peter Zeneo	50	do	Gentleman	Pennsylva.	do	
	Francis Raphael	62	do	do	do	do	
	John Deal	23	do	Merchant	Ireland	Nova Scotia	
	Cepeana Bendelo	32	do	Baker	Italy	U. States	
	Daniel Dunlap	26	do	Bricklayer	Ireland	do	
	George Savell	25	do	Trader	G. Britain	G. Britain	Schooner Cherub, William Athearn.
	Terence Cannal	35	do	Papermaker	do.	do	
	J. M'Gregor and wife	24	do	Carpenter	do	U. States	
	Waller Rabb	30	do	Papermaker	do	do	
	Wm. Garreg and wife	24	do	Servant	do	do	
	Mark Dixon	24	do	Farmer	do	do	
	John Fitzpatrick	20	do	Farmer	do	do	
	John Clark	25	do	Tinker	France	Canada	Ship Warren, Webb.
	John Leonard	22	do	Farmer	England	U. States	Schooner Cherub, William Athearn.
	William Bancroft	23	do	Mechanic	Nova Scotia	do	
	William Bird	20	do	Merchant	U. States	do	
	N. G. Carnes	28	do	do	do.	do	Ship Falcon, Joseph W. Sears.
	John Shephard	35	do	do	England	do	
	George Phillips	56	do	Umbrellamaker	do	do	

Name	Age	Sex	Occupation			Remarks
Henry Phillips	14	male	Umbrellamaker	England	U. States	Brig Swift, Amos Hill.
Margaret Phillips	21	female		do	do	Schooner Victory, Samuel Barker.
Frances Phillips	17	do		do	do	
Martha Phillips	16	male		do	do	Ship Jasper, T. Crooker.
James Rogerson	26	female	Laborer	do	do	Ship Persia, H. Hale.
Mary Baker	28	male		do	do	Schooner Abigail, Howe Davidson.
Thomas Davidson	4			do	do	
James Dey	28	do	Merchant	U. States	do	
William Lamb	30	da	Gentleman	do	do	Schr. Alpha & Omega, Wm. H. Wallace.
Samuel Baker	43	do	Trader	do	do	Brig Matilda, James Coffin.
J. T. Marshall	17	do		do	do	
Jesse Waln	38	do	Merchant	do	do	
James Wilson	29	do	Gardener	Scotland	do	Schooner Eliza, Asa Keith.
New London.						
T. H. Cushing.						
Plymouth.						
Levi Fagar.						
James Murphy	25	do	Cordwainer	Ireland	do	Schooner Lucy, Nathaniel Crosby, jr.
J. A. Estery	22	do	Blacksmith	U. States	Hartford	
S. M'Kentey	31	do	Laborer	Ireland	America	
M. Marr	38	do	Merchant	U. States	Virginia	Brig Copernican, George Henchman.
Prentiss Scudder	22	do	Mariner	do	U. States	Ship William, C. W. Noyes.
Edgartown, Mas.						
Thos. Cooke, jr.						
Aaron Scudder	21	do	do	do	do	
Ephraim Meozarvey	31	do	do	do	do	
Nathan Pecket	23	do	do	do	do	
John Roberts	34	do	do	England	do	
Clarissa Ellis	28	female		do	do	
Clarissa Ellis, jr.	6	do		do	do	
Emily Ellis	4	do		do	do	
Charlotte Ellis	2	do		do	do	
Angeline Ellis	1	do		do	do	
Harriet Ellis	6	do		do	do	
David W. Thirlkill	22	male	Gentleman	do	do	
Wm. W. Bray	28	do	do	do	do	
William Gardner	36	do	Farmer	do	do	
Thomas Gardner	27	do	do	do	do	
Thomas Gardner, jr.	16	do	do	do	do	
Abraham Gardner	12	do	do	do	do	
Mary Gardner	18	female		do	do	
Thomas Brown	40	male	Gentleman	do	do	
Thomas Neyel	35	do	do	do	do	

LIST of Passengers, &c.—Quarter ending March 31, 1820.

Custom House, with the name of the Collector.	Names of Passengers.	Age.	Sex.	Occupation.	Country to which they belong.	Country of which they intend to become inhab's	Ship or Vessel, with the Name of the Master or Commander.
EDGARTOWN, Mas. Thos. Cooke, jr.	Thomas Trustrum	50	male	Butcher	England	U. States	Ship William, C. W. Noyes.
	William Eldrid	36	do	Farmer	do	do	
	George Eldrid	22	do	do	do	do	
	Sarah Eldrid	28	female		do	do	
	Betsey Eldrid	10	do		do	do	
	Sarah Eldrid	8	do		do	do	
	Mary Eldrid	6	do		do	do	
	William Eldrid, jr.	4	male		do	do	
	Charles Eldrid	2	do		do	do	
	Henry Eldrid	6	do		do	do	
	Sarah Eman	25	female	do	Ireland	do	Brig Climax, Jared Fisher.
	Mitchel Lyons	24	male		do	do	
	James Doyle	14	do		do	do	
	Patrick Doyle	11	do		do	do	
	Bridget Doyle	8	female		do	do	
	Mary Doyle	6	do		do	do	
	Reuben F. Coffin	28	male	do	U. States	do	Ship Thomas, John Brown.
	Jos. Kaldwell	22	do	Mariner	do	do	
	Andrew Compton	30	do	do	do	do	Schooner Zephyr, K. Ripley.
	Elizabeth Cowan	21	female	Merchant	do	do	Schooner Rising Sun, Lott Doane.
	Uriah Lyons	22	male	do	Ireland	do	Brig Pallas, Jacob Leifler.
	Eben. Wheelwright	30	do	Mariner	U. States	do	Brig St. Clair, Joseph Hooper.
	Joseph Walker	26	do	Trader	do	do	Sloop Hero, John Trow.
PORTLAND AND FALMOUTH. Isaac Ilsley.	One man, &c. unknown						
	Joseph Wittum	40	male	Seaman	do	do	Sloop Favorite, John Trow.
	Mrs. Wittum	80	female				

Name	Age	Sex	Occupation	Country	Country	Vessel
Child	13	male			U. States	Schooner Packet, Ebenezer Small.
Child	8	do			do	
Mary Probyn	22	female	Schoolmistress	England	do	
Henry Croford	29	male	Cutler	Ireland	do	
John Small	29	do	Baker	do	do	
Samuel Sampson	24	do	Cutler	England	do	
Jethro Bancroft	21	do	Merchant	U. States	do	Schooner Enterprise, David Jones, jr.
Silas Smith	25	do	do	do	do	
Orange M. Ferress	22	do	do	do	do	
Neal Shaw	23	do	Indigo planter	do	do	
Wm. U. Green	33	do	Merchant	do	G. Britain	Schooner Albert, Jno. Shackford.
Samuel Campbell	35	do	do	G. Britain	do	Ship Com. Preble, Edward Bray.
Archibald Gaute	18	do	do	do	do	Schooner Lucretia, George Kimball.
Nathaniel Milby	20	do	Farmer	do	do	
Patrick Powar	30	do	Ship carpent'r	St. John	St. John	Sloop Milledgeville, George Knight.
Thomas Pettingell	55	female				
Mrs. Pettingell	20	do				
Mrs. Pettingell	18	do				
James Whitney	24	male				
Dis. of Portsmouth & Norfolk, James Johnson.						
Wm. Merret	35	do	Merchant	Canada	Canada	Schooner Wm. and Jos. Thomas Rocke.
John Ansley	24	do	Farmer	New York	New York	
James Jackson	40	do	Gentleman	New Hamp.	New Hamp.	
Edward Dale	28	da	do	St. John	St. John	
George Chadwick	25	do	House carpt'r	do	do	
Daniel Cunningham	30	do	Blockmaker	New York	New-York	
John C. Saunders	32	do	Farmer	U. States	U. States	Brig Hibernia, James Fitzsimons.
Darius Woodland	23	do	Merchant	do	do	
Matthew Reardon	26	do	Clerk	do	do	
Hugh Mayne	28	do	do	Ireland	do	
James Cappels	30	do	Teacher	do	do	Brig John and Adeline, Joshua Folger.
Wm. Hutton	31	do	Farmer	do	do	
Conway Whittle	22	do	Physician	U. States	do	
Catharine Folger	27	female		do		
Jane Parsons	22	do	Servant	Isl. Bermuda	Isl. Bermuda	Ship Governor Hawkins, M. Carr.
John Higginson	55	male	Ship master	U. States	U. States	
John Stephenson	25	do	do	do	do	Schooner Charles K. Mallory, B. Bissell.
Francis Barts	40	do	Supercargo	do	do	
Henry Keele	32	do	Ship master	do	do	

LIST of Passengers, &c.—Quarter ending March 31, 1820.

Custom House, with the name of the Collector.	Names of Passengers.	Age.	Sex.	Occupation.	Country to which they belong.	Country of which they intend to become inhab's	Ship or Vessel, with the name of the Master or Commander.
Dis. of Portsmouth & Norfolk, James Johnson.	David Robertson	23	male	Merchant	Scotland	U. States	Brig Andromache, E. Farnham.
	John Freeman	40	do	Merchant	England	do	Schooner George, Robert Hall.
	Cornelius Mathews	38	do	Victualler	U. States	do	Ship Higson, Jno. Johnston.
	James M'Carthy	18	female	Clerk	Ireland	do	
	Lucy Mackay	24	do		do	do	
	Mary Ann Mackay	5	male		do	do	
	John Mackay	7	female		do	do	
	Catharine Mackay	3			do	do	
	Thomas Smith	45	male	Mariner	U. States	St. Domingo	Schooner Beluga, Charles Lynn.
	Gabriel Justian	24	do	Merchant	St. Domingo	U. States	
	James Steward	31	do	Stone cutter	Scotland	do	Schooner Only Daughter, Jno. Ellis.
	Thomas Oxley	35	do	Teacher math's	England	do	
	Elizabeth Oxley	35	female		do	do	
	Thomas Oxley, jr.	7	male		do	do	
	Elizabeth Oxley, jr.	5	female		do	do	
	Samuel Harris	45	male	Ship master	U. States	do	Ship Virginia, Reuben Fisher.
	George Kipper	29	do	Merchant	England	do	
	William Brown	17	do	Clerk	do	do	
	Thomas B. Bell	40	do	Cutler	Ireland	do	Brig Hammer, James M. Pollard.

LIST of Passengers, &c.—Quarter ending June 30, 1820.

Custom House, with the name of the Collector.	Names of Passengers.	Age.	Sex.	Occupation.	Country to which they belong.	Country of which they intend to become inh'bts.	Ship or Vessel, with the Name of the Master or Commander.
PHILADELPHIA, John Steele.	Robert Connell	28	male	Merchant	Ireland	U. States	Brig Rose in Bloom, S. Scull
	John M'Kausky	28	do	do	do	do	
	Robert Harvey	24	do	Schoolmaster	do	do	
	James Hunter	23	do	Farmer	do	do	
	W. C. Johnston	21	do	Teacher	do	do	
	Robert Craig	23	do	Farmer	do	do	
	David Martin	24	do	Laborer	do	do	
	John M'Kinstry	28	do	do	do	do	
	John Dougherty	35	female	Farmer	St. John, N.B.	do	Schooner Infant, Samuel Anderson.
	Nancy Dougherty	30	do		do	do	
	Margaret Dougherty	30	do		do	do	
	John Dougherty, jr.	6	male		do	do	
	Elizabeth Lewis	24	female		G. Britain	do	Ship Tuscarora, Wm. West.
	Anna Hallworth	36	do		do	do	
	Alfred Hallworth	4	male		do	do	
	Anna Hallworth, jr.	infant	female		do	do	
	Jane Leigh	21	male		do	do	
	Robert Petty	28	female	Farmer	do	do	
	Ann Petty	28	male		do	do	
	Ashton Barlow	23	female	Farmer	do	do	
	Francis Filton	35	male		do	do	
	Hannah Filton	14	female		do	do	
	Mary B. Filton	12	do		do	do	
	Thomas Filton	10	male		do	do	
	Samuel Filton	7	do		do	do	
	Francis Filton	5	do		do	do	
	William Filton	3	do		do	do	

LIST of Passengers, &c.—Quarter ending June 30, 1820.

Custom House, with the name of the Collector.	Names of Passengers.	Age.	Sex.	Occupation.	Country to which they belong.	Country of which they intend to become inhab's	Ship or Vessel, with the name of the Master or Commander.
Philadelphia, John Steele.	Richard Smitherst	22	male	Carter	G. Britain	U. States	Ship Tuscarora, Wm. West.
	Richard Gaunt	50	do	Farmer	do	do	
	Jonathan Hutton	24	do	Clerk	do	do	
	Edward Grundy	20	do	Farmer	America	do	
	Richard Hardman	33	do	Farmer	G. Britain	do	
	Wm. Bailly	65	do	Shoemaker	do	do	
	Andrew Story	17	do	Merchant	do	do	
	Howard Sims	24	do	Brewer	America	do	
	Frederick Gaul	54	do	Merchant	do	do	
	Samuel Conly	30	do	do	do	do	
	John Bacon	32	do		do	do	
	William Orange	23	do	Farmer	England	do	Ship Tontine, E. Turley.
	Benjamin Orange	17	do	do	do	do	
	Richard Wilson	23	do	Gentleman	do	do	
	Jane Wilson	50	female		do	do	
	Mary Wilson	18	do.		do	do	
	John Rudge	35	male		do	do	
	Henry Moss	24	do	Stationer	Scotland	do	
	George Anderson	28	do	Farmer	do	do	
	Robert Anderson	25	do	do	do	do	
	Ann Anderson	25	female		do	do	
	David Wallace	26	male	Farmer	England	do	
	John Jakes	50	do	do	do	do	
	John Thompson	17	do	do	do	do	
	Thomas Calvert	14	do	do	do	do	
	Sarah Noon	68	female		do	do	
	John Kelty	30	male	Gentleman	England	England	Ship Catharine, Robert Young.

Name	Age	Sex	Occupation			Vessel
Mathias Stewart	35	male	Laborer	U. States	U. States	Brig Harp, Charles Landgrain.
Jane Stewart	30	female	None	do	do	
Albert Flood	26	male	Laborer	do	do	
Jeremiah Cochrane	30	do	Cooper	do	do	
C. Barry	36	do	Merchant	do	do	Brig Hannah, A Latour.
J. Monsanta	38	do	do	Trinidad	do	
E. Mendoza	16	do		U. States	do	
H. Quig	36	do	Soap boiler	Spain	Spain	Brig Zeno, L. Slade.
Manuel Bellis	40	do	Merchant	do	do	
Pedro Tavoana	34	do	Mariner	do	do	
Manuel Fernandez	12	do		U. States	U. States	
Anthony White	23	do	do	France	do	
Francis Marcus	26	do	Merchant	U. States	do	Shooner Nymph, T. D. Kennedy.
George Lewis	25	do	Mariner	do	do	
William Philips	40	do	Supercargo	St. Domingo	do	Ship Brandt, George W. Steinhaur.
Mrs. P. Gausche & son	30	female		do	do	
Mrs. M. Gausche	26	do		U. States	do	
Maria C. Smith	35	do		do	do	
Wilhelmina Smith	11	do		France	France	
John Chaban	26	male	Merchant	France	France	Schooner Almira, B. Eldridge.
Miss Claudin Boyer	21	female		do	do	
Louisa Boyer	11	do		St. Domingo	U. States	
Francisco Perez	22	male	Merchant	do	do	
G. W. Moise		do	Mariner	France	do	
John Purdy	60	do	Merchant	do	do	
Mr. Perpignan	45	do	do	U. States	do	Brig La Hermione, Stephen Veyssore.
Mr. Duford	21	do	do	England	do	
Dennis Cragg	38	do		do	do	Ship Election, George Roberson.
Jane Smith	46	female	Victualler	do	do	
John Hollinsbe	47	male		do	do	
Mary Hollinsbe	21	female	Victualler	do	do	
John Hollinsbe	35	male		do	do	
Margaret Mills	36	female		do	do	
Mary Cox	50	do		do	do	
Charles Benson	27	male	Gardener	do	do	
Wm. Hamilton	37	do	Grocer	do	do	
Robert A. Grys	33	do	Farmer	do	do	
John Day		do	Harnessmaker	da	da	

LIST of Passengers, &'c.—Quarter ending June 30, 1820.

Custom House, with the name of the Collector.	Names of Passengers.	Age.	Sex.	Occupation.	Country to which they belong.	Country of which they intend to become inhab's	Ship or Vessel, with the name of the Master or Commander.
PHILADELPHIA, John Steele.	Wm. Shirman Smith	21	male	Clerk	England	U. States	Ship Election, George Roberson.
	Charles Wood	21	do	Leatherdress	do	do	
	John Johnson	36	female	Carpenter	Ireland	do	
	Ann Johnson	37	male		do	do	
	John Harnett	25	female	Carpenter	do	do	
	Ann Harnett	30	male	Shoemaker	do	do	
	Jeremiah Leasy	48	do	Farmer	England	do	
	Elisha Gedge	41	female		do	do	
	Jane Gedge	36	do		do	do	
	Elizabeth Amos	26	do		do	do	
	Martha Varndell	27	male	Farmer	do	do	
	John Wooldridge	48	female		do	do	
	Sarah Wooldridge	37	male	Merchant	do	do	
	Richard Atherton	38	female		do	do	
	Esther Atherton	29	male		do	do	
	William Atherton	7	do		do	do	
	Henry Atherton	6	do		do	do	
	John Atherton	4	female		do	do	
	Ann Esther Atherton	10	do		do	do	
	Isabella Atherton	2	do		do	do	
	Frances Atherton	5	male		do	do	
	Richard Atherton	8	do		do	do	
	William Wooldridge	4	do		do	do	
	James Amos	6	do		do	do	
	Theodore Amos	5			do	do	
	Francina Amos	4	female		do	do	
	Edward Mills	3	male		do	do	

Name	Age	Sex	Occupation	Country	Destination	Remarks
Mary Ann Cox	9	female			do	
Frederick Geo. Gedge	16	male			do	
James C. Gedge	12	do			do	
Christian H. Gedge	7	do			do	
Wm. Henry Gedge	4	do			do	
Chas. Edw. Gedge	2	do			do	
Elizabeth H. Gedge	15	female		Philadelphia	do	
Sarah Ann Gedge	0 2	do		Bermuda	Bermuda	
Jacob Neff*	24	male	Merchant	England	U. States	*Died on the voyage, March 20, 1820.
Joseph Shaw	28	do	do	Gonaives	St. Thomas	Brig Junius, George Duntor.
William Henry	26	do	do	U. States	U. States	
John Henry	25	do	do	do	do	
James Guffer	28	female	Servant	do	do	
Nancy	27	male	Merchant	do	do	
C. Tupess	45	do	Cabinetmaker	Spain	do	Schooner Philadelphia, P. Hall.
James Hughes	30	do	Mariner	U. States	do	
David Duchan	35	do	Cabinetmaker	do	do	
William Kean	25	do	Merchant	do	do	
A. Roberts	25	do	do	do	do	
R. Bango	35	do	do	Ireland	do	
Francis Silva	50	female	Lady	U. States	do	Brig Trident, Edward Duston.
Mrs. Mayo	40	male	Merchant	do	do	
Palanga	30	do	do	G. Britain	do	
I. M. Meynie	35	do	do	do	do	
Huffman	50	do		do	do	
Michael Aiken	23	female	Spinster	do	do	Schooner Dorcas Ann, S. Fisher.
Martha M'Mullin	39	male	Currier	do	do	Ship William Penn, James Hamilton.
John Jefferson	10	do	Farmer		do	
Edmund Jefferson	48	do			do	
John Fentun	7	do			do	
John Fentun, jr.	11	do	Spinster		do	
Fentun	38	female	do		do	
Nancy Hollowell	11	do	do		do	
Hannah Hollowell	7	do			do	
Sally Hollowell	2	do			do	
Nancy Hollowell, jr.	14	male			do	
John Hollowell	12	do	do		do	
Daniel Hollowell		do			do	

LIST of Passengers, &c.—Quarter ending June 30, 1820.

Custom House, with the name of the Collector.	Names of Passengers.	Age.	Sex.	Occupation.	Country to which they belong.	Country of which they intend to become inhab's	Ship or Vessel, with the name of the Master or Commander.
PHILADELPHIA, John Steele.	William Hollowell	10	male		G. Britain	U. States	Ship William Penn, James Hamilton.
	Ely Hollowell	4	do		do	do	
	John Armstrong	26	do	Farmer	do	do	
	John Armstrong, jr.	3	do		do	do	
	Letty Armstrong	32	female		do	do	
	Jane Armstrong	3	do		do	do	
	Letty Armstrong, jr.	5	do		do	do	
	Eliza Armstrong	18	do		do	do	
	M. Viesch	32	male	Draftsman	France	France	
	Daniel Perkins	27	do	Merchant	U. States	U. States	Brig Howard, Jos. Perkins.
	E. P. Lord	21	do	do	do	do	
	Hannah Crompton	27	female		England	do	Ship Rebecca Sims, Dl. Brenton.
	Samuel Crompton	2	male		do	da	
	James Pierounet	13	do		do	do	
	Mary Mahin	22	female		do	da	
	Harriet Mahin	3	do		do	do	
	Margaret Mahin	2	do		do	do	
	John Hurry	20	male	Merchant	do	do	
	James Findly	67	do	Gardener	do	do	
	Mrs. Campbell	35	female		Nova Scótia	do	Schooner Nancy, Thomas Warren.
	J. H. Turner	53	male	Merchant	Italy	do	Schooner M'Donough, John Reading.
	John Alderson	40	do	do	G. Britain	do	Brig Meta, William Wilkie.
	John T. Cox	38	do	do	U. States	do	Schooner Lydia and Mary, A. Burns.
	David B. Noñes	38	do	Supercargo	do	do	Schooner St. Helena, Alexr. Taylor.
	Lewis T. Pratt	22	do	do	do	do	
	Sophia M'Laughlin	40	female		Ireland	do	
	Daniel Boyd	45	male	Farmer	do	do	Ship Conestoga, Wm. Marshall.

Name	Age	Sex	Occupation		U. States
John Andrew	70	do	Laborer	Ireland	do
Mary Andrew	60	female	Farmer	do	do
David Andrew	22	male		do	do
Eliza Andrew	26	female		do	do
Francis Andrew	15	male	do	do	do
Hugh Hanegan	60	do	Laborer	do	do
Catharine Hanegan	20	female		do	do
Hugh Hanegan, jr.	17	male	do	do	do
Thomas Hanegan	18	do	do	do	do
Patrick Bradley	30	do	do	do	do
Eleanor Kaine	25	female		do	do
Thomas Leonard	30	male	Farmer	U. States	do
Biddy Rogan	21	do	Spinster	Ireland	do
Sarah Hume	40	male	Farmer	do	do
John M'Clure	35	do	Merchant	do	db
Wm. Cavenaugh	20	female		U. States	do
Eliza Arbuckle	18	do		Ireland	do
Jane Arbuckle	25	male	Farmer	do	do
James Cummins	24	female		U. States	to
Hannah Neilson	17	do		Ireland	do
Eleanor M'Girr	22	do	do	do	do
Bridget M'Girr	25	male		do	do
Patrick Smith	25	female	do	do	do
Rose Smith	54	do		do	do
Juliet Smith	25	do		do	do
Mary Smith	30	male	do	U. States	do
Robert Hill	20	do	do	do	do
James M'Causland	50	do	do	Ireland	do
William Hunter	21	do	do	U. States	do
David Blackburn	25	do	do	Ireland	do
Henry Sproul	20	female		do	do
John Nelson	30	male	do	do	do
Catharine Tracy	20	female		do	do
William Lowry	1	do		do	do
Mary Lowry	42	male	Merchant	U. States	do
Mary Lowry, jr.	35	do	Servant	do	do

Barque Ossipee, James Stanbury.

LIST of Passengers, &c.—Quarter ending June 30, 1820.

Custom House, with the name of Collector.	Names of Passengers.	Age.	Sex.	Occupation.	Country to which they belong.	Country of which they intend to become inhab's	Ship or Vessel, with the name of the Master or Commander.
PHILADELPHIA. John Steele.	Henry Bosley	35	male	Servant	U. States	U. States	Barque Ossipee, James Stanbury.
	S. Lavens	30	do	Merchant	do	do	
	William Martin	26	do	do	do	do	
	Philip Haezell	43	do	Chairmaker	do	do	
	Benjamin Viall	44	do	Chandler	do	do	
	Michael Mitchell	45	female		do	do	
	Mary Mitchell	26	female		do	do	
	Mrs. Morris	32	do	Baker	do	do	
	Edward Ryan	22	male	Jeweller	do	do	
	John Graves	28	do		do	do	Schooner Minerva, S. Barclay.
	Mr. Murphy	28	do	Gentleman	do	do	
	Mr. Holland	21	do	do	do	do	
	Mr. Hoagh	40	do	do	do	do	
	Mr. Gillard	38	do	Merchant	do	do	Brig Joseph, John Graves.
	William Burnham	26	do		do	do	
	John Izard	22	do	Carpenter	do	do	
	Asa Copeland	25	do	Gentleman	do	do	
	John Casanova	20	do	Laborer	Britain	do	Sloop Jones Hull, George Prince.
	Samuel Davenald	40	do		do	do	
	Thomas Evans	16	female		no	do	
	Rebecca Evans	9	male		do	do	
	David Davenald	4	female		do	do	
	Sarah Davenald	36	male		do	do	
	John Davenald	1	female		do	do	
	Hannah Davenald	6	do		do	do	
	Mary Davis	18	male	Divine	do	do	
	Samuel Hill	80					

Name	Age	Sex	Occupation	Country	Destination	Ship
Mary Ann Hill	25	female		G. Britain	U. States	Brig James Coulter, Wm. F. Hill.
Sarah Ann Hill	5	do		do	do	
Charles Callacan	25	male	Merchant	U. States	do	
Joel Z. Reynolds	26	do	do	do	do	
Patrick Hayes	55	do	do	do	do	
Lenso de Forest	26	do	do	do	do	
Francis Matthews	22	do	do	G. Britain	do	
Joseph Posante	22	do	do	do	do	
J. More	25	do	Shoemaker	do	do	Ship Bingham, Wm. Fleming.
J. Wright	30	do	Gardener	do	do	
J. M'Cauley	30	do	do.	do	do	
T. Moreley	28	do	Farmer	do	do	
Robert Sheeyog	18	do	do	do	do	Brig Mary Ann, James Sheal.
J. G. Sheeyog	16	do	do	U. States	do	
Anson Buchanan	35	do	de	Ireland	do	
Hugh Aikin	26	do	Merchant	do	do	
Edward Guest	23	do		do	do	
Eliza School	14	female		do	do	Ship Æolus, Abraham Bunker.
Mary School	10	do		do	do	Brig Charlotte Laurence, Thomas Hunt.
Martha School	8	do		do	do	
Rose M'Mullen	14	male	Laborer	do	do	
James M'Bride	20	do	do	do	do	
William Elliott	20	do	do	do	do	
Dennis Mackey	25	do	do	do	do	
Dennis Macken	25	do	do	do	do	
Pat Hegarty	30	do	do	do	do	
James Orr	28	do	do	do	do	
John Barr	24	do	do	do	do	
David Gray	20	do	do	do	do	
Henry Gray	12	do	do	do	do	
William Gray	24	do		do	do	
William Kane	21	do	Farmer	do	do	
Margaret Kane	16	female	Wife	do	do	
Mary Ann Kearney	20	do	Maid	do	do	
Magaret M'Genley	30	do	do	do	do	
Priscilla Dougherty	10	do	Wife	do	do	
James Dougherty	19	male		do	do	
Giles Kane		female		do	do	

LIST of Passengers, &c.—Quarter ending June 30, 1820.

Custom House, with the name of the Collector.	Passengers.	Age.	Sex.	Occupation.	Country to which they belong.	Country of which they intend to become inhab's	Ship or Vessel, with the name of the Master or Commander.
Philadelphia, John Steele.	Sarah Kane	16	female	Laborer	Ireland	U. States	Brig Mary Ann, James Sheal.
	Hugh Kane	22	male	do	do	do	
	John Davis	24	female		do	do	
	Mary Rogers	25	male		do	do	
	Jonathan Johnson	30	male	do	do	do	
	Thomas Porter	37	female	do	do	do	
	Eliza Porter	35	male	Wife	do	do	
	Andrew Porter	18	female	Laborer	do	do	
	Margaret Porter	17	male		do	do	
	Edward Mitchell	24	female		do	do	
	Mary Mitchell	22	male	Wife	do	do	
	John Gardiner	28	do	Cabinetmaker	G. Britain	do	Ship James, Thomas Anderson.
	James M'Kell	28	do	do	do	do	
	John Harrison	43	female	Turner	do	do	
	Mrs. Harrison	27	male		do	do	
	David S. Shuter	27	do		U. States	do	Ship Halcyon, Isaac S. Worster.
	David S. Getting	22	female	Doctor	do	do	
	Alice Dewhurst	25	male		do	do	
	George Dewhurst	8	do		do	do	
	Charles Dewhurst	1	female		do	do	
	Mary Ann Dewhurst	6 7	male	Farmer	do	do	
	James Clayton	25	do	do	do	do	
	Joseph Leach	35	female		do	do	
	Margaret Leach	40	male		do	do	
	James Leach	5	do		do	do	
	Joseph Leach, jr.	3	do		Scotland	do	
	John Campbell	50					

Name	Age	Sex	Occupation			Ship
Agnes Campbell	50	female		Scotland	U. States	
Agnes Campbell, jr.	15	do		do	do	
Elizabeth Campbell	13	do		do	do	
Jane Campbell	10	do		Ireland	do	
Eliza Middleton	25	male	Shoemaker	do	do	
Charles O'Neil	27	do	do	Scotland	do	
John O'Neil	29	do	Farmer	G. Britain	do	
Robert Grave	22	female	do	do	do	
Benjamin Wright	32	male		do	do	
Hannah Wright	27	do		do	do	
William Wright	5	do		do	do	
John Wright	2	female		do	do	
Mary Wright	1	male	Merchant	do	do	
Benjamin Shaw	47	do		do	do	
John Harrison	17	do	Laborer	do	do	
William Palaney	29	female		do	do	
Jane Paxter	10	male	Gentleman	do	do	Brig Free Ocean, Adam Bausch.
Patrick Griffin	61	female		do	do	
Ellen Griffin	50	male	Officer	do	do	
John Griffin	26	female		do	do	
Anna Griffin	14	do	Gentleman	do	do	
Mary Ann Griffin	21	male		do	do	
Patrick Griffin, jr.	22	female		do	do	
Bridget Denny	9	do	Housewife	do	do	
Mary Denny	7	do		do	do	
Ann Denny	30	male		do	do	
Catharine Denny	3	do	Clerk	do	do	
Thomas Denny	2	do	Farmer	do	do	
John White	28	do	do	do	do	
Thomas Cooper	20	do	Merchant	U. States	do	
John Leahy	22	do	Engineer	France	France	Brig Perseverance, Jacob Armstrong.
Israel Israel	24	do	do	do	U. States	
M. Baudisson	30	do	Carpenter	France	do	
Trudon Desormes	40	do	Mariner	U. States	do	
John Rambier	30	do	Merchant	do	do	Brig Rose R. Pickle.
William Morrison	45	do	do	do	do	Brig South America, Charles Gotier.
Adam Ashburner	22	do		do	do	
James Crawford	35	do		do	do	

LIST of Passengers, &c.—Quarter ending June 30, 1820.

Custom House, with the Name of the Collector.	Names of Passengers.	Age.	Sex.	Occupation.	Country to which they belong.	Country of which they intend to become inhab's	Ship or Vessel, with the Name of the Master or Commander.
PHILADELPHIA, John Steele.	John Stewart	30	male	Merchant	U. States	U. States	Brig South America, Charles Gotier.
	Isaac Field	31	do	do	do	do	
	Martha Field	28	female	Wife	do	do	
	James Field	8	male		do	do	
	Catharine Congo	18	female	Servant	do	do	
	Henry Francis	35	male	do	do	do	
	Henry Francis, jr.	10	do	do	do	do	Ship Pennsylvania, William Bunce.
	Eloiza G. Tarry	30	female	Lady	do	do	
	Elizabeth S. Tarry	9	do		do	do	
	M. Taylor	45	do	Lady	France	do	
	M. R. Tignabe	35	do	do	do	do	
	G. R. Tignabe	4	male		do	do	
	Mark Warner	39	do	Mariner	U. States	do	Schooner Maria, William Kennedy,
	S. P. Tull	28	do	Merchant	do	do	
	John W. Watson	40	do	Farmer	Scotland	do	Schooner Eliza Jane, Jona. Wheeler. Ship Sisters, John Miller.
	David M'Lish	30	female	Wife	do	do	
	Icobel M'Lish	18	do	Spinster	do	do	
	Icobel Robertson	45	male	Laborer	do	do	
	James Morris	40	do	do	do	do	
	Archibald Smeton	35	do	do	do	do	
	John Mercer	45	do	Merchant	England	do	Ship Cleveland, James Mackey
	James St. Perinnot	45	female	Wife	do	do	
	Susan St. Perinnot	20	do	Child	do	do	
	Mary Ann St. Perinnot	18	do	do	do	do	
	Susan St. Perinnot, jr.	18	male	do	do	do	
	Thomas St. Perinnot	16	female	do	do	do	
	Sophia St. Perinnot						

Name	Age	Sex	Occupation	Country	Destination	Ship
Eliza St. Perinnot	10	female	Child	England	U. States	
John St. Perinnot	11	male	do	do	do	
Robert St. Perinnot	9	do	do	do	do	
Caroline St. Perinnot	7	female	do	do	do	
William St. Perinnot	5	male	do	do	do	
Alfred St. Perinnot	10	do	do	do	do	
Henry Pierce	29	do	Merchant	do	do	
James Rattle	36	do	do	do	do	
Sarah Rattle	35	female	Wife	do	do	
Cecelia Rattle	14	do	Child	do	do	
John Rattle	13	male	do	do	do	
Samuel Rattle	11	do	do	do	do	
William Rattle	9	do	do	do	do	
Mary Rattle	7	female	do	do	do	
Eliza Rattle	3	do	do	do	do	
Henry Rattle	5	male	do	do	do	Ship Benjamin, Michael Webb.
James Rattle	1 6	do	do	do	do	
Morgiana Rattle	28	female	do	do	do	
Child	1 6	female	do	do	do	
George Sibley	29	male	Merchant	do	do	
James Sibley	8	do	Child	do	do	
William Sibley	2	do	do	do	do	
Ann Sibley	30	female	Wife	do	do	
Solomon Sibley	4	male	Child	do	do	
George Sibley, jr.	1 9	do	do	do	do	
George Sparring	20	do	Merchant	do	do	Snow Jane, Patrick Thorn.
William Harrington	20	do	do	do	do	Ship Little Cherub, Jno. M'Keene.
Sarah Hoodley	20	female	Lady	do	do	
Mrs. M'Clean	40	do	do	do	do	
John Mossop	35	male	Hatter	France	do	
William Salter	20	do	Farmer	Scotland	do	
Pignatelly Cercheira	53	do	Lieut. Gen.	Italy	do	
Elliphiner Cercheira	50	female		France	S. America	
Elizabeth	32	do	Servant	da	do	
William Castles	50	male	Farmer	Ireland	U. States	Schooner Independence, Ephraim Haynes.
Judith Castles	50	female		do	do	
Judith Castles, jr.	14	do		do	do	
Robert Castles	11	male		dq	do	

LIST of Passengers, &c.—Quarter ending June 30, 1820.

Custom House, with the name of the Collector.	Names of Passengers.	Age.	Sex.	Occupation.	Country to which they belong.	Country of which they intend to become inhab's	Ship or Vessel with the name of the Master or Commander.
PHILADELPHIA, John Steele.	Thomas Kennedy	43	male	Farmer	Ireland	U. States	Schooner Independence, Ephraim Haynes.
	Rachel Kennedy	40	female		do	do	
	Benjamin Kennedy	20	male		do	do	
	Margaret Kennedy	18	female		do	do	
	Ann Kennedy	15	do		do	do	
	Thomas Kennedy, jr.	13	male		do	do	
	James Flannagan	40	do	do	do	do	
	Elizabeth Flannagan	38	female	do	do	do	
	Charles Camell	25	male		do	do	
	Margaritta Camell	4	female		do	do	
	Owen Flannagan	3	male		do	do	
	Rose Flannagan	2	female		do	do	
	John Wilson	30	male	do	do	do	
	Elizabeth Murrey	27	female		do	do	
	William Hasety	30	male	do	do	do	
	Catharine Morrow	26	female		do	do	
	George Grier	60	male	do	do	do	
	Elizabeth Grier	55	female		do	do	
	Eliza Grier	36	do		do	do	
	Joseph Grier	34	male	do	do	do	
	James Grier	30	do	do	do	do	
	Frances Grier	27	female		do	do	
	Mary Grier	16	do	do	do	do	
	Alexander Grier	27	male	do	do	do	
	Sarah Grier	17	female		do	do	
	George Grier	21	male	do	do	do	
	George Grier, jr.	7	do		do	do	

Brig Concord, Benjamin Cozens.

Name	Age	Sex	Occupation	Country	Destination
Sally Grier	5	female		Ireland	U. States
Redmond Grier	3	male		do	do
Phebe Grier	2	female		do	do
J. Grier	5	male		do	do
Margaritta Grier	3	female		do	do
Sally Grier	7	do		do	do
William Martin	26	male	Farmer	do	do
Agnes Martin	22	female		do	do
George Carson	23	male	do	do	do
Samuel Adrane	13	do		do	do
Joseph Adrane	11	do		do	do
William Costly	24	female	do	do	do
Jane Costly, jr.	22	do		do	do
Jane Costly	24	do		do	do
Jane Mulroy	50	male		do	do
David Mulroy	60	female	do	do	do
Jane Creders	25	male		do	do
Rose Smith	50	female		do	do
William Henning	56	do	do	do	do
Mary Henning	30	male	do	do	do
Sarah Holiday	24	do	do	do	do
G. Henning	30	do	do	do	do
George Henning	22	female		do	do
Jonathan Henning	18	do		do	do
James Henning	28	do		do	do
James Carney	26	female		do	do
Nancy Henning	23	do		do	do
Sarah Henning	18	male	do	do	do
Sarah Henning, jr.	17	do		do	do
Jonathan Henning	60	female		do	do
George Butler	40	male	Merchant	G. Britain	do
Elizabeth Butler	11	female		do	do
Anna M. F. Butler	9	male		do	do
Norman W. H. Butler	6	female		do	do
Almira Butler	9	do	do	do	do
Georgiana Barton	36	male	do	do	do
Samuel Ramsay	15	do		do	do
S. T. Ramsay					

LIST of Passengers, &c.—Quarter ending June 30, 1820.

Custom House, with the Name of the Collector.	Names of Passengers.	Age.	Sex.	Occupation.	Country to which they belong.	Country of which they intend to become inhb'ts.	Ship or Vessel, with the name of the Master or Commander.
Philadelphia, John Steele.	John Ghouchard	32	male	Merc't ant	G. Britain	U. States	Schooner Pegasus, Alexander Todd.
	J. Lovett	40	do	Mariner	U. States	do	Brig Farmer's Nancy, Isaac Isaacs.
	J. B. Sevett	35	do	Merchant	do	do	
	Nichols Vite	34	do		Italy	do	Brig Mary, —— Campbell,
	George Hawkins	30	do	do	U. States	do	
	William Erwin	20	do	Gentleman	Prussia	do	
	John Mayer	56	do	Clergyman	U. States	do	
	Mary Mayer	56	female	Lady	St. Croix	do	
	A. Ruan	13	do		do	do	
	Carle Severs	5	male	Boy	Gottenburg	do	
	Peter Cruse	35	do	Mariner	U. States	do	Schooner Two Brothers, Harvey Seal.
	Henry H. Smith	22	do	Merchant	do	do	
	Ezekiel Wysham	35	do	do	Spain	do	Brig Mary and Aschsah Ann, F. Bouquet.
	Carlos de Veroni	20	do	do	Germany	do	
	George Zingroff	30	female		G. Britain	do	Brig Rising Sun, Blanchard.
	Nancy Jackson	25	male		do	do	
	James Jackson	4	do	Supercargo	U. States	do	
	B. F. Herbesh	23	do	Farmer	G. Britain	do	Schooner Albert, Asa Bly.
	Edward Phillips	22	female		do	do	Ship Kensington, Charles Hamilton.
	Mary Phillips	48	do		do	do	
	Jane Phillips	20	do		do	do	
	Ann Phillips	14	male		do	do	
	George Phillips	10	do		do	do	
	William Phillips	5	do		do	do	
	Martin Lynch	44	do	Laborer	do	do	
	Thomas Jones	53	do	Farmer	do	do	
	Catharine Jones	23	female		do	do	

Name	Age	Sex	Grocer / Farmer	G. Britain	U. States
Ann Jones	21	female			do
Richard Beckerton	23	male	do	do	do
David Stevens	51	do	do	do	do
David Jones	37	do	do	do	do
Cadwalader Roberts	26	do	do	do	do
John Edwards	25	do		do	do
Evan Davis	42	female		do	do
Jane Davis	41	female		do	do
Elizabeth Davis	12	do		do	do
William Davis	9	male	do	do	do
Evan Davis	33	do		do	do
Evan Evans	33	do	do	do	do
Mary Evans	35	female	do	do	do
Thomas Jones	22	male.		do	do
John Bowen	40	do	do	do	do
Mary Morris	18	female		do	do
William Morris	17	male		do	do
Richard Evans, jr.	8	do		do	do
Richard Evans	45	do	do	do	do
Ann Evans	43	female		do	do
Edward Evans	42	male		do	do
Mary Evans	12	female		do	do
Jane Evans	11	do		do	do
Elizabeth Evans	9	do		do	do
Thomas Davis	40	male	do	do	do
Thomas Davis, jr.	16	do		do	do
Mary Davis	12	female		do	do
Robert Davis	11	male	do	do	do
John Cadwalader	33	do		do	do
Sarah Cadwalader	40	female		do	do
John Cadwalader	8	male		do	do
William Watkin	24	do	do	do	do
John Jones, jr.	24	do	do	do	do
John Owens	37	do	do	do	do
Grace Owens	36	female		do	do
John Jones	30	male	do	do	do
Elizabeth Jones	35	female		do	do
Jane Jones	7	do		do	do

LIST of Passengers, &c.—Quarter ending June 30, 1820.

Custom House, with the name of the Collector.	Names of Passengers.	Age.	Sex.	Occupation.	Country to which they belong.	Country of which they intend to become inhb's.	Ship or Vessel, with the name of the Master or Commander.
PHILADELPHIA, John Steele.	David Griffith	26	male	Farmer	G. Britain	U. States	Ship Kensington, Charles Hamilton.
	Mary Griffith	27	female		do	do	
	James Molineux	12	male		do	do	
	James Croft	46	do	Merchant	do	do	
	David Evan Jones	37	female	Farmer	do	do	
	Dorothy Jones	40	do		do	do	
	Mary Jones	16	do		do	do	
	Sarah Jones	12	do		do	do	
	James Davis	36	male	Minister	do	do	
	Thomas Humphreys	45	do	Farmer	do.	do	Schooner Infant.
	Edward Boyle	26	do	Tailor	Ireland	do	
	Agnes Boyle	26	female	Wife	do	do	
	John Boyle	4	male		do	do	
	William Boyle	2	do		do	do	
	Neal Madden	53	do		N. Brunwick	do	
	Sally O'Donnel	19	female	Servant	Ireland	do	
	Jane Thompson	20	do	do	do	do	
	Gale Dudgen	20	male	Seaman	do	do	
	Edward Guscher	21	do	Laborer	do	do	
	James Gelday	28	do	do	St. Andrews	do	Schooner Trader, John M'Knight.
	John Chancellor	60	do	Weaver	do	do	
	Ann Chancellor	55	female	do	do	do	
	Thomas Chancellor	26	male	do	do	do	
	Robert Chancellor	24	do	do	do	do	
	John Chancellor	22	do	do	do	do	
	William Chancellor	20	do	Shoemaker	do	do	
	Jos. Chancellor	18	do	Clerk	do	do	

Name	Age	Sex	Occupation	St. Andrews	U. States
James Chancellor	16	male	Weaver	do	do
Jane Chancellor	23	female	do	do	do
Ann Chancellor	20	male	do	do	do
John M'Maury	28	do	do	do	do
John Martin	23	do	do	do	do
Mary Martin	23	do	do	do	do
James Meurder	21	male	Farmer	do	do
Hugh Watson	21	do	Baker	do	do
Joseph Dickson	20	do	Farmer	do	do
John Duff	35	do		do	do
Edward Duff	17	male	Weaver	do	do
Matthew Duff	11	do		do	do
Ann Duff, jr.	9	female		do	do
George Duff	8	male		do	do
John Duff	5	do		do	do
Moses Marcheller	9	do		do	do
William Dugan	22	do	Farmer	do	do
John Dugan	10	do		do	do
Ruth Dugan	8	female		do	do
Adam Dugan	11	male		do	do
William Burns	21	do	Clerk	do	do
Jane Burns	17	female	Wife	do	do
Daniel Murphy	20	male	Baker	do	do
Barney Savage	21	do	Tailor	do	do
William Gill	24	do	Blacksmith	do	do
Grace Gill	26	female	Wife	do	do
Robert Gill	20	male	Smith	do	do
Robert Gill, jr.	3	do		do	do
Sally Smith	40	female	Millener	do	do
Nancy Smith	18	male	do	do	do
Samuel Smith	16	male		do	do
Grace Smith	14	female		do	do
Jane Smith	11	do		do	do
Andrew Smith	9	male		do	do
Sally Smith	5	female		do	do
James Timing	22	male	Carpenter	do	do
Bridget Timing	20	female	Wife	do	do
Robert Maxwell	22	male	Carpenter	do	do

LIST of Passengers, &c.—Quarter ending June 30, 1820.

Custom House, with the name of the Collector.	Names of Passengers.	Age.	Sex.	Occupation.	Country to which they belong.	Country of which they intend to become inhab's	Ship or Vessel, with the name of the Master or Commander.
PHILADELPHIA, John Steele.	Hugh Martin	23	male	Farmer	St. Andrews	U. States	Schooner Trader, John M'Knight.
	Sarah Carr	25	female	Milliner	do	do	
	William Accall	26	male	Shoemaker	do	do	
	Ann Accall	28	female	Wife	do	do	
	James Accall	24	male	Shoemaker	do	do	
	Alexander Ervin	22	do	Farmer	do	do	
	Jane Lanerdy	24	female	Milliner	do	do	
	Agnes Scammell	64	do	Confectioner	U. States	do	
	Clayton Hollingshead	27	male	Merchant	do	do	
	F. Pomroy	31	do	do	do	do	Brig Commodore Perry, Joshua Barclay.
	E. Pollit	23	do	do	do	do	
	V. Lepinoy	25	do	do	do	do	
	L. Brechinan	28	do	do	do	do	
	P. Lacoste	66	do	do	do	do	
	P. Mitchell	23	do	do	do	do	
	Selina Predell	28	female		Denmark	do	
	Alexander Gordon	46	male	Farmer	G. Britain	do	
	Alexander Gordon,jr.	13	do	do	do	do	
	Samuel M'Dowell	21	do	do	do	do	
	Andrew Hay	33	do	do	do	do	Ship Missouri, Jacob Brush.
	William Hammerton	34	do	do	do	do	
	Mary Hammerton	30	female		do	do	
	James Hammerton	7	male		do	do	
	Ellen Hammerton	5	female		do	do	
	George Hammerton	3	male		do	do	
	John Hammerton	1	do		do	do	
	Edward Brenan	44	do	Gentleman	do	do	

Name	Age	Sex	Occupation	Country	Destination	Ship
William M'Cammon	17	male	Farmer	G. Britain	U. States	
Eliza Thompson	35	female	do	do	do	
Alexander Rodgers	43	male		do	do	
Wm. H. Thompson	9	do	do	do	do	
George Gilmore	28	do		do	do	
William Bigham	60	female	do	do	do	
Betty Bigham	60	do		do	do	
Mary Bigham	19	do		do	do	
Nancy Bigham	10	do		U. States	do	Schooner Little George Eyre, A. Moore.
Betty Bigham	8	do		do	do	
Robert R. Stewart	27	male	Supercargo	do	do	
John M'Kittera	27	male	do	do	do	
Francis Fearis	29	do	Captain	do	do	
John Latiman	30	do	Planter	Cuba	Cuba	
Chivaleau	50	do	Morocco dress.	Ireland	U. States	
John Watson	39	do	Farmer	New-York	do	
E. Watson	22	female		Ireland	do	
O. Devan	24	male		do	do	
H. Devan	25	female		do	do	
Mrs. Burley	60	male	Clerk	do	do	
James Burley	16	do	Schoolmaster	do	do	
T. Johnston	18	do	Farmer	do	do	
Mitchell Hoover	26	do	do	do	do	
W. Monaugher	60	do	do	do	do	Schooner George, Benjamin Betry.
E. Monaugher	60	do		do	do	
P. Monaugher	20	do		do	do	
W. Monaugher, jr.	15	do		do	do	
James Monaugher	11	do	Farmer	do	do	
P. Monair	8	do	do	do	do	
I. O. Harro	24	do		do	do	
M. Harro	30	do		do	do	
I. O. Harro, jr.	5	de	Farmer	do	do	
Isabel Harro	3	female	do.	do	do	
Samuel Moore	28	male	Weaver	do	do	
M. Moore	20	do	do	do	do	
Manny Moore	17	do	do	do	do	
R. M'Donald	25	do		do	do	
E. M'Donald	68	do		do	do	

LIST of Passengers, &c.—Quarter ending June 30, 1820.

Custom House, with the name of the Collector.	Names of Passengers.	Age.	Sex.	Occupation.	Country to which they belong.	Country of which they intend to become inhab's	Ship or Vessel, with the name of the Master or Commander.
Philadelphia, John Steele.	I. M'Donald	7	male	We'ver	Ireland	U. States	Schooner George, Benjamin Berry.
	I. Colwell	30	do		do	do	
	Sarah Clements & child	34	female	Farmer	do	do	
	I. Wallose	19	male	do	do	do	
	C. M'Laughlin	20	do		do	do	
	S. M'Dermott	30	do		do	do	
	Betsey M'Dermott	11	female		do	do	
	I. M'Dermott	7	do		do	do	
	Nancy M'Dermott	9	do		do	do	
	Thomas M'Dermott	4	male		do	do	
	Patrick M'Dermott	16	do		do	do	
	B. M'Dermott	19	do	Farmer	do	do	
	I. Smyth	30	do	do	do	do	
	G. Marshall	24	do	do	do	do	
	D. M'Donald	24	do	do	do	do	
	I. Funey	22	do		do	do	
	Mrs. M'Entee	38	female	Weaver	do	do	
	John M'Entee	20	male	do	do	do	
	E. M'Entee	18	female	do	do	do	
	Nancy M'Entee	13	male		do	do	
	W. M'Entee	11	do	do	do	do	
	M. Noble	22	female		do	do	
	Martha Noble	15	female		do	do	
	S. Duffy	22	male	Distiller	do	do	
	W. Hopkins	52	do	do	do	do	
	R. Orr	19	do		do	do	
	S. M'Dermot	20	do		do	do	

Name	Age	Sex	Occupation		Country	Destination	Ship
John Graham	38	male	Farmer		Ireland	U. States	Brig Collector, Nathaniel Blanchard.
Ellen Graham	30	female	Wife		do	do	
James Graham	10	male			do	do	
Thomas Graham	9	do			do	do	
William Graham	6	do			do	do	
John Graham, jr.	3	do			do	do	
William Carts	21	do	do		do	do	
James Jackson	26	do	do		do	do	
Martha Jackson	21	female			do	do	
Sarah Jackson	22	do			do	do	
James Gibson	18	male			do	do	
Margaret Gibson	16	female	do		do	do	
William Chapman	50	male			G. Britain	do	British ship John & Sarah, W. Belton.
William Chapman, jr.	19	do			do	do	
Joseph Chapman	15	do			do	do	
George Chapman	12	do			do	do	
Mary Chapman	10	female			do	do	
Thomas Reader	72	male			do	do	
George Reader	32	do			do	do	
Elizabeth Reader	38	female			do	do	
Elizabeth Reader, jr.	2	do			do	do	
Mary Hirwin	28	do			do	do	
Thomas Lawson	48	male			do	do	
Elizabeth Lawson	13	female			do	do	
John Pearson	12	male			do	do	
John Cox	38	do			do	do	
Mary Cox	37	female			do	do	
George Cox	13	male			do	do	
Elizabeth Parkison	33	female			do	do	
George Sheppard	22	male			do	do	
Rebecca Jones	58	female			do	do	
James Moss	18	male			do	do	
James Hargrave	18	do			do	do	
William Pearcy	50	do			do	do	
Joseph Pearcy	10	do			do	do	
Thomas Hingham	18	do			do	do	
William Belt	26	tio			do	de	
Thomas Major	21	do			do	do	

LIST of Passengers, &c.—Quarter ending June 30, 1820.

Custom House, with the Name of the Collector.	Names of Passengers.	Age.	Sex.	Occupation.	Country to which they belong	Country of which they intend to become inhab'ts	Ship or Vessel, with the name of the Master or Commander.
Philadelphia, John Steele.	Thomas Pearson	18	male	Laborer	G. Britain	U. States	British ship Jno. and Sarah, W. Belton.
	Thomas St. John	30	do	Baker	Ireland	do	Schooner Three Friends.
	Arthur Christy	23	do	Weaver	do	do	
	Thomas Conn	27	do		do	do	
	Margaret Conn	23	female		do	do	
	Sarah Conn	27	do		do	do	
	Thomas Walsh	52	male	Laborer	do	do	
	Cabias Walsh	16	female		do	do	
	Bridget Walsh	37	do		do	da	
	William Roach	22	male	do	do	do	
	Jerome Maher	27	do	Cooper	do	do	
	Edmund Maher	24	do	Laborer	do	do	
	Patt Murphy	64	female	do	P. E. Island	do	
	Grace Taylor	56	male		U. States	do	
	Owen O'Brien	52	do	do	do	do	
	Timothy Whiting	35	do	Merchant	Ireland	do	
	John Dugle	30	female	Laborer	do	do	
	Eleanor Dugle	22	do		do	do	
	Jane Kelly	14	male		do	do	
	James Dugle	4	female		de	do	
	Eleanor Dugle	4	male		do	do	
	Thomas M'Coller Kelty	1	do		do	do	
	John Dugle, jr.	4	do		do	do	
Newbern, Francis Hawks.	Joseph S. Fowles	27	do	Merchant	U. States	Bermuda	Schooner Maine, Thomas Emery
Richmond, James Gibbon.	Thomas Spring	62	do	Farmer	England	U. States	Ship Galen.
	Margaret Spring	52	female			do	

Name	Age	Sex	Occupation	Country	U. States	Ship
Sydner Spring	22	male		England	do	
Archibald Spring	18	do		do	do	
George Spring	15	do		do	do	
Henry Spring	13	do		do	do	
John D. Spring	11	do		do	do	
Hannah Sharman	25	female		do	do	
James Price	41	male	Farmer	do	do	
Mary Price	42	female		do	do	
James Price, jr.	17	male		do	do	
Thomas Price	14	do		do	do	
Mary Price	12	female		do	do	
Ann Price	9	do		do	do	
William Stokes	42	male	do	do	do	
John Price	5	do		do	do	
Sarah Brown	22	female		do	do	
Edward Fanningly	28	male	Joiner	do	do	
Harriet Fanningly	29	female		do	do	
Lewis Wilde	27	male	Gardener	do	do	
Hannah Wilde	30	female		do	do	
John Murry	38	male	Carpenter	do	do	
Mary Murry	22	female		do	do	
Charles Murry	6	male		do	do	
Mary Ann Wilde	5	female		do	do	
Eliza Wilde	9	do		do	do	
Thomas Crawley	16	male	Laborer	Ireland	do	Ship Glide.
Joseph Bell		do		do	do	
James Boddon		do		do	do	
Z. Boddon		do		do	do	
Mary Crowthers		female		do	do	
James Crowthers		male		do	do	
Mary Ann Crowthers		female		do	do	
Eliza Crowthers		do		do	do	
John Allen	37	male	Merchant	England	do	Ship Tobacco Plant.
Mrs. Allen	25	female		do	do	
Charles F. Ralphman	38	male		do	do	
Henry Villoniss	38	do		do	do	
Mary Sipley	38	female		do	do	

LIST of Passengers, &c.—Quarter ending June 30, 1820.

Custom House, with the name of the Collector.	Names of Passengers.	Age.	Sex.	Occupation.	Country to which they belong.	Country of which they intend to become inhab's	Ship or Vessel, with the Name of the Master or Commander.
Richmond. James Gibbon.	Liguiffin	45	male	Horse doctor	France	U. States	Brig Agnes.
	G. Breasit	20	do	Clerk	do	do	
	—— Huckley	18	do		England	do	
	James Hean	23	do	Farmer	do	do	Ship Henry Clay.
	Jane Roach	44	female	Stationer	do	do	
	Malloda M. Roach	18	do	do	do	do	
	Louisia Jane Roach	13	do	Merchant	do	do	
	James Oliver	37	do		do	do	
	Mary Oliver	37	female		do	do	
	Jane Oliver	9	do		do	do	
	John Oliver	7	male		do	do	
	Thomas Oliver	34	do	Farmer	do	do	
	Agnes Oliver	32	female		do	do	
	Thomas Oliver	10	male		do	do	
	Grace Gould	48	female		do	do	
	John May	25	male		do	do	
	Jessey White	24	do		do	do	
	Elizabeth Appling	45	female		do	do	
	Elizabeth Appling, jr.	19	do		do	do	
	Mary Ann Appling	17	do		do	do	
	William Appling	14	male		do	do	
	Sarah Appling	13	female		do	do	
	Charles Appling	11	male		do	do	
	Thomas Appling	9	do		do	do	
	John Appling	7	do		do	do	
	Celia Appling	5	female		do	do	
	Robert Fisher	32	male	Farmer	do	do	

Name	Age	Sex	Occupation	Country	U. States	Ship
NEWPORT, Chris. Ellery.						
George L. Baker	30	male	Schoolmaster	England	do	Schooner Buffalo, John Hau..
Elizabeth J. Baker	27	female		do	do	
George W. Baker	6	male		do	do	
Emma J. Baker	8	female		do	do	
Elias J. Baker	4	male		do	do	
Alfred Baker	1	do		do	do	
Thomas Lemon	35	do	Basketmaker	do	do	Brig Nereus, James Easton
Arnisse Lemon	48	female		do	do	
William Meserve	35	male	Victualler	U. States	do	
Timothy Cornwell	29	do	do	do	do	
Col. Samuel Swett	39	do	Gentleman	do	do	
Lucia G. Swett	30	female	Wife	do	do	
John Temple Palmer	20	male	Gentleman	do	do	
William Kermit	20	do	Merchant	do	do	
Antonio Leven	27	do	Servant	do	do	Brig Oswego.
A. Baldwin	28	do	Merchant	do	do	
C. Schwartz	20	do	do	do	do	Schooner Marmion.
BALTIMORE, J. H. M'Culloch.						
Dennis Marsh	25	do	do	do	do	Ship Ceres.
Jane Frowsdale	17	female		England	do	
J. Schofield	36	male	Farmer	do	do	Ship Jason.
P. Dougherty	28	do	do	Ireland	do	
A. Hamilton	20	female		do	do	
J. Hamilton	11	male		do	do	
G. Hamilton	17	do		do	do	
R. Hamilton	12	do	do	do	do	
M. Kelly	20	female		do	do	
M. Darvittle	61	do		do	do	
William Frith	19	male	do	do	do	
J. Higgonson	25	female		do	do	
J. Reunmons, jr.	55	male	Boatbuilder	U. States	do	Schooner Telegraph.
James Reunmons	25	do	do	do	do	
J. Delano	20	do	do	do	do	
S. Clayworth	25	do	do	England	do	Brig Wellington.
J. Boardman	26	do		do	do	
J. Hodkinson	23	do	Farmer	do	do	
A. Hodkinson	21	do	Shoemaker	do	do	
B. Hodkinson	20	female	Farmer	do	do	

LIST of Passengers, &c.—Quarter ending June 30, 1820.

Custom House, with the name of the Collector.	Names of Passengers.	Age.	Sex.	Occupation.	Country to which they belong.	Country of which they intend to become inhb's.	Ship or Vessel, with the name of the Master or Commander.
Baltimore, J. M'Culloch.	A. Orrall	29	female		England	U. States	Brig Wellington.
	W. Arrall	8	male		do	do	
	S. Arrall	6	do		do	do	
	L. Arrall	1	female		do	do	
	E. Arrall	3	do		do	do	
	James Williams	41	male	Mariner	do	do	
	A. Williams	21	female		do	do	
	S. Arrall	1	do		do	do	Brig Morris.
	J. Walker	35	male	Merchant	U. States	do	
	M. Walker	24	female		do	do	
	Sarah	20	do	Servant	England	England	Schooner Sam.
	J. A. Ready	19	male	Gentleman	France	W. Indies	Brig Chatsworth.
	J. Diones	45	do	Merchant	do	do	
	J. Balno	23	female	Seamstress	Italy	U. States	
	P. Dettind	35	male	Merchant	U. States	do	
	M. Gibson	27	do	Mariner	Ireland	do	
	P. Rurick	30	do	Gardener	do	do	
	D. Moore	35	do	Stonecutter	W. Indies	W. Indies	
	L. Drinkwater	34	do	Fruit merch't	U. States	U. States	
	A. Davis	30	do	Merchant	do	do	
	G. Montgomery	34	do	Mariner	Ireland	do	Schooner Harriet.
	F. Welsh	36	do	Stonecutter	U. States	do	
	P. Barnes	40	do	Merchant	do	do	Schooner Annthea Bell
	C. I. Burckle	40	do	do	do	do	Ship Philip.
	J. Yearson	58	do	Mariner	do	do	
	P. A. Harthouse	21	do	Merchant	do	do	
	L. Rhibers	45	do	do	do	do	

Name	Age	Sex	Occupation			Ship
William Hale	30	do	do	do	do	Schooner Ins.
D. I. A. Arreamas	50	do	Gentleman	Mexico	Temporary	Schooner Ceres,
S. Silvester	45	do	Mariner	U. States	U. States	
S. Demoland	48	do	Planter	Cayenne		Schooner Philedini.
H. Perry	45	female	Mariner	U. States	do	
A. Comple	35	male	Merchant	do	do	Schooner Eliza.
J. Bernabeau	27	do	Mechanic	do	do	Schooner Sally.
C. Wegaud	25	do	Mariner	do	do	
J. Taylor.	21	do	do	do	do	
A. Gunonson	50	do	Merchant	do	do	Brig G. P. Stevenson.
B. I. Tonkapff	49	do	do	do	do	
William Eckell	26	do	Gentleman	do	do	
J. Turrell	50	do	Mariner	do	do	Sloop Thomas and Eliza.
J. M'Knight	48	do	Merchant	do	do	Schooner Duly Ann.
B. D. Pitts	29	do	do	do	do	Schooner Col. Ramsay
John Mills	21	do	Officer	W. Indies	W. Indies	
J. G. E. Taggs	23	do	Mariner	U. States	U. States	
J. Brown	49	do	Merchant	do	do	Brig Margaret.
A. Fauler	30	do	do	do	do	
Garro	30	do	Mechanic	do	do	
Delosle	35	do	Merchant	do	do	
J. Payo	40	do	Tobacconist	Spain	do	
G. Draper	24	do	do	U. States	do	Sloop Active.
R. Draper	22	do	do	do	do	
E. Draper	50	do	do	do	do	
J. Draper	20	female	do	do	do	
J. M'Gill	27	male	Grocer	do	do	
W. Kincaid	28	do	Merchant	do	do	Ship Medford.
M. Murphy	65	do	Farmer	Ireland	do	
Wm. Murphy	11	do		do	do	
H. Wainwright	40	do	Merchant	St. Domingo	St. Domingo	Schooner Sterling.
H. Dubois	40	do	Cabinetmaker	U. States	U. States	
D. Ghio	35	do	Merchant	do	do	
Samuel Hilman	25	do	Cooper	do	do	Schooner Nancy.
Samuel Laurens	24	do	Merchant	Ireland	do	
J. Young	21	do	do	England	do	
D. Wilson	50	do	Mariner	U. States	do	Schooner Atlantic.
D. Wingett	45	do	Farmer	do	do	Ship Rolla.

LIST of Passengers, &c.—Quarter ending June 30, 1820.

Custom House, with the name of the Collector.	Names of Passengers.	Age.	Sex.	Occupation.	Country to which they belong.	Country of which they intend to become inhab's	Ship or Vessel, with the name of the Master or Commander.
BALTIMORE, J. H. M'Culloch.	G. Dander	25	male	Mariner	France	Temporary	Brig Cashier.
	B. M. Bosworth	30	do	Supercargo	U. States	U. States	
	Polly and 2 children	35	female	Wife of a rigger	Halifax	do	Schooner Harriet.
	J. C. Burnham	25	male	Merchant	U. States	do	Schooner Telegraph.
	J. Francis	39	do	do	do	tto	Brig Harriet.
	J. Pearson*	32	do	do	do	*Died at sea	Brig Ann.
	J. D. Work	25	do	do	do	do	Brig Eros.
	J. D. Went	25	do	do	do	do	
	C. G. Snow	25	do	Mariner	do	do	
	C. Hudgeon	35	do	do	do	do	
	J, M'Civer	40	female	Hatter	Ireland	do	Schooner Maria.
	Mrs. M'Civer	38	female		do	do	
	A. M'Civer	14	male		do	do	
	J. M'Civer	10	do		do	do	
	E. M'Civer	8	female		do	do	
	G. A. Wills	22	male	Merchant	U. States	do	Schooner Fountain.
	A. Shannon	22	do	Tailor	Ireland	do	
	Mrs. Shannon	22	female	Tailoress	do	do	
	S. Denny	38	male	Mariner	U. States	do	Schooner Samuel Smith.
	S. Register	28	do	Doctor	do	do	
	—Barton	25	do	Mariner	do	do	
	—Smith	35	do	do	da	do	
	John Smith	24	do	do	do	do	Schooner President.
	William Atkinson	37	do	Merchant	do	do	Brig William and Thomas.
	J. Rich	28	do	do	do	do	Schooner Col. G. Armistead.
	J. Gold	35	do	do	do	do	
	I. J. Hassenclever	40	do	do	do	do	

Name	Age	Sex	Occupation	Country to which they belong	Country they intend to inhabit	Ship
H. Adelare	36	male	Gentleman	U. States	U. States	Brig Virginia.
William Rorno	40	do	do	Spain	do	
J. M'Fadden	26	do	Merchant	U. States	do	
William Furlong	26	do	Mariner	do	do	Brig Clio.
S. Daniel	7	female		do	do	Ship William Penn
G. Patterson	26	male	Merchant	do	do	
Wm. B. Zanbeggar	28	do	do	do	do	Brig Maryland
P. Adrian	25	do	do	do	do	Ship Franklin.
Wm. C. Somerville	35	do	Planter	do	do	
Lenox Birkhead	25	do	Physician	do	do	
R. Riddle	20	do	Gentleman	do	do	
L. Tiernan, jr.	19	do	do	do	do	
J. Tait	45	do	Merchant	Scotland	Temporary	
J. Tait, jr.	18	do	do	do	do	
Y. Burkenshaw	26	do	Whitesmith	England	U. States	
Mrs. Burkenshaw	24	female		do	do	
Mary Burkenshaw	7	do		do	do	
R. Chapman	45	male	Farmer	do	do	
Mrs. Chapman	34	female		do	do	
G. Chapman	14	male		do	do	
E. Chapman	13	female		do	do	
M. Chapman	8	do		do	do	
C. Chapman	10	male		do	do	
A. Chapman	6	female		do	do	
M. Martin	20	male	Farmer	Ireland	do	Brig Thetis.
J. M'Antee	22	male	Laborer	England	do	
G. Parker	63	do	Farmer	do	do	
S. Parker	10	do		do	do	
E. Palmer	45	female		do	do	
Y. Palmer	10	do	Laborer	do	do	
Z. Palmer	5	male		do	do	
J. Darks	29	female		do	do	
Mary Darks	23	male		do	do	
E. Thomas	31	female	do	do	do	
A. Thomas	25	male		do	do	
J. Thomas	6	female	do	do	do	
Wm. Austie	21	male		do	do	
R. Mullikin	32	do	Merchant	do	do	Schooner Thomas Tenant.

LIST of Passengers, &c.—Quarter ending June 30, 1820.

Custom House, with the name of the Collector.	Names of Passengers.	Age.	Sex.	Occupation.	Country to which they belong.	Country of which they intend to become inhab's	Ship or Vessel, with the name of the Master or Commander.
BALTIMORE, J. H. M'Culloch.	John Spier	39	male	Watchmaker	Ireland	U. States	Schooner Franklin.
	Mary Spier	47	female		do	do	
	I. Spier	14	male		do	do	
	S. Spier	12	female		do	do	
	William Spier	10	male		do	do	
	Samuel Spier	7	do		do	do	
	Wm. Cargill	68	do	Gardener	do	do	
	J. Cargill	28	female		do	do	
	R. Smith	18	do		do	do	
	S. Smith	16	do		do	do	
	J. Schee	35	male	Consul U. S.	U. States	do	Schooner Amphion.
	J. Penn	30	do	Merchant	do	do	
	J. Mahony	22	do	Laborer	Ireland	do	Ship Jno. Bukly.
	S. Kemp	20	do	do	do	do	
	J. Kemp	8	do		do	do	
	M. Flinn	22	female		do	do	
	E. Flinn	13	do		do	do	
	P. Flinn	5	male		do	do	
	M. Linch	30	do	do	do	do	
	J. Linch	9	do		do	do	
	M. Purdy	35	do	do	do	do	
	M. Smithurd	25	do	do	do	do	
	M. Smithurd	18	female		do	do	
	J. O'Brien	35	male	Merchant	do	England	Schooner Brutus.
	D. O'Brien	35	do	do	do	U. States	Schooner Rebecca.
	C. Foulac	22	do	Watchmaker	do	do	Schooner Quiroga.

Name	Age	Sex	Occupation	Country	Country	Vessel
EDGARTOWN, Thos. Cooke, Jr.						
E. F. P. P. Hinshilwood	22	male	Gentleman	Halifax	Nova Scotia	Schooner Liberty, Joseph Tyler.
John Allen	30	do	Mariner	do	U. States	
George Warren	12	do	do	N. Spain	do	Schooner Favorite, Samuel Tate.
William Israel	36	do	Merchant	U. States	do	Brig Delegate, Charles Cushman.
Elizabeth Israel	29	female		do	do	
Hannah Israel	10	do		do	do	
Israel Israel	6	male		do	do	
Michael Israel	5	do		do	do	
Ann Israel	3	female			do	
John Joseph Israel	1	male			do	
George Georgison	18	do	Servant	E. Florida	do	Schooner Sally, Alfred Easton.
Jonathan Gales	32	do	Laborer	U. States	do	
Dominicus Hanson	24	do	do		do	
Amos W. Merrybee	22	do	do		do	
Henry H. Murphy	13	do	Mariner		do	Schooner Dove, Oliver Price.
James Eastman	28	do	do		do	
Israel Small	25	do	do		do	
James Trugant	17	do	do		do	
SAVANNAH, A. S. Bullock						
Guillaume Cannapeau	45	do	Shoemaker	France	do	Schooner Phanton, Joseph Bruchet.
John Dominique	42	do	Carpenter	do	do	
Don Antonio Durette	35	do	Merchant	Spain	do	
Don Jose M. Leyba	28	do	do	do	do	
James Dickson	50	do	do	England	do	The Georgia, C. Varnum.
George Law	36	do	do		do	
Peter Dennis	20	do	Body servant		do	
Lewis Morault	29	do	Tailor		do	
Daniel Andrews	23	do	Merchant		do	Schooner Kitty, Peter Douville.
Fine Swarsey	26	female	Cook			
Robert Wright	39	male	Carpenter	U. States		Brig John Burgwin, Samuel Perry.
Wm. R. Boone	21	do	Merchant			Schooner Hills, J. Hills.
Daniel Coyle		do	do	Ireland		
John Cannon		do	do			
Eliza Kelly	25	female	Lady	Dublin	do	Ship Mount Vernon, A. Rowson.
Marius M'Flury	65	male	Farmer	Liverpool	do	
Edward Mooney	21	do	Clerk	do	do	
James Downy	25	do	Laborer	do	do	
Mary Downy	25	female	Spinster	do	do	
William Higgins	24	male	Laborer	do	do	

LIST of Passengers, &c.—Quarter ending June 30, 1820.

Custom House, with the name of the Collector.	Names of Passengers.	Age.	Sex.	Occupation.	Country to which they belong.	Country of which they intend to become inhab's	Ship or Vessel, with the name of the Master or Commander.
SANDUSKY, Peter F. Ferry.	Helen Waugh	28	female	Spinster	Liverpool		Ship Mount Vernon, A. Rowson.
	One infant						
	George Cummins	25	male	Wheelwright	Canada	U. States	Boat Sloop Rigger, Michael Fox.
	Daniel W. Corey	25	do	Cooper	U. States	do	Brig Juno, Seth Talbot.
	Benjamin Weeks	32	do	Mariner	do	do	Ship Charlotte, Solomon Tyler.
	James M. Brown	23	do	Jeweller	do	do	Schooner Experiment, Daniel Payne.
	Minza Sweet	26	do	Carpenter	do	do	Brig Sall and Hope, James M. Blinn.
	James E. Rhodes	25	do	do	do	do	
	William Wilbour	26	do	Mason	do	do	
	Jeremiah Stutson	18	do	Carpenter	do	do	
	James E. Hubbard	17	do	do	do	do	
	Alfred Barton	29	do	Mariner	do	do	Brig Fame, Isaac Bowen,
	Welcome A. Greene	24	do	Merchant	do	do	
	Theodore Stanwood	19	do	Mariner	do	do	
	Mark A. Smith	22	do	do	do	do	
	Solomon R. Nunes	51	do	Merchant	Surinam	Surinam	Brig Beaver, Spooner Ruggles.
DELAWARE, A. M'Lane.	John Lees	21	female	Weaver	Ireland	U. States	Schooner Ice Plant, Thomas Bunker.
	Mary Lees	22	do	Wife	do	do	
	Wm. Marshall	31	male	Farmer	do	do	Schooner Madison, Leach D. Price.
	Mary Marshall	29	female	Wife	do	do	
	Wm. Marshall, jr.	7	male		do	do	
	Andrew Marshall	6	do		do	do	
	Henry Marshall	3	do		do	do	
	James Marshall	2	do		do	do	
	J. M'Maine and wife*						* Were landed at Booth bay by permission of the Collector,
BRISTOL, B. Bates.	Doctor Caleb Miller	34	do	Physician	U. States	do	Brig Caroline, James Luther.
	Atwell Richmond	30	do	Mariner	do	do	

Esick Greenman	32	male	Mariner	U. States	U. States	Brig Francis, George W. Carr.
Sanford Pearse	22	do	do	do	do	Schooner Phœbe, G. F. Usher.
Robert Wall	35	do	Cordwainer	do	do	Schooner Enterprize, George Wheaton.
John H. Oaks	26	do	Gentleman	do	do	
Charles Allen	22	do	Carpenter	do	do	
John A. Pratt	19	do	do	do	do	
John Bowen	26	do	Mariner	do	do	Brig Matilda, James Coffin,
David Walker	13	do	do	do	do	
George R. Dewey	24	do	Carpenter	do	do	
Matthew Allen	20	do	do	do	do	
Ransalaer Merrill	20	do	do	do	do	
John Gardner	40	do	do	do	do	
Charles C. Starkey	20	do	do	do	do	Brig Eliza Ann, Seth Bartol.
Daniel Fuller	40	do	do	do	do	
Moses Studen	18	do	do	do	do	
Coomer Hail	20	do	Seaman	do	do	Brig Jno. Smith, Norman Hill
Nathaniel Goff	20	do	Ordinary	do	do	
William B. Wood	23	do	Landsman	do	do	Brig Catharine, Wilsman.
Levi Shearman	25	do	Cooper	do	do	
Martin Salisbury	34	do	do	do	do	
James M'Kensie	27	do	Mariner	do	do	Sloop Lawrence, Buckley.
James Cunningham	33	do	Carpenter	do	do	
Philip Robinson	38	do	Merchant	do	do	
John D. Silva	33	do	do	do	do	Ship South Boston, Campbell.
F. Le Page	21	female	do	do	St. Augustine	
Mary Lindsay	39	do	Spinster	do	U. States	
Harriet Frith	17	do	do	do	do	
—— Peck	38	male	Mariner	Spain	St. Domingo	Schooner Intrepid, Peizant.
Charles Sully	36	do	Merchant	Britain	U. States	Ship Prince Madoc, Shoate,
Mrs. Williams	29	female	do	do	do,	
Georgiana Buntin	12	do		do	do	
Jesse Buntin	8	male		do	do	
William Buntin	7	do		do	do	
Alvin Sortie	30	do	Trader	France	St. Domingo	
Francis Hogg	57	do	Farmer	Britain	U. States	
William Ireson	30	do	Merchant	do	do	
John Stewart	28	do	do	do	do	
James M'Cully	18	do	Farmer	do	do	Brig Susan, Pollock.

CHARLESTON,
James R. Pringle,

LIST of Passengers, &c.—Quarter ending June 30, 1820.

Custom House, with the name of the Collector.	Names of Passengers.	Age.	Sex.	Occupation.	Country to which they belong.	Country of which they intend to become inh'bts.	Ship or Vessel, with the Name of the Master or Commander.
CHARLESTON, James R. Pringle.	Stephen M'Cully	17	male	Farmer	Britain	U. States	Brig Susan, Pollock.
	Henry Irwin	22	do	do	do	do	
	John Murchie	28	female	do	do	do	
	Lapai Loefleur	21	do	Spinster	U. States	Nantz	
	Galbaud	22	male	Servant	France	do	Brig Confiance, Heraud.
	P. Machallette	40	do	Merchant	U. States	U. States	Schooner Fame, Sherry.
	John Sennett	25	do	Trader	Britain	do	
	John Burk	23	do	do	do	do	
	Joseph Barden	28	do	do	Spain	Havana	
	Gregory Hexemera	35	do	do	do	do	
	Antonio More	25	do	Physician	do	do	* Died on the passage.
	Aaron Lyon*	30	do	Laborer	U. States	U. States	
	Michael M'Cobb	35	do	Baker	Britain	do	Brig Edward, Collier.
	James Maynard	37	do	Barber	do	do	Ship Friends, Watson.
	William Maynard	16	do	Turner	do	do	
	George Levan	39	do		do	do	
	Joseph Gilchrist	13	do		do	S. Augustine	Schooner Margaret,
	John Durbee	30	do		Spain	U. States	Schooner Mary.
	Mrs. Brown		female	Lady	U. States	do	Ship Adriana, Drew.
	Harriet Brown	5	do		Britain	do	
	Augustus Brown	3	male		do	do	
	Caroline Brown	2	female		do	do	
	Francis Peyre, jr.	25	male	Planter	U. States	do	
	Robert Child	29	do	Mechanic	do	do	
	Joseph Dehagres	30	do	Merchant	Spain	do	
	Harriet	25	female	Servant	G. Britain	do	
	Capt. L. Curtois	52	male	Mariner	France	do	Ship Greyhound, West.

Name	Age	Sex	Occupation	Of what country	To what country	Ship
Madam Courtois	28	female	Merchant	France	U. States	Schooner Susan, M. Busher.
Lewis Courtois	6	male		do	do	
Samuel Cook	37	do	do	U. States	do	
Hugh M'Nary	26	do	Planter	do	do	
Thomas Briggs	37	do	Doctor	France	France	Ship Virginia, Martin.
Monsieur Martin	25	do		do	do	
Madam Martin	20	female		G. Britain	do	
Alexander Gregg	24	male	Baker	do	U. States	Brig Phœbe, Anderson.
Gilbert Taylor	24	do	Farmer	do	do	
Henry Janny	60	do	Laborer	do	do	Ship Pocahontas, Howland.
Robert Janny	55	do	do	do	do	
Mary Janny	46	female		do	do	
Harriet Janny	23	do		do	do	
Louisa Janney	20	do		do	do	
Mary A. Janny	17	do		do	do	
Ellen Janny	15	do		do	do	
Elizabeth Janny	13	do		do	do	
Margaret Janny	12	do		do	do	
Michael Harvey	32	male	Mechanic	U. States	do	Schooner Comet, T. Bates.
Polly Queck	30	female	Spinster	do	do	
Rebecca Buire	45	do	do	do	do	
James Chambore	38	male	Dyer	Germany	do	Sloop General Washington, I. Bulkley.
Andrew Friddle	30	do	Merchant	U. States	do	
Nicholas Gardiner	30	do	Mariner	Spain	do	
John M. Sanchez	22	do	Merchant	do	do	
John Pellessier	26	do	do	do	do	
George W. Ogden	40	do	do	U. States	do	
James Shaddock	18	do	Mariner	do	do	
James M'Gregor	30	do	merchant	G. Britain	do	Ship Roger Stewart.
Hippolite Grove	28	do	do	France	do	Schooner Sisters, W. Grain.
John Stewart	28	do	do	Britain	do	Brig Sea Gull, W. Hubble.
Rachael de Pass	18	female	Merchant	U. States	do	Schooner Jane.
Samuel Goodrey	30	male	do	do	do	
Adolphus Eschen	24	do	do	do	do	
John Lopez	35	do	do	do	do	
Henry Heldebram	32	do	do	Hamburg	do	
Isabella Heldebram	45	female	do	do	do	
John Machoen	18	male	do	Britain	do	Ship Ceres.

LIST of Passengers, &c.—Quarter ending June 30, 1820.

Custom House, with the name of the Collector.	Names of Passengers.	Age.	Sex.	Occupation.	Country to which they belong.	Country of which they intend to become inhab's	Ship or Vessel, with the name of the Master or Commander.
CHARLESTON, S. C. Jas. R. Pringle.	Marshall Luker	23	male	Cabinetmaker	U. States	U. States	Schooner Mary Ann, J. Bonnell.
	George Scott	22	do	Shoemaker	do	do	
	Joseph Matthews	45	do	Trader	do	do	Schooner Carrier.
	Seth Austin	48	do	Merchant	do	do	
	Jonathan Rathbone	28	do	do	G. Britain	do	
	Edward King	15	do	Yeoman	do	do	
	Wm. Clark	15	female	do	do	do	Ship Isabella.
	Mrs. Dalton	45	male	Lady	do	do	
	D. Wood & 2 children	25	do	Tailor	do	do	Ship Jane, Cumming.
	Hugh Livingston	45	do	Mariner	do	do	
	James Smith	23	do	Clerk	do	da	
	Hugh Oliver	25	female	do	do	do	
	Agnes Oliver	24	male	Laborer	do	Kentucky	Brig Catharine, Wilson.
	William Craig	20	do	None	U. States	do	
	William Jerry	28	do,	do	do	Cuba	
	L. Blauton	35	do	Trader	Spain	Bath	
	Antonio Garrier	35	do	Mariner	U. States	New York	Steam ship Robert Fulton.
	Jacob Drummond	32	do	Merchant	Holland		
	William Dustch	28	do		Spain		
	Manuel Fernandez	60	do				
	Peter Pelow	35	do				
	Pedres Isagalate	40	female		U. States		
	Venison Salsald		do	Servant	Spain		
	Mrs. O'Brian	35	male	Laborer	Britain	N. Carolina	Ship Mary & Susan.
	Ingliso and servant		do	None	do	do	
	Andrew Munroe	58	femal.				
	Christiana Munroe	18					

Name	Age	Sex	Occupation	Country	Destination	Ship
James O'Conner	25	male	Laborer	G. Britain	Charleston	Sloop James Vincent,
Nathaniel G. Clary	35	do	Merchant	U. States		Schooner Susan Susan Rusher.
Andw. M'Dowell	32	do				
G. Ward	30	do				
D. Sanchez	24	do				
John Taylor	25	do				
—— Devaureoux	24	do	Merchant	Spain	St. Augustin	Schooner Susan, Buscher.
—— Perrier	24	do	Mariner	U. States	Columbia	
—— Carrier	59	do	do	Spain	St. Augustin	
—— Fortune	19	do	Merchant	do	Columbia	
Francis Burke	30	do	Trader	U. States	St. Augustin	Schooner Mary Ann, Hillan.
Asa Harmon	28	do	Mariner	do	do	
Asa Harmon, jr.	38	do	Clerk	G. Britain	do	
William Kinneau	25	do	Merchant	do	do	
James Hamilton	24	do	do	U. States	do	Schooner Antelope, Lewis.
Michael O'Conner	22	do	do	G. Britain	do	
John Curling	22	do	Mariner	U. States	do	
John G. Wade	52	do	Cooper	Scotland	do	Brig Upton, Noah Downs.
James Kerr	32	do	Merchant	do	do	
John Cooper	38	do	Farmer	England	do	
Andrew Erving	11	female	do	do	do	
John Erving	19	male		do	do	
Sarah Erving	28	do	Merchant	Nova Scotia	do	
John Erving	29	female	Watchmaker	England	do	
Robert M. Barry	3	male		do	do	
John Yates	2	do		do	do	
Jane Yates	32	female	Farmer	Ireland	do	Schooner Sally, Peleg Griffin.
Samuel Yates	26	male	Laborer	do	do	
John Yates	45	do	Farmer	do	do	
Peter M'Dermot	32	do	do	do	do	
Fanny M'Dermot	22	do	Weaver	do	do	
John Sculling	24	do	Farmer	do	do	
Terry Owens	15	do	do	da	do	
Peter M'Clain	15	do		do	do	
James Goodfellow	1	de			do	
Hugh Sculling						
Daniel Sculling						
John Goodfellow						

Dis. or Belfast, Daniel Lane.

LIST of Passengers, &c.—Quarter ending June 30, 1820.

Custom House, with the name of the Collector.	Passengers.	Age.	Sex.	Occupation.	Country to which they belong.	Country of which they intend to become inhab's	Ship or Vessel, with the name of the Master or Commander.
BELFAST, Daniel Lane.	Rose ˙ culling	34	female	Spinster	Ireland	U. States	Schooner Sally, Peleg Griffin.
	Mary Owens	40	do	do	do	do	
	Alla Goodfellow	22	do	do	do	do	
	Ann Sculling	13	do	do	do	do	
	Susan Sculling	11	do	do	do	do	
	Catherine Sculling	8	do	do	do	do	
	Mary Sculling	3	do	do	do	do	
EDENTON, Saml. Treadwell.	Nathl. Lightburn	33	male	Merchant	Bermuda	Bermuda	Schr. Ruby, Jonathan Foster.
	Richard Conyer	33	do	Servant	do	do	
DIS. PORTSMOUTH, T. Upham.	Robert Fitzgerald	30	do	Shoemaker	Ireland	U. States	Schooner Pink, A. Trefethen.
	Asa B. Yesspon	30	do	Mariner	Connecticut	Connecticut	Schooner Alexander, Alex. Middleton
PORTLAND, &c. Isaac Ilsley.	Winston Bradford	47	do	do	U. States	U. States	Schooner Harmony, Allison Harmon.
	Wm. Pierce	20	do	Miller	Ireland	Maine	
	Ellice M'Corley	22	female	Housemaid	do	do	
	Supply C. Thurin	16	male	Merchant	U. States	U. States	Brig Alexander, E. Robinson.
	Patrick Quinlan	20	do	Mariner	Ireland	Ireland	
	Robert Crookshanks	60	do	Merchant	St. John, N.B.	On a visit	Schooner Recover, John Deering.
	William Widgery	25	do	do	U. States	U. States	Sloop Aurora, Ira Bradford.
	Mr. March	35	do	Laborer	do	do	
NEW LONDON, T. H. Cushing.	Sidney Thaxter	44	do	Baker	do	do	Brig Adela, Eli B. Allen.
	Wm. Henry Barker	21	do	Gentleman	Jamaica	Jamaica	
	Wm. Henry	31	do	Servant	do	do	
	Jachin B. Peirera	31	do	Gentleman	Brazil	Brazil	Brig Pizarro, David Churchill.
	Wm. C. Bellincourt	22	do	Merchant	Portugal	Portugal	
BARNSTABLE, J. L. Green.	Jane Boyd	35	female		Scotland	U. States	Sloop Hunter, Winthrop Sears.
	Thos. Appleby	45	male		New-York		Schooner Hope, Elnathan Lewis.
	Peter Peterson	8	do		St. Thomas		

Name	Age	Sex	Occupation	Country	Country	Ship
John Voyel	40	male	Laborer	Germany	U. States	Schooner Carlen, Asa Scudder.
Anna Voyel	27	female	do	U. States	do	
Mary Murphy	19	do	do	do	do	Schooner Fame, Abijah Hawley.
Samuel Maltby	35	male	Shoemaker	G. Britain	do	
John Calvan	40	do	Merchant	St. Croix	do	Schooner Edward, John Carlisle.
Francis Mitchell	28	do	W. In. Planter	Spain	Ireland	Schooner Hibernia, H. Graham.
Diego Real	45	do	Merchant	U. States	U. States	
A. Alvaris	35	do	do	do	do	
Thomas P. Harper	25	do	Citizen	Spain	do	Brig Volant, D. W. Wiley.
Salvador Felix	40	do	do	do	do	
Joseph M. Garcier	30	do		U. States	do	
Nicholas Paulman	15	do		do	do	
Robert Hinnah	45	do	Merchant	U. States	do	Schooner Active, R. Howland.
Robert Elliot	50	do	Gentleman	Ireland	do	Schooner Combine, W. R. E. Boyed.
Isaac Francis	45	do	do	do	do	
John Cornwall	20	do	do	New York	do	
John Scarlett	17	do	Clerk	Ireland	do	
Jane Francis	25	female	Wife to Francis	do	do	
M. Bertrand	35	male	Cooper	France	do	Brig Spartan, J. Cooper.
Domingo Storine	33	do	Gentleman	Italy	do	Brig Bee, Wm. Gray.
Gasper Nichol	28	do	Coppersmith	Bavaria	do	
Mary Nichol	30	female	do	Wirtemberg	do	
Jacob George	19	male	Shoemaker	do	do	
Philip Witidman	19	do	do	do	do	
Lewis Capanell	26	do	Gentleman	Trieste	do	
Catharine Querreau	29	female	Mariner	U. States	do	Ship Virginia, P. Querreau.
Richard Cole	33	male	Domestic	Halifax	do	Brig Hippomenes, Samuel Bourne.
Margaret Short	23	female	do	Curracoa	do	
John Curriel	25	male	Merchant	U. States	Curracoa	
John Geryee	28	do	do	do	U. States	Ship Gleaner, Jno. O. Ziull.
E. W. Waring	23	do	do	Ireland	do	
S. A. Duplex	18	female	do	do	do	
Christopher Bant	20	male	do	do	do	Ship Maria, George Duplex.
Jane Hunt	16	female	do	do	do	
Ann Hunt	11	do	do	do	do	
Catharine M'Carthy	36	do	do	do	do	
Catharine M'Carthy	14	do	do	do	do	
Mary M'Carthy	10	do	do	do	do	

FAIRFIELD
Walter Bradley.
NEW YORK,
David Gelston.

LIST of Passengers, &c.—Quarter ending June 30, 1820.

Custom House, with the name of Collector.	Names of Passengers.	Age.	Sex.	Occupation.	Country to which they belong.	Country of which they intend to become inhab's.	Ship or Vessel, with the name of the Master or Commander.
New York, David Gelston.	James M'Carthy	12	male		Ireland	U. States	Ship Maria, George Duplex.
	Peggy M'Carthy	7	female		do	do	
	John M'Carthy	5	male		do	do	
	Thomas M'Carthy	3	do		do	do	
	John Punch	25	do		do	do	
	James Callender	27	female		do	do	
	Catharine Crough	43	female		do	do	
	Margaret Crough	17	do		do	do	
	Mary Crough	10	do		do	do	
	Michael Crough	15	male		do	do	
	John Crough	12	do		do	do	
	William Crough	8	do		do	do	
	Thomas Crough	6	do		do	do	
	Hannah Horsford	24	female		do	do	
	Margaret Horsford	3	do		do	do	
	Mary Harrington	30	do		do	do	
	Biddy Hau	22	do		do	do	
	James Flinn	24	male		do	do	
	James Gorham	59	do	Merchant	G. Britain	G. Britain	Brig Greyhound, Thomas Bedson.
	Sally Hopkins	50	female		do	do	
	Betty Perkins	25	do		do	do	
	Sarah Bates	35	female		do	do	
	George Dunbar	30	male	Merchant	U. States	U. States	
	James Jeryer	29	do		do	do	
	Mrs. Jeryer	29	female		do	do	
	Betty Hynaas	14	do		do	do	
	James Hynaas	3	male		do	do	

Name	Age	Sex	Occupation			Vessel
John Hymaas	5	male		U. States	U. States	Schooner Vestal, Jno. Blackburn.
Elizabeth Hymaas	7	female		do	do	
Betsey M'Kindlay	15	do		do	do	
Nancy James	24	do		do	do	
John Richards	25	male		do	do	
John Nowland	53	do	Shipwright	do	do	
Owen M'Glue	30	do	Bookbinder	do	do	
Alexander Maxwell	31	do	Merchant	G. Britain	Canada	Schooner James Monroe, James Rogers.
Ann Wilson	28	female		do	do	
Ann Wilson	4	do		do	U. States	
Eliza Wilson	2	do		do	do	
Helen Griffiths	23	do	Servant	do	do	
John Lawton	27	male	Merchant	do	do	
Gen. Don Fra. Vives	44	do	S. Ambassador	Spain	Spain	
M. Salmon	28	do	Secret'y to do.	do	do	
Don J. Sanchez Boado	25	do	Cal. Artillery	do	do	
Don Antonio Donis	22	do	Lieut. do	do	do	
Sebastian Vedal	31	do	Servant	do	do	
Randall Lees	26	do	Draper	do	do	
Betsey Holt	24	female		G. Britain	U. States	
John Holt	4	male		do	do	
I. G. M'Iivish	36	do	Merchant	do	Canada	
Joseph Wingley	24	do	do	do	U. States	
Thomas Burnett	48	do	Civil engineer	do	Canada	
Alexander M'Donald	43	do	Farmer	do	do	
George Sampson	31	do	Merchant	do	U. States	
John Lord	21	do	do	do	do	
C. S. Tattersall	25	do	do	do	de	
I. C. Beffinsteau	40	do	Late in the army	do	Canada	
Sampson Fordge	25	do	Collier	do	U. States	
Solomon Fordge	27	do	do	do	do	
Anna Fordge	32	female		do	do	
William Shephard	34	male	Merchant	do	do	
Sarah Kindall	27	female		do	do	
Mrs. Dunlap	48	do		do	do	
Jane Dunlap	12	do		do	do	
Matthew Dunlap	14	male		do	do	
Joseph Tutton	30	do	Servant	do	Canada	

LIST of Passengers, &c.—Quarter ending June 30, 1820.

Custom House, with the Name of the Collector.	Names of Passengers.	Age.	Sex.	Occupation.	Country to which they belong.	Country of which they intend to become inhab's	Ship or Vessel, with the Name of the Master or Commander.
New-York, David Gelston.	Alexander Jaffray	31	male	Teacher	Scotland	America	Camillus, Joseph Boyer.
	Don. M'Lean	30	do	Laborer	do	do	
	John Anderson	22	do	do	do	do	
	John Stewart	25	do	do	do	do	
	William Niven	25	do	do	do	do	
	William Breckenridge	30	female		do	do	
	Margaret M'Pherson	6	male		do	do	
	M. M'Pherson	3	do		do	do	
	B. M'Pherson	1	female		do	do	
	Margaret M'Pherson	30	do		do	do	
	Eliza Ure	6	male		do	do	
	William Ure	4	do		do	do	
	John Ure	1	female		do	do	
	Eliza Ure	40	do	Farmer	do	do	
	Margaret M'Cullum	18	male	Wife	do	do	
	D. M'Cullun	16	do	Child	do	do	
	William M'Kee	30	female	Merchant	do	do	
	Eliza M'Kee	30	male	do	do	do	
	Robert M'Kee	3	do	Gentleman	Teneriffe	do	Brig Diligence, James Jones.
	Lamaco Baudes	38	do	Merchant	do	U. States	
	Jose Ramos	16	do	do	U. States	G. Britain	Schooner Grampus, Robert Davie.
	Edward Abeile	21	do	do	G. Britain	do	Schooner Charlotte Corday, I. G. Russell
	David Merrit	54	do	Shipmaster	do	do	
	L. Burns	38	do	Carpenter	America	America	
	William Kellog	30	do		do	do	
	David Matthews	30	do				
	Francis Euice	25	do				

Name	Age	Sex	Occupation	Country	Country	Ship
Benjamin Euice	28	male	Carpenter	America	America	Schooner General Jackson, I. B. Nicholas
Jacob Mires	26	do	do	do	do	
William Webbey	20	female	do	do	do	
Jane Wallace	40	do	Spinster	do	do	Schooner Sisters, Charles Winslow.
Hannah Wallace	18	do	do	do	do	
Money Wallace.	16	do	do	do	do	
James Martin	36	male	Mason	U. States	U. States	
A. Bragas	38	do	Merchant	Havana	do	
J. Ragand	35	do	do	France	do	
I. D. Correy.	23	do	do	U. States	do	
J. Le Brun	24	do	Mariner	do	do	
A. Dacken	16	female	Spinstress	Havana	do	
Augustus Newman	20	male	Gentleman	U. States	U. States	Brig Columbia, Walter Midlen.
Reault de Mombray	35	do	Lawyer	France	do	Brig Belvidere, William Jocelin.
James Standring	35	do	Farmer	G. Britain	do	Ship Helen, Jon. Hillman.
William Ball	28	do	Laborer	do	do	
I. Lutherwaite.	44	do	do	do	do	
Walter King	39	do	Shopkeeper	do	do	
James King	12	do.	do.	do	do	
John M'Kendick	17	do	do	do	do	
George M'Keorcher	32	do	Laborer	do	do	
R. Keorcher	30	female	do	do	do	
M. Keorcher	10	do	do	do	do	
B. M'Keorcher	7	do	do	do	do	
E. M'Keorcher	4	do	do	do	do	
John M'Keorcher	1	male	do	do	do	
Sarah Herson	28	female	do	do	do	
Peter Harvey	32	male	Gardener	do	do	
Anthony Baker	33	do	Cordwainer	do	do	
E. Roberts	30	do	Minister	do	do	
John Shepherd	25	do	Clerk	do	do	
Mary Harvey	26	female	do	do	do	
John Dikeman	24	male	Merchant	U. States	do	Schooner Royal Oak, James Allen.
A. Avey	42	do	do	do	do	Schooner Vestal, Jno. Blackburn.
Eliza Vincent	31	female	do	do	do	Brig Visitor, Charles Thomas.
Jane Vincent	11	do	do	do	do	
John Dowling	35	male	Coppersmith	do	do	Schooner Eliza Ann, Chas. W. Cahoon.
Martin Leney	45	do	Supercargo	de	do	

LIST of Passengers, &c.—Quarter ending June 30, 1820.

Custom House, with the name of the Collector.	Names of Passengers.	Age.	Sex.	Occupation.	Country to which they belong.	Country of which they intend to become inhab's	Ship or Vessel, with the name of the Master or Commander.
New-York. David Gelston.	Joseph Anderson	10	male	Mariner	U. States	U. States	Sloop McDonough, J. Pratt.
	Raphael Gonsales	19	do	Merchant	Cuba	do	Brig Polly, Charles Brownall.
	Lewis Lino	14	do		do	Spain	Brig Mechanic, I. C. Ray.
	Nicholas Brunet	10	do	Mechanic	do	do	
	Edmund Dupont	26	do		New-York	New York	schooner Fairplay, P. Scoyen.
	William Radcliff	42	do	Minister	England	England	Sloop Herald, William Flay.
	Mrs. Radcliff	35	female		do	do	
	Stephen Wheeler	29	male	Mariner	do	do	
	Robert Lockhart	40	do	Supercargo	G. Britain	U. States	Brig Milford, William Glenny.
	Thomas Bacchus	31	do	Shipmaster	U. States	do	Schooner John, John Soreland.
	Thomas Willock	35	do	Merchant	do	do	
	George Brown	21	do	do	do	do	
	D. Ogden	25	do	do	do	do	
	Volney Roberts	22	do	Mason	do	do	
	Levi Grant	27	do	do	do	do	Schooner Magnet, B. Waite, jr.
	Thomas Hughes	39	do	Merchant	England	do	Schooner Andrew Jackson, N. Gillet.
	Susan Hughes	30	female		do	do	
	William Hughes	infant	male		do	do	
	Mary Brown	35	female	Servant	Africa	do	
	Jacob Beach	30	male	Mariner	England	England	
	James Brown	34	do	Mechanic	do	Boston	
	L. Johnson	21	do	do			
	I. I. Theband	23	do	Merchant	U. States	U. States	Brig Joseph, P. Morris.
	James Newell	23	do	Seaman	do	do	Schooner Jane, P. Fowler.
	M. A. Dupony	15	do	Merchant	France	do	Ship Nimrod, Joel Center
	Francis Demandelers	24	do	Currier	do	do	
	John Nixon	48	do	do	St. John	St. John	Sloop Betsey, B. Young

Name	Age	Sex	Occupation			Vessel
Frederick O'Brien	35	male	Cooper	U. States	U. States	Brig Brothers. J. Gardner.
Catherine Lambert	28	female		do	do	
John Shepherd	45	male	Merchant	Amsterdam	no	Schooner Logan, S. Holmes.
Jacob Kloppenburd	30	do	do	U. States	Amsterdam	
Silvanus Gifford	35	do	do	do	U. States	Brig Onslow, R. Snow.
E. W. Sage	30	do	do	do	do	
George Webster	8	do		do	do	
Scipio	20	do	Servant	do	do	Ship General Hand, Dl. Fitch.
Michael Hogan	53	do	U. S. service	do	do	
A. H. Wood	23	do	do	do	do	
Samuel Grael	48	do	do	do	do	
Edward W. Waldo	32	do	do			
John Murdock	43	do	do	Spain		
John Averheff	12	do	For education	France		
J. Caberet	6	do	Merchant	do		
Monsieur Martin	40	do	do	do		
John M'Donald	42	do	do	U. States		
Samuel M'Lellem	24	do	Ship master	do	do	Schooner Eliza Pagott, R. Waterman.
William Black	22	do	Merchant	G. Britain	do	
John Smith	46	do	do	U. States	do	Brig Bordeaux, B. Butman.
Justin Boche	22	do	do	England		
Chas. A. Davis	23	do	do	S. Carolina	Charleston	Brig Eunice, J. W. Sterling.
John Bird	21	do	do	do	do	
Daniel Shebit	24	do		U. States	do	Brig Clarissa, Jno. A. Millian.
George Holmes	29	do	do	Spain	U. States	
Domingo Pueria	36	do		U. States	Spain	
Joseph Garrat	24	do		do	U. States	
Richard Spight	19	do	do		do	
V. Radarguez	48	do	Steward	New York		
Charles	9	do	Seaman	Ireland	do	Sloop Bright Phœbus, N. Bristol.
John Allen	28	do	Merchant	do	New-York	Schooner Atlantic, James Hamon.
Andrew Lloyd	35	do	Milliner	do	do	
Mary Lloyd	39	female	do	do	do	
Sarah Hamilton	19	do		do	do	
Robert Lloyd	8	male			do	
Samuel Lloyd	5	do	Laborer		do	
James Leech	24	do			do	
Eleanor Leech	24	female			do	

LIST of Passengers, &c.—Quarter ending June 30, 1820.

Custom House, with the name of the Collector.	Names of Passengers.	Age.	Sex.	Occupation.	Country to which they belong.	Country of which they intend to become inhab's.	Ship or Vessel with the name of the Master or Commander.
New York, David Gelston.	Wm. J. Leech	3	male		Ireland	New York	Schooner Atlantic, James Hamon.
	Matilda Leech	7	female				
	Hugh Loriman	25	male				
	Sally Loriman	23	female				
	John Leech	46	male				
	Mary Leech	36	female				
	James Wilkerson	8	male				
	Geo. Kamohan	25	do	Weaver			
	Wm. Kisland	25	do	Lawyer			
	John Anderson	26	do	Merchant	G. Britain	U. States	Ship Iris, J. B. Smith.
	James Dougherty	35	do	Farmer	do		
	Ann Dougherty	30	female		do		
	William Dougherty	5	male		do		
	John Dougherty	3	do				
	Owen M'Cabe	30	do				
	Sarah M'Cabe	27	female				
	Margaret M'Cabe	28	do				
	Margaret M'Cabe	2	do				
	Margaret Cartwright	20	do				
	William Cochran	50	male	Laborer	U. States		
	Thomas Cochran	45	do		G. Britain		
	Dennis Baxter	20	do				
	John Smith	35	do			New York	Schooner Edward, John Carlisle
	Robert Spies	30	do	Merchant	do		
	Mary Wiggins	24	female	Spinster	do		
	David Wiley	26	male	Weaver	do		
	David Chalms	16	do	Farmer	do		

Name	Age	Sex	Occupation			
John Wilson	17	male	Farmer	Britain	New York	
Thomas Naylor	25	do	Seaman	do	do	
James Mitchell	27	do	Painter	do	do	
Wm. Zinse	32	do	do	do	do	
John Anderson	30	do	Farmer	do	do	
Wm. Thedan	32	do	do			
James Patterson	27	do	Weaver			
B. M'Guien	26	do	Shoemaker			
James Robertson	25	do	Farmer			
C. Hamilton	50	db.	do			
John Mexon	19	do	Weaver			
James Parker	25	do	Shoemaker			
Mary Parker	32	female	Farmer			
A. Pollox	20	male	Spinster			
H. M'Cay	13	do	Farmer			
Margaret M'Grotes	38	female	Spinster			
Mary Languin	20	do	do			
Catherine Patterson	20	do	do			
Ann M'Farland	40	do				
Catherine M'Farland	48	do				
Margaret Patterson	13	do				
Margaret Dennand	50	do				
Ann Patterson	18	do				
Mary Duffy	30	do				
Lewis M'Laughlin	28	do				
Susan Dale	18	male				
Eleanor Dale	28	female				
Grace Dale	40	do				
Susan Bryan	16	do				
John Walsh	20	do	Gentleman	G. Britain	G. Britain	
Wm. P. Walsh	40	male	do	do	do	
W. Williams	2, 6	do	Farmer	U. States	U. States	
John Edin	20	do	Laborer	G. Britain	do	
Jane Edin	70	do				
Ann Edin	27	female				
Matthew Edin	58	do				
John A. Maire	21	male	Farmer	Germany		Schooner Loire, Isaac Bassett.
	20	do				

LIST of Passengers, &c.—Quarter ending June 30, 1820.

Custom House, with the name of the Collector.	Names of Passengers.	Age.	Sex.	Occupation.	Country to which they belong.	Country of which they intend to become inhb's.	Ship or Vessel, with the name of the Master or Commander.
New York, David Gelston.	C. G. Kuntz	24	male	Farmer	Germany	England	Schooner Loire, Isaac Bassett.
	Edward Boyd	28	do	Gentleman	England	do	
	Edward Bland	25	do	do	do	U. States	
	E. W. Fetch	22	do	Merchant	U. States	do	
	Wm. Peter	22	do	do	do		
	Kirby Dalrymple	50	female				
	Ann Dalrymple	45	male				
	Grant Dalrymple	3	do				
	Thomas N. Brown	34	female	Farmer	France	America	
	Mary Brown & 4 child.	28	female				
	John P. Gofry	22	male	Merchant			
	Ann C. Gofry*	58	female		America		* Died on the voyage, 24th May, 1820.
	Angle De Pare	51	male	Farmer		France	
	Wm. Fenwick	21	do	Merchant	France		
	Moses Shepherd	19	do			America	
	Victor Tancette	26	do	do		U. States	
	John C. Dernelly, wife & 4 children	42	do		do		
	John L. Demelly	24	do	Farmer	U. States	America	
	Henry Aisqueth	20	do	Merchant		U. States	
	C. A. De Renamie	38	do	Barber			
	Victor Villeneure	39	do	do			
	Wm. Boandner	40	do	Merchant	Ireland	U. States	
	Thos. Charlton	24	do	Farmer	do		
	Mary Charlton	24	female		do		
	Henry Charlton	1	male		do		
	George Kerr	22	do	do			

Name	Age	Sex	Occupation			Ship
John Kerr	20	male	Farmer	Ireland	U. States	
Bryan O. Keeke	22	do	do	do	do	
Owen O. Rorke	15	do	do	do	do	
Wm. Wallace	22	do	do	do	do	
Martin Kilroy	28	do	do	do	do	
John Bing	24	do	do	do	do	
Catharine M'Dermot	23	female		do		
Sarah Boonan	25	do		New York		
Bridget Boonan	3	do				
Joseph Sirtane	48	male	Merchant	U. States	U. States	Schooner Olive Branch, R. Duggs.
Joseph Augustine	21	do	do	Cuba	Cuba	
Peter Recoras	27	do		do	do	
—Belafond	43	do	Teacher	France	U. States	Ship L'African, Jno. Ganechi,
Penelope Belafond	27	female	do	do	do	
J. Bullivard	20	male	Merchant	do	do	
—Dupasquier	19	do	do	do	do	
J. Doumout	27	do	Farmer	do	do	
J. L. Boussey	39	do	Merchant	do	do	
Mrs. Grogean	34	female		do	do	
W. Grogean	41	do		do	do	
Fanny Grogean	4	do		do	do	
Lucy Grogean	2	do		do	do	
Sophia Grogean	14	do		do	do	
Lucian Grogean	12	male		do	do	
Louis Constant	8	do		do	do	
Augusta	13	female		do	do	
Wm. M'Gillevery	50	male	Merchant	G. Britain	G. Britain	Albion, Jno. Williams.
Ann M'Gillevery	15	female		do	do	
Magdalene M'Gillevery	12	do		do	do	
Agnes Shaw	50	do		do	do	
C. W. Grant	36	do		do	do	
Margaret Nicholson	25	male		U. States	U. States	
Robert Mixon	21	female		do	do	
Samuel Zerball	32	do		do	do	
Samuel Cobb	58	do		do	do	
Sarah Cobb	48	female		do	do	
Sarah J. Cobb	17	do		do	do	
Eliza Inches	40	do		do	do	

LIST of Passengers, &c.—Quarter ending June 30, 1820.

Custom House, with the Name of the Collector.	Names of Passengers.	Age.	Sex.	Occupation.	Country to which they belong.	Country of which they intend to become inhab's	Ship or Vessel, with the name of the Master or Commander.
New-York, David Gelston.	Susan Inches	37	female		U. States	U. States	Albion, Jno. Williams.
	Joseph G. Fry	33	male		do	do	
	Tristam Barnard	69	do		do	do	
	David Watkinson	42	do	Merchant	G. Britain	da	
	James Brown	32	do		U. States	do	
	John Lusston	32	do	do	do	do	
	Rebecca Jeffcoat	42	female		do	do	
	Isabella Jeffcoat	16	do		do	do	
	Margaret Jeffcoat	7	do		do	do	
	Henry Jeffcoat	3	male		do	do	
	Lewis Bliss	26	do	do	do	do	
	Thomas Dixon	27	female		do	do	
	Isabella Lenox	25	male		do	do	
	Julius Idemenou	31	female		France	France	
	Mary M'Kay	34	female		G. Britain	U. States	
	James M'Kay	12	male		do	do	
	John M'Kay	10	do		do	do	
	Patrick M'Kay	4	do		do	do	
	Elizabeth Kelly	30	female		do	do	
	Thos. Wragg	17	male	Farmer	do	do	
	Josiah Wragg	18	do	do	do	do	
	Thomas Allan	34	do		do	do	
	James King	50	do		do	do	
	James E. Esther	47	do	Engineer	do	do	
	Henry Pullan	26	do		do	G. Britain	
	Isabella Leek	18	female		G. Britain	U. States	
	Peter Campbell	32	male	Merchant	do	do	Brig Percival, James Scott

Name	Age	Sex	Occupation			Vessel
James Ramsay	24	male	Laborer	G. Britain	U. States	
Robert Wighton	22	do	Merchant	do	do	
Alexander Stewart	27	do	Carpenter	France	do	
Charles Raymond		female	Merchant	U. States	do	Schooner Catharine, D. Hepburn.
Mrs. Pepin		do		do	do	
Miss Pepin		do		do	do	
Mrs. Hayden		do		do	do	
Sarah Brown		do		do	do	
Susan Wheeland					do	
Ths. W. C. Moore	24	male	do	do	do	
Lt. Benjamin Cooper	25	do	Navy	do	do	
Sarah Armstrong	35	female		do	do	
Eliza Anderson	13	do		do	do	
Maria Griscovla	18	do		do	do	
Mary O'Brien	22	do		do	do	Ship Blooming Rose, E. Kingsbury.
Samuel Townshend	40	male	Millwright	do	N. Scotia	Ship Elizabeth, Wm. S. Tabor.
Richard Moore	20	do	Farmer	N. Scotia	do	
A. Playson	38	do	Merchant	do	U. States	
Warner Miller	28	do	do	U. States	do	Schooner Fair Polly, Edward Lewis.
Seth Hayden	40	do	Gentleman	do	do	
Gideon Davenport	33	do	Carpenter	do	do	
Charles Turner	31	do	do	do	do	Schooner Milo, P. Allin.
Mr. Innis	51	do	Manufacturer	do	do	
Edward Innis	12	do	do	do	do	
Wm. Innis	4	do	do	do	do	Ship Magnet, James M'Kee.
Catharine Lewis	16	female	Servant	do	do	
H. Fowler	24	male	Supercargo	Bristol	England	
Charles Ward	27	do	Merchant	G. Britain	G. Britain	
H. Ward	27	female		do	do	
Ruth Cambery	35	do		do	do	Schooner Nancy, Reuben Crowell.
Thomas Cambery	22	male		do	do	
Wm. Tilton	30	do		do	do	
C. Carnon	25	do		do	do	
James Biggot	30	do		do	do	
Elsay Biggot	25	female		do	do	
T. Nown	25	do		U. States	U. States	
John Baker	30	male	Farmer	do	do	
Henry Lambert	35	do		do	do	

LIST of Passengers, &c.—Quarter ending June 80, 1821.

Custom House, with the name of the Collector.	Names of Passengers.	Age.	Sex.	Occupation.	Country to which they belong.	Country of which they intend to become inhab's	Ship or vessel, with the name of the Master or Commander.
New York, David Gelston.	Elizabeth Lambert	31	female		U. States	U. States	Ship Nancy, Reuben Crowell.
	Ann Lambert	22	do		do	do	
	Mary Lambert	18	do		do	do	
	Benjamin Clark	30	male		do	do	
	Ann Clark	28	female		do	do	
	Richard Logan	22	male		do	do	
	Thomas Appbery, jr.	40	do	Merchant	do	do	
	John Slaiging	50	do	Weaver	G. Britain	de	Schooner Mercator, M. D. Griffing.
	C. H. Vn. Brunt	24	do	Physician	U. States	do	
	Mary Fairbanks	26	female	Governess	do	do	
	Jno. Felix Dominic	44	male	Jeweller	Hayti	Hayti	
	Jno. Campbell	25	do	Farmer	Scotland	U. States	Schooner Marion, S. J. Merrill.
	Jane Montgomery	24	female		do	do	
	Ths. Stephens	26	male	do	England	do	
	Wm. Stephens	32	do	do	do	do	Ship Criterion, S. Avery.
	Charles Oliver	28	do	Merchant	U. States	do	
	Samuel Stephens	28	do	do	England	do	
	George Stephenson	56	do	do	do	do	
	M. Luccock	22	do	do	do	do	
	Mary Jackson	28	female		do	do	
	Eleanor Mair	20	do		do	do	
	Mary Stephens	19	do		do	do	
	Mrs. Piper & infant	35	do		do	do	
	Mrs. Fletcher	26	do		do	do	
	Josiah Vincent	50	male		do	do	
	Hannah Vincent	50	female	Farmer	do	do	
	Wm. Farfort	45	male		do	do	

Name	Age	Sex	Occupation	Country	Destination
Mary Farfort	40	female		England	U. States
Michael Farfort	12	male		do	do
Aaron Farfort	5	do		do	do
George Mitchell	45	female		do	do
Sarah Mitchell	40	male		do	do
John Paul	40	do		do	do
James Futa	35	do		do	do
John Kinsley	35	do		do	do
Mrs. Benham	30	female		do	do
William Benham	8	male		do	do
Joshua Stead	35	do		do	do
Mrs. Stead	35	female		do	do
George Stead	8	male		do	do
Joseph Stead	7	do		do	do
Henry Stead	6	do		do	do
Thomas Stead	5	do		do	do
Caroline Stead	4	female		do	do
Frederick Stead	3	male		do	do
John Stead	2	do		do	do
Robert Stead	1	do		do	do
Joseph Harrison	40	do	Farmer	do	do
Aaron Davis	38	do	do	do	do
William Funch	32	do		do	do
Samuel A. Barnet	50	do		do	do
Mrs. Barnet	50	female		do	do
William Barnet	25	male		do	do
Levi Nathan	50	do		do	do
James Haywood	20	do		do	do
Nicholas Menache	25	female	Merchant	do	do
Mrs. Menache, 2 child'n	24	do		Trinidad	do
Miss Menache	23	female		do	do
William Bruce	2	do		do	do
A servant	14	male			do
do	35				do
T. Leplace	35	male	Merchant	France	do
Isaac Packara	37	do	do	U. States	do
Thomas H. Madox		do	Mariner	do	do
Adam Champlain	40	do	Shipmaster	America	America

LIST of Passengers, &c.—Quarter ending June 30, 1820.

Custom House, with the name of the Collector.	Names of Passengers.	Age.	Sex.	Occupation.	Country to which they belong.	Country of which they intend to become inhab'ts	Ship or Vessel, with the name of the Master or Commander.
New-York, David Gelston.	Jelin Durosuan	32	male	Merchant	America	America	Ship Criterion, S. Avey.
	Fernando Povarer	11	do		Spain	Spain	
	Sarah Spear	35	female	Housekeeper	U. States	U. States	
	Henry Spear	2	male		do	do	
	Sarah Cuff	35	female	Housekeeper	do	do	
	John Cuff	8	male		do	do	
	Charles L. Reg		do	Merchant	do	do	
	Antonio Benauch		do		Spain	do	
	S. Benauch				do		
	C. Benauch				do		
	C. White			Servant	U. States		
	Joseph Bryan*	37	male	Merchant	Pernambuco		*Died on the voyage.
	A child	5	female				
	A child	4	do				
	2 servant girls	14 & 10	do				
	Mrs. Hector	35	de		Scotland	U. States	Schooner Betriere, Jacob Haws.
	Eliza Hector	10	do		do	do	
	James Hector	8	male		do	do	
	Margaret Hector	6	female		do	do	
	Charlotte Hector	3	do		do	do	
	Ellen Ross	19	do		do	do	
	William Ashton	28	male	Tallowchandler	Ireland	France	Brig Agnes, M. Sandford.
	P. Beabeau	24	do	Merchant	Point Petre	U. States	Brig Mechanic, J. Wright.
	Nichodemus Viel	21	do	Farmer	U. States	do	
	S. Blackwood	21	do	Merchant	do	do	
	James D. Scott	26	do	Mariner	do	do	
	William Brooks	26	do	House carpen,	do	do	

Name	Age	Sex	Occupation	G. Britain	U. States	Ship
Richard G. Clanchy	35	male		G. Britain	U. States	Ship Eliza Ann, William Malcom?
Mary Clanchy	28	female		do	do	
Peter Clanchy	7	male		do	do	
Margaret Clanchy	10	female		do	do	
Hugh Clanchy	6	female		do	do	
Maria Clanchy	4	male		do	do	
John Clanchy	2	do		do	do	
Joseph Clanchy	5	do		do	do	
Jno. Dundam	29	do	Publican	do	do	
Thomas Henson	37	do	Farmer	do	do	
Peggy Heald	50	female	Servant	do	do	
Betty Donnelly	27	do		do	do	
Mary Donnelly	10	do		do	do	
James Donnelly	7	male		do	do	
Kitty Donnelly	4	female		do	do	
William Wade	30	male		do	do	
John Healy	30	do		do	do	
John Gaflaher	50	do		do	do	
Michael M'Mahon	28	do		do	do	
George Crumby	28	do	Mechanic	England	do	Brig Hope, Egbert Smith.
Jared Procker	27	do	do	do	do	
Burret Keeler	30	do	do	do	do	
John Brown	42	do	do	do	do	
R. Turner	47	do	do	do	do	
George Smith	23	do	do	do	do	
George Major	50	do	do	do	do	
Cruse Jones	37	do	do	do	do	
John Paterson	25	do	do	do	do	
Miles Magran	50	do	do	do	do	
Edward State	23	do	do	do	do	
Joel B. Nott	24	do	Merchant	U. States	do	Ship Garonne, Edward Whiting.
Frederick Hickey	40	do	Gentleman	do	Canada	Ship Atlantic, W. Mattock.
Robert M'Kobb	25	do	Capt. B. navy	G. Britain	do	
Jasper Vandenburg	35	do	Merchant	do	do	
David Handyside	26	do	do	do	do	
Robert Cowise	23	do	do	do	do	
Robert Conick	25	do	do	do	do	
William Smith	47	do	do	do	do	

LIST of Passengers, &c.—Quarter ending June 30, 1820.

Custom House, with the name of the Collector.	Names of Passengers.	Age.	Sex.	Occupation.	Country to which they belong.	Country of which they intend to become inhab's.	Ship or Vessel, with the Name of the Master or Commander.
New York, David Gelston.	Stephen Yarwood	35	male	B. Nav.	G. Britain	Canada	Ship Atlantic, W. Matlock.
	Henry Neimire	39	do.	Gentleman	Germany	U. States	
	Isaac Pickford	34	do.	Merchant	U. States	do	
	Julia Barrie	30	female	Lady	G. Britain	do	
	Julia Barrie	20	do	do	do	do	
	Charles Smither	35	male	Servant	do	do	
	Michael Robson	55	do	Farmer	do	do	
	Eliza Robson	57	female		do	do	
	Joseph Robson	22	male		do	do	
	James Robson	20	do	do	do	do	
	Henry Robson	17	do	do	do	do	
	John Banks	29	do	do	do	do	
	John Horn	29	female		do	do	
	Lucy Horn	27	do		do	do	
	William Horn	3	male		do	do	
	John Smith	15	do	do	do	do	
	John Pickford	38	do	do	do	do	
	Geo. Whitehead	43	do	Merchant	Ireland	do	Ship Mirror, B. Shepherd.
	Peter M'Laughlin	20	do	Farmer	do	do	
	Michael Omally	20	do		France	do	
	Labrure Ducoudray	32	do		Charlestor	do	
	A. Ceregg	44	do	Merchant	New York	New York	
	G. R. Barker	21	do	Cutler	France	U. States	
	P. Barrel	21	do	Merchant	New York	New York	Brig Virginia, J. Servemteau.
	W. Fostin	19	do	Ropedancer	France		
	Gedean	31	do		France		
	Gedean	21	female		do		

Name	Age	Sex	Occupation	Nativity	Destination	Ship
Cailatt	28	male	Merchant	France	U. States	Brig Ocean, N. S. Bend.
James Burt	37	do	Mechanic	U. States	do	
J. Boggin	18	do	Carpenter	do	do	
Peter Stepney	26	do	Gentleman	G. Britain	do	
Wm. Bronell	27	do.	Surgeon	do	do	
Wm. Hutton	23	do	Merchant	do	do	
Jos. Spencer	42	do	Farmer	do	do	Ship Lady Gallatin, J. Barker.
John Francis	54	female		do	do	
Mary Francis	41	do		do	do	
Ann Francis	6	do		do	do	
Mary Francis	9	do		do	do	
Dorothy Francis	4	male		do	do	
John Francis	13	do		do	do	
Samuel Reynolds	36	female		do	do	
Mary Reynolds	32	male		do	do	
Thomas Reynolds	4	female		do	do	
Mary Reynolds		female		do	do	
Richard Haves	49	male	do	do	do	
John Haves	6	do		do	do	
Humphrey Lowe	36	do		do	do	
Lenah Lowe	40	female		do	do	
Maria Lowe	10	do		do	do	
David Lowe	14	male		do	do	
Thos. Kinsay	46	do		do	do	
Ann Kinsay	45	female		do	do	
James Kinsay	20	male		do	do	
Lydia Kinsay	16	female		do	do	
Stephen Kinsay	18	male		do	do	
Hannah Kinsay	12	female		do	do	
Evan Kinsay	10	male		do	do	
Edward Kinsay	8	do		do	do	
Betsey Kinsay	6	female		do	do	
Charles Kinsay	4	male		do	do	
David Kinsay	infant	do		do	do	
Ann Roberts	22	female		do	do	
Wm. Wilson	28	male	Cloth dresser	do	do	
Benj. North	22	do		do	do	
Wm. Green	22	do		do	do	

LIST of Passengers, &c.—Quarter ending June 30, 1820.

Custom House, with the Name of the Collector.	Names of Passengers.	Age.	Sex.	Occupation.	Country to which they belong.	Country of which they intend to become inhb'ts.	Ship or Vessel, with the name of the Master or Commander.
New York, David Gelston.	John Cattver	29	male	Farmer	G. Britain	U. States	Ship Lady Gallatin, J. Barker.
	John Davis	24	do	do	do	do	
	Hugh Jones	21	do		do	do	
	Jane Roberts	30	female		do	do	
	Benson Roberts	31	male		do	do	
	Benjamin Powell	30	do	Minister	do	do	
	Mary Powell	27	female		do	do	
	Abigail Powell	4	do		do	do	
	Alorth Powell	3	do		do	do	
	Selina Powell	infant	do		do	do	
	Geo. Steer	24	male	Confectioner	do	do	
	Mary Steer	22	female		do	do	
	Wm. Longdon	22	male	Farmer	do	do	
	Jno. Zaster	20	do	do	do	do	
	Wm. Douglass	22	do	Cordwainer	do	do	
	Thos. Beekman	22	do	do	do	do	
	James Beekman	29	do	Farmer	do	do	
	George Nales	24	male	Clerk	do	do	
	Ellen Nales	30	female		do	do	
	Sarah Nales	10	do		do	do	
	John Aldridge	40	male		do	do	
	Esther Aldridge	24	female		do	do	
	Cyrus Aldridge	17	male		do	do	
	Alfred Aldridge	15	do.		do	do	
	James Stokes	42	do	Surveyor	do	do	
	Esther Jones	36	female	Spinster	do	do	
	John J. Dughurst	32	male	Joiner	do	do	

Name	Age	Sex	Occupation			Ship
Thomas Leigh	55	male	Weaver	G. Britain	U. States	Ship Hercules, N. Cobb.
Thomas Leigh	12	do		do	do	
Edward Greaves	42	do	Merchant	England	do	
Elizabeth Greaves	38	female		do	do	
Luke Barker	30	male	Surgeon	do	do	
Joseph Nowell	31	do	Merchant	do	do	
James Eddy	21	do	Physician	New-York	do	
Elizabeth Asterhold	31	female		England	do	
Nancy Asterhold	5	do		do	do	
James Gee	25	male	Laborer	do	do	
John Matthews	24	do		do	do	
Jane Matthews	39	female		do	do	
Margaret Matthews	33	do		do	do	
Helena Matthews	14	do		do	do	
Jane Matthews	39	do		do	do	
Thomas Matthews	33	male		do	do	
David Matthews	14	do		do	do	
John Matthews	12	do		do	do	
Charlotte Matthews	10	female		do	do	
J. Matthews, & 3 others	8	do		do	do	
John Haworth	9	male		do	do	
James Maxwell	26	do		do	do	
James Harper	20	do		do	do	
Joseph Bottomly	30	do		do	do	
Mrs. Bottomly	18	female		do	do	
William Blanker	30	male		do	do	
Ralph Thompson	26	do		do	do	
George Athwood	25	do		do	do	
James Broadly	24	do		do	do	
Edward Kidd	23	do		do	do	
George Scott	27	do		do	do	
James Wright	28	do		do	do	
Theophilus Watkins	26	do		do	do	
John Bolton	30	do		do	do	
Sarah Gee	24	female		do	do	
Francis Maxwell	22	male	Merchant	U. States	do	Brig Orizimbo, William Paty.
L. Mallett	20	do		do	do	
James Milliner	24	do			do	

LIST of Passengers, &c.—Quarter ending June 30, 1820.

Custom House, with the name of the Collector.	Names of Passengers.	Age.	Sex.	Occupation.	Country to which they belong.	Country of which they intend to become inhab's	Ship or Vessel, with the name of the Master or Commander.
New-York, David Gelston.	E. Bates	22	male	Carpenter	U. States	U. States	Brig Orizimbo, William Paty.
	Benjamin H. Talbot	23	do	Merchant	do	do	
	E. A. Talbot	15	do.	Clerk	G. Britain	do	
	Thomas Mather	25	do.	Doctor	do	do	
	James M'Kensie	45	do	Tailor	do	do	
	Thomas Lick	40	do.	Farmer	do	do	
	Charles Boyd	19	do.	Cooper	do	do	
	Agnes Larnard	50	female		do	do	
	Ann M'Kensie	50	do		do	do	
	Janet Bruce	35	do		do	do	
	Mary Bruce	10	.do.		do	do	
	Margaret Bruce	7	do		do	do	
	William Bruce	40	male	Merchant	England	do	Schooner Mars, Jno. Stenman.
	William H. Kelly	40	female	Mariner	U. States	do	
	William R. Russle	52	male		England	England	
	William Foster	36	do	Merchant	do	do	
	John Holmes, jr.	43	do	Physician	do	do	
	Ebenezer Shepherd	30	do	Gentleman	U. States	U. States	Emulation, George Paddock.
	Theodorus Bliss	50	female		do	do	
	Sarah Bliss	45	do		do	do	
	Sarah Ann Bliss	16	male		do	do	
	Robert Bliss	14	female	Servant	do	do	
	Harriet Bregwill	16	male	Farmer	do	do	
	Thomas Shipley	49	do		do	do	
	Thomas Shipley	17	do		do	do	
	George B. Jones	19	do	Merchant	do	do	
	Charles Daniels	46					

Name	Age	Sex	Occupation			Ship
Ann Daniels	28	female		U. States	U. States	
Samuel Daniels	1	male		do	do	
Ann Bell	48	female	None	do	do	
Elizabeth Bell	17	do		do	do	
Anna Bell	11	do		do	do	
Frances Bell	17	do		do	do	
Eliza Bell	9	do		do	do	
Joseph Bell	4	male		do	do	
Madam Pachat	77	female		Switzerland	do	Ship Lunion, Bellingerville.
M. Fallen	19	male	Laborer	do	do	
Susan Fallen	15	female		do	do	
Abraham Fallen	49	male	Laborer	do	do	
Mrs. Fallen	49	female		do	do	
Jennet Fallen	27	do		St. Croix	St. Croix	
Mrs. Barbara Regulau	9	do		do	do	
Hannata Regulau	38	male	Merchant	France	U. States	Ship Chase, J. Baxter, jr.
Charles Bouneau	23	do		England	do	
Samuel Harriot	24	do	Shipmaster			
William Bellony	35	do	Merchant	Scotland	Scotland	
Duncan Cunningham	27	do	Shipmaster	Scotland	U. States	Schooner Diana, S. W. M'Pherson.
Thomas Hughes	30	female	Merchant	do	do	
Mary Hughes	8	do		do	do	
Mary Richardson	62	male	Farmer	do	do	
John Dick	64	female		do	do	
Mary Dick	52	male		do	do	
Altan Dick	27	do		do	do	
John Dick	6	female		do	do	
Mary M'Phan	47	male	Merchant	do	do	
Charles Orr	40	female		do	do	
Margaret Orr	40	male		do	do	
Thomas Orr	50	female		do	do	
Jennet M'Austin	12	female		do	do	
Jane Orr	9	do		do	do	
Charles Orr	1	male		New-York	New-York	
John Orr	48	do.	Merchant	Scotland	Scotland	Ship Harriet, J. O. Bull.
Robert Thompson	19	do	do	do	do	
James Taylor	40	do	do		do	
Alexander Orr		do			do	

LIST of Passengers, &c.—Quarter ending June 30, 1820.

Custom House, with the name of the Collector.	Names of Passengers.	Age.	Sex.	Occupation.	Country to which they belong.	Country of which they intend to become inhb's.	Ship or Vessel, with the name of the Master or Commander.
New York, David Gelston.	Thomas Orr	4	male	Merchant	Scotland	U. States	Ship Harriet, J. O. Bull.
	George Lawson	60	do	Farmer	do	do	
	William Lawson	24	do		do	do	
	Andrew Holmes	35	do		do	do	
	Margaret Holmes	26	female		do	do	
	Robert Holmes	1	male		do	do	
	John Camett	31	do		do	do	
	Wm. M'Kean	39	do	Clerk	do	do	
	David Amery	35	do		do	do	
	Robert Nicholl	25	do		do	do	
	Wm. Dobbie	25	do	Farmer	do	do	
	Walter Gow	26	do		do	do	
	Duncan M'Gregor	32	female		do	do	
	Mary M'Gregor	60	do		do	do	
	Ann M'Gregor.	24	do	Clerk	do	do	
	Catharine M'Gregor	45	male		do	do	
	John Holmes	20	do		England	do	Ship Caledonia, P. G. Foodick.
	James Hall	22	do		do	do	
	James Gibson	16	female		do	do	
	John Gow	1	male		do	do	
	Susan Wilkes	36	do		do	do	
	Henry Wilkes	14	do		do	do	
	John A. Wilkes	13	do		do	do	
	S. M. Wilkes	5	female		do	do	
	James Wilkes	11	do		do	do	
	Ann A. Wilkes	7			do	do	
	F. J. Wilkes	4			do	do	

Ship Cincinnatus, A. H. Griswold.

Name	Age	Sex	Occupation	Country	Destination
William Wilkes	1	male		England	U. States
Julia Ann M'Evoy	19	female	Servant	do	do
Edward Fletcher	19	male	Manufacturer	do	do
John Williams	20	do	Laborer	G. Britain	do
John Palmer	44	do	Farmer	do	do
Hannah Palmer	40	female		do	do
Augusta S. Palmer	14	do		do	do
Emily Palmer	12	do		do	do
Reuben Palmer	10	male		do	do
Nelson Palmer	8	do		do	do
Walter Palmer	5	do		do	do
Alfred Palmer	2	do		do	do
John Haver	23	do	Miller	do	do
Matthew Telfair	24	do	Farmer	do	do
Frederick Pentril	36	do		Germany	do
Gotting Modinger	26	do		do	do
Luke Searle	41	do		G. Britain	do
Reginal Kirkpatrick	20	do.		do	do
Arthur Kirkpatrick	27	do		do	do
Eliza Kirkpatrick	22	female		do	do
Thomas Kirkpatrick	11	male		do	do
Jane Kirkpatrick	9	female		do	do
Richard Galwarthy	50	male		do	do
Francis Farm	29	do		do	do
William Farm	19	do		do	do
Thomas Farm	7	do.		do	do
Ann Farm	11	female		do	do
Mary Brittle	47	do		do	do
Louisa Brittle	17	do		do	do
Ann Brittle	17	do		do	do
Harriet Brittle	9	do		do	do
Francis Brittle	6	male		do	do
Sarah Carpenter	41	female		do	do
Mary Eliza Carpenter	16	do		do	do
Jane Carpenter	14	do		do	do
Caroline Carpenter	7	do		do	do
Louisa Carpenter	5	do		do	do
George Carpenter	3	male		do	do

LIST of Passengers, &c.—Quarter ending June 30, 1820.

Custom House, with the name of the Collector.	Names of Passengers.	Age.	Sex.	Occupation.	Country to which they belong.	Country of which they intend to become inhab's	Ship or Vessel, with the name of the Master or Commander.
New York, David Gelston.	Emily Carpenter	1	female		Britain	U. States	Ship Cincinnatus, A. R. Griswold.
	Hannah Meyers	35	do		do	do	
	George Europe	16	male		do	do	
	Thomas Maris	22	do		do	do	
	Edward Neube	36	do		do	do	
	Sally Maria Fairer	26	female		do	do	
	Maria Fairer	6	do		do	do	
	Leonora Fairer	5	do		do	do	
	Wm. H. Fairer	4	male		do	do	
	Charles Fairer	3	do.		do	do	
	Ann Martha Fairer	1	female		do	do	
	R. R. Wormley	36	male	Royal navy	do	do	
	J. Ban.	40	do.	Merchant	do	do	
	J. G. Scharch	20	do	do	Austria	do	
	L. S. Parmley	25	do	Dentist		N. York	
	John N. Loyd	36	do	Gentleman		do	Ship S. Ca. Packet, S. B. Pinkham.
	P. Floyd	29	female	Lady			
	James Van Beheal	25	male	Gentleman	America		
	Ann Beheal	22	female				
	Julia Beheal	3	do				
	James Bush	7	male				
	Eli Burrith	46	do	Physician			
	Eliza Codwise	46	female	Lady			
	Jane Smith	35	do				
	Mary Snyder	24	do				
	Louisa Jackson	24	do				
	Augustus Blackmore	50	male				

Name	Age	Sex	Occupation	Country	Country	Vessel
E. Delfore	45	male	Merchant	U. States	U. States	Schooner Ariosto, James Smith.
John Campbell	18	do	Physician	Scotland	G. Britain	Brig Aurora, Peter Milne.
Francisco Banetts	60	do	Merchant	Portugal	U. States	Brig Louisa Cecilia, Jno. Daring.
Valentine Smattes	32	do	do	Portugal	Portugal	
Isaac Nunes	18	do	Servant	do	do	
Antonie Desants	12	do	do	do	do	
J. J. Lawrence	29	do	Landholder	England	England	Schooner Lady's Delight. J. Benedict.
J. J. Lawrence	1	female		do	do	
Julia Lawrence	8	male		do	do	
James Lawrence	6	female	Servant	do	do	
Ann Naughan	22	male		do	da	
Peter Meadu	19	female		do	do	
Sally Lawrence	12	female		do	do	
Charles Pigson	12	male	Gentleman	G. Britain		Brig Commerce, Isaac Little.
John A. Black	33	do	Servant	do	U. States	
Norris Hoare	25	do	Merchant	U. States	dor	Schooner Lewis, Jon. Sears.
James Craig	25	do	Weaver	do	Boston	Ship Justine, Andrew Tombs.
Thomas Owen	25	do	Farmer	G. Britain	do	
Mary Owen	22	female		do		
Patrick Brown	24	male	Tanner, &c.	Ireland	N. York	Schooner Charlotte Corday, J. G. Russel.
Joseph Clark	23	do	Gentleman	G. Britain	G. Britain	
John S. Nally	55	do	do	U. States	U. States	
Wm. Gilbert	23	do	do	G. Britain	Britain	
Wickhear Brou	24	do	do	U. States	U. States	
James Wilstock	34	do	Merchant	do	do	Brig Amelia, James Nile.
K. Gothfroid	32	do	do	Saxony	do	Brig Hesper, Jacob Stephens.
G. Angmoz	24	do	Marinemaster	Germany	do	
F. H. Orloh	20	do	Merchant	Prussia	do	
Charles Mesewer	42	do	Seaman	do	do	
Chris. Harke	27	do	Laborer	Oldenberg	do	
S. F. Peterson	41	do	Merchant	Germany	do	
Hermoine Peterson	22	female		Prussia	do	
George Trumbull	25	male	do	U. States	do	Brig Frederick, Charles Auner.
Mrs. Trumbull	76	female		do	do	
George Trumbull	60	male	do	do	do	
M. Trumbull	20	female		do	do	
Ann Trumbull	25	do		do	do	

LIST of Passengers, &c.—Quarter ending June 30, 1820.

Custom House, with the name of the Collector.	Names of Passengers.	Age.	Sex.	Occupation.	Country to which they belong.	Country of which they intend to become inhab's	Ship or Vessel, with the name of the Master or Commander.
New-York, David Gelston.	C. Hicks	20	female		U. States	U. States	Brig Frederick, Charles Auner.
	N. Cartwright	19	male	Gentleman	G. Britain	G. Britain	
	A. Kenny	20	do		do	do	
	H. W. King	23	do		do	do	
	Ira Munson	29	do	Mechanic	U. States	U. States	
	A. P. Blanchard	41	female	do	do	do	
	Abigail Smith	29	female		do	do	
	John Smith	18	male	Gentleman	do	do	
	Harriet Kirby	16	female	Seamstress	do	do	
	Charlotte Kirby	16	do	do	do	do	
	John Carr	32	male	Carpenter	do	R. Island	
	Wm. Fayer	44	do	do	do	U. States	
	Felix Campbell	26	do	do	N. Hampsh.	do	
	James Ferguson	22	do	Stonecutter	U. States	do	
	Thomas Sommerville	23	do	Laborer	Ireland	do	Schooner John Dickerson, John Baush.
	H. Miller	7	female		do	do	
	A. Harris	25	do		do	do	
	Henry Onsill	18	male	Carpenter	do	do	
	Mary M'Connell	20	female		do	do	
	Elizabeth M'Connell	50	do		do	do	
	James Findlay	31	male	Weaver	do	do	
	Samuel Pepper	22	do	do	do	do	
	Jno. Davidson	22	do	Clerk	do	do	
	Robert Dunlap	31	do	Farmer	do	do	
	David West	25	do	Cartman	U. States	do	
	Jno. Elliott	23	do	Shoemaker	do	do	
	Michael Roberts	25	do	Weaver	do	do	

Name	Age	Sex	Occupation			Ship
Gilbert Laing	35	male	Farmer	Scotland	do	
Elizabeth Harris	22	female		do	do	
Robert Wilson	10	male		do	do	
Wm. Wilson	3	do.		do	do	
E. Wilson	13	female		do	do	
Betsey Humes	15	do		do	do	
James Wilson	1	male		U. States	do	
Elizabeth Phillips	28	female		do	do	
Thomas Phillips	3	male		do	do	
Margaret Phillips	1	female		do	do	
Thomas Major	45	male	Farmer	Scotland	do	
Jno. Donaldson	32	do	Blacksmith	do	do	
Agnes Donaldson	24	female		do	do	
William Donaldson	4	male		Ireland	do	
Elizabeth Harris.	24	female		do	do	
Thomas Jolly	9	male		do	do	
Jane Robinson	7	female		do	do	
Hannah Smith	12	female		do	do	
Mary Phillips	5	do,		U. States	France	Brig Orleans, Thos. C. Brown,
Auguste Risotal	23	male	Merchant	France	do.	
Jean B. Guerard	20	do	do	do	U. States	
Peter Brock	50	do	Mariner	U. States	do	
C. Pink	21	do	Baker	England	do	
C. Jones	36	do	Mariner	U. States	do	
Wm. Capper	24	da	Farmer	G. Britain	do	Ship Illinois, Jas. Funk,
Robert Hyslop	47	do	do	do	do	
John Hyslop	40	dq	do	do	do	
John M'Evers	33	do	do	do	do	
John Midgley	50	do	do	do	do	
Benj. Midgley	18	do	do	do	do	
John Shannon	27	do	do	do	do	
John Joyet	32	do	do	do	do	
John Baxter	42	dq	do	do	do	
Henry Patterswell	32	do	Gentleman	England	do	
Wm. Miles	50	female	do	do	do	
Miss S. Miles	17	female		do	do	Ship Thames, Norman Peck.
Miss E. Miles	15	do		do	do	
John R. Maqes	50	male		Germany	do	

LIST of Passengers, &c.—Quarter ending June 30, 1820.

Custom House, with the name of the Collector.	Names of Passengers.	Age.	Sex.	Occupation.	Country to which they belong.	Country of which they intend to become inh'bts.	Ship or Vessel, with the Name of the Master or Commander.
New York, David Gelston.	Wm. Smith	31	male		America	U. States	Ship Thames, Norman Peck.
	B. Ansell	24	do		England	do	
	J. S. Chapman	21	do		Canada	do	
	J. L. Brucks	32	do		do	do	
	R. G. Hollins	23	do		Germany	do	
	R. M. Rensie	33	do		America	do	
	James Aikens	52	do		do	do	
	D. A. Didrach	23	do		do	do	
	Wm. Sprague	31	do		England	do	
	James Lance	32	do		do	do	
	J. S. Probert	36	do	Carpenter	do	do	
	John White	26	do	Blacksmith	do	do	
	Wm. B. Denison	26	do	Land surveyor	do	do	
	Catherine Denison	25	female		America	do	
	Wm. H. Denison	3	male		do	do	
	P. B. Denison	2	do		do	do	
	Thomas Lefevre	25	do	Farmer	England	do	
	Sarah Lefevre	29	female		do	do	
	Wm. Lefevre	2	male		do	do	
	Rebecca Frisby	22	female		do	do	
	M. A. Frisby	1	do		do	do	
	Fanny Monk	63	do		do	do	
	Amelia Monk	22	do		do	do	
	Sarah Monk	5	do		do	do	
	Jas. Brambleber	34	male		do	do	
	Fanny Brambleber	30	female		do	do	
	Chas. Clarke	37	male		do	do	

Name	Age			England	U. States	Ship Amity, George Maxwell.
Charlotte Clarke	33	female		do	do	
Thomas Clarke	12	male		do	do	
George Clarke	9	do		do	do	
Hannah Clarke	7	female		do	do	
J. Turner	4	male		do	do	
Wm. Clatton	1	do		do	do	
Thos. Wall	53	do		do	do	
Richard Stiles	30	do		do	do	
Mary Stiles	7	female		do	do	
George Stiles	4	male.		do	do	
Samuel Dare	1	do		do	do	
Wm. Cox		do		do	do	
John Reid		do		do	do	
Sarah Reid		female		do	do	
Susan Reid		do		do	do	
John Carter		male		do	do	
Benj. Carter		do		do	do	
S. Abrahams		do		do	do	
Robert Abrahams		female		do	do	
Fanny Reymer		male.		do	do	
James Reymer		do		do	do	
G. R. Reymer		do		do	do	
F. M. Reymer		female		do	do	
O. S. W. Reymer		do		do	do	
Peter Watkinson	35	male	Farmer	do	do	
Hannah Watkinson	35	female		do	do	
E. Watkinson	13	do		do	do	
Maria Watkinson	11	male		do	do	
Thos. Watkinson	7	female		do	do	
Mary Hartley	35	do		do	do	
Sally Hartley	12	do		do	do	
Enelby Hartley	13	male		do	do	
Ann Hartley	6	female		do	do	
Thomas Hartley	4	do		do	do	
Sarah Marshall	30	do		do	do	
Mary Marshall	6			do	do	
Rebecca Marshall	3			do	do	
Sarah Marshall	1			do	do	

LIST of Passengers, &c.—Quarter ending June 30, 1820.

Custom House, with the name of the Collector.	Names of Passengers.	Age.	Sex.	Occupation.	Country to which they belong.	Country of which they intend to become inh'bs.	Ship or Vessel, with the name of the Master or Commander.
New York, David Gelston.	Mary Dakin	28	female		England	U. States	Ship Amity, George Maxwell.
	Esther Dakin	7	do		do	do	
	Mary Ann Dakin	2	do		do	do	
	Maxwell Dakin	3	male		do	do	
	David Lancaster	24	do	Painter	do	do	
	John Beaumont	34	do	Merchant	do	do	
	John Jackson	23	do	Druggist	do	do	
	Henry Baines	24	do	Surgeon	do	do	
	Smith Pyne	17	do		do	do	
	Thos. Woodhead	21	do.	Merchant	U. States	do	
	Mary Ann Woodhead	23	female	None	do	do	
	Thos. Feenn	30	male	Physician	England	do	
	Adeline Pratt	19	female		do	do	
	Chas. Botherom	29	male	Merchant	U. States	do	
	James Massom	28	do	do	do	do	
	John A. Donnell	23	do.	Physician	do	do	
	Wm. Howard	34	do	Merchant	do	do	
	Hannah Hart	25	female		England	do	
	Betty Hart	20	do		U. States	do	
	John Harwood	21	male	do	do	do	Brig Greyhound, S. Bedsen.
	—McDonald	19	do	do	do	do	
	Saml. P. Bishop	13	do		do	do	
	Margaret Chidsey	17	female	Lady	do	do	
	Margaret Proyan	20	do		do	do	
	Bridget Dorothy	25	do		do	do	
	Betsey Kirby	3	do		do	do	
	Edwd. Allen	21	male	Merchant	do	do	

Name	Age	Sex	Occupation	Country	Country	Ship
Edward Glascow	23	male	Clerk	Ireland	U. States	Schooner Enterprize, J. Dunham
Alexander Hosack	45	do	Physician	America	America	Ship Clothier, Jno. Owens.
Scott H. Smith	25	do	Supercargo	do	do	
—— Sorre	30	do	Servant	do	do	
Lewis Therassen	36	do	Merchant	Ireland	Ireland	Scnooner Edward, G. W. Grice.
Thomas Moreau	40	do	Seaman	G. Britain	U. States	Brig Penelope, George Page.
Edward Codd	41	do	Merchant	do	do	Brig Superb, Daniel Aymer
Catharine Codd	30	female		do	do	
Billy	11	male	Servant	do	do	
Francis W. M'Nae	25	do	Merchant	do	do	
Nathl. Butterfield	31	do,	do	do	do	
Nathl. Butterfield	24	do,		do	do	
Jane Davenport	40	female		do	do	
John D. La Port	22	male	Merchant	Italy	America	Schooner Sally, Jno. Whitehead.
Daniel Rogers	44	female	Supercargo	America	U. States	Brig Rolla, James Morrison.
M. Morallo	22	male	Merchant	Spain		Schooner Maria Theresa, Andrew Smith.
I. L. Baclin	28	do		U. States		
N. De Lard	56	female		do		
Mrs. De Lard	35	do		do		
—— De Lard	10	male		do		
—— De Lard	8	do		do		
—— De Lard	6	do		do		
—— De Lard	4	do		do		
—— De Lard	2	do		do		
R. Moulard	23	do	Merchant]	France	do	
—— Macriel	19	do	Servant-	U. States	do	
I. Stearns Hurd	24	do	Physician	do	do	
John Baxter	25	do	do	do	do	
Louis De Sangurs	22	do	Merchant	do	do	
Henry Sheldon	29	do		do	do	Ship Belle, E. Huntington.
Jno. W. Wainwright	16	do		do	do	
Mrs. Carnes	22	female		do	do	
Miss Carnes	2	do		do	do	
Miss Wainwright	18	do		do	do	
Mrs. Hardy	42	do		do	do	
Miss Hardy	19	do		do	do	
I. S. Burtch	42	male	Physician	St. Thomas	Denmark	
Irem Guillard	44	do	Merchant	France	U. States	

LIST of Passengers, &c.—Quarter ending June 30, 1820.

Custom House, with the name of the Collector.	Names of Passengers.	Age.	Sex.	Occupation.	Country to which they belong.	Country of which they intend to become inhab's	Ship or Vessel, with the name of the Master or Commander.
New-York, David Gelston.	Juste Lancaster	23	male		France	U. States	
	Elizabeth Le Grand	27	female		Ireland	do	
	Mary Perrin	23	do		do	do	
	Louis Couverchel	32	male	Gaudener	France	France	
	Mr. Couverchel	23	do		do	do	
	Auguste Aurevay	22	do	Clerk	G. Britain	do	
	George Winter	33	do	Sailmaker	do	G. Britain	
	Mary Winter	26	emale		do	do	
	George Winter	6	male		do	do	
	William Winter	5	do		do	do	
	Jno. Winter	4	do		do	do	
	— Winter	2	do		do	do	
	John Jackson	24	do	Carpenter	do	do	
	Alexander Manzin	13	do	Sailor	do	do	
	James Russle	32	do	Laborer	England	U. States	Ship Martha, Seth Freeman.
	William Wiley	27	do	do	do	do	
	Matthew Matchell	32	do	do	do	do	
	Ann Matchell	32	female		do	do	
	Edward Querden	31	male	Laborer	do	do	
	Martha Querden	26	female		do	do	
	Ann Querden	6	do		do	do	
	James Querden	3	male		do	do	
	Elizabeth Querden	1	female		do	do	
	John Stone	30	male	Laborer	do	do	
	James Kenan	35	do	do	do	do	
	Heby Kenan	24	female		do	do	
	Margaret Kenan	4	do		do	do	
	Charlotte Todd	40	do	Lady	Quebec	Quebec	Ship Hector, J. Gillender.

Name	Age	Sex	Occupation			Ship
John B. Broome	29	male	Farmer	England	U. States	Ship Hector, J. Gillender.
R. P. Broome	25	do	Merchant	do	Cuba	
John Wragg	24	do	do	Montreal	Montreal	
H. G. Bouthellier	23	do	B. army	England	do	
John Pullen	37	do	Merchant	do	U. States	
John M. Bledsow	44	do.	Gentlemen	do	do	
Samuel Trodsham	27	do	Merchant	do	do	
Thomas Williams	44	dq	do	do	do	
Ann & Sarah Williams	19	female		do	do	
George Williams	19	male		do	do	
Emma Williams	19	female		do	do	
Mary & Betsy Williams	12	do		do	do	
Hannah Williams	3	do		do	do	
Thomas Bradley	42	male	Joiner	do	do	
Eliza Bradley	52	female		do	do	
Mary Bradley	21	do		do	England	
Thomas Bradley	15	male		do	U. States	
Samuel Clamsha	44	do	Merchant	do	do	
William M'Gibbon	26	do	Farmer	do	do	
John Grears	23	do	Servant	Scotland	do	Brig Sarah, Joseph Badger.
R. Tram	21	do	Laborer	do	do	
Fanny Whitaker	18	female	Seamstress	do	do	
A. Marlin	40	do	Lady	do	do	
D. M'Gregor	19	male.	Clerk	do	do	
John Douglass	38	do	Merchant	do	do	
R. Tentason	28	do	Farmer	do	do	
William Sawyer	23	dq	do	do	do	
I. Graham	28	do	Weaver	do	do	
J. Walker	30	do,	Carpenter	do	do	
Anna Kennier	25	female	Servant	do	do	
Anna M'Farland	20	do.	do.	do	do	
P. M'Lauren	28	male	Farmer	do	do	
A. M'Lauren	28	do	do	do	do	
J. M'Lauren	20	do		do	do	
Ann Johnson	35	female		do	do	
H. Johnson	12	do		do	do	
I. M'Lauren	21	male		do	do	
J. Johnson	30	do		do	do	

LIST of Passengers, &c.—Quarter ending June 30, 1820.

Custom House, with the name of the Collector.	Names of Passengers.	Age.	Sex.	Occupation.	Country to which they belong.	Country of which they intend to become inhab's	Ship or Vessel, with the name of the Master or Commander.
New York. David Gelston.	Charles J. Vandston	12	male		Scotland	U. States	Brig Sarah, Joseph Badger.
	Wm. J. Vandston	6	do		do	do	
	Edward Vandston	8	do		do	do	
	J. J. Vandston	2	do		Ireland	do	Schooner Dublin Packet, J. Coles.
	John Evans	25	do	Merchant		do	
	Thomas Evans	19	do			do	
	Wm. Evans	17	do			do	
	Robert Page	23	do.	Farmer		do	
	Roger Hawkins	23	do.	do	Ireland	do	
	Mary Gnagan	20	female	Spinster	do	do	
	Bridget Haydon	40	do		do	do	
	Joanna Haydon	7	do		do	do	
	Margaret Haydon	5	do		do	do	
	Wm. Haydon	3	male.		do	do	
	Mary Ann Hayden	1	female		do	do	
	Francis Harry	30	do	Laborer	do	do	
	Mary Harry	7	do		do	do	
	Mrs. Smith	35	do		do	do	
	John Smith	10	male		do	do	
	Robert Smith	8	do		do	do	
	Fanny Smith	3	female		do	do	
	Margaret Nowland	22	do		do	do	
	James Hanlon	30	male		do	do	
	Rose Hanlon	30	female		do	do	
	Robert H. Moran	27	male		do	do	
	Richard Dempsey	23	do		do	do	
	Thomas Dempsey	25	do		do	do	

Ship Magnet, D. S. Ogden.

Name	Age	Sex	Occupation	Country	Destination
Wm. Oyckbown	30	male		do	U. States
Arthur Smith	30	do		Ireland	do
Catharine Smith	30	female		do	do
James Smith	5	male		do	do
James Marlin	20	do		do	do
John Stewart	22	do		do	do
Bell Cowan	22	female		do	do
Mary Cowan	19	male		do	do
Matthew M'Coonon	33	do		do	do
Edward Collins	24	female		do	do
Ann Collins	21	male		do	do
Thomas Hart	20	do		do	do
Francis Thompson	40	do		do	do
Samuel Gothings	18	female		G. Britain	do
Elizabeth Pardow	40	male		do	do
Francis Pardow	18	female		do	do
Helen Pardow	16	female		do	do
Julia Pardow	12	male		do	do
George Pardow	4	do		do	do
Jas. & Austin Pardow	3 & 9 mo.	-do,-		do	do
James Warwick	30	female	Merchant	do	Canada
Elizabeth Warwick	25	male		do	do
Richard Warwick	4	do		do	do
Charles Warwick	3	female		do	do
Helen Warwick	1	male		do	do
Justice Penn	24	do	Merchant	do	U. States
Wm. Blackwood	32	do	do	do	do
Alexander Thaine	35	do	do	do	do
Andrew Patterson	36	do	do	do	do
James M'Jarvis	30	do	do	do	do
Wm. Stephens	30	do	do	do	do
Peter M'Cutchen	30	do	do	do	do
John Cooper	20	do	do	do	do
Wm. Brown	25	do	Laborer	do	do
Jacob Foster	23	do	do	do	do
Robert Humphreys	20	do	do	do	do
Robert Humphreys	20	do	do	do	do
John Humphreys	18	do	do	do	do

LIST of Passengers, &c.—Quarter ending June 30, 1820.

Custom House, with the name of Collector.	Names of Passengers.	Age.	Sex.	Occupation.	Country to which they belong.	Country of which they intend to become inhab's	Ship or Vessel, with the name of the Master or Commander.
New York, David Gelston.	James Slossen	23	male	Shoemaker	G. Britain	U. States	Ship Magnet, D. S. Ogden.
	Daniel R. Jacobs	28	do	Grocer	do	do	
	Nicholas Reid	28	do	Farmer	do	do	
	Christopher Reid	23	do	Laborer	do	do	
	James Buchanan	30	do	Lawyer	do	do	
	J. Robinson	34	do	Laborer	do	do	
	George Walton	50	do	Shoemaker	do	do	
	Patrick Riley	28	do	Laborer	do	do	
	John David	21	female	Cordwainer	do	do	
	Jane David	34	do		do	do	
	Mary Woodward	32	do		do	do	
	Ann Woodward	20	do		do	do	
	Charlotte Woodward	21	do		do	do	
	Naomi Woodward	18	do		do	do	
	Elizabeth Wellington	28	male		do	do	
	John Baines	35	do	Merchant	do	do	
	A. Sportwodod	45	do	Shoemaker	do	do	
	Edwin Millington	2	do		do	do	
	Robert Blackstock	35	do	Farmer	do	do	
	Thomas Golden	30	do	do	do	do	
	C. Clairngburne	45	female	do	do	do	
	Thomas Barton	30	male	do	do	do	
	Agnes Gilmore	22	female		do	do	
	Frederick Spencer	40	do	Mariner	do	do	
	Jane Spencer	32		Spinster	do	do	
	Eliza Spencer	40		do	do	do	
	Mary Woodward	11			do	do	

Ship Alexander Mansfield, H. Beanes.

Name	Age	Sex	Occupation	G. Britain	U. States
Edward Jacobs	3	male			U. States do
Robert Befers	28	do	Farmer	Ireland	do
John Befers	26	do	do	do	do
Henry Millen	30	do	do	do	do
Isaac Moore	28	do	do	U. States	do
Jane Kown	25	female	Lady	do	do
Nancy Bennet	28	do	do	Ireland	do
Patrick Conner	28	male	Farmer	do	do
Neil Collins	26	do	Chandler	do	do
John Strain	21	do		do	do
Mary Strain	21	female		do	do
Samuel M'Kay	33	male	Carpenter	do	do
Patrick M'Knice	22	do	Weaver	do	do
John Ganet	20	do	Farmer	do	do
Andrew Bable	14	do		do	do
Wm. Robinson	25	do	Gardener	do	do
Robert M'Kown	26	do	Farmer	do	do
Mary Robinson	25	female		do	do
Wm. M'Kown	28	male		U. States	do
Jane Hewitt	20	female	do	do	do
Samuel Clark	30	male	Spinster	do	do
Hannah Clark	22	female	Farmer	do	do
Joseph Clark	18	male		do	do
Samuel Agnew	21	do.	Bricklayer	Ireland	do
Alexander Fran	27	do		do	do
James Coulan	39	do		do	do
Margaret Coulan	6	female		do	do
Thomas Coulan	15	male		do	do
John Coulan	17	do		do	do
James Scott	45	do		do	do
Elizabeth Scott	32	female		do	do
Eliza Scott	6	do		do	do
James F. Scott	4	male		do	do
Grace Scott	5	female		do	do
Eleanor Kenedy	34	do	Spinster	do	do
Wm. Harrison	21	male	Carpenter	do	do
James Harrison	19	do	Whitesmith	do	do
Robert Harrison	36	do		do	Jn

LIST of Passengers, &c.—Quarter ending June 30, 1820.

Custom House, with the name of the Collector.	Names of Passengers.	Age.	Sex.	Occupation.	Country to which they belong.	Country of which they intend to become inhab's	Ship or Vessel, with the name of the Master or Commander.
NEW-YORK. David Gelston.	Catharine Gibson	47	female	Spinster	Ireland	U. States	Ship Alexander Mansfield, H. Beanes.
	Hamilton Davis	44	male	Farmer	do	do	
	Sarah Davis	15	female		do	do	
	Allen Davis	13	male		do	do	
	Wm. Davis	11	do		do	do	
	Hamilton Davis	9	do		do	do	
	Arthur Davis	9	female		do	do	
	Peggy Jane Davis	6	male		do	do	
	Francis Davis	1	do		do	do	
	James Davis	3	do		do	do	
	Wm. Couroy	24	do	do	do	do	
	James Rogers	36	do	do	do	do	
	Betty Rogers	30	female		do	do	
	Nancy Rogers	22	do	Spinster	do	do	
	Elizabeth M'Leod	30	do	Farmer	do	do	
	Arthur M'Donnel	36	male	Military	England	do	Schooner Union, Henry Brown.
NORFOLK, James Johnson.	Charles Kemp	15	do	do	do	do	
	Richard Reynett	25	do	do	do	do	
	Robert Egan	21	do	Planter	U. States	do	Schooner Esther & Sally, A. Orum.
	James Bradshaw	45	do	Merchant	do	do	Ship Phil Tabb, G. C. Whaler.
	William Angus	31	do	Sea captain	do	do	Sloop Invincible, W. H. Bliss.
	John Gorham	30	do	Carpenter	do	do	Schooner Alpha, Jno. W. Hall.
	Stephen Haynie	32	do	Planter	do	do	Schooner Agawam, Wm. H. Rott.
	John Beard	33	do		Ireland	do	Ship Foster, N. Moran.
	George Weightman	15	do		do	do	
	Benjamin White	26	do	Farmer	Ireland	do	
	William Strachan	30	do	Shipmaster	Halifax	do	Schooner Lydia, D. Reed.

Name	Age	Sex	Occupation	Country	Destination	Ship / Remarks
Elisha Hall	28	male	Ship master	U. States	U. States	Ship Comet, Wm. Coxon.
Thos. Stiles	30	do	Gardener	England	do	
Miss Duncan	30	female		Scotland	do	Schooner Mary, D. Driver.
Geo. Wood*	30	male	Merchant	U. States	do	* Jumped overboard, and was drowned.
Thos. Lancaster	34	do	do	do	do	
Judah Lord	34	do	do	do	do	
H. Leon	85	do	Ship master	Ireland	do	Brig Alonzo, Jno. Canaway.
Robt. Cook	44	do		do	do	Ship Hyson, Jno. Johnson.
Jerry Denover	21	do		do	do	
Lewis Minchin	27	do		do	do	
John Murphy	19	do		do	do	
Mary Hartnet	24	female		do	do	
Eliza Douthet	26	do		do	do	
Jno. M'Guire	42	male	Laborer	do	do	
David Welsh	34	do	do	do	do	
Wm. Martin	19	do	Farmer	do	do	
Philip Delany	22	do	Carpenter	do	do	
Lawrence Cranny	38	do	Laborer	do	do	
Edmund Alun	29	do	do	do	do	
Robert Wynne	27	do	Carpenter	do	do	
Patrick Bryan	28	do	Laborer	do	do	
John Austin	25	do	do	do	do	
Johanna Shehan	28	female		do	do	
Catherine Murphy	13	do		do	do	
Mary Joyce	24	do		do	do	
Mary Walsh	29	do		do	do	
Johanna Conner	30	do		do	do	
Wm. Shenan	4	male		do	do	
Johanna Conner	4	female		do	do	
Mary Joyce	2	do		do	do	
Bridget Welsh	1	do		do	do	
John Joyce	2	male		do	do	
Peggy Welsh	7	female		do	do	
R. J. Hogan	24	male	Clerk	G. Britain	G. Britain	Brig Sophronia, S. Harding.
H. Almand, jr.	24	do	Mariner	U. States	U. States	
Benj. Hatchbings	38	do	Supercargo	do	do	
Wm. Bolgians	21	do	Merchant	do	do	
Stephen J. Seymour	25	do		Bermuda	Bermuda	Schooner Hero, Thos. Travers.

LIST of Passengers, &c.—Quarter ending June 30, 1820.

Custom House, with the name of the Collector.	Passengers.	Age.	Sex.	Occupation.	Country to which they belong.	Country of which they intend to become inhab's	Ship or Vessel, with the name of the Master or Commander.
Norfolk, James Johnson.	John —	10	male	Apprentice	Bermuda	Bermuda	Schooner Hero, Thos. Travers.
	Wm. Gibson	20	do	Clerk	U. States	U. States	Schooner Ghent, J. Folger.
	Francis Osburn	21	do	do	do	do	
Boston and Charlestown, H. A. S. Dearborn.	B. Cunningham	60	do.	Farmer	Halifax	do	Schooner Gen. Green, J. Bears.
	S. Cunningham	40	female		do	do	
	A. Cunningham	10	male		do	do	
	G. Cunningham	9	female		do	do	
	Morton Cunningham	7	female		do	do	
	Charlotte Cunningham	5	female		do	do	
	Miss Morton	30	do		do	do	
	Sarah Cunningham	20	do		do	do	
	Thos. Rafferty	50	male		do	do	
	Mrs. Rafferty	30	female		do	do	
	Jane Gordon	25	do		do	do	
	Wm. Stearns	20	male		do	do	
	J. Atwood	18	do		do	do	
	John Prior	50	do		do	do	
	John Prior, jr.	40	do		do	do	
	Mrs. Bancroft	30	female		do	do	
	J. Bancroft	6	male		do	do	
	Mrs. Fullerton	30	female		do	do	
	A. Fullerton	7	do		do	do	
	Mrs. M'Nab	38	do		do	do	
	Sarah Laffer	15	do		do	do	
	Mrs. Mansfield	50	do		do	do	
	Miss Mansfield	15	do		do	do	
	Ellena Porter	20	do		do	do	

Name	Age	Sex	Occupation	Halifax	U. States	
Mr. Neal	25	male		Halifax	U. States	
Jas. Foley	26	do		do	do	
Mary Percival	22	female		do	do	
J. Percival	10	male		do	do	
A. Percival	7	do.		do	do	
John Percival	5	do		do	do	
Wm M'Cloud	14	do		do	do	
James Sample	20	do	Farmer	Ireland	do	
John Carr	64	do	do	England	do	
Andrew Carr	25	do	Brasier	do	do	
Joseph Barker	25	do	Shoemaker	U. States	do	
Elisha Hathway	22	do	Merchant	Germany	do	Ship Commerce, H. Peterson.
Chas. L. Baker	23	do	do	G. Britain	do	
Cormac Godfrey	26	do	Wheelwright	do	do	
James Slater	52	do	Tanner	do	do	
Samuel Barber	22	da	Joiner	do	do	
Robert Barber	23	dq		do	do	
Ann Barber	4	female		do	do	
Samuel Barber	1	male		do	do	
Jas. Bentley	55	do	Seaman	do	do	
Wm. Bentley	29	do		do	do	
Ann Bentley	28	female		do	do	
Wm. Bentley	6	male		do	do	
Elizabeth Armby	30	female		do	do	
Mary Ann Armby	9	do		do	do	
Wm. Armby	38	male	Plaisterer	do	do	
Cardin Armby	1	do		do	do	
Thomas Armby	1	do		do	do	
Amelia Bullock	27	female		do	do	
Jas. Wood	33	male	Merchant	Ireland	Ireland	Schooner Mary & Martha, L. Bangs.
Benj. B. Lecwitt	22	do	do	Eastport	Eastport	Sloop Anson, John Ross.
H. Lecwitt	20	do	Yeoman	Charleston	Charleston	
James Newland	25	do	do	New-York	New-York	
James Casseday	22	do	do	Nova Scotia	Nova Scotia	
Thos. Turnbull	22	do	do	do	do	
John Ryan	60	do	Iron founder	Ireland	Boston	
Patrick King	26	do	Yeoman	do	do	
Philip Crane	30	do		do	do	

LIST of Passengers, &c.—Quarter ending June 30, 1820.

Custom House, with the Name of the Collector.	Names of Passengers.	Age.	Sex.	Occupation.	Country to which they belong.	Country of which they intend to become inhab's	Ship or Vessel, with the name of the Master or Commander.
BOSTON AND CHARLESTOWN, H. A. S. Dearborn.	Dennis Curmody	30	male	Mathematician	Ireland	Boston	
	Mary Dunn	35	female		do	do	
	Mary Brinon	28	do		do	do	
	Kitty Brinon	4	do		do		
	Thomas Barkley	28	male	Merchant	St. Croix	England	Brig Mary, Hugh M'Pherson.
	John M'Colon	23	do	Laborer	Ireland		Schooner Castine Packet, R. K. Blodget.
	John Toy	23	do	do	do		
	Daniel M'Coley	22	do	Seaman	do		
	Pat M'Gawy	25	do	Laborer	do		
	Andw. M'Cawley	38	do	do	do		
	James Gibbons	17	do	do	do		
	Jas. Blas	43	do	Weaver	do		
	Edw. Swaney	32	do	Laborer	do		
	Hugh Ray	34	do	do	do		
	Mrs. Ray	30	female		do		
	Jas. Brown	15	male	do	do		
	Mary Brown	22	female		do		
	Eliza Brown	20	do		do		
	Priscilla Holmes	19	do	Supercargo	U. States	U. States	Schooner Little Sarah, Jno. Tildom.
	John Drummond	22	male	Mariner	do	on a visit	Brig Palafox, Noble Maxwell.
	David Evans	57	do	Merchant	England	U. States	Schooner Abigail, Joshua Elwell.
	Thomas Crocker	22	do	do	U. States	do	
	James Leslie	27	do	Butcher	do	do	
	John Emmerson	27	do	Merchant	do	do	
	John Macomb	22	do		do	do	
	John M. Smith	18	do		do	do	
	George Knight	34	do	Sailor	do		

Name	Age	Sex	Occupation	Country	Destination	Ship
Nathaniel Clark	23	male		U. States	do	Brig Galen, U. Keating.
2 Servants	24	female		do	do	
Mrs. Knight	35	male	Tailor	do	do	
Samuel Pickering	28	do	Shipmaster	do	do	Ship Ceres, J. B. Lincoln.
E. S. Manning	40	do	Trader	Ireland	do	Schooner Syren, S. Emery.
Patrick Welsh	30	do	Blacksmith	Nova Scotia	do	Brig Ellen, E. Merrill.
I. Cummings	25	do	Mason	U. States	do	Brig Hope and Sally, D. Oliver.
—— Pratt	23	do	Merchant	France	do	Brig Romp, U. Crosby.
Louis Bounimon	27	do	Clergyman	Halifax	do	Ship Atticus, J. Westcott.
Rev. Th. G. M'Innis	35	do	Merchant	U. States	do	
Joseph Mark	32	female		England	do	
Ann Wood	1	male		do	do	
Twentyman Wood	8	female		do	do	
Mr. Brown	36	male		do	do	
Mrs. Brown	36	female		do	do	
George A. Eames	34	male	Merchant	U. States	do	Schooner Penguin, Thomas Soule.
Daniel C. Robinson	36	do	do	do	do	Sloop Milledgeville, George Knight,
Charles C. M'Donald	19	do		St. John	do	
Patrick M'Gaw	17	do		Ireland	do	
Catharine Maypole	45	female		U. States	do	
Betsey M'Gaw	19	do		Ireland	do	
Catharine Wade	24	do		St. John	do	
Jacob Pike	26	male	Cooper	U. States	do	Ship Ten Brothers, M. Bond.
Joseph C. Swan	27	do	Mariner	do	do	Brig Syren, Elisha Small.
Charles C. Hooper	31	do	do	do	do	
John H. Wood	27	do	do	do	do	
I. D. Western	29	do	do	do	do	
R. W. Ray	24	do	Gentleman	do	do	
S. T. Locke	30	do	Doctor	do	do	
Antonio Madagrouza	19	do	Servant	do	do	
Lydia Savage	23	female	Servant	Cuba	do	Schooner Pocahontas, E. Sears.
Josephine ——	25	do	do	U. States	do	
Arthur Savage	31	male	Merchant	do	do	
Adam Beasly		do	Mariner	Scotland	do	
James Nichols	22	do	Weaver	do	do	Schooner Woolwich, D. G. Scott.
James Wilmer	22	do	Coppersmith	do	do	
Richard Richards	52	do	Ropemaker	England	do	
Mary Richards	30	female			do	

LIST of Passengers, &c.—Quarter ending June 30, 1820.

Custom House, with the Name of the Collector.	Names of Passengers.	Age.	Sex.	Occupation.	Country to which they belong.	Country of which they intend to become inhab's	Ship or Vessel, with the Name of the Master or Commander.
BOSTON AND CHARLESTOWN, H. A. S. Dearborn.	William Richards	6	male		England	U. States	Schooner Woolwich, D. G. Scott.
	Joseph Richards	2	do		do	do	
	John Richards	4	do		do	do	
	Charles Heynos	20	do		Ireland	do	
	David Reid	25	do	Tailor	Scotland	do	
	R. Graham	24	do	Shoemaker	do	do	
	Mary Graham	20	female	Slater	do	do	
	William King	21	male		do	do	
	David King	19	do	Weaver	do	do	
	William Loomis	35	do		do	do	
	Edward Templeton	32	do	Ropemaker	do	do	
	Jennet Bell	40	female	Weaver	do	do	
	James Porter	28	male	Trader	U. States	do	Schooner Albert, Jno. Shackford.
	Daniel Smith	23	do	Blacksmith	do	do	
	Samuel Raymond	42	do	Brickmaker	do	do	
	Valentine Boyer	45	do	Baker	France	do	
	Simon B. Robee	49	do	Laborer	Halifax	Halifax	
	Elizabeth Robee	30	female		do	do	
	Edward Wallace	22	male	Merchant	do	do	
	Miss E. Wallace	26	female		do	do	
	Robert Dawson	30	male	Merchant	do	do	
	France D. Conner	24	do	do	do	do	
	M. E. Mott	21	do	do	do	do	
	John Richardson	25	do		do	do	Brig George Atwood, Marwick.
	Mersey White	30	female		do	do	Brig Fawn, Thomas Hedge.
	Edward Hickey	20	male	Servant	do	do	Schooner General Greene, I. Bears.
	Sarah H. Ellen	19	female	do	do	do	

Name	No.	Sex	Occupation		Ship
Ellen White	1	female		Halifax — Halifax	
Mrs. Gibbs	31	do		do — do	
John Gibbs	2	male		do — do	
John Basden	38	do	Shipmaster	U. States — U. States	Schooner Union, A. W. Sheafe.
Olwin Basden	23	do		do — do	
Ann Basden	3	female		do — do	
Dorothy B. Basden	14	do		Bermuda — do	
Peter Coffin	42	male	Merchant	U. States — do	Ship Clio, Caleb Heath.
W. James	21	do	Laborer	do — do	
Sarah James	30	female		do — do	
Ann James	2	do		do — do	
Robert Higham	42	male	Farmer	do — do	Brig Belisarius, J. D. Groce.
Gilbert Deblois	38	do	Merchant	do — do	
Don Domingo Monteull	32	do	do	Havana — Havana	
Robert M'Kown	32	do	Mariner	U. States — U. States	Brig Edwin, James B. Moore.
Joseph Steele	46	do	Shipmaster	do — do	Brig Barbary, Robert Turner.
E. A. Newton	35	do	do	do — do	
Sarah T. Newton	28	female		do — do	Brig Eunice, Jno. Howe.
Simon M. Openheimer	21	male	Dyer	Frankfort — do	
Andrew Smith	35	do	Hairdresser	U. States . — do	
Elizabeth Smith	33	female		do — do	
John A. Smith	12	male		do — do	
William H. Smith	10	do		do — do	
Michael C. Smith	8	do		do — do	
George M. Smith	6	do		do — do	
Charles H. Smith	3	do		do — do	
Frederick A. Smith	7	do		do — do	
Susanna Smith	43	female		Holland — do	Schooner Cherub, William Athern.
Richard W. Rowland	27	male	Merchant	G. Britain — G. Britain	
William Haswell	50		do	U. States — U. States	Schooner Salmon, Jno. Kelly.
Ebenezer Clapp	35		do	do — do	Schooner General Brewer, Thomas Rodgers.
Henry Gleason	30			do — do	
Samuel Topliff	45			England — do	
Charles Fisher	19			do — do	
John A. Anderson	25			do — do	
Robert Chantee	91		Farmer	do — do	
Charles Noacha	18		do	do — do	
Mrs. Giilchrist	25	female		U. States — do	

LIST of Passengers, &c.—Quarter ending June 30, 1820.

Custom House, with the name of the Collector.	Names of Passengers.	Age.	Sex.	Occupation.	Country to which they belong.	Country of which they intend to become inhab's	Ship or Vessel with the name of the Master or Commander.
BOSTON AND CHARLESTOWN, H. A. S. Dearborn.	Mrs. Clark	30	female		U. States	U. States	Schooner General Brewer, Thomas Rodgers.
	Miss Tuttle	20	do		do	do	
	George Clark	35	male	Mariner	do	do	Ship Alert, Daniel C. Baron.
	William B. Jackson	25	do	do	do	do	
	Edward King	76	do	Gentleman	Halifax	do	
	Agnes King	46	female	Lady	do	Halifax	Schooner Victory, Samuel Parker.
	George Sewall	30	male	Trader	do	do	
	Leonard Geldard	22	do	do	do	do	
	James Dool	23	do	do	do	do	
	Samuel Baker	43	do	Butcher	do	U. States	
	Helen Fitz Patrick	34	female	Brewer	.	do	
	James Fitz Patrick	15	male	do	do	do	
	John Stacy	16	do	Farmer	Ireland	do	
	Edward Sanderson	24	do	Cooper	U. States	do	
	Patrick Mahony	34	do	Servant	Ireland	do	
	Margaret Morris	17	female	do	do	do	Brig Climax, J. Fisher.
	Elizabeth Gahagaw	33	do	do	do	do	
	Mary Shendan	30	do	do	do	do	
	Mary Potts	26	do		do	do	
	Joseph Potts	23	male	do	do	do	
	Bridget Kernan	28	female		do	do	
	Rose Kernan	2	do		do	do	
	Patrick M'Kenna	26	male	Farmer	U. States	do	Schooner Eagle, Abel Johnson.
	Labena Sears	29	do	Mariner	do	do	Schooner Olive Branch, Thomas Sampson.
	Joseph Tompkins	25	do	Seaman	do	do	Schooner Mary and Nancy, S. Prescott.
	Samuel Winter	43	do	Carpenter	England	do	
	Jane Winter	42	female		do	do	

Name	Age	Sex	Occupation	Country	Country	Ship
Will'am Winter	13	male		England	U. States	
Fanny Winter	14	female		do	do	
Eliza Winter	10	do		do	do	
Jane Winter	8	do		do	do	
Mary Winter	5	do		do	do	
Helen Winter	3	male		do	do	
Samuel Winter	1	do		do	do	
Charles Winter	7	do		do	do	
Nathan Dodd	47	do	Shoemaker	do	do	Brig Harriet Newell, Robert Thâire.
Austin Dodd	27	do	do	do	do	Schooner New Packet, Obed Snow.
Richard Dodd	19	do	Laborer	do	do	
Michael Dodd	16	do	do	do	do	
Wm. Dodd	14	do	do	do	do	
Gabriel Dodd	12	do	do	do	do	
Andrew Buchanan	20	do	Seaman	Scotland	N.Brunswick	
George Croates	28	female	Merchant	G. Britain	G. Britain	
Catharine Wise	25	male		U. States	U. States	
Walter W. Adams	5	do		do	do	
George Weston	21	do	Merchant	do	do	Ship Herald, Philip Fox.
Nathan Bacon	42	do	do	-do-	do	
J. Van Lenniss	48	do	do	Turkey	do	
J. Whitehead	49	do	do	England	do	
John Loring	30	do	do	do	do	Brig Mary, David Loring,
Wm. Cant	18	do	do	G. Britain	do	Brig Frederick, H. E. Fridge,
Patrick Jurdon	25	do	Servant	Ireland	do	
George Jackson	32	do	Seaman	U. States	do	
John Gray	30	do	do	Martinique	no	
Mr. Bardel	12	female	Merchant	do	do	
Joseph Barcel	20	male		U. States	do	Brig Union, R. H. Wade.
Mary Dunlivie	2	do		do	do	Schooner Sally, J. Hibbert.
Stephen Dunlivie	1	do		do	do	
John Dunlivie	12	do		Bermuda	do	
Wm. Frost	26	do	Merchant	Creole	do	
John Thompson	2	do	Seaman	U. States	do	
Daniel Hill	23	do	do	do	do	
John Domingo	25	do		France	do	
Wm. Dalmes		female	Manufacturer	England	do	Ship Catharine & Eliza, J. Portilby
Lady						

LIST of Passengers, &c.—Quarter ending June 30, 1820.

Custom House, with the name of the Collector.	Names of Passengers.	Age.	Sex.	Occupation.	Country to which they belong.	Country of which they intend to become inhb's.	Ship or Vessel, with the name of the Master or Commander.
BOSTON AND CHARLESTOWN, H. A. S. Dearborn.	Three children						Ship Catharine & Eliza, J. Portilby.
	John Lambert	26	male	Confectioner	England	U. States	Brig Columbia, B. Loring.
	Gaspard Vatteau	21	do	Sailor	St.Bartholo'w	do	
	Simon Johns	18	do	do	Havre	do	Schooner Only Son, G. Rowley.
	Alphius Weeks	35	do	Farmer	U. States	do	Sloop Favorite, E. Jones.
	Wm. Fox	47	do	Mariner	do	do	Brig Mary, N. Barker.
	Elias Cuby	42	do	do	G. Britain	do	
	David Baxter	32	do	Merchant	U. States	do	
	John C. Page	22	do	do	do	do	
	Edmund Sawyer	45	do	Mariner	do	do	Brig Governor Carver, P. Holmes.
	James Brown	32	do	Farmer	do	do	Brig Helen, C. Belham.
	Peter D. Alderman	22	do	Paperhanger	Bremen	do	Ship Minerva, S. Eames.
	John A. Pillette	31	do	Gentleman	France	do	Ship Mercury, G. J. Prince.
	Jno. H. Green	30	do	Merchant	U. States	do	Ship London Packet, C. Tracy.
	Jno. Aldersey	33	do	do	do	do	
	Henry Cullen	25	do	Artist	G. Britain	do	
	Samuel Jackson	18	do		do	do	
	Mary Ann Jackson		female		do	do	
	Child	8				do	
	John Smith	23	male	Painter	U. States	do	
	Robert Smith	24	do	Farmer	do	do	
	Aaron Upjohn	25	do	Cooper	England	do	
	Mary Upjohn	25	female		do	do	
	Harriet Green	21	do		do	do	
	Elizabeth Odell	36	do		do	do	
	Mary Odell	17	do		do	do	
	Samuel Maen	19	male	Mariner	do	do	

Name	Age	Sex	Occupation	From	To	Ship
James Green	29	male	Baker	England	U. States	Schooner Seven Friends, W. Ross.
John M'Bridge	18	do	Merchant	Ireland	do	Brig Sam, J. Upton.
John Tontaine	37	do	do	U. States	do	
Lawrence Taures	25	do	do	do	do	
S. D. Ward		do	Surveyor	do	do	Brig Trim, Larkin Turner.
Richard S. Hackley		do	late U. S. con.	do	do	Brig Edward Foster, J. Cathway.
Samuel Thompson		do	Gentleman	do	do	
Enoch ——		do	Servant	do	do	
Wm. S. Dorr	23	do	Merchant	do	do	Schooner Hope, David Scott.
G. H. Apthorp	28	do	do	do	do	
—— Emmerson	32	do	Dealer	do	do	Schooner Liberty, Hemrick.
Benjamin Smith	30	do	Merchant	do	do	Ship Sally, Robert B. Edes.
Thomas W. Langdon	23	do	do	do	do	Brig Romp, N. Crosly.
Mary C. Davis	22	female	Mantuamaker	Halifax	Halifax	
Joseph Dixey	28	male	Seaman	Ireland	U. States	Schooner Miller, A. Brooks.
L. Slung	22	do	Merchant	U. States	do	
R. Bartlett	25	female	do	do	do	
Mrs. Noyes and 2 child.	60	male		do	do	
Mr. Gold		do		do	do	
Wm. M. Deblois	20	do	Confectioner	N. Scotia	N. Scotia	Schooner Cherub, Wm. Athern.
Felix Anncloth	18	do	Farmer	do	do	
Jno. M. Nutt	25	do	Fisherman	Ireland	do	
Jno. Delany	21	do	Baker	Scotland	Halifax	
Wm. Taylor	38	do	Merchant	G. Britain	Boston	
Jno. Williamson	44	do	Trader	U. States	U. States	Schooner General Greene, Wm. Athern.
Edward Hugly	55	do	Carpenter	do	do	
James Malowny	37	female	Farmer	Ireland	do	
Samuel Blythe	38	male		do	do	
Margaret Blythe	14	female		do	do	
George Blythe	12	male		do	do	
Ann Blythe	9	female		do	do	
Samuel Blythe	2	male		do	do	
Margaret Blythe	6 weeks	do	Farmer	do	do	
Jno. Blythe	20	do	do	do	do	
George Cummings	40	do	Painter	do	do	
Dennis Hannegan	28	do	Chandler	do	do	
Wm. Nott	28			do	do	
Wm. Lyon				do	do	

LIST of Passengers, &c.—Quarter ending June 30. 1820.

Custom House, with the name of the Collector.	Names of Passengers.	Age.	Sex.	Occupation.	Country to which they belong.	Country of which they intend to become inhab's	Ship or Vessel, with the Name of the Master or Commander.
BOSTON AND CHARLESTOWN, H. A. S. Dearborn.	Ann Thatch	16	female		Halifax	U. States	Schooner General Greene, Wm. Athern.
	Nathaniel Scobie	15	male		N. Scotia	do	Brig Nautilus, H. J. Defres.
	Jose P. Flagnat	21	do	Mariner	Spain	Havana	Brig Harvard, Thomas Rodgers.
	Samuel Beal	27	do	Carpenter	U. States	do	
	Peter Smith	31	female	do	do	do	Schooner Victory, Samuel Burkee.
	Eliza B. Horner	30	male		Scotland	do	
	Philip Brazer	32	do	Seaman	do	do	
	George Hawkins	34	do	do	U. States	do	
	Wm. Snaith	40	do	Cordwainer	do	do	Schooner Lane, J. Miller.
	Isaac M. Hawes	25	do	Merchant	do	do	Brig Lascar, A. Gifford.
	Aaron Hadson	45	do	do	St. Johns	St. Johns	Schooner General Brewer, Thomas Rodgers.
	Joel Brand	25	do	do	do	do	
	James Hendrick	45	do	do	U. States	U. States	
	George Neul	58	do	do	do	do	
	Charles Craft	33	do	do	do	do	
	Benjamin Dodd	24	do	do	do	do	
	Jer. Fowler	29	do	Shipwright	do	do	
	Jno. Smith	30	do	Merchant	do	do	
	Seth Grammer	31	do	do	do	do	
	Jared Allen	30	do		do	do	
	E. F. Drury	35	do	Joiner	do	do	
	Andrew Withington	64	do		do	do	
	Jenet Burnbire	45	female		do	do	
	Melisher Sikes	26	do		do	do	
	Lucinda Ballard	20	do		do	do	
	Nelson Weston	12	male		do	do	
	Horatio G. Buttrick	42	do	Farmer	do	do	Schooner Cherub, Wm. Athern.

Name	Age	Sex	Occupation			Ship
Benjamin Ball	36	male	Farmer	U. States	U. States	Schooner Governor, J. Hutchins.
Alexr. Mitchell	28	do	Fair trader	do	do	Schooner Lingan, N. B. Wright.
Jas. A. Creighton	21	do	Butcher	Nova Scotia	do	Ship General Greene, J. Bears.
Wm. C. M'Koy	26	do	Merchant	Scotland	do	
Chas. M'Cartha	25	do	Butcher	Ireland	do	
Jno. Robinson	26	do	Hatter	Nova Scotia	Nova Scoti	
Captain L. Ponce	30	do	Mariner	Porto Rico		
Henry Benson	17	do		U. States	U. States	
Wm. Chevers	27	do	Merchant	St. Johns	St. Johns	
Margaret Drinkwater	40	female		Halifax		
Jas. Morton	28	male		do		
James Dowell	25	do		do		
Martha Bowers	20	do		do		
James Gibbs	20	do		do		
Edwd. Thaxter	15	do		do		
Jas. Dunlap	56	do	Farmer	U. States	U. States	Ship Aurora, Thos. Atherton.

LIST of Passengers, &c.—Quarter ending September 30, 1820.

Custom House, with the name of the Collector.	Names of Passengers.	Age.	Sex.	Occupation.	Country to which they belong.	Country of which they intend to become inhab's	Ship or vessel, with the name of the Master or Commander.
BALTIMORE, J. H. M'Culloch.	Wm. Schley	30	male	Merchant	England	U. States	Schooner P. S. of Baltimore.
	D. Cliffe	45	female		do	do	Ship William & Henry, of Newport.
	E. Cliffe	16	do		do	do	
	M. Cliffe	15	do		do	do	
	A. Cliffe	11	male		do	do	
	Henry Cliffe	13	do		do	do	
	A. Cliffe	7	do		do	do	
	G. Cliffe	3	do		do	do	
	S. Cox	36	do		do	do	
	J. Cox	21	do		do	do	
	H. Sauderland	25	do	Draper	do	do	
	S. Sauderland	25	female	Farmer	do	do	
	G. Sauderland	4	do		do	do	
	Wm. Crosland	42	male	Carpenter	do	do	
	E. Crosland	30	female		do	do	
	J. Crosland	3	male		do	do	
	G. Crosland	1	do		do	do	
	M. Chapman	30	female		do	do	
	E. Chapman	11	do		do	do	
	S. Chapman	8	do		do	do	
	J. Parrot	24	male	Tailor	do	do	
	M. Farrot	28	female		do	do	
	G. Beausnout	35	male	Clothier	do	do	
	J. Taylor	34	do	Weaver	do	do	
	T. Gollier	25	do	Shoemaker	do	do	
	E. Gollier	19	female		do	do	
	J. Highet	27	male	Cabinetmaker	do	do	

Schooner Azariah, of Baltimore.

Name	Age	Sex	Occupation	Nativity	Destination
J. Highet	19	female		England	U. States
M. Bird	17	do		do	do
Wm. Brossare	50	male	Farmer	do	do
J. Parry	24	do		do	do
R. Penney	35	do	do	do	do
W. Penney	33	do	do	do	do
J. Penney	45	female		do	do
J. Penney	11	do		do	do
D. Penney	9	male	do	do	do
T. Price	18	do		do	do
S. Jones	26	female	do	do	do
L. Davies	40	male		do	do
M. Davies	35	female		do	do
M. A. Davies	6	do		do	do
D. Davies	4	male	do	do	do
M. Pugh	75	female	do	do	do
T. Jones	20	male	do	do	do
Wm. Jones	30	do		do	do
Wm. Williams	30	do		do	do
E. Williams	30	female	do	do	do
W. Williams	3	male		do	do
W. Williams	1	do		do	do
W. Williams	45	do		do	do
J. Williams	40	female		do	do
M. Williams	18	do		do	do
H. Williams	14	do		do	do
J. Williams	11	do		do	do
D. Williams	9	male		do	do
W. Williams	7	do		do	do
S. Williams	3	do		do	do
J. Williams	6	female		do	do
W. Prosser	40	male	Shoemaker	do	do
A. Prosser	22	female		do	do
Wm. Prosser	11	male		do	do
J. Prosser	3	do		do	do
M. A. Prosser	1	do		do	do
J. Green	30	do	Merchant	U. States	do
B. Bedford	35	do	Mariner	do	do

LIST of Passengers, &c.—Quarter ending September 30, 1820.

Custom House, with the Name of the Collector.	Names of Passengers.	Age.	Sex.	Occupation.	Country to which they belong.	Country of which they intend to become inhb'ts.	Ship or Vessel, with the name of the Master or Commander.
BALTIMORE, J. H. M'Culloch.	I. Smith	18	male	Mariner	U. States	U. States	Schooner Azariah, of Baltimore.
	G. Smith	22	do	do	do	do	
	I. Spier	56	do	Farmer	Ireland	do	
	M. Spier	56	female		do	do	
	T. Spier	17	male		do	do	
	R. Spier	14	do		do	do	
	I. Glass	14	female		do	do	
	T. M'Bride	27	male	Farmer	do	do	
	R. M'Bride	23	female	Nurse	do	do	
	A. M'Bride	3	male		do	do	
	I. Tailor	28	female		do	do	
	I. Broads	22	male	Farmer	do	do	
	E. Magnerain	22	female		do	do	
	I. Tailor	17	male		do	do	
	I. Tailor	2	female		do	do	
	I. Tailor	1	male		do	do	
	R. Hill	25	do	Farmer	do	do	
	E. Hill	22	female		do	do	
	S. Hill		male		do	do	
	I. Hoger	28	do	Tailor	do	do	
	A. Hoger	24	female		do	do	
	R. Hoger	7	do		do	do	
	E. Hoger	2	do		do	do	
	S. Hoger	5	do		do	do	
	G. Keapatrick	63	male	Farmer	do	do	
	M. Keapatrick, & 3 chil.	60	female	None	do	do	
	B. Poor	25	male	Merchant	U. States	do	Schooner Madeira Packet, of Salem.

Name	Age	Sex	Occupation	Country	Destination	Ship
S. Dix	26	male	Merchant	U. States	U. States	Schooner William, of Baltimore.
L. Donald	25	do	Mariner	Scotland	do	Ship Clara, of Baltimore.
I. Hultz	35	do	Shoemaker	Germany	do	Sloop Jones, Hale, of Portland.
M. Thomas	58	do	Farmer	England	do	
I. Scott	40	do	Shoemaker	do	do	
M. Scott	36	female		do	do	
I. Scott	15	male		do	do	
G. Scott	11	do		do	do	
I. Scott	9	do		do	do	
T. Scott	9	do		do	do	
Wm. Scott	5	do		England	do	
L. Phillips	22	do		do	do	
T. Morgan	32	do		do	do	
S. M'Kee	24	do		do	do	
Robert Lindsay	20	do	Farmer	do	do	
M. Lindsay	24	female		do	do	
J. Lindsay	4	male		do	do	
R. Lindsay	2	do		do	do	
A. Lindsay	18	female	Farmer	do	do	
M. Maggonge	21	male		do	do	
M. M'Marker	21	do		do	do	
S. Green	30	do		do	do	
M. Green	12	do		do	do	
I. Green	10	do		do	do	
R. Green	7	do		do	do	
S. Dodds	25	do		do	do	
M. Dodds	4	do		do	do	
M. Logen	4	do		U. States	do	Brig Edward, of Baltimore,
I. Logen	26	male	Farmer	do	do	Ship James, of Bremen.
P. Baldwin	36	do	Mariner	do	do	
I. D. Rusdesepedden	21	female	Blockmaker	Germany	do	
E. Z. Thorner	30	male	Farmer	do	do	
I. Kedzinger	40	do		do	do	
C. Ganganette	17	female		do	do	
M. Swarendrubber	48	do	Farmer	do	do	
C. Swarendrubber	38	male		do	do	
C. Swarendrubber	28	female		do	do	
M. Swarendrubber	4	do		do	do	

LIST of Passengers, &c.—Quarter ending September 30, 1820.

Custom House, with the name of the Collector.	Names of Passengers.	Age.	Sex.	Occupation.	Country to which they belong.	Country of which they intend to become inhab's	Ship or Vessel, with the name of the Master or Commander.
BALTIMORE, J. H. M'Culloch.	C. T. Chlabach	69	male		Germany	U. States	Ship James, of Bremen.
	M. Chlabach	59	female		do	do	
	I. Chlabach	33	male		do	do	
	A. Chlabach	20	female		do	do	
	M. Chlabach	24	do		do	do	
	D. Chlabach	17	male		do	do	
	I. Algerie	26	do	Farmer	do	do	
	M. Algerie	28	female		do	do	
	M. Algerie	8	male		do	do	
	D. Coisch	40	do	Farmer	do	do	
	M. Coisch	35	female		do	do	
	I. Coisch	13	male		do	do	
	M. Coisch	11	female		do	do	
	E. Hendrick	40	male	Farmer	do	do	
	I. Kampff	32	do	do	do	do	
	I. Kampff	33	do	do	do	do	
	M. Gangrinche	28	do	Tailor	do	do	
	M. Gangrinche	28	female		do	do	
	C. Swargendober	22	male	Farmer	do	do	
	E. Swargendober	44	female		do	do	
	C. Orendorf	13	do		do	do	
	T. Sloer	24	male	Tailor	do	do	
	C. Brenneman	24	do	Farmer	do	do	
	Maria Brenneman	24	female		do	do	
	E. Brenneman	45	do		do	do	
	I. Brenneman	19	male		do	do	
	Daniel Brenneman	15	do		do	do	

				Germany	U. States	Ship Amazon, of Baltimore.
M. Brenneman	13	female		de	do	
C. Brenneman	10	do		do	do	
I. Brenneman	8	male		do	do	
I. Discombes	6	do		do	do	
E. Gallivitze	21	do	Gardener	do	do	
C. Holeman	20	do	Farmer	do	do	
G. Guester	36	do	Merchant	do	do	
G. Winter	28	do	Blacksmith	do	do	
W. Feeman	23	do	Mechanic	do	do	
C. Aukamp	30	do	do	do	do	
M. Muller	33	do	Merchant	do	do	
T. G. Weber	23	do	Tailor	do	do	
I. H. Myer	28	do	Farmer	do	do	
I. I. Myer	30	do	do	do	do	
I. Breddin	25	do	Blacksmith	do	do	
A. Boheme	32	do	do	do	do	
A. Little	40	female	Staymaker	England	do	
M. Little	20	do	Mantuamaker	Ireland	da	
G. Graff	62	male	Farmer	do	do	
I. Goff	30	do	do	de	do	
M. Goff	23	female		do	do	
Mary Goff	3	do		do	do	
H. Goff	24	do		do	do	
W. Tyrell	24	male	Laborer	da	do	
P. Cullen	25	do	do	do	do	
L. Cullen	18	do	Farmer	do	do	
P. Grace	55	do	Currier	do	do	
C. Grace	45	female		do	do	
I. Grace	24	male	do	do	do	
M. Grace	21	female		do	do	
H. Grace	19	do		do	do	
M. Grace	18	do		do	do	
A. Grace	14	do		do	do	
M. Grace	9	do		do	do	
R. Walsh	44	male	Joiner	do	do	
C. Walsh	44	female		do	do	
I. Walsh	20	male	Laborer	do	do	
M. Walsh	18	do	do	do	do	

LIST of Passengers, &c.—Quarter ending September 30, 1820.

Custom House, with the name of the Collector.	Names of Passengers.	Age.	Sex.	Occupation.	Country to which they belong.	Country of which they intend to become inhab's	Ship or Vessel, with the name of the Master or Commander.
BALTIMORE, Jas. H. M'Culloch.	B. Walsh	16	female		Ireland	U. States	Ship Amazon, of Baltimore.
	W. Walsh	14	male		do	do	
	J. Walsh	10	do		do	do	
	J. Shannon	40	female	Farmer	do	do	
	A. Shannon	40	female		do	do	
	M. Shannon	16	do		do	do	
	D. Shannon	12	male		do	do	
	A. Shannon	10	female		do	do	
	A. Shannon	8	male		do	do	
	J. Shannon	6	do		do	do	
	C. Shannon	4	do		do	do	
	M. A. Shannon	10	female		do	do	
	T. Walsh	22	male	do	do	do	
	N. Philan	19	do	Clerk	do	do	
	A. Philan	21	female		do	do	
	G. Philan	24	male	Joiner	do	do	
	A. Philan	20	female		do	do	
	M. Dalton	28	male	Laborer	do	do	
	M. Dalton	19	female		do	do	
	D. Farrell	27	male	Farmer	do	do	
	M. Doyle	27	do	Laborer	do	do	
	T. Crawley	37	female	do	do	do	
	J. Hartigan	30	male	Fisherman	do	do	
	M. Hartigan & 5 childn.	36	male	Laborer	do	do	
	M. Bryan	26	do	do	do	do	
	T. Bryan	19	do		do	do	
	J. Bryan	45	female		do	do	

Name	Age	Sex	Occupation			Vessel
M. Crane	30	male	Laborer	Ireland	U. States	
M. Crane	22	do	do	do	do	
M. Ryan	21	do	do	do	do	
J. Butler	30	do	do	do	do	
J. Whelan	44	female		do	do	
M. Whelan	35	do	Laborer	do	do	
M. Whelan	6	male	do	do	do	
J. Whelan	3	do	do	do	do	
B. Rice	44	do	Farmer	do	do	
J. Morrisy	23	do		do	do	
T. Flemming	22	do	Laborer	do	do	
J. Brying	30	do		do	do	
H. Roche & H.	30	female	Farmer	do	do	
W. Roche	28	do		do	do	
J. Roche	5	do		do	do	
H. Brown	3	male	Laborer	do	do	
G. Rodemond	28	do		do	do	
L. Boland	25	do		do	do	
J. Murphy	25	do	Farmer	do	do	
P. Harrell	28	do		do	do	
P. Tobin	35	male		do	do	
E. Tobin	26	female		do	do	Brig Ann, of London.
I. Tobin	15	male	do	do	do	
B. Tobin	7	female	Merchant	do	do	
P. Tobin	30	male	Laborer	do	do	
G. Goddard	20	do	do	do	do	
Robert Waugh	26	do	do	do	do	
T. Donaho	26	do		do	do	
P. Donaho	23	do	do	do	do	
S. Grant	30	female	Clerk	do	do	
M. Morrison	50	male	Laborer	do	do	
S. Morrison	18	do	do	do	do	
P. M'Namarr	24	do		do	do	
T. Maulan	16	do	Merchant	do	do	
S. M'Namarr	21	do	Seaman	U. States	do	Schooner Mariner, of Baltimore.
P. Harrison	40	do		do		
F. Ashurr	30	do				
J. Benjamin	20	do				

LIST of Passengers, &c.—Quarter ending September 30, 1820.

Custom House, with the name of Collector.	Names of Passengers.	Age.	Sex.	Occupation.	Country to which they belong.	Country of which they intend to become inhab's	Ship or Vessel, with the name of the Master or Commander.
BALTIMORE, J. H. M'Culloch.	E. Leawan	36	male	Blacksmith	U. States	U. States	Brig Thomas & Edward, of Bristol.
	J. Rogers	27	do	Merchant	do	do	
	J. Griffing	28	do	Mariner	England	do	Schooner Iris, of Baltimore.
	T. Barch	45	do	Merchant	do	do	Ship Gen. Smith, of Baltimore,
	M. Barch	40	female		do	do	
	T. Barch, jr.	16	male	do	do	do	
	T. Barch	36	do	Miller	do	do	
	M. Barch	30	female		do	do	
	H. Barch	7	female		do	do	
	C. Barch	5	male		do	do	
	J. Barch	3	male		do	do	
	M. Barch	2	female		do	do	
	M. Barch	1	do		do	do	
	M. Sawkins	35	female	Limner	do	do	
	J. Sawkins	15	male		do	do	
	E. Sawkins	13	female		do	do	
	J. Sawkins	11	do		do	do	
	L. Sawkins	7	do		do	do	
	P. Sawkins	4	do		do	do	
	M. Sawkins	2	do		do	do	
	J. Surly	23	male	Butcher	do	do	
	G. Surly	11	do		do	do	
	S. Surly	18	female		do	do	
	Wm. Blake	37	male	Cloth dresser	do	do	
	T. Labourne	26	do		do	do	
	T. White	29	do	Carpenter	do	do	
	H. White	2	female		do	do	

Name	Age	Sex	Occupation	Country	U. States	Ship
T. White	5	male		England	do	Ship General Smith, of Baltimore.
J. White	1	female		do	do	
C. Johnson	20	do	Laborer	do	do	
William West	24	male	Weaver	do	do	
J. Brown	43	do	Carpenter	U. States	do	
T. Jurnet	44	do	Merchant	do	do	
A. B. Rogers	30	do	Mariner	do	do	
T. D. Galloway	40	do	Merchant	England	do	
J. M'Curdy	40	do	Herdsman	do	do	
I. Little	31	do	Farmer	do	do	
W. Rawling	25	do	do	do	do	
I. Rawling	22	do	do	do	do	
I. Leunce	32	do	do	do	do	
I. Burnes	21	do	do	do	do	
E. Tryer	31	female		do	do	
A. Tryer	30	male		do	do	
I. Tryer	9	female		do	do	
A. Tryer	7	male		do	do	
M. Tryer	4	female		do	do	
T. Hadwine	20	male	Merchant	do	do	Schooner Valona, of Baltimore.
I. Hadwine	22	female		do	do	
M. Hadwine	16	do		do	do	
E. Hadwine	28	male		do	do	
Wm. Coipland	30	do	Laborer	do	do	
A. Hughes	28	female	Basketmaker	do	do	
F. Hughes	26	male		do	do	
G Cunningham	31	do	Farmer	do	do	Ship Athens, of New-York.
Wm. Nicholson	45	do	do	do	do	
R. Green	49	female		do	do	
M. Green	22	male		do	do	
T. Green	13	do	Farmer	do	do	
I. Green	15	female	do	do	do	
C. Green	9	do		do	do	
E. Green	33	male		do	do	
T. Walsh	28	do	Cooper	do	do	
H. M'Thee	21	female	Laborer	do	do	
M. M'Thee	3	male		do	do	
I. M'Thee				do	do	

LIST of Passengers, &c.—Quarter ending September 30, 1820.

Custom House, with the name of the Collector.	Names of Passengers.	Age.	Sex.	Occupation.	Country to which they belong.	Country to which they intend to become inh'bs.	Ship or Vessel, with the name of the Master or Commander.
BALTIMORE, Jas. H. M'Culloch.	I. Shienne	34	male		England	U. States	Ship Athens, of New-York.
	R. Pearce	30	do		do	do	
	C. Austin	32	do		do	do	
	R. Schutte	25	do		U. States	do	
	I. Burnham	23	do	Seaman	England	do	
	I. Hider	28	do	do	U. States	do	
	I. Bardier	24	do	do	Spain	Spain	
	D. Snowden	40	do	Merchant	U. States	U. States	
	I. G. Barreton	40	female	do	do	do	
	I. M. Beuretter	30	female	Baker	do	do	
	M. M. Beuretter	1	male	None	do	do	
	I. Farrar	29	male	Farmer	England	do	
	M. Farrar	25	female		do	do	
	H. Farrar	5	male		do	do	
	A. Farrar	3	do		do	do	
	I. Price	34	male	Harnessmaker	do	do	
	M. Price	33	female		do	do	
	I. Price	9	male		do	do	
	R Price	7	do		do	do	
	I. Coales	47	do	Blacksmith	do	do	
	T. Wood	40	do	Shoemaker	do	do	
	E. Wood	40	female		do	do	
	E. Wood	21	do		do	do	
	I. Dodson	48	male	Farmer	do	do	
	E. Dodson	49	female		do	do	
	I. Dodson	23	male	Shoemaker	do	do	
	C. Dodson	17	female		do	do	

Name	Age	Sex	Occupation	England	U. States	
P. Dodson	14	male	Farmer	do	do	Ship Sally, of New-Castle.
R. Clopehan	28	do	Farmer	do	do	
A. Clopehan	35	female	Butcher	do	do	
I. Beane	27	male		do	do	
P. Baines	49	do	Farmer	do	do	
M. Baines	28	female	do	do	do	
E. Baines	20	male	do	do	do	
H. Baines	14	female	do	do	do	
T. Meek	12	do		do	do	
H. Meek	24	male		do	do	
I. Maddle	20	do		do	do	
I. Rhodes	20	do		do	do	
S. Beaumont	24	do		do	do	
Wm. Beaumont	36	female		do	do	
I. Beaumont	14	male		do	do	
H. Beaumont	13	do		do	do	
I. Beaumont	12	do		do	do	
T. Beaumont	10	do		do	do	
I. Beaumont	9	do		do	do	
G. Beaumont	7	do		do	do	
B. Beaumont	6	do		do	do	
I. Miller	2	female	Weaver	do	do	
S. Miller	31	male		do	do	
T. Richards	7	female	Draper	do	do	
R. Ellis	23	male	Weaver	do	do	
I. Hughes	20	female		do	do	
H. Hughes	26	do		do	do	
H. Hughes	20	male		do	do	
R. H. Dowson	29	do	Farmer	do	do	
R. Adams	21	female	Clerk	do	do	
A. Adams	21	male	Bricklayer	do	do	
T. Murphy	19	do	Farmer	do	do	
S. W. Banaclough	20	female	do	do	do	
A. Banaclough	49	male		do	do	
I. Spreunell	13	female	Farmer	do	do	
I. Spreunell, jr	34	male	do	do	do	
I. Marshall	25	do	do	do	do	
	39			do	do	

LIST of Passengers, &c.—Quarter ending September 30, 1820.

Custom House, with the name of the Collector.	Names of Passengers.	Age.	Sex.	Occupation.	Country to which they belong.	Country of which they intend to become inhab's	Ship or Vessel, with the name of the Master or Commander.
BALTIMORE, Jas. H. M'Culloch.	S. Marshall	39	female	Farmer	England	U. States	Ship Sally, of New-Castle.
	I. Marshall	19	male	do	do	do	
	W. Marshall	15	do	do	do	do	
	I. Marshall	13	do		do	do	
	T. Marshall	9	do		do	do	
	A. Marshall	8	female		do	do	
	C. Marshall	5	male		do	do	
	T. Hollands	20	do	Farmer	do	do	
	R. Ward	50	do	do	do	do	
	E. Ward	45	do		do	do	
	M. Ward	22	do		do	do	
	I. Ward	20	do	Farmer	do	do	
	I. Ward	13	do	do	do	do	
	I. Ward	37	do	do	do	do	
	T. Murphy	35	female		do	do	
	I. Murphy	15	do		do	do	
	H. Murphy	7	male		do	do	
	I. Murphy	33	do	Laborer	do	do	
	A. Ellwood	28	female		do	do	
	E. Ellwood	19	do		do	do	
	S. Ellwood	11	do		do	do	
	B. Ellwood	9	do		do	do	
	A. Ellwood	17	male	Laborer	do	do	
	I. Millet	32	female		do	do	
	E. Cooper	17	do		do	do	
	M. Cooper	11	do		do	do	
	S. Cooper	35	male	Laborer	do	do	
	W. Stone						

Name	Age	Sex	Occupation	Country	U. States	Vessel
A. Stone	36	female		England	do	Ship Sally, of New-Castle.
C. Stone	15	do		do	do	
E. Stone	10	male		do	do	
I. Stone	6	do		do	do	
T. Barton	40	female		do	do	
B. Barton	22	male	Shoemaker	do	do	
I. Holland	50	male		do	do	
I. Barmingham	29	do	Currier	do	do	
M. Barmingham	34	do	Laborer	do	do	
P. Lee	39	do	do	do	do	
M. Lee	34	female	do	do	do	
A. M'Ardle	22	male		do	do	
T. Gudwine	40	do		do	do	
A. Murphy	3 w.	female		do	do	
Robt. Conn	66	male	Laborer	Ireland	do	Schooner Infant, of Boston.
A. Conn	26	do	do	do	do	
R. Conn, jr.	22	do	Farmer	do	do	
I. Conn	17	do	do	do	do	
I. Conn	60	female	do	do	do	
C. Conn	19	do	do	do	do	
E. Conn	23	do		do	do	
R. Conn	23	do		do	do	
G. Bully	32	male	Farmer	do	do	
Mrs. Bully	28	female		do	do	
Wm. Davidson	30	male	Farmer	do	do	
E. Davidson	22	female		do	do	
R. Davidson	18	male		do	do	
Wm. M'Kown	28	do	Farmer	do	do	
Mrs. Kown	24	female	do	do	do	
I. Miscumbell	22	male	Tailor	do	do	
I. Pinkerton	28	do	Farmer	do	do	
Mrs. Pinkerton	48	female		do	do	
I. M'Cable	54	male	Farmer	U. States	do	Brig Mary, of Baltimore.
Wm. Davidson	40	do	Mariner	do	do	
C. Simmons	30	do	Merchant	do	do	
Wm. T. Stewart	28	do	Seaman	do	do	Schooner Lady of the Lake, of Baltimore.
Wm. Brown	29	do	do	do	do	
T. Sheets	25	do	do	do	Io	

LIST of Passengers, &c.—Quarter ending September 30, 1820.

Custom House, with the name of the Collector.	Names of Passengers.	Age.	Sex.	Occupation.	Country to which they belong.	Country of which they intend to become inhab's	Ship or Vessel, with the name of the Master or Commander.
BALTIMORE, J. H. M'Culloch.	D. Kreiger	33	male	Farmer	Switzerland	U. States	Ship Plato, of Duxbury.
	C. Lagenbuhl	27	female		do	do	
	M. Stanfer	55	male		do	do	
	J. Lagenbuhl	25	do	do	do	do	
	T. Kommell	50	do	do	do	do	
	J. Burgy	34	male		England	do	Ship Pocahontas, of Baltimore.
	M. Jones	22	female		do	do	
	M. Jones	51	do	do	do	do	
	T. Jones	20	male		do	do	
	B. Jones	10	female		do	do	
	E. Jones	24	male	do	do	do	
	F. Farcett	26	male	Clothier	do	do	
	L. Farcett	20	female		do	do	
	H. Farcett	10	do		do	do	
	J. Lavesly	47	male	Farmer	do	do	
	E. Lavesly	37	female		do	do	
	T. Lavesly	7	male		do	do	
	M. Lavesly	6	female		do	do	
	Wm. Lavesly	5	male		do	do	
	M. Lavesly	3	female		do	do	
	J. Lavesly	1	male		do	do	
	H. Hughes	30	female		do	do	
	J. Hughes	7	male		do	do	
	A. Hughes	1	female		do	do	
	A. Aubry	22	do		do	do	
	J. Aubry	10	male		do	do	
	M. Aubry	8	female		do	do	

Ship Newburyport, of Newburyport:

Name	Age	Sex	Occupation	England	U. States
9. Aubry	3	female		do	do
C. Aubry	1	do		do	do
E. Karney	33	male		do	do
I. Karney	12	female		do	do
M. Karney	7	male		do	do
R. Karney	4	do	Laborer	do	do
J. Best	31	do	Clothier	do	do
J. Henshaw	26	do	Tailor	do	do
R. Williams	25	do	Brassfounder	do	do
J. Kinnerty	22	do	Farmer	do	do
T. Pike	35	do		do	do
M. Williams	5	female		do	do
J. Pike	21	do		do	do
A. Gucca	23	male	Butcher	do	do
J. Termpher	45	do	Farmer	do	do
W. Flemming	50	do		do	do
A. Nuttle	28	da	Plumber	do	do
R. Nuttle	23	da	Farmer	do	do
A. Thompson	41	do	do	do	do
W. Thompson	40		Cabinetmaker	do	do
M. Thompson	50			do	do
W. Kingborn	32		Farmer	do	do
P. Kingborn	11			do	do
R. Whitehead	36		do	do	do
M. Whitehead	36			do	do
J. Brassington	22		Gardener	do	do
H. Brassington	26			do	do
N. Burchill	39		Shopkeeper	do	do
C. Burchill	39			do	do
E. Knight	42			do	do
W. Noon	36		Farmer	do	do
M. Noon	13	female		do	do
E. Noon	39	do		do	do
M. Noon	11	do		do	do
J. Noon	9	do		do	do
T. Booth	18	male	Butcher	do	do
T. Hill	48	do	Farmer	do	do
F. Hill	47	female		do	do

LIST of Passengers, &c.—Quarter ending September 30, 1820.

Custom House, with the name of the Collector.	Names of Passengers.	Age.	Sex.	Occupation.	Country to which they belong.	Country of which they intend to become inhab's	Ship or Vessel, with the name of the Master or Commander.
BALTIMORE, J. H. M'Culloch.	J. Knight	38	male	Farmer	England	U. States	Ship Newburyport, of Newburyport.
	M. Knight	29	female		do	do	
	J. Therby	13	male		do	do	
	T. Bunby	28	do	do	do	do	
	Wm. Baker	27	do	Butcher	do	do	
	J. Jockman	57	do	Farmer	do	do	
	J. Jockman	12	do	do	do	do	
	J. Candle	29	do	do	do	do	
	J. Hayet	35	do	do	do	do	
	J. Shield	28	do	Butcher	do	do	
	R. Wallace	26	do	Shopkeeper	do	do	
	J. Robinson	44	do	Butcher	do	do	
	J. Wilson	38	do	Farmer	do	do	
	A. Wilkinson	34	do		do	do	
	H. Wilkinson	32	female		do	do	
	G. Vickars	31	male	do	do	do	
	E. Vickars	21	female		do	do	
	J. Hann	38	male	Collier	do	do	Brig Brothers, of Leith.
	C. Hann	40	female		do	do	
	B. Hann	19	male	do	do	do	
	S. Hann	17	female		do	do	
	M. Hann	15	do		do	do	
	C. Hann	10	do		do	do	
	J. Hann	8	male		do	do	
	T. Hann	6	do		do	lo	
	M. Hann	6	do		do	do	
	J. Hann	5	female		do	do	

Name	Age	Sex	Occupation		U. States	Ship
E. Hann	3	female		England	do	
T. Ayre	27	male	Farmer	do	do	
A. Ceffrosh	22	do	Laborer	do	do	
C. Elliot	30	female		do	do	
C. Elliot	8	male		do	do	
J. Elliot	6	female		do	do	
J. Elliot	3	female		do	do	
T. Elliot	6	do		do	do	
Waggerman	28	male	Farmer	Germany	do	Brig Venus, of Baltimore.
Steimnyer	45	do	Carpenter	do	do	
Fexlyr	22	do		do	do	
H. Graves	25	do	Printer	England	do	
R. Beveridge	25	do	Merchant	do	do	Ship Belvidera, of Baltimore.
Mrs. Southern	44	female		do	do	
J. Stewart	17	male		do	do	
J. Murdock	16	do		do	do	
J. Noble	14	do		do	do	
J. Carse	32	do		do	do	
Y. Smith	30	do	Clothier	G. Britain	do	Brig Governor Myers, of Philadelphia.
J. Smith	19	do	do	do	do	
Z. Smith	62	female		do	do	
R. Pow	44	male	Farmer	do	do	
B. Pow	52	female		do	do	
G. Pow	19	male	do	do	do	
B. Pow	16	female		do	do	
A. Pow	12	male		do	do	
A. Armesta	22	female		do	do	
T. Wilkinson	41	male	Laborer	do	do	
A. Wilkinson	43	female		do	do	
J. Wilkinson	12	male		do	do	
T. Wilkinson	9	do		do	do	
B. Wilkinson	7	do		do	do	
J. Wilkinson	4	female		do	do	
R. Southern	29	male	Farmer	do	do	
G. Southern	30	female		do	do	
M. Southern	2	do		do	do	
R. Senior	43	male	do	do	do	
E. Senior	15	do		do	do	

LIST of Passengers, &c.—Quarter ending September 30, 1820.

Custom House, with the name of the Collector.	Names of Passengers.	Age.	Sex.	Occupation.	Country to which they belong.	Country of which they intend to become inhab's	Ship or Vessel, with the name of the Master or Commander.
BALTIMORE, J. H. M'Culloch.	R. Senior	10	male		G. Britain	U. States	Brig Governor Myers, of Philadelphia,
	M. A. Senior	8	do		do	do	
	J. Senior	6	do		do	do	
	J. Spencer	20	do	Laborer	do	do	
	A. Molscroft	21	do	Painter	do	do	
	A. Spencer	54	female		do	do	
	E. Spencer	22	do		do	do	
	M. Spencer	20	do		do	do	
	S. Spencer	17	do		do	do	
	J. Young	22	male	Merchant	U. States	do	Schooner Nancy, of Baltimore.
	F. Lacople	35	do	do	do	do	
	J. S. Solomon	30	do	do	do	do	
	A. Mayard	41	female	Lace merch't	France	France	
	J. Roland	35	male	Servant	do	do	
	E. Von Drunks	40	do	Gentleman	Germany	U. States	Brig Unity, of Baltimore.
	D. Von Drunks	30	female		do	do	
	R. Leusard	40	male	Merchant	do	do	
	9. L. Harme	37	do	do	do	do	
	J. Kloninger	37	do	Baker	do	do	
	P. Matzer	19	do	Miller	do	do	
	M. Truitz	19	do	Cooper	do	do	
	C. Woelstein	22	female	Servant	do	do	
	C. Lauber	23	do	do	do	do	
	J. Diehl	22	male	Smith	do	do	
	A. M. Diehl	25	female	Servant	do	do	
	J. Lauber	38	male	Farmer	do	do	
	G. Lauber	19	do	do	do	do	

Brig Unity, of Baltimore.

Name	Age	Sex	Occupation		U. States
L. Hick	17	male	Baker	do	do
N. Cohn	42	do	Butcher	do	do
G. Bohmer	32	do	Smith	do	do
C. H. Sutter	43	do		do	do
I. Fluce	32	do	Baker	do	do
N. Waefer	62	do	Farmer	do	do
O. Medinger	16	do	do	do	do
G. Lucit	17	do		do	do
C. Borighuger	16	do	Farmer	do	do
L. De Viller	17	do	Merchant	do	do
J. Felt	49	do	Tailor	do	do
M. Felt	54	female		do	do
I. Felt	11	male		do	do
T. Wolf	17	do	Baker	do	do
J. D. Beyrer	18	do		do	do
G. Wolf	15	do		do	do
J. J. Lais	22	do	Farmer	do	do
F. Struckling	17	female		do	do
J. Wolfer	19	male	Servant	do	do
I. Hussard	18	do	Butcher	do	do
I. Hockler	19	do	do	do	do
D. Fischer	19	female	Miller	do	do
D. Byyer	20	do	Servant	do	do
E. Wolf	26	do	do	do	do
D. Schmeid	20	do	do	do	do
I. H. Bruch	41	male	Baker	do	do
I. Ingleman	22	do	Cooper	do	do
C. Mezyer	20	do	Merchant	do	do
I. C. Lang	26	do	Butcher	do	do
I. H. Mozar	26	do	Merchant	do	do
I. Zinmer	35	do	Farmer	do	do
I. Husgel	28	do		do	do
E. F. Meyer	40	do	Cabinetmaker	do	do
P. F. Marechal	24	do		do	do
W. R. Leinwold	17	do		Holland	do
I. De Linn	52	do	Merchant	do	do
E. De Linn	11	do		do	do
B. De Linn	18	female		do	do

LIST of Passengers, &c.—Quarter ending September 30, 1820.

Custom House, with the Name of the Collector.	Names of Passengers.	Age.	Sex.	Occupation.	Country to which they belong.	Country of which they intend to become inhab's	Ship or Vessel, with the Name of the Master or Commander.
BALTIMORE, J. H. M'Culloch.	H. De Linn	16	female		Holland	U. States	Ship Unity, of Baltimore.
	A. De Linn	9	do		do	do	
	S. De Linn	7	do		do	do	
	R. De Linn	5	male		do	do	
	A. Liv asor	21	do	Merchant	do	do	
	L. Benjamin	36	female	do	do	do	
	B. Benjamin	28	male		do	do	
	S. Benjamin	5	female		do	do	
	E. Benjamin	3	female		do	do	
		6	do		do	do	
	I. Muller	28	male	Nailmaker	Germany	do	
	J. Hoffman	20	do	Smith	do	do	
	F. Leyer	16	do	Baker	do	do	
	J. Ellis	34	do	Seaman	do	do	
	E. Luis	42	female		do	do	
	C. Luis	17	male		do	do	
	8 children under 15	15	male	Physician	do	do	
	T. Schneider	36	do	Gentleman	Spain	do	
	J. Medind	45	do	Farmer	Germany	do	Schooner Young Man's Companion, of Balt.
	I. I. Muller	42	female		do	do	Ship Massasoit, of Baltimore.
	A. M. Muller	42	do	Farmer	do	do	
	C. M. Muller	18	male		do	do	
	J. M. Muller	17	female		do	do	
	A. A. Muller	15	do		do	do	
	D. A. Muller	13	do		do	do	
	M. Muller	12	do		do	do	
	J. C. Muller	11	do		do	do	

Ship Massasoit, of Baltimore.

Name	Age	Sex	Occupation	Germany	U. States	Died.
J. H. Muller	7	male		do	do	
J. G. Muller	5	do		do	do	
C. Muller	3	do		do	do	
R. F. Muller	6	female		do	do	
J. G. Grubman	32	male	Farmer	do	do	
E. R. Grubman	6	do		do	do	
J. Grubman	4	do		do	do	
M. F. Bahrl	45	do		do	do	
A. M. Bahrl	43	do	Farmer	do	do	
I. G. Bahrl	13	female		do	do	
M. F. Bahrl	6	male		do	do	
G. Bahrl	4	do		do	do	
I. Eckstan	27	do	Farmer	do	do	
B. Eckstan	70	do		do	do	
E. Bakenger	28	do	Tailor	do	do	
A. M. Bakenger	24	female		do	do	
S. Leopolin	19	do		do	do	
J. M. Weiland	45	male	Blacksmith	do	do	
C. Weiland	41	female		do	do	
G. A. Weiland	18	male	Blacksmith	do	do	
C. Weiland	13	female		do	do	
C. Weiland	9	do		do	do	
J. M. Eckstein	42	male	Farmer	do	do	
M. Eckstein	39	female		do	do	
J. M. Eckstein	15	de		do	do	
J. G. Eckstein	2	male		do	do	
G. P. Hoffman	44	do	Farmer	do	do	
A. M. Hoffman	45	female		do	do	
A. B. Hoffman	18	do		do	do	
G. P. Hoffman	10	male		do	do	
G. M. Hoffman, jr.	7	do		do	do	
E. Hoffman	37	do		do	do	
S. T. Hoffman	33	female		do	do	
G. F. Hoffman	4	male		do	do	
D. Hoffman	3	do		do	do	
E. S. Hoffman	2	female		do	do	
J. F. Hout	40	male	Farmer	do	do	
E. M. Hout	38	female		do	do	

LIST of Passengers, &c.—Quarter ending September 30, 1820.

Custom House, with the Name of the Collector.	Names of Passengers.	Age.	Sex.	Occupation.	Country to which they belong.	Country of which they intend to become inhab's	Ship or Vessel, with the name of the Master or Commander.
BALTIMORE, J. H. M'Culloch.	C. F. Hout	12	male		Germany	U. States	Ship Massasoit, of Baltimore.
	A. W. Hout	10	female		do	do	
	E. C. Hout	7	male		do	do	
	F. Hout	2	do		do	do	
	J. Ecksteen	37	do	Farmer	do	do	
	J. Ecksteen	11	do		do	do	
	G. F. Molin	4	do		do	do	
	M. C. Molin	28	do		do	do	
	C. Molin	25	female	Tailor	do	do	
	C. F. Konkelin	21	male		do	do	
	E. Konkelin	36	do		do	do	
	E. F. Konkelin	36	female	Farmer	do	do	
	B. Hacksey	11	male		do	do	
	M. Schwertzein	70	female		do	do	
	J. G. Hillenger	48	male	do	do	do	
	M. Hillenger	44	female		do	do	
	G. A. Hillenger	23	male	do	do	do	
	J. G. Hillenger	11	do		do	do	
	B. Hillenger	21	female		do	do	
	J. G. Mafer	50	male	Cabinetmaker	do	do	
	S. Mafer	52	female		do	do	
	C. Mafer	37	male	do	do	do	
	J. Schruber	66	do	Tailor	do	do	
	J. G. Schruber	24	do	Farmer	do	do	
	E. D. Makin	36	female	Seamstress	do	do	
	J. Hemans	40	male	Farmer	do	do	
	G. M. Hoffman	37	do	do	do	do	

					U. States	Died.
D. Hemans	33	female		Germany	do	
M. Hemans	8	male		do	do	
L. Schreider	49	do	Ropemaker	do	do	
R. Schreider	36	female		do	do	
F. Schreider	16	male		do	do.	
S. Schreider	30	do		do	do	
C. Fush	26	female	Farmer	do	do	
R. D. Brannying	30	male	do	do	do	
I. I. Brannying	9	do		do	do	
I. Scheartman	52	female	Carpenter	do	do	
A. Scheartman	46	male		do	do	
D. Scheartman	15	female		do	do	
C. Scheartman	13	do		do	do	
C. Scheartman	24	male		do	do	
I. Scheartman	21	do	Carpenter	do	do	
I. G. Steintress	26	do	Baker	do	do	
G. J. Wholoff	50	do	Shoemaker	do	do	
I. M. Wholoff	17	do	do	do	do	
J. M. Marfer	24	do	Weaver	do	do	
C. Filler	40	do	Farmer	do	do	
J. D. Nicholas	26	do	Weaver	do	do	
D. Wiseman	26	do	Merchant	do	do	
E. Helichre	38	female		do	do	
M. Matthews	23	male	Clerk	U. States	do	Brig Leopard, of Baltimore.
I. Delany	26	do	do	England	do	
S. H. Harnes	27	do	Merchant	U. States	do	Schooner Harriet, of Baltimore.
D. Walker	38	do	do	do	do	
H. H. Curtis	23	do	do	Scotland	do	Schooner Alert, of Baltimore.
D. Riddle	21	do	Plasterer	do	do	Ship Oryza, of Baltimore.
G. Ford	24	do	do	do	do	
R. Lawson	12	do	do	do	do	
T. Mullikin	37	do	Smith	do	do	
M. Mullikin	30	do		do	do	
M. M'Donald	21	female		do	do	
H. M. Jenners	22	do	Merchant	U. States	do	Schooner Patriot, of Baltimore.
H. C. Cook	22	male	Seaman	do	do	
D. C. Brien	28	do	Merchant	do	do	
I. Grant	41	do	Carpenter	England	do	

LIST of Passengers, &c.—Quarter ending September 30, 1820.

Custom House, with the name of the Collector.	Names of Passengers.	Age.	Sex.	Occupation.	Country to which they belong.	Country of which they intend to become inhab's.	Ship or Vessel, with the name of the Master or Commander.
BALTIMORE, Jas. H. M'Culloch.	G. Weston	40	male	Laborer	England	U. States	Ship Liverpool Packet, of Portsmouth.
	M. Weston	39	female		do	do	
	I. Dusnoss	34	male	Laborer	do	do	
	E. Dusnoss	33	female		do	do	
	T. Belcher	24	male	Rulemaker	do	do	
	I. Grant	19	do	Butcher	do	do	
	I. Johnston	34	do	Painter	do	do	
	W. Robinson	49	do	Tailor	do	do	
	A. Robinson	19	female		do	do	
	G. Gorius	25	male	Basketmaker	do	do	
	C. Burley	17	do	Laborer	do	do	
	A. Clough	35	do	do	do	do	
	T. Cribank	26	do	Butcher	do	do	
	F. Haig	41	female	do	do	do	
	H. Haig	15	do	do	do	do	
	T. Hoggin	46	male	Farmer	do	do	
	I. Hoggin	56	female		do	do	
	I. Hoggin	22	male	Farmer	do	do	
	I. Reid	46	do	Laborer	do	do	
	P. Jafflock	30	do	do	do	do	
	A. Wilson	21	do	do	do	do	
	J. Sepior	22	do	Farmer	do	do	
	H. Baker	40	do		do	do	
	J. Baker	40	female		do	do	
	H. Baker	3	male	Farmer	do	do	
	W. Briggs	26	do,	do	do	do	
	T. Briggs	3	do		do	do	

Name	Age		Occupation	England	U. States
W. Whitaker	23	male	Farmer	do	do
P. Gasciogne	49	do	do	do	do
M. Gasciogne	40	female	Merchantess	do	do
A. Barker	2	do		do	do
T. Hollingsworth	26	male	Tanner	do	do
R. Lee	60	do		do	do
N. Cunningham	25	do	Laborer	do	do
W. Hoy	28	do	do	do	do
W. Gordon	28	do	do	do	do
M. Gordon	30	female		do	do
M. Gordon	2	do		do	do
I. Wainwright	27	male	Cordwainer	do	do
D. Boole	55	do	Farmer	do	do
R. Haythornwaite	44	do	do	do	do
M. Haythornwaite	25	female		do	do
R. Haythornwaite	6	male		do	do
E. Haythornwaite	5	female		do	do
R. Haythornwaite	4	male		do	do
M. Haythornwaite	2	female		do	do
C. Belfield	32	do		do	do
T. Belfield	12	male		do	do
W. Belfield	10	do		do	do
A. Belfield	7	female		do	do
H. Belfield	5	male		do	do
C. Belfield	2	female		do	do
E. O. Hanlow	21	male	Gentleman	do	do
W. Robinson	25	do	Farmer	do	do
H. Wilmot	28	do	Gentleman	do	do
I. Breary	47	do	Farmer	do	do
G. Ramesden	28	do	Gardener	do	do
G. Moolen	27	du	Laborer	do	do
S. Thornhill	18	do	Gardener	do	do
T. Sharpless	38	do	Farmer	do	do
E. Sharpless	35	female		do	do
M. Sharpless	12	do		do	do
A. Sharpless	10	do		do	do
A. Sharpless	8	do		do	do
B. Sharpless	6	do		do	do

LIST of Passengers, &c.—Quarter ending September 30, 1820.

Custom House, with the name of the Collector.	Names of Passengers.	Age.	Sex.	Occupation.	Country to which they belong.	Country of which they intend to become inhab's	Ship or Vessel, with the name of the Master or Commander.
BALTIMORE, J. H. M'Culloch.	I. Sharpless	4	male		England	U. States	Ship Liverpool Packet, Portsmouth.
	H. Sharpless	3	female		do	do	
	H. Mursden	29	male	Farmer	do	do	
	J. Fielding	45	do	Laborer	do	do	
	H. M. Gibson	22	do	Baker	do	do	
	L. Bennett	21	do	Laborer	do	do	
	W. Thornbrook	46	do	Farmer	do	do	
	Mrs. Thornbrook	36	female		do	do	
	P. Gillard	26	male	do	do	do	
	T. Gillard	23	do	do	do	do	
	C. Gillard	22	do	do	do	do	
	L. Gillard	18	do		do	do	
	E. Gillard	17	do		do	do	
	C. Gillard	15	female		do	do	
	R. Gillard	12	male		do	do	
	S. Crosker	33	do	Farmer	do	do	
	M. Crosker	24	female		do	do	
	W. Williams	28	male	Laborer	do	do	Brig Millen Don Ersten, of Rotterdam.
	S. Williams	24	female		do	do	
	W. Williams	5	male		do	do	
	J. Swatile	40	do	Farmer	do	do	
	B. Swatile	44	do		do	do	
	G. Swatile	14	do		do	do	
	B. Swatile	44	female		do	do	
	G. Swatile	14	male		do	do	
	N. Gilbert	30	do	Farmer	do	do	
	T. Bryant	30	do	Laborer	do	do	

Name	Age	Sex	Occupation	Country	U. States	Vessel
J. Cary	35	male	Laborer	England	do	
J. C. Palmer	22	do	Merchant	do	do	
L. Palmer	22	female	Laborer	do	do	
J. Cooper	40	male	Farmer	do	do	
E. Cossins	39	do		do	do	
S. Cossins	26	female	Merchant	do	do	
R. I. Jackson	23	female	do	do	do	
S. Jackson	58	male		do	do	
A. Jackson	57	female		do	do	
H. Jackson	20	do	do	do	do	
E. Jackson	16	do		do	do	
Wm. Grant	13	male		do	do	
H. Grant	30	female	Farmer	do	do	
P. Romuil	34	male		do	do	
S. Romuil	59	female		do	do	
E. Romuil	14	do	do	do.	do	
J. Crawford	40	do		do	do	
H. Crawford	12	male		do	do	
J. Canon	26	de	Servant	U. States	do	Brig Eliza, of Philadelphia.
F. Grant	26	do	Merchant	do	do	
C. H. Decker	30	do	do	do	do	Schooner Virginia, Ross, of Baltimore.
A. Favor	50	do	do	do	do	Schooner Adeline, of Baltimore.
M. Launey	42	do	do	do	do	
J. B. Navior	38	do	do	do	do	
A. Compte	25	do	do	do	do	Schooner Dandy, of Baltimore.
J. V. Mumford	25	do	do	do	do	
L. Pomille	21	do	Mariner	do	do	
A. Thompson	54	do	Merchant	England	do	Schooner Alexander, of Baltimore.
A. Shaw	30	do	do	U. States	do	
R. W. Gardner	30	do	do	do	do	Brig Canada, of Baltimore.
G. A. Welles	21	do	do	do	do	Schooner Maria, of Baltimore.
F. Knapp	35	do	do	St. Domingo	do	
L. Gloudon	22	do	do	do	do	
B. Coppeau	18	do	do	do	do	
P. D. Porter	36	do	do	U. States	do	Schooner Fox, of Baltimore.
R. Currell	26	do	do	do	do	Schooner Arethia, of Baltimore.
J. J. Myer	25	do	do	do	do	

LIST of Passengers, &c.—Quarter ending September 30, 1820.

Custom House, with the name of the Collector.	Names of Passengers.	Age.	Sex.	Occupation.	Country to which they belong.	Country of which they intend to become inhab's	Ship or Vessel, with the name of the Master or Commander.
BALTIMORE, J. H. M'Culloch.	William G. Witherall	22	male	Clerk	U. States	U. States	Schooner Columbus, of Baltimore.
	I. Larney	28	do	Laborer	Ireland	do	Brig Ayres, of Machias.
	I. Wash	30	do	Blacksmith	England	do	
	R. Allen	30	do	Seaman	U. States	do	
	I. Knap	32	do	Mariner		do	Schooner Armunda, of Baltimore.
	T. Curren	35	do	Merchant	Spain	do	
	I. Gold	38	do	Mariner	U. States	do	Ship Balloon, of Baltimore.
	William G. Hearle	23	do	Tobacconist	Saxony	do	
NANTUCKET, M. J. Morton.	William Pastor	25	do		Prussia	do	Ship Ruby, P. C. Myrick.
	I. I. George Carnahl	18	do		Bremen	do	
	John H. Poppie	18	do		do	do	
	Henry H. Jorning	36	do		England	do	Brig Neptune.
WALDOBOROUGH, D. M. Cobb.	William Anderson	40	do	Merchant	U. States	do	
	Maria Louisa Anderson	25	female	Spinster	do	do	
	Charlotte E. Tully	22	do	Servant	England	do	
	Edmund Meddowcrift	42	male	do	W. Indies	do	
	John Middleton	24	do	Lady	U. States	do	
NEWPORT, C. Ellery.	Ellen Carrington	60	female	do	Turks Island	Turks Island	Schooner Baltic, D. Bailey.
	Mrs. Frith	18	do	Servant	do	U. States	
	Miss Frith	19	do	Lady	do	do	
	Matilda Frith	30	do	do	England	do	Ship Amazon, J. R. Tillinghast.
	Lucy Richardson	7	do		do	do	
	Ann Richardson	4	do		do	do	
	Lucy Richardson	19	do	do		do	
PROVIDENCE, Thomas Cole.	John Amory	20	male	Seaman	U. States	do	Ship General Hamilton, E. Talbot.
	John P. Troding	25	do	Merchant	Sweden	do	Ship Asia, Jno. H. Ormsbee.
	John W. Macy		do	do	U. States	do	Brig Emerald, Thomas Peane.

	Name	Age	Sex	Occupation		U. States	Remarks
NEWARK, James Hawke.	B. S. Burling	25	male	Merchant	U. States	U. States	Sloop Edward, Samuel Sampson.
	— Victor	25	do	Servant	do	do	Sloop Fly, Charles S. Rawlings.
	John Jameison	26	do	Shipwright	England	do	
	Edward Jones	40	do	Mariner	U. States	do	Brig Jason, Elijah Willis.
	John F. Fasset	21	do	Merchant	do	do	
	George Devereaux	23	do	do	do	do	
	Peleg Tupper	25	do	Mariner	England	do	Schooner Rufus King, James Wallace.
	Henry Fulger	26	do	Merchant	U. States	do	Brig Planter, R. Rheidernierte.
	Neil M'Neil	24	do	Seaman	St. Barts	do	Schooner Robert Lenox, Joseph Gould.
	Henry Baintin	50	do	do	U. States	do	
	Stephen M. Chester	25	do	Merchant	do	do	Ship Eagle.
	David Hoyt	28	do	Mariner	England	do	
GEO. TOWN, D. C. John Barnes.	David Martin	28	female		do	do	
	Alice Kyle	57	do		do	do	
	Mary Martin	22	do		do	do	
	Mary Martin	18	do		do	do	
	Helen Martin	30	do		do	do	
	Wm. Goodfellow	46	male	Carpenter	do	do	Brig Penopea, Crabtree.
	George Goodfellow	1	do		do	do	
	John Graham		do	Min. U. S. at Rio [Janeiro]	U. States	do	
	Mrs. Graham		female		do	do	
	John Graham		male		do	do	
	Richard H. Graham		do		do	do	
	Frank		female	Servt. of Mr. G.	do	do	
	Anna		do	do	do	do	
	Mary		do	do	do	do	
	Milly		do	do	do	do	
	Patty		do	do	do	do	
	Peter White		male	Seaman	do	do	} Put on board at Rio Janeiro, by the American Consul.
	William Hale		do	do	do	do	Sloop Express, Knight.
	Thomas Robinson	24	male	Carpenter	Ireland	do	
	Richard Morris	26	do	Cooper	do	do	
	Michael H. Gehagen	20	do	Gardener	do	do	
	James Hornenton	28	do	do	do	do	
ALEXANDRIA, H. Peake.	Andrew Fleming	28	do	Mariner	U. States	do	Schooner Elizabeth, Eaton.
	Henry Cunningham	26	do	do	do	do	
	Henry Own	24	do	do	do	do	Schooner Malvina, Fulton.
	Alexander Semmes	23	do	do	do	do	

LIST of Passengers, &c.—Quarter ending September 30, 1820.

Custom House, with the Name of the Collector.	Names of Passengers.	Age.	Sex.	Occupation.	Country to which they belong.	Country of which they intend to become inhb'ts.	Ship or Vessel, with the name of the Master or Commander.
ALEXANDRIA, H. Peake.	Frederick Goverman	24	male	Mariner	U. States	U. States	Schooner Malvina, Fulton.
	John Butler	24	do	do	do	do	Schooner Aretas, Andrew Johnston.
	Silas Hall	63	do	Farmer	do	do	Schooner Factor, Alexander Hubbs.
	Hannah Hall	53	female		do	do	
	George Weltaen	47	male	Mariner	England	do	
	W. C. Baxter	40	do	do	U. States	do	
	John Howe, jr.	29	do	do	do	do	
	Wm. Smith	34	do	do	do	do	
	S. S. Worth	21	do	do	do	do	
	I. C. Baxter	12	do	do	do	do	
	Thomas Rogers	50	do	Merchant	do	do	Brig Alexander, Samuel Davis.
	John Richardson	49	do	do	do	do	Schooner Fame, Reuben York.
	Ebenezer Corey	25	do		do	do	
	Mary Cooledge	40	female		do	do	
PORTLAND AND FALMOUTH, Isaac Ilsley.	Joseph Cooledge	7	male		do	do	Brig Nimrod, F. Blanchard.
	Joseph Gunison	20	do	Merchant	do	G. Britain	
	William Dickson	23	do	do	Ireland	do	
	Patrick Russell	24	do	do	do	do	
	Jane Noble	30	female	Housewife	do	U. States	
	Catharine Noble	1	do		do	do	
	Robert Noble	5	male		do	do	
	Arthur Noble	3	do		do	do	
	James Veal	45	do	Merchant	U. States	do	
	Ann Veal	35	female		do	do	
	Margaret Veal	14	do		do	do	
	John Veal	12	male		do	do	
	Sarah Veal	10	female		do	do	

Name	Age	Sex	Occupation			Vessel
Richard Collins	27	male	Seaman	U. States	U. States	Brig Fox, Moses Hall.
Joseph Wilson	22	do	do	do	do	Schooner Recover, Jno. Seering.
Pollard	26	do	Merchant	G. Britain	G. Britain	Sloop Favorite, Ezra Jones.
Joshua Richardson	50	do	Merchant	U. States	U. States	
Mrs. Richardson	40	female	do	do	do	
Miss Richardson	4	do	do	do	do	
Master Richardson	2	male	do	do	do	
James Sears	40	do	Merchant	do	do	Schooner Enterpize, D. Jones.
D. Harman	42	do	Blacksmith	do	do	
Freeman Pope	25	do	do	do	do	
James Gould	30	do	Carpenter	do	do	
James Alden	46	do	Seaman	do	do	
James Shaw	23	do	Saddler	do	do	
Harriet Shaw	25	female	Mantuamaker	do	do	
Edward Moulton	20	male	Mason	do	do	Sloop Ranger, F. Smith.
Samuel Ham	20	do	do	do	do	
Edward Starboard	14	do	Laborer	do	do	
Nathaniel D. Poor	24	do	Merchant	do	do	Schooner Clothier, A. Gray.
Joseph Burton	25	do	do	do	do	
Stephen Thomas	46	do	do	do	do	
Henry	35	do	Servant	do	do	
William Harper	35	do	Mariner	do	do	Schoonor Fanny, Packet, J. Waite.
William Hancy	26	do	Potter	do	do	
George Nash	18	do	do	do	do	
Isaac Pearson	19	do	Schoolmaster	do	do	
Benjamin Kelly	18	do	Merchant	do	do	
Mary Hale	41	female	do	do	do	
Martha Goold	18	do	do	do	do	
John Dodd	40	male.	Farmer	Ireland	do	Sloop Rachel, William Field.
Mrs. Dodd	36	female	do	do	do	
Margaret Dodd	8	do	do	do	do	
Robert Dodd	11	male	do	do	do	
David Dodd	6	do	do	do	do	
Mary Dodd	4	female	do	do	do	
John Dodd	2	male	do	do	do	
Joseph Dodd	1	do	do	do	do	
Alexander Porter	60	do	Farmer	do	do	
Mrs. Porter	62	female	do	do	do	

LIST of Passengers, &c.—Quarter ending September 30, 1820.

Custom House, with the name of the Collector.	Names of Passengers.	Age.	Sex.	Occupation.	Country to which they belong.	Country of which they intend to become inhab's	Ship or Vessel, with the name of the Master or Commander.
PORTLAND AND FALMOUTH. Isaac Ilsley.	Jane Porter	30	female		Ireland	U. States	Sloop Rachel, W. Field.
	James Porter	28	male	Farmer	do	do	
	Mary Porter	18	female		do	do	
	A. Porter	20	male		do	do	
	Hutchinson Porter	32	male	Farmer	do	do	
	James Melvin	50	female	do	do	do	
	Isabella Melvin	45	do		do	do	
	Elizabeth Melvin	18	do		do	do	
	Mary Melvin	16	do		do	do	
	Jane Melvin	14	do		do	do	
	Mary Melvin, jr.	13	do		do	do	
	Mary Melvin	36	male		do	do	
	Hugh Ardur	25	do	Farmer	do	do	
	John Alexander	43	male	do	do	do	
	Mary Alexander	46	female		do	do	
	Thomas Alexander	4	male		do	do	
	Elias Alexander	1	do		do	do	
	Michael Oaks	32	do	Farmer	do	do	
	Catharine Hannagan	30	female		do	do	
	Margaret Hannagan	32	do		do	do	
	Nicholas Hannagan	27	male	Farmer	do	do	
	Joseph Dela	16	do		do	do	
	Elizabeth Buckner	30	female		U. States	do	Schooner Dolphin, J. Pote.
	John Sawyer	20	male		do	do	
	John Babcock	21	do		do	do	
	Charles Collins	21	do		do	do	
	John Williams	36	do	Mariner	do	do	

Name	Age	Sex	Occupation			Brig Nimrod, F.C. Blanchard.
Mr. Smith	35	male	Doctor	U. States	U. States	
Mr. Pettingell	28	do	Carpenter	St Johns	St. Johns	
Mr. Riggs	21	do	Merchant	do	U. States	
Mr. Bartlett	40	female	Tailor	do	do	
Miss Beck	25	do		do	do	
Miss Berry	25	do		do	do	
Miss Rigges	23	do		do	do	
Miss Ross	18	do		do	do	
John Cambell	25	male	Mechanic	Ireland	do	
James Cambell	1	female		do	do	
Ann Cambell	20	do		do	do	
Eliza Smith	15	do		do	do	
Jane Smith	14	do		do	do	
John Brady	30	male	Farmer	do	do	
Gilbert Brady	70	do		do	do	
Sarah Lovett	34	female		do	do	
Rebecca Brady	50	do		do	do	
Gilbert Brady	17	male		do	do	
John Graham	14	do	Farmer	do	do	
Robert Smith	22	do	do	do	do	
James Smith	21	do	Weaver	do	do	
Thomas O'Neil	25	do		do	do	
Isabella O'Neil	24	female		do	do	
Mary Jane O'Neil	2	do		do	do	
Elizabeth Potter	16	do		do	do	
Margaret Potter	14	do		do	do	
H. Potter	10	do		do	do	
Jane Potter	8	do	Farmer	do	do	
James Woodman	22	male		do	do	
Mary Woodman	26	female		do	do	
Catharine Johnson	27	do		do	do	
John Harden	35	male		do	do	
Jane Harden	30	female		do	do	
William Harden	12	male		do	do	
Sarah Harden	10	female		do	do	
Alex. Harden	8	male		do	do	
Mary Harden	7	female		do	do	
Eleanor Harden	5	do		do	do	

PHILADELPHIA, John Steele.

24

LIST of Passengers, &c.—Quarter ending September 30, 1820.

Custom House, with the name of the Collector.	Names of Passengers.	Age.	Sex.	Occupation.	Country to which they belong.	Country of which they intend to become inh'bs.	Ship or Vessel, with the name of the Master or Commander.
PHILADELPHIA, John Steele.	Robert Harden	3	male		Ireland	U. States	Brig Nimrod, F. C. Blanchard.
	Harding Harden	1	do		do	do	
	James Williamson	23	female		do	do	
	Agnes Williamson	20	do	Weaver	do	do	
	Rachel Williamson	13	male		do	do	
	Adam M'Nally	70	female	Farmer	do	do	
	Jane M'Nally	61	female		do	do	
	William M'Nally	25	male		do	do	
	Ellen M'Nally	23	female		do	do	
	Andrew M'Nally	20	male	Merchant	do	do	
	James M'Kee	28	do		do	do	
	Sarah M'Kee	28	female		do	do	
	William M'Kee	6	male		do	do	
	Charlotte M'Kee	3	female		do	do	
	James M'Kee	1	male		do	do	
	James Jenkins	37	do		do	do	
	James Jenkins	11	do		do	do	
	Robert Jenkins	8	do		do	do	
	John Jenkins	4	do		do	do	
	Geo. Comtaulo	59	do		U. States	do	Ship Electra, G. Robinson.
	Eliza Comtaulo	21	female		G. Britain	do	
	Sophia Comtaulo	18	do		do	do	
	George Comtaulo	13	male		do	do	
	John Comtaulo	42	do		do	do	
	Richard Pettit	42	do		do	do	
	Elizabeth Pettit	42	female		do	do	
	Elizabeth Sutton	32	do		do	do	

Name	Age	Sex	Occupation		
Charlotte Sutton	4	female		G. Britain	U. States
George Sutton	7	male		do	do
John Mortimer	8	do		do	do
Ann Mortimer	34	female		do	do
Cecilia Mortimer	24	do.		do	do
Emma Mortimer	4	do		do	do
Hampden Mortimer	3	male		do	do
Samuel Bilbrough	1	do			do
William Harris	30	do			do
William V. Anderson	22	do		U. States	G. Britain
Thomas Allsopp	21	do		G. Britain	U. States
Bernard Bayley	28	do		do	G. Britain
Henry Paul	41	do		do	U. States
Thomas R. Cuppy	23	do	Carpenter	do	do
Letitia Cross	19	female		do	do
George Ball	34	male	Carpenter	do	do
Eliza Ball	31	female		do	do
Eliza Ball	2	do		do	do
George Ball	1	male		do	do
Richard Young	28	do	Farmer	do	do
Mary Young	28	female		do	do
Ambrose Garret	36	male	Clergyman	do	do
Elizabeth Garret	42	female		do	do
Charles Dolby	25	male	Farmer	do	do
Henry Homer	40	do	do	do	do
John Thompson	50	do	Gardener	do	do
Sarah Thompson	35	female		do	do
Eliza Thompson	6	do		do	do
Sarah Thompson	1	do		do	do
Samuel Gibbs	45	male	Farmer	do	do
Eliza Gibbs	40	female		do	do
Eleanor Gibbs	17	do		do	do
Maria Gibbs	15	do		do	do
Leonel Gibbs	12	do		do	do
Robert Gibbs	9	male		do	do
Edna Gibbs	6	female		do	do
John Gibbs	3	male		do	do
William Redman	21	do	Shoemaker	do	do

LIST of Passengers, &c.—Quarter ending September 30, 1820.

Custom House, with the name of the Collector.	Names of Passengers.	Age.	Sex.	Occupation.	Country to which they belong.	Country of which they intend to become inhab's	Ship or Vessel, with the name of the Master or Commander.
PHILADELPHIA, John Steele.	Eliza Cooper	57	female		U. States	U. States	Ship Electra, G. Robinson.
	Catharine Cooper	17	do		do	do	
	Eliza Cooper	14	do		do	do	
	Ezekiel Cooper	10	male		do	do	
	Emeline Cooper	8	female		do	do	
	Joseph Brett	20	male	Butcher	do	do	
	William Tomlin	17	do	Farmer	do	do	
	John Gibbs	27	do	Blacksmith	do	do	
	John Newberry	17	do	Com. merch.	do	do	
	Christopher Abel	36	do	Farmer	G. Britain	do	
	Sarah Webb	36	female		do	do	
	Charles R. Webb	6	male		do	do	
	Rebecca Webb	4	female		do	do	
	Eliza Webb	3	do		do	do	
	Susan Webb	1	do		do	do	
	Charles Benice	16	male	Bootmaker	do	do	
	William Archer	51	do	Farmer	do	do	
	William Lambert	65	do		do	do	
	Mary Lambert	58	female	Farmer	do	do	
	Ebenezer Lambert	21	male	do	do	do	
	James Rowe	30	do		do	do	
	Mary Rowe	27	female		do	do	
	Mary Rowe, jun.	6	do		do	do	
	Elizabeth Rowe	3	do		do	do	
	Rebecca Rowe	2	do		do	do	
	Richard Burton	47	male	Carpenter	do	do	
	Anna Burton	38	female		do	do	

Name	Age	Sex	Occupation	G. Britain	U. States	Ship
Francis W Burton	17	male		G. Britain	U. States	
Mary Ann Burton	15	female		do	do	
Frederick Burton	12	male		do	do	
Richard Burton	29	do	Carpenter	do	do	
Elizabeth Burton	31	female		do	do	
Elizabeth Burton, jun.	5	do		do	do	
Ann Burton	4	do		do	do	
William Burton	1	male		do	do	
Jenet Jones	22	female		do	do	
Ambrose Orr	25	male	Farmer	do	do	
George Smith	22	do	do	do	do	
John Blacklock	18	do	do	do	do	
Walter Leyden	50	do	Tailor	do	do	
Robert Keightly	39	do	Carpenter	do	do	
Violetta Keightly	33	female		do	do	
Robert Keightly, jun.	12	male		do	do	
Hannah Keightly	11	female		do	do	
William Keightly	9	male		do	do	
Ann Keightly	8	female		do	do	
Maria Keightly	6	do		do	do	
Henry Keightly	3	male		do	do	
Edmund Keightly	1	do		do	do	
Daniel Osgood	42	do	Physician	Havana	Havana	Brig Margaret, I. Hall.
Rachael Osgood	31	female		do	do	
Edwin Osgood	9	male		do	do	
Emma Osgood	11	female		do	do	
Rosa	36	do	Servant	do	do	
Antonio Risal	42	do		do	U. States	Brig Commodore Porter, J. L. Kay.
Manuelle Garro	20	do		do	do	
Cheimba	30	do	Servant	do	do	
Raymond Baryo	22	male		do	do	
James Brian	11	do		St. Croix	do	
H. Brian	9	do		do	do	
William Borland	40	do	Farmer	Ireland	do	Schr. Enterprize.
Mary Borland	35	female		do	do	
Hannah Borland	9	do		do	do	
Robert Borland	8	male		do	do	
Elizabeth Borland	4	female		do	do	

LIST of Passengers, &c.—Quarter ending September 30, 1820.

Custom House, with the name of Collector.	Names of Passengers.	Age.	Sex.	Occupation.	Country to which they belong.	Country of which they intend to become inhab's	Ship or Vessel, with the name of the Master or Commander.
Philadelphia, John Steele.	Isabella Borland	1	female		Ireland	U. States	Schooner Enterprize.
	John Borland	20	male	Farmer	do	do	
	Jane Barns	23	female		do	do	
	John Sampson	31	male	Laborer	do	do	
	Hugh Lindsay	20	do	do	do	do	
	Samuel Caskey	29	do	Farmer	do	do	
	Mary Ann Caskey	29	female		do	do	
	Mary Caskey	8	do		do	do	
	Margaret Caskey	5	do		do	do	
	Rebecca Caskey	3 6	do		do	do	
	Sally Caskey		do		do	do	
	Bryan M'karney	22	male	Laborer	do	do	
	Wm. Highlands	30	do	Shoemaker	do	do	
	Nancy Highlands	70	female	Spinster	do	do	
	Mary Highlands	36	do	do	do	do	
	Jane Highlands	28	do	do	do	do	
	Jenny Highlands	25	do	do	do	do	
	Nancy Highlands	8	do		do	do	
	Francis Della	50	male	Farmer	do	do	
	Isab:lla Della	45	female		do	do	
	Nancy Della	16	do		do	do	
	Margery Della	14	do		do	do	
	Michael Della	12	male		do	do	
	Isabella Della	8	female		do	do	
	James Johnson	24	male	Farmer	do	do	
	Andrew C. Lemon	31	do		do	do	
	Elizabeth Lemon	20	female		do	do	

Name	Age	Sex	Occupation	Native of	Destination	Vessel
Sally Boland	24	female		Ireland	U. States	
Catharine Duley	26	do		do	do	
John Forsyth	19	male	Weaver	do	do	
James Dougless	22	do	do	do	do	
James Holmes	18	do		do	do	
Nancy Bird	45	female	Milliner	do	do	
Matthew Knox	25	male		do	do	
Elizabeth Dorety	18	female		G. Britain	do	Brig Christopher, Rowe,
James Donlevy	8	male		U. States	do	
Wm. Thompson		do.		do	do	
J. P. Maddock		do.		do	do	
J. H. Chapman		do.		do	do	
N. G. Bayne		do		G. Britain	do	
J. Ellerbee		do		do	do	
R Dean		do		do	do	
H. Shinkle		do		do	do	
Mr. Redman		do		do	do	
Mrs. Redman, son & daughter		female		do	do	
Mrs. Miles		do		do	do	
Mrs. Fairer & 2 child'n		do		do	do	Brig Hannah, A. Latour.
Mrs. Brandon	40	do		do	do	
Mr. Brandon	22	male	Gentleman	do	do	
G. Mason	24	do	do	do	do	
H. Haynes	18	do	do	do	do	
Doctor Rascome	26	do	Physician	do	do	
H. Hays	38	do	Gentleman	do	do	
Mr. Albaner	62	do'	do	do	do	
Mrs. Gills	11	female	Servant	do	do	
Mrs. Dennis	35	male	do	do	do	
James Smith	30	female	Schoolmaster	do	do	Ship Natchez, J. A. Warnack,
Sarah Smith	37	male		do	do	
P. Carroll	35			U. States	do	Brig Trident, Dustin.
Michael Miller	35	do	Mariner	do	do	
Wm. Mason	40	do	Merchant	do	do	
M. Alkin	55		Farmer	do	do	
Mrs. Faux	22	female	Lady		do	Sloop Betsey, B. Young.
Jos. Boyd	57	male		Ireland	do	

LIST of Passengers, &c.—Quarter ending September 30, 1820.

Custom House, with the Name of the Collector.	Names of Passengers.	Age.	Sex.	Occupation.	Country to which they belong.	Country of which they intend to become inhab's	Ship or Vessel, with the Name of the Master or Commander.
PHILADELPHIA, John Steele.	Wm. Boyd	25	male	Farmer	Ireland	U. States	Sloop Betsey, B. Young.
	James Boyd	11	do		do	do	
	Martha Boyd	49	female		do	do	
	Eliza Boyd	13	female		do	do	
	Mary Boyd	16	male		do	do	
	Thos. Mackey	22	do		do	do	
	Robert Mackey	12	female		do	do	
	Sarah Mackey	25	do		do	do	
	Jane Mackey	45	do		do	do	
	Eliza Mackey	14	male		do	do	
	John S. Reuns	10	do		do	do	
	Andrew Reuns	60	female		do	do	
	Mary Wane	28	do		do	do	
	Mary Jane Wane	24	do		do	do	
	Martha Wane	2　6	male		do	do	
	Wm. Petters	9	do		do	do	
	James Petters	28	do		do	do	
	John Petters	7	female		do	do	
	Mary Petters	4	do		do	do	
	Hannah Petters	27	male		do	do	
	W. M'Laughlin	1　6	female		do	do	
	Mary Rickey	26	do		do	do	
	Hannah Rickey	36	do		do	do	
	H. Dauby	5	female		do	do	
	Margaret Dauby	17	do		do	do	
	Biddy Dauby	15	do		do	do	
	Rosetta Dauby	11			do	do	

Name	Age	Sex	Occupation			Ship
Ave Dauby	9	female		Ireland	U. States	
Philip Dauby	6	male		do	do	
Robert Coyle	20	do		do	do	
Mary Coyle	20	female		do	do	
R. Coyle	28	male		do	do	
Reuben M'Clentush	1	female		do	do	
Mary Geniles	18	female		do	do	
Eliza Geniles	18	do		do	do	
John Galaus	28	male		do	do	
John Blasdel	23	do		do	do	
Wm. Moore	38	female	Farmer	G. Britain	do	Schooner Hope & Polly, J. Baxter.
Mary Moore	38	female		do	do	
Martha Moore	14	do		do	do	
Jane Moore	12	do		do	do	
Elizabeth Moore	10	do		do	do	
John Moore	8	male		do	do	
James Moore.	3	do		do	do	
Nancy Moore	2	female		do	do	
Mary Moore		do		do	do	
John Stunkard	45	male	do	do	do	
Mary do. & 5 child'n	42	female		do	do	
Jane Hodge	25	do		do	do	
Mary Miller	20	do		do	do	
Mary Saylia	20	do		do	do	
Robert Hunter	19	male		do	do	
Wm. Martin	24	do	Tailor	do	do	
Susanna Bell	50	female		do	do	
James Long	34	male		do	do	
Rose Donally & 5 chil'n	40	female		do	do	
Robert Gold	33	male		do	do	
Wm. Shardon	30	do		do	do	
Nathan White	25	do		do	do	
Susanna White	25	female		do	do	
John M'Ilvaine	23	male		do	do	
James Cunningham	24	do	Merchant	U. States	do	Schooner Philadelphia, P. Hall.
Joseph Fernander	27	do	do	do	do	
Francis Adams	28	do	Sea captain	do	do	
James Doyle	25	do	do			

25

LIST of Passengers, &c.—Quarter ending September 30, 1820.

Custom House, with the Name of the Collector.	Names of Passengers.	Age.	Sex.	Occupation.	Country to which they belong.	Country of which they intend to become inhab's	Ship or Vessel, with the name of the Ma... or Commander.
PHILADELPHIA, John Steele.	Mary Ramsden & 4 chil.	33	female		G. Britain	U. States	Schooner Philadelphia, P. Hall.
	F. Silva	30	male		do	do	
	M. Donougher	45	do		do	do	
	F. Melizet	35	do		do	do	
	Mrs. Muller	30	female		do	do	
	Daniel Giraud	35	male	Merchant	do	do	Schr. Marius, H. H. Williams.
	Benjamin Williams	74	do		do	do	
	Joseph Williams	42	do		do	do	
	R. Williams & 4 children	26	female		do	do	
	Mary Kelly	18	do		do	do	
	Sarah Brien & 2 children	28	do		do	do	
	Mary Keskith	32	do		do	do	
	Catharine Miller	59	do		do	do	
	William Ellis	15	male		do	do	
	R. Worthington	28	do	Farmer	do	do	
	M. Worthington & 2 ch.	24	female		do	do	
	Thomas Towar	21	male	Farmer	do	do	
	William Holderness	68	do	Merchant	do	do	
	Samuel Hadden	26	do	Farmer	do	do	
	John M'Gowan	25	do	Laborer	do	do	
	Ann Hill and child	50	female		do	do	
	Daniel M'Faoren	21	male	Laborer	Havana	Havana	Brig Caledonia, Jarvis.
	I. Porey	25	do	Clerk	do	do	
	Peter Diego	19	do		G. Britain	U. States	
	F. Diego	12	male		U. States	do	
	Margaret Smith	26	female		G. Britain	do	Schr. Decatur, John Hopkins.
	Thomas Galen	65	male	Carpenter	G. Britain	do	

Name	Age	Sex	Occupation	Country		Ship
Mary Galen	60	female	Laborer	G. Britain	U. States	Schr. Decatur, John Hopkins.
Johnson Galen	21	male	Merchant	do	do	
W.liam Bartlett	25	do	Supercargo	U. States	do	Brig D. Moffat, Charles Snowden.
S. Stutgard	35	do	Servant	do	do	
Joseph Homo	12	do	Merchant	do	do	
John Grovillo	40	do	Seamen	Spain	do	
Alexander Barnet	30	do	Merchant	U. States	do	Schr. Margaret, Thomas Wilson.
Isaac Nash	20	do	Farmer	G. Britain	do	
Thomas Thousley & 6 child.	48	female	Servant	do	do	
S. Thousley & child	46	do	do	do	do	
H. Gillespie & child	32	male	Farmer	do	do	Schr. Jefferson, J. Howard.
Thomas M'Grath & 2 ch.	24	do		do	do	
Samuel Osburne	40	female	Farmer	do	do	
Mary Osburne	38	do		do	do	
Mary Osburne	24	female		do	do	
William Osburne	24	male	Farmer	do	do	
James Osburne	20	do	do	do	do	
Samuel Osburne	18	do		do	do	
Catharine Osburne	16	female		do	do	
Betsey Osburne	14	do		do	do	
Francis Daisley	50	male	Farmer	do	do	
Ann Daisley & 3 childr.	50	female		do	do	
Andrew Ramsay	25	male	Farmer	do	do	
John M'Bride	19	do	Servant	do	do	
Bell Blackburn	25	female	do	do	do	
Elizabeth Steel	26	do	do	do	do	
Hugh Campbell	23	male	Laborer	do	do	
John Martin	26	do	Gentleman	do	do	
Mrs. ?. Hissand & child	45	female		do	do	Brig Columbia, William Midler.
C. Hissand & 4 children	22	do		do	do	
Henry Spears	25	male		do	do	Schooner Antelope, Kennedy.
W. .m Bell	27	do	Merchant	do	do	
Antonio Moor	38	do		Austria	do	
Aaron Smith	21	do	Merchant	U. States	do	Brig Olive Branch, D. L. Bingham.
John A. Monges	21	do	do	G. Britain	do	
John Searle	21	do	do	do	do	
Thomas Ansley	46	do	Farmer	U. States	do	Brig Melita, A. Pastonus.
William Todd	16	do	do	do	do	

LIST of Passengers, &c.—Quarter ending September 30, 1820.

Custom House, with the name of the Collector.	Names of Passengers.	Age.	Sex.	Occupation.	Country to which they belong.	Country of which they intend to become inhb's.	Ship or Vessel, with the name of the Master or Commander.
PHILADELPHIA, John Steele.	John Hamilton	50	male	Farmer	Ireland	U. States	Ship Prosperity, Childs.
	Patrick M'Laughlin	60	do	do	do	do	
	Owen M'Laughlin	30	do	do	do	do	
	Mary M'Laughlin	18	female	Spinster	do	do	
	C. Scanlin	21	do	do	do	do	
	William Spence	22	male	Laborer	do	do	
	Ann M'Farland	27	female	Spinster	do	do	
	Daniel Brown	22	male	Laborer	do	do	
	W. Stevenson	19	do	Spinster	do	do	
	John M'Allan	22	do	Laborer	do	do	
	Alexander Ernley	22	do	do	do	do	
	Hugh M'Cannon	22	do	do	do	do	
	William Armstrong	23	do	do	do	do	
	Margaret Armstrong	22	female	Spinster	do	do	
	Robert M'Clarnes	30	male	Laborer	do	do	
	John Thompson	20	do	do	do	do	
	Robert Foxman	18	do	do	do	do	
	Andrew Dixon	28	do	do	do	do	
	John Murney	24	do	do	do	do	
	Jane Brown	21	female	Spinster	do	do	
	B. M'Allen	20	male	Laborer	do	do	
	Samuel Spence	25	do	do	do	do	
	Owen Boyle	25	do	do	do	do	
	Daniel M'Gulagh	25	do	do	do	do	
	Samuel Horner	22	do	do	do	do	
	H. Scanlin	19	do	do	do	do	
	James Banter	30	do	Farmer	do	do	

Name	Age	Sex	Occupation		U. States
John Conoway	18	male	Farmer	do	do
John M'Alwin	25	do	Laborer	do	do
James Lery	20	do	do	do	do
Ezekiel Mann	25	do	do	do	do
S. Butler	25	do	do	do	do
Pat. Butler	24	do	do	do	do
M. Cornay	25	do	do	do	do
Francis Frazer	25	do	do	do	do
Patrick M'Nally	20	do	do	do	do
Ann M'Nally and child	21	female	Spinster	do	do
Robert P. Little	26	male	Merchant	do	do
Benjamin Pottage	24	do	Coppersmith	do	do
Catharine M'Laughlin	18	female	Servant	do	do
Roger Gough	59	male	Farmer	do	do
Rebecca Gough	54	female		do	do
Edward Gough	33	male		do	do
Sarah Gough	25	female		do	do
Mary Gough	21	do		do	do
Elizabeth Gough	12	do		do	do
William Hait	37	male	Gardener	do	do
Martha Hait	30	female		do	do
Jonathan Rudman	48	male	Farmer	do	do
Susan Rudman & 4 chil.	53	female		do	do
George Nutall	25	male	Farmer	do	do
George Fox	46	do	Miller	do	do
Ann Fox & 3 children	39	female		do	do
Robert Ward	36	male	Weaver	do	do
Ellen Sunman & 8 chil.	38	female		do	do
Alfred Smart	30	male	do	do	do
Esther Smart	32	female		do	do
Thomas Hinchliff	38	male	do	do	do
Sarah Hinchliff	38	female		G. Britain	do
Nathaniel Whiston	30	male	Painter	do	do
Edward Hodges	25	do	Shoemaker	do	do
William France	50	do	Weaver	do	do
John Sexton	34	do	do	do	do
William Kemp	31	do	do	do	do
Leonard Rusby	24	do	do	do	do

Ship Nancy, Bray.

LIST of Passengers, &c.—Quarter ending September 30, 1820.

Custom House, with the name of the Collector.	Names of Passengers.	Age.	Sex.	Occupation.	Country to which they belong.	Country of which they intend to become inhab's	Ship or Vessel, with the name of the Master or Commander.
PHILADELPHIA, John Steele.	Robert Peck	21	male		G. Britain	U. States	Ship Nancy, Bray.
	William Hill	22	do		do	do	
	William Whitall	26	do		do	do	
	George Oxley	24	do		do	do	
	John Philips	33	do		do	do	
	Nathaniel Clegg	36	do		do	do	
	Benjamin M'Loby	36	do		do	do	
	Edward Price	22	do		do	do	
	Nicholas Johns	37	do		do	do	
	Edward Hodges	16	do	Merchant	do	do	
	Wm. F. Knight	20	do	Carpenter	do	do	
	George Green	35	do		do	do	Ship Tontine, E. Turtis.
	Mrs. Green	40	female		do	do	
	Jane Green	28	do		do	do	
	John Duncan	50	male	Farmer	do	do	
	Eliz. Duncan &7 childr.	45	female		do	do	
	Jane M'Culloch	18	do		do	do	
	Dennis Harkin	30	male	Tailor	U. States	do	
	Stephen Curcer	44	do	Merchant	Ireland	do	Ship Brandt, G. W. Steinhaven.
	John Loge	28	do	Dyer	England	do	Schooner Madison, F. Jones.
	Mary Grigg	20	female	Mantuamaker	do	do	
	Han. Humbly & 2 chil.	25	do		do	do	
	Mary Humbly	27	do		do	do	
	R. M'Cloud	36	do		do	do	
	John Baird	37	male	Laborer	Ireland	do	
	Mary Baird & 3 children	28	female		do	do	
	William King	23	male	Merchant	U. States	do	Brig Hannah, A. Latour.

Name	Age	Sex	Occupation	Country	Destination	Ship
Samuel Jackson	57	male	Seaman	G. Britain	U. States	Brig Belvidere, W. Jordan.
Thomas B. Townsend	39	do	Clothier	do	do	
Jane Townsend & 4 chil.	31	female		do	do	
Letitia H. Carroll	27	male	Lady's maid	Prussia	do	
Gerard Shmingler	39	female	Tailor	do	do	
R. Shmingler	37	male		G. Britain	do	
Charles Foster	30	do	Seaman	Ireland	do	
Jno. Savage	40	female	Merchant	England	do	
Isa. Seagrave & child	30	do		do	do	
Sarah E. Pattison	40	do	Spinster	do	do	
Mary Jefferson	26	do		do	do	
Miary Parker & child	41	do		do	do	
F. Bainton	28	male	Tallow-chandler	do	do	
W.lliam Bainton	27	do	Farmer	do	do	
John Parker	46	do	do	do	do	
Grace Bainton & child	28	female		do	do	
Ann. Bainton	61	do		do	do	
Robt. Topham & child	42	male	Farmer	do	do	
C. Topham & 2 childr'n	41	female		do	do	
George Wilson	42	male		do	do	
Sarah Wilson & 5 chil.	41	female		do	do	
Samuel Harrison	25	male	Farmer	do	do	
John Cowtan	21	do	do	do	do	
Thomas Lea	30	do	do	do	do	
Michael Bracker	45	do		do	do	
Mary Bracker & 5 chil.	35	female		do	do	
Mary Walker & 3 chil.	40	do		do	do	
James Bond	47	male		do	do	
Mary Bond & child	40	female		do	do	
Sarah Renner & child	27	do		do	do	
Sarah Otis & 5 children	36	do		do	do	
Marg. Jackson & child	22	do		do	do	
Mary Hurst	50	do		do	do	
Sarah Hurst & 6 chil.	30	do		do	do	
Sarah Broom & 3 chil.	36	do		do	do	
Thomas Hurst	40	male	Manufacturer	Italy	do	Brig Superior, M. Dixon.
Joseph Felungo	25	do	Merchant	England	do	Ship Dido, J. E. Mathew.
Mr. Inskeep	35	do	Farmer		do	

LIST of Passengers, &c.—Quarter ending September 30, 1820.

Custom House, with the name of the Collector.	Names of Passengers.	Age.	Sex.	Occupation.	Country to which they belong.	Country of which they intend to become inhab's	Ship or Vessel, with the Name of the Master or Commander.
PHILADELPHIA, John Steele.	Mrs. Inskeep & child	27	female		England	U. States	Ship Dido, J. E. Mathew.
	Mr. Swannell	24	male	Farmer	do	do	
	Mr. Ludeker	25	do		Germany	do	
	Mr. Lees	24	do	Supercargo	U. States	do	
	Mr. Le Roy	21	do	Merchant	do	do	
	Mr. Chacon_	30	do	Consul	Spain	do	
	Mr. Levy	32	do	Jeweller	France	do	
	Mr. E. Lea	25	do	Gentleman	U. States	do	
	Mrs. Millerdon	22	female		G. Britain	do	Ship John, Thurston.
	G. Goldsmith	21	male	Farmer	do	do	
	A. Archer	41	do	Merchant	do	do	
	I. Macafee	25	do	Hairdresser	do	do	Brig Laura, J. Haskell.
	M. Macafee	23	female		do	do	
	Harriet Hughes	20	do		do	do	
	M. Herring	30	male	Laborer	do	do	
	E. Curley	24	do	do	do	do	
	M. M'Kenney	31	female		do	do	
	C. Cunningham	14	do		do	do	
	L. Bouner	35	male	Baker	Germany	do	Ship Sachem, Edward Fennell.
	N. Miller	35	do	Mariner	U. States	do	
	John Mackafee	26	do	Farmer	Ireland	do	
	M. Mackafee & children	26	female		do	do	
	Moses Black	30	male	Brazier	do	do	Schooner Pilgrim, R. Cozens.
	Jane Black & 2 children	28	female		do	do	
	Martha Moose	22	do		do	do	
	Francis Cunningham	70	male	Farmer	do	do	
	Jane Cunningham	60	female		do	do	

Name	Age	Sex	Occupation		U. States
William Cunningham	20	male	Farmer	Ireland	do
Jane Cunningham	28	female		do	do
John Duncan	60	male		do	do
Eliza Duncan & 6 childr.	45	female		do	do
Jane M'Culloch	18	do		do	do
Dennis Harkin	30	male	Tailor	do	do
Stephen Currier	44	do	Merchant	do	do
John Loge	28	do	Dyer	do	do
Mary Grigg	20	female	Mantuamaker	England	do
Hannah Humbly & child	25	do		do	do
Mary Humbly	27	do		do	do
R. M'Cloud	36	do		Ireland	do
John Baird	37	male	Laborer	do	do
Mary Baird & 3 children	28	female		do	do
William King	23	male	Merchant	U. States	do
Samuel Jackson	37	do	Seaman	do	do
Thomas B. Townshend	39	do	Clothier	G. Britain	do
J. R. Townshend & 3 ch.	31	female		do	do
James Townshend	18	male		do	do
Letitia H. Carroll	27	female	Servant	do	do
Gerard Shmingler	39	male	Lady's maid	Prussia	do
Regana Shmingler	37	female	Tailor	do	do
Ann Ayling & 3 children	29	do		G. Britain	do
John Dodgson	38	male	Farmer	do	do
Deb. Dodgson & 3 chil.	40	female		do	do
John Waterhouse	24	male	Tailor	do	do
Eliz. Taylor & 2 childr.	28	female		do	do
Frank Neild	34	male	Farmer	do	do
Betty Neild & child	35	female		do	do
John Quinn	35	male	Laborer	do	do
Mary Falkner & 2 chil.	30	female		do	do
Jane Dowling & 3 chil.	30	do		do	do
John Robinson	70	male	Farmer	do	do
John Robinson, jr.	40	do	do	do	do
Hannah Robinson	34	female		do	do
Mary Robinson	30	do		do	do
Ann Robinson & 6 chil.	42	do		do	do
Mary Acomack	60	do		do	do

LIST of Passengers, &c.—Quarter ending September 30, 1820.

Custom House, with the name of the Collector.	Names of Passengers.	Age.	Sex.	Occupation.	Country to which they belong.	Country of which they intend to become inhab's	Ship or Vessel, with the name of the Master or Commander.
PHILADELPHIA, John Steele.	Frederick Beycats	23	male	Clerk	G. Britain	U. States	Schooner Pilgrim, R. Cozens.
	Anne Beycats	20	female		do	do	
	Wm. Butcher	25	male		do	do	
	Wm. F. Smith	22		Laborer	do	do	
	Thomas Smith	18		Farmer	do	do	
	Jos. Bagnall	16		Servant	do	do	
	John Heywood	18		Baker	do	do	
	Ann Thistlewait	28			do	do	
	Agnes Thistlewait	27			U. States	do	
	Rebecca Waln	70			G. Britain	do	
	Margaret Wright	27		Blacksmith	do	do	
	John Salmon	20		Laborer	do	do	
	Daniel M'Farlan	27		Baker	do	do	
	James Claridge	22			do	do	
	Esther Claridge	23		do	do	do	
	Joseph Claridge	27		Joiner	do	do	
	Thos. Smith	21		do	do	do	
	Joseph Smith	25		Bookseller,	do	do	
	Maria Ann Smith	22			do	do	
	Stephen Maddox	27			do	do	
	Mary Hornbrook and 2 children	50			do	do	
	G. Ernshaw	16		Farmer	do	do	
	Ann Ernshaw	64			do	do	
	Mary Ernshaw	21			do	do	
	Hannah Ernshaw	74			do	do	
	Thos. Langley	30		Laborer	do	do	Ship Superior, Jno. Hamilton.

Name	Age	Sex	Occupation	Country	Destination	Ship
Ann Langley & child	25			G. Britain	U. States	
Sarah Holroyd & do.	25			do	do	
Thomas Baxter	30		Laborer	do	do	
M. Baxter & 3 children	28			do	do	
Mary Bell	18				do	
M. Dombrowsky	45		Officer	Germany	do	Ship Governor Hawkins, C. Bower.
J. G. Franks	45		Gentleman	do	do	
Jno. N. Gluer	32		do	do	do	
H. G. Polk	22		do	do	do	
Frederick Classin	25	male	Baker		do	
Jno. G. Schmoke	27	do	Farmer		do	
G. P. Gledeschtz	25	do	Servant		Canton	
Redwood Fisher	38	do	Merchant	U. States	U. States	Ship William Savary, Thos. Arnold
Samuel D. Lees	22	do	do	do	do	
Ahing	40	do	Servant	Canton	do	Schooner Ajax, Jno. Rice.
Benj. J. Shair	39	do	Merchant	U. States	do	
Robert	39	do	Chairmaker	do	do	
Robert Beattie	22	do	Farmer	G. Britain	do	
Samuel Beattie	24	do	do		do	
Matthew Roberts	38	do	do		do	Brig Rising Sun.
Gilbert Cruit	50	do	do		do	
John Cruit	33	do	do		do	
Susan Cruit	20	female	Dressmaker		do	
Margt. Hego & 5 child'n	40	do			do	
Hugh M'Gowan	39	male	Mariner		do	
Charles M'Fargart	34	do	Stone mason		do	
Sarnpson Pant	18	do	Weaver		do	
Wm. Moore	30	do	Farmer		do	
Manuel Corvelo	20	do	Merchant	Spain	do	Brig Water Witch, Kean.
Edmund W. Robinson	24	do	Teacher	U. states	do	Schooner Ilsley, D. Loring.
Thos. Brown	19	do	Toolmaker	G. Britain	do	Brig Mary & Achsah Ann, Bousquel.
Jno. Le Grase	20	do	Shoemaker	U. States	do	
Case	25	do	Missionary	do	do	
Danl. Hilliar	30	do		G. Britain	do	Schooner. St. Helena, C. Cory.
Mrs. Hilliar & child	32	female		do	do	
Jane	34	do	Servant	do	do	
Jno. Beucker	13	male		St. Thomas	do	
Jas. Mimunky & 9 chil'n	48	do	Farmer	G. Britain	do	Ship Niagara, N. Gookin.

LIST of Passengers, &c.—Quarter ending September 30, 1820.

Custom House, with the name of the Collector.	Names of Passengers.	Age.	Sex.	Occupation.	Country to which they belong.	Country of which they intend to become inhab's	Ship or Vessel with the name of the Master or Commander.
PHILADELPHIA. John Steele.	John Breckenridge	22	male	Farmer	G. Britain	U. States	Ship Niagara, N. Gookin.
	Hugh Breckenridge	22	do	do	do	do	
	John Johnson	19	do	do	do	do	
	John Munair	22	do	do	do	do	
	James Culbertson	21	female		do	do	
	Jane Culbertson	20	male	Tailor	do	do	
	Alexander Brown	21	female		do	do	
	Jane Brown	22	female	Farmer	do	do	
	Wm. Griffin	30	male		do	do	
	Isaba. Griffin & 2 chil'n	26	female		do	do	
	Agnes Reid	22	do.	do	do	do	
	Robert Armour	62	male	do	do	do	
	David Watson	28	do.		do	do	
	Jane Watson & child	26	female	Tinsmith	do	do	
	Alexr. Clark	24	male	Farmer	do	do	
	Neal Muloy	22	do	do	do	do	
	Jas. Watson	24	do	do	do	do	
	Donald M'Munky	19	do	Merchant	do	do	
	John Shaw	36	do	Umbrellamak.	do	do	
	Jarvis Askin	60	do		do	do	
	Martha Askin	23	female	Merchant	do	do	
	James Brodie	22	male	Farmer	do	do	
	Wm. Russell	18	do		do	do	
	John Armour	29	do		do	do	
	Jane Armour	27	female		do	do	
	Elizabeth Armour	23	male		do	do	
	Duncan Stewart	22	do	do	do	do	

Name	Age	Sex	Occupation	Country	Destination	Ship
Robert Watson	22	male	Farmer	G. Britain	U. States	Ship Warrington, L. Dunbar.
James Watson	20	do	do	do	do	
Margaret Watson	18	female		U. States	do	
Lewis Chastant	30	male	Merchant	do	do	
A. Beyac	39	do	do	do	do	
S. P. Dantreroche	35	do	do	do	do	
A. Tourtelot	23	do	do	do	do	
P. Knappe	18	female		do	do	
C. Knappe	38	male		do	do	
P. Meifren	20	do	do	France	do	
J. Baptiste	17	male	do	do	do	
B. Dapuy	21	do	do	do	do	
E. Wolf	21	do	do	do	do	
B. Samuel	23	do	do	do	do	
M. Davis	28	do	Seaman	Spain	do	Brig Louisiana, J. P. Hart.
Antonio Lewis	21	do	Supercargo	U. States	do	Schooner Albert, Ira Bly.
Leeson H. Simmons	20	do	Gentleman	do	do	
Josiah Lachart	25	do	Merchant	Germany	do	Brig Leader, J. Jones.
Andrew Thompson	23	do	Baker	do	do	
V. T. Wachmuth	28	female	do	do	do	
S. C. Baurshacks	14	male	do	do	do	
G. Escher	18	do	Turner	do	do	Schooner Bee, John Martin.
Henry Davids	25	do	Organist	do	do	
John Althaus	26	do	Merchant	Spain	Havana	Schooner Hannah, Samuel Owens.
Raman Sierra	28	do	do	Italy	do	
Lorenzo Pacher	28	do	do	Spain	do	
Francis de Mavros	30	do	Baker	G. Britain	do	
Jas. Wilson	23	female	do	do	do	
Ann Wilson & 4 child'n	30	do		do	do	
Mary Clifer	30	male	Laborer	do	do	
Dennis Carey	23	do	do	do	do	
P. Fitzgerald	23	do	do	do	do	
David Con	23	female	do	do	do	
Sarah Con & child	34	male	do	do	do	
John Cartlow	28	do	do	do	do	
Wm. Mahan	59	do	Farmer	do	do	Ship Stranger, Jno. Riley.
Rich. Woodhouse	48	female	do	do	do	
Mrs. do. & 4 child'n		female		do	do	

LIST of Passengers, &c.—Quarter ending September 30, 1820.

Custom House, with the name of the Collector.	Names of Passengers.	Age.	Sex.	Occupation.	Country to which they belong.	Country of which they intend to become inhb's.	Ship or Vessel, with the name of the Master or Commander.
PHILADELPHIA, John Steele.	Jos. Hornby	30	male	Farmer	G. Britain	Havana	Ship Stranger, Jno. Reilly.
	Mary do. & 4 chil'dn	27	female	do	do	do	
	Wm. Hinds	26	male	do	do	do	
	Edmd. Taylor	28	do		do	do	
	Thos. Taylor	22	do		do	do	
	Mary do. & 3 child'n	25	female		do	do	
	Mrs. Wilcox & 3 do.	26	do		do	do	
	Jno. Dickson	36	male		do	do	
	D. Martin	22	male		do	do	
	Peter Whitaker	36	do	Merchant	do	do	Brig Hibernia, H. Hutchinson.
	Thos. Andrews	33	do	do	do	do	
	M. Walker & 3 child'n	40	female		do	do	
	Franklin Didier	25	male	Surgeon	U. States	do	Ship Telegraph, H. Coffin.
	Henry Chatard	16	do	do	do	do	
	Michael Devine	24	do	Servant	G. Britain	do	
	Ann Devine & child	26	female		do	do	
	Thos. Mithvin	23	male	Teacher	do	U. States	
	Sarah Birch	16	female		do	do	
	Nathan Jennings	19	male	Farmer	do	do	
	Hannah Lane & child	55	female		do	do	
	John Lonsdale	40	male		do	do	
	Mary Sussman & child	32	female	Horse dealer	do	do	Ship Bainbridge, J. Berry.
	Matthew Lanswall	50	male		do	do	
	Hannah Lanswall	30	female		do	do	
	William Orient	48	male	Farmer	do	do	
	Sarah do. & 4 child'n	47	female		do	do	
	Robert Hunt	22	male	do	do	do	

Name	Age	Sex	Occupation		U. States	Ship
Ann Hunt and child	24	female		G. Britain	U. States	
Thomas Heard	28	male		do	do	
Jane Burnist	70	female	Servant	do	do	
Phœbe Heard	32	do		do	do	
John Sellary	23	male		do	do	
Ann Sellary	23	female		do	do	
James Stopman	26	male	Laborer	do	do	Ship Jane, T. S. Luberg.
James Bayne	48	do	Ship owner	do	do	Brig Two Brothers, J. Laws.
Ed. Garret and 2 child.	42	do	Farmer	do	do	Brig Pilot, S. Fenton.
John Quaas	40	do	Cabinetmaker	Portugal	do	
Robert Smith	30	do	Physician	U. States	do	
George Regnault	26	do	Paperhanger	do	do	
E. Regnault and 5 chil.	30	female		do	do	
J. Wigmore	50	male	Gentleman	do	do	
Paul Balash	25	do	do	do	do	
George Walters	26	do	Cooper	do	do	Brig Georgetown Packet, S. Woodhouse.
J. R. Lawrence	22		Merchant	do	do	Brig M. Hope, H. Strefether.
Margaret M'Niel & 2 ch.	30	female	Seamstress	G. Britain	do	
John Tobin	24	male	Schoolmaster	do	do	
James M'Ginnis	55	do	Laborer	do	do	
Patrick Hogan	18	do	Merchant	U. States	do	
Julia Granberry	28	female	Lady	do	do	
Samuel Nash	18	male	Mariner	G. Britain	do	
Robert Mortrage	23	do.	Servant	do	do	Brig True American, S. G. Yorke.
Michael M'Man	23	do	Laborer	Ireland	do	
John M' Daniel	21	do	do	do	do	
Robert Cooper	24	do	Weaver	do	do	
Daniel Mooney	27	do	do	do	do	
George Platt	34	do	Merchant	U. States	do	Schr. Harriet Newall, John Carter.
George W. Tatem	28	do	Mariner	do	do	Schr. Eagle, H. King.
Horton	28	do	do	Denmark	do	
Wm. Lanham	50	do	Painter	G. Britain	do	
John Picoiu	37	do	Mariner	Spain	do	
Ralph Baggaley	29	female	Farmer	G. Britain	do	Ship Factor, Wm. H. Sheed.
Ann Baggaley & 4 chil.	31	male		do	do	
Sarah Goldthorp	35	do	Farmer	do	do	
Edmund Atkinson	42	male	Carpenter	do	do	Ship Liverpool Packet, J. Birket.
James Willis		do		do	do	

LIST of Passengers, &c.—Quarter ending September 30, 1820.

Custom House, with the name of the Collector.	Names of Passengers.	Age.	Sex.	Occupation.	Country to which they belong.	Country of which they intend to become inhab's	Ship or Vessel, with the name of the Master or Commander.
PHILADELPHIA. John Steele.	John Calvert	26	male	Farmer	G. Britain	U. States	Ship Liverpool Packet, J. Birket.
	William Cartmer	52	do	do	do	do	
	M. Cartmer & 8 child.	44	female		do	do	
	James Holmes	30	male	Farmer	do	do	
	John Pig	27	do	do	do	do	
	John L. Hodgson	60	do	Surgeon	do	do	
	James Graham	32	do	Schoolmaster	do	do	
	Agnes Workman	27	female		do	do	
	John Ferguson	29	male	Tailor	do	do	
	Mary Ferguson & 4 ch.	29	female		do	do	
	James Irving	47	male	Tailor	do	do	
	Ann Irving & 3 children	47	female		do	do	
	Robert Ross	21	male	Draper	do	do	
	George Bell	23	do	do	do	do	
	Thomas Pearson	22	do	Farmer	do	do	
	Thomas Cartmer	25	do	Carpenter	do	do	
	William Gibson	42	do	Stonecutter	do	do	
	Ann Gibson & 6 childr.	44	female		do	do	
	Thomas Milbern	45	male	Farmer	do	do	
	Isabella Milbern & 7 ch.	48	female		do	do	
	James Brayton	42	male	do	do	do	
	Isaac Brown	24	do	do	do	do	
	John Rennison	40	do	Tailor	do	do	
	Jane Rennison & 6 chil.	43	female		do	do	
	Isaac Lawson	37	male	Farmer	do	do	
	Henry Bousfield	36	do	Shopkeeper	do	do	
	Richard Bousfield	30	do	do	do	do	

Schooner Telegraph, S. L. Blanchard.

Name	Age	Sex	Occupation	Country belonging	Country destination
William Muney	25	male	Farmer	G. Britain	U. States
William Percival	67	do	do	do	do
Esther Rotherby	12	female		do	do
Henry I. Sharpe	22	male	Merchant	Ireland	do
James M'Carter	36	do	Laborer	do	do
Peggy M'Carter	24	female		do	do
James M'Carter	26	male	Laborer	do	do
James Wallace	27	do	do	do	do
Thomas Dugan	21	do	do	do	do
Charles Dugan	22	do	do	do	do
Charles Walker & child	52	female		do	do
Elizabeth Walker & ch.	50	female		do	do
Daniel O'Neal	22	male		do	do
A. O'Neal & 2 children	38	female		do	do
Patrick O'Neal	23	male		do	do
Nancy O'Neal & 2 chil.	22	female		do	do
Andrew How	17	male	Laborer	do	do
Thos. Vance & child	33	do	do	do	do
Margaret Vance	54	female		do	do
Rebecca Vance	23	do		do	do
Alexander Wilkey	30	male	Weaver	do	do
Samuel Stevenson	40	do	Farmer	do	do
Daniel Conahaut	55	do	Tailor	do	do
Nelly Conahaut	21	female		do	do
John Brown	17	male	Farmer	do	do
Brady Bracils	24	do		do	do
Mary Ann M'Cally	12	female		do	do
Nancy Wilson	45	do		do	do
James Morris	16	male		do	do
Elizabeth Conyham	51	female		do	do
Francis Montgomery	22	male	Farmer	do	do
Agnes Montgomery	26	female		do	do
Nancy M'Farland	45	do		do	do
William Progue	21	male	Farmer	do	do
Richard S. Dunn	21	do	do	do	do
Dennis Moran	25	do	Weaver	do	do
Daniel L. O. Donaldson	32	do		G. Britain	do
George Greaves	41	do	Farmer	do	do

LIST of Passengers, &c.—Quarter ending September 30, 1820.

Custom House, with the name of the Collector.	Names of Passengers.	Age.	Sex.	Occupation.	Country to which they belong.	Country of which they intend to become inhab's	Ship or vessel, with the name of the Master or Commander.
Philadelphia, John Steele.	Sarah Greaves & 3 chil.	37	female		G. Britain	U. States	Schooner Telegraph, J. L. Blanchard.
	James Musgrave	26	male	Farmer	do	do	
	W. Musgrave & 3 chil.	25	do		do	do	
	Francis Cottam	26	female	Farmer	do	do	
	Mary Cottam & 3 chil.	20	male		do	do	
	Vincent Cottam	46	do	Farmer	do	do	
	William Sampson	45	female		do	do	
	M. A. Sampson & 8 chil.	59	male	Farmer	do	do	
	James Melvin	62	female		do	do	
	Isabella Melvin	25	female		do	do	
	Elizabeth Melvin	20	do		do	do	
	Mary Melvin	18	do		do	do	
	Jane Melvin	40	do		do	do	
	Mary Melvin	13	do		do	do	
	Mary Moore	25	male	Farmer	do	do	
	Hugh Irwin	26	do	do	do	do	
	Joseph Delany	64	do	do	do	do	Sloop Rachel, William Field.
	Alexander Porter	60	female		do	do	
	Jane Porter	25	do		do	do	
	Jane Porter, jr.	22	do		do	do	
	Ann Porter	18	do		do	do	
	Mary Porter	24	male	Farmer	do	do	
	James Porter	20	do	do	do	do	
	Hichman Porter	40	do	do	do	do	
	John Dodd	39	female		do	do	
	Eliz. Dodd & 6 children	28	male	Farmer	do	do	
	John Alexander						

Name	Age	Sex	Occupation	G. Britain	U. States	Ship
Mary Alexander & 2 ch.	30	female	Farmer		do	Schooner Horatio, C. Hallet.
Michael Oaks	20	male	Farmer	do	do	
Cath. Flanagan & child	24	female	do	do	do	
Nicholas Hanna	20	male		Ireland	do	
George Black	30	do		do	do	
Jane Black	25	female	Weaver	do	do	
William Pollard	25	male	do	do	do	
James Black	25	do	do	do	do	
Michael Bradley	27	do		do	do	
Mrs. Bradley	23	female	Spinster	do	do	
Jno. Murray	28	male	Farmer	do	do	
Mary Danby & 4 chil.	37	female	Spinster	do	do	
Richard Dizant	30	male	Farmer	do	do	
Mrs. Dizant & 2 chil.	25	female	Spinster	do	do	
Owen Maun	28	male	Farmer	do	do	
M. Maun	26	female	Spinster	do	do	
Edward Clark	37	male	Weaver	do	do	
S. Clark & 6 children	28	female	Spinster	do	do	
Peter Markee	26	male	Weaver	do	do	
Thomas Markee	24		Laborer	do	do	
M. Duffee & 7 children		do	do	do	do	
D. M'Ibee & 6 children		do	do	do	do	
Mr. M'Fadden		do,		do	do	
Mrs. M'Fadden & child		female		do	do	
Mrs. Crawford & 2 chil.		do		do	do	
P. Doonan		male		do	do	Schooner Morning Star, M. Drinkwater.
E. Bill & 5 children		do		do	do	
Isaac Coleman		do		do	do	
M. Bothy		do		do	do	
L. Keene		do		do	do	
I. M'Divot		do		do	do	
L. M'Kindwick		do		do	do	
Thos. Caves & 2 chil.		do		do	do	
I. Orr		do		do	do	
I. Anderson		do		do	do	
S. Anderson		do		do	do	
B. Baine		do		do	do	
W. Cisket		do		do	do	

LIST of Passengers, &c.—Quarter ending June 30, 1820.

Custom House, with the name of the Collector.	Names of Passengers.	Age.	Sex.	Occupation.	Country to which they belong.	Country of which they intend to become inhab's	Ship or Vessel, with the name of the Master or Commander.
PHILADELPHIA, John Steele.	J. Malony		male		Ireland	U. States	Schooner Morning Star, M. Drinkwater.
	J. Kelly		do		do	do	
	M. Bordon		do		do	do	
	G. Hannon		do		do	do	
	A. N. Black		do		do	do	
	E. Alexander		do		do	do	
	J. Alexander		do		do	do	
	James Thompson	22	do	Laborer	G. Britain	do	Brig Ceres, Patterson.
	John Polen	20	do	do	do	do	
	Francis Wrey	21	do	do	do	do	
	William Waring	30	do	do	do	do	
	Jno. Waring	21	do	do	do	do	
	H. Horatius	30	do	do	do	do	
	Francis Wilson	23	do	Merchant	do	do	
	Jane Wilson & child	22	female		do	do	
	Hannah Quinn	58	do		do	do	
	Mary Mellon	22	do		do	do	
	William M'Evoy	24	male	Laborer	do	do	
	Rosa M'Evoy & child	55	female		do	do	
	Mary Moore	23	do		do	do	
	Allen Patterson	22	male	Laborer	do	do	
	George Dawson	16	do	Farmer	do	do	
	Marg. Warren	17	female	Spinster	do	do	
	Bill Nichols & 3 chil.	25	do	Merchant	do	do,	
	Samuel Crawford	17	do	Clergyman	do	do	
	Jno. Kennedy	35	do		do	do	
	Hessey Kennedy & child	25	do		do	do	

Name	Age	Sex	Occupation	G. Britain	U. States	Ship
Samuel Smith	19	male	Merchant	do	do	
James Smith	12	do	Laborer	do	do	
George Smith	27	do	Farmer	do	do	
Mrs. M'Kee	25	female	do	do	do	
William Ritchie	22	male	Farmer	do	do	
William Alexander	35	do		do	do	
Margaret Service	12	female	Spinster	do	do	
Hugh Dickson	35	male	Clergyman	do	do	
Rose Doyle and child	27	female	Laborer	do	do	
George Gray	35	male	Farmer	do	do	
William Hunter	40	do		do	do	
Robert Neal	26	do		do	do	
Ann J. Stewart	22	female		do	do	Schooner Cherub, William Athearn.
Mrs. Patterson	28	do	Spinster	do	do	
R. Bemis	40	male	Merchant	do	do	
William Cottrell	29	do	do	St. Johns	do	
Edward Thitts	25	do	Shoemaker	do	do	
Augustus Broadbent	26	do	Merchant	England	do	
Joshua Bunting	27	do	do	U. States	do	
John Gardner	35	do	Fisherman	do	do	Brig Calcutta, J. S. Winslow.
Greenleaf Morris	22	do	Merchant	do	do	
Henry Blanchard	37	do	do	do	do	Brig Eight Sons, D. Low.
Jos. L. Hiesk	13	do	Glass manufac.	Germany	do	
James Stafford	38	do	Seaman	U. States	do	Schr. Neptune, E. Jewitt.
Ashbel Shelburn	36	do	do	do	do	Schr. Tekeli, Lyman Carlow.
Thomas Jones	20	do	Merchant	do	do	Schr. Planter, George Lapham.
M. Birds	25	do	Mariner	G. Britain	do	Brig Alert, E. Snow.
Benjamin Morgan	37	do	Merchant	U. States	do	Schr. General Brewer, Thomas Rodgers.
Charles Grant	28	do	do	do	do	
William H. Tyler	23	do	do	do	do	
Josiah Hastings	31	do	do	do	do	
Cyrus Chemry	22	do	do	do	do	
Mrs. Whitney and ch.	32	female		do	do	
Mrs. Price	35	do		do	do	
Mrs. Wheeler	35	do		do	do	
Mrs. Howard	28	do		do	do	
Mrs. Rodgers	24	do		do	do	
Mrs. Poole	21	do		do	do	

BOSTON AND CHARLESTOWN, H. A. S. Dearborn.

LIST of Passengers, &c.—Quarter ending September 30, 1820.

Custom House, with the name of the Collector.	Names of Passengers.	Age.	Sex.	Occupation.	Country to which they belong.	Country of which they intend to become inhab's	Ship or Vessel, with the name of the Master or Commander.
Boston and Charlestown, H. A. S. Dearborn.	Mrs. Miller	18	female		U. States	U. States	Schooner General Brewer, Thomas Rodgers.
	Lucy Wiston	13	do		do	do	
	Mrs. Robinson	26	do		do	do	
	E. B. Homer	30	do		Nova Scotia	Nova Scotia	
	Salome Tasden	56	do		do	do	
	John M'Neil	39	male		do	do	
	James Kirby	30	do	Printer	U. States	U. States	
	Leonard D. Gildart	21	do	Trader	Ireland	do	
	Jos. T. Smith	27	do	Mariner	do	do	Brig Rebecca, Henry Snow,
	John Lewis	34	do	do	do	do	
	John Voyle	31	do	do	do	do	
	John Thomas	30	do	do	do	do	
	John Williams	36	do	do	do	do	
	William Smith	31	do	do	do	do	
	George Sager	38	do	do	do	do	
	Peter Johnson	32	do	do	do	do	
	Antonius Boniface	34	do	do	do	do	
	John Delacruz	45	do	do	do	do	
	Domingo Ambrosio	21	do	do	do	do	
	Francis Fernandez	41	do	do	do	do	
	Joseph Martini	40	do	do	do	do	
	Adolphus Lacoste	21	do	do	do	do	
	Emml. Fernandez	20	do	do	do	do	
	Antonio Gunwales	28	do	do	do	do	
	Jos. I. King	26	do	do	do	do	
	Kemp Southcomb	26	do	Midshipman	do	do	Put on board the Rebecca as a guard.
	Jas. K. Wallette		do		do	do	

Name	Age	Sex	Occupation	Native Country	Destination	Ship
John Hansbury		male	Seaman	Ireland	U. States	
Jos. Pewe		do	do	do	do	
M. Ireland		do	do	do	do	
Blackman		do	Cook	U. States	do	
Robert Morland	35	do	Merchant	do	do	Brig Neptune's Barge, Samuel Watts.
Caleb Sherman	25	do	Farmer	Halifax	Halifax	Brig Romp, N. Crosby.
Thomas Cassaday	38	do	Painter	Boston	U. States	
Lewis Bailey	25	do		Halifax	Halifax	
George Creighton	53	do		Nova Scotia	U. States	
John Garino	22	do	Ploughman	Halifax	do	
Susan Goodwin	21	female	Milliner	St. Johns	do	
Mary Cummins	33	do		Ireland	do	
Edward Eaton	22	male	Weaver	Halifax	Halifax	
Brinton Gardner	20	do	Laborer	U. States	U. States	
Martin Newton	36	do	Sailor	do	do	
David Hall	33	do	do	do	do	
John Titus	34	do	Cook & stewa.	do	do	Brig Telemachus, Geo. Wood.
Peter Parodi	39	do	Carpenter	Italy	do	
Francis Robbins	44	do	Bricklayer	U. States	do	
John Pratt	29	do	Merchant	do	do	
John Wilson	30	do		do	do	
Mary E. Landais & 3 ch.	30	female		Martinico	N. Brunswick	Brig Olive, J. Lincoln.
Capt. William Lovitt	35	male	Seaman	St. Johns	do	Schr. Aristides, T. M'Intire.
Capt. H. Lovitt	40	do	do	do	do	Schooner Enterprize, J. Morton.
D. Peas	30	do	Merchant	Lubec	do	
Miss Peas	30	female		do	do	
I. F. Taxon		male	Merchant	do	do	
Isseachar Masters		do	Sea captain	U. States	U. States	
William Cole		do		do	do	
Samuel G. Bradlie		do		do	do	Ship Paragon, D. Wilds.
Bill		do		Sandwich Isl.	do	
George B. Bolton	50	do	Gentleman	New York	New-York	Schooner Victory, Samuel Barker.
William Chever	27	do	Merchant	Newfoundl.	Boston	
Adolphus Emerson	23	do	Butcher	Roxbury	Roxbury	
John Duvall	23	do	Trader	Halifax	Halifax	
Francis Fulham	38	do	Spinster	Ireland	New York	
William Canaan	31	do	Carpenter	do	Connecticut	
Patrick Callahan	36	do	Gardener	do	Boston	

LIST of Passengers, &c.—Quarter ending September 30, 1820.

Custom House, with the name of the Collector.	Names of Passengers.	Age.	Sex.	Occupation.	Country to which they belong.	Country of which they intend to become inh'bts.	Ship or Vessel, with the Name of the Master or Commander.
BOSTON AND CHARLESTOWN, H. A. S. Dearborn.	Lewis Goodwin	37	male	Mariner	U. States	U. States	Schr. Zephyr, T. Ripley.
	Chas. Copriel	42	do	Gentleman	do	do	
	Geo. Tyson	22	do	Merchant	do	do	Schr. Cherub, Wm. Athearn.
	Jno. Smith	31	female	Farmer	do	do	
	Mrs. Smith	27	male		G. Britain	G. Britain	
	Wm. Murdoch	19	do	Merchant	Boston	Boston	Schr. General Greene, J. Bears
	James M'Nab	30	do	do	do	do	
	W. A. Brabine	28	female	do	do	do	
	Mrs. Hoop	20	male		do	do	
	Thos. Walsh	40	female		do	do	
	Mrs. Walsh	36			do	do	
	Francis G. Clark	29	male	Mariner	U. States	U. States	Ship Gallatin, S. Towne.
	Peter Ekinson	36	do	Carpenter	Sweden	do	Brig Samaritan, Benj. Gray.
	J. Jughune	35	do	Merchant	G. Britain	N.Brunswick	Sloop Milledgeville, G. Knight.
	Captain Clark	35	do	Mariner	N. Brunsw'k	do	
	Captain Smith	40	female	do	do	do	
	Mrs. Smith	49	male	Mechanic	do	do	
	G. Winslow	30	female	Lady	U. States	U. States	
	Mrs. Morton	36	male	Carpenter	Portland	Portland	
	Mr. Walker	30	do	Merchant	Maine	Maine	
	Mr. Putnam	25	female		Boston	Boston	
	Allice Clark	25	male	Tailor	Canada	Canada	
	S. Stephen	40	do	Farmer	N.Brunswick	N.Brunswick	
	Mr. Harman	16	do	do	Maine	Maine	
	G. Edmonds	18	do	do	Gloucester	Gloucester	
	J. Litchfield				do		
	R. Therr		do	do	Nova Scotia	U. Canada	

Name	Age	Sex	Occupation	From	To	Ship
John Downing	28	male	Cordwainer	N. Brunsw'k	N. Brunsw'k	Ship Eagle, Wm. H. Davis.
Wm. H. Davis	40	do	Mariner	U. States	U. States	
Eliab Grimes	27	do	do	do	do	
John Guvin	23	do	do	do	do	Schr. Paragon, R. Sesson.
A. M. D. Hart	28	do	Merchant	Holland	do	
J. P. Fisher	30	do	Mariner	U. States	do	
Lieut. A. M'Kenzie	22	do	B. officer			
L. G. Hamilton	25	do	Merchant	Teneriffe		Schr. Albert, J. Sharkfen.
James Bonce	24	do	Gentleman	U. States	Boston	
Caleb Merritt	54	do	Merchant	N. Brunsw'k	N. Brunsw'k	Schr. Dolphin, J. Pole.
John Milligan	48	do		Boston	Boston	
Eliza Buchanan	30	female		Eastport.	Eastport	
John Sawyer	20	male		do	do	
John Bullock	21	do		dp	do	Brig Hope, Geo. B. Hall.
Chas. Collins	29	do		do	do	
Fredk. W. Camerford	35	do	Mariner	U. States	U. States	Put on board by the Consul.
Edward Briggs	30	do	do	do	do	Schr. Rob Roy, M. Thompson.
Caleb Easton	25	do	do	do	do	Ship Jasper, T. Crooker.
John Snyder	29	do	do	do	do	
Gaston Grord	16	do	Gentleman	Martinico	Martinico	
Nathaniel Pierce		do	Mariner	U. States	U. States	
Jas. Blakhest		do		G. Britain		
Eleanor Salver		do		do		Ship Meteor, R. Glover.
E. Appleton	35	do	Merchant	U. States	do	Ship Suffolk, J. T. Trott.
Saml. Massey & child	35	do	Farmer	England	do	Ship Hope & Sally, D. Oliver.
William Arnote	15	do	Mariner	U. States	do	Brig Havre Packet, M. Libby.
B. J. L. Jeune	19	do		Amsterdam	do	Brig Archer, C. Dexter.
Philip Ammidon	42	do	Merchant	U. States	do	Brig Catherine, A. Windsor.
F. Chapeau	35	do	do	France.	do	Ship Mercury, Samuel Nicholls.
Lambert Dexter	25	do	do	U. States	do	
Saml. B. Bradford	24	do		do	do	Schr. Exertion, Jas. Windsor.
Jas. Roberts & 2 child'n	22	do		Scotland	do	
John Richardson	25	do	Printer			Schr. Cherub, Wm. Athearn.
Jno. L. Leuston	22	do	Trader	Nova Scotia	Nova Scotia	Brig Jane, Chas. Hart.
Benj. Brookhouse	21	do	Farmer	U. States	do	
John Smith	16	do	Seaman	do	U. States	Schr. Victory, Saml. Barker.
John Cassaday	37	do	do	Halifax	Halifax	
Miss A. White	30	do		Haverhill	Haverhill	

LIST of Passengers, &c.—Quarter ending September 30, 1820.

Custom House, with the Name of the Collector	Names of Passengers	Age	Sex	Occupation	Country to which they belong.	Country of which they intend to become inhb'ts	Ship or Vessel, with the name of the Master or Commander.
BOSTON AND CHARLESTOWN, H. A. S. Dearborn.	Thos. Edwards	25	male	Artist	England	England	Schooner Victory, Samuel Barker.
	Adolphus Emmerson	25	do	Butcher	Roxbury	Roxbury	
	John Hutton	27	do	Merchant	N. London		
	John Dunnell	25	do	Trader	Scotland	Nova Scotia	
	Edwd. Kearney	32	do	do	Boston	Boston	
	Thos. Christy	21	do	Hatter	Scotland	do	
	John Boyd	28	do	Farmer	do	Kentucky	
	Eliz. do. & 2 child'n	26	female			do	Schr. Lucy, N. Williams.
	Edmund Hopkins	30	male	Laborer	Dublin	do	
	Patrick Thanny	25	do	do	Cork	do	
	John Micklemac	26	do	do	do	do	
	Benj. B. Etter	27	do	Watchmaker	Halifax	Pernambuco	Schr. Edward, John Carlisle.
	Daniel Gibbs	25	do	Mariner	U. States	U. States	
	B. H. Shirland	23	do	Shoemaker	do	do	
	Margaret Glend	24	female	Seamstress	St. John	do	
	Mary Moore	20	do	do	do	do	
	Wm. Stafford	40	male	Farmer	G. Britain	do	
	Fanny do. & 5 child'n	40	female			do	
	Thos. Scott	24	male	do	do	do	
	Patrick Convall	21	do	do	do	do	Schr. George, Stephen Berry.
	Mary Cary & child	55	female			do	
	Nancy Colvin	22	do	Laborer	Ireland	do	
	Chas. Boyles	27	male	do	do	do	
	John Derning	26	do	Tailor	do	do	
	James Cook	56	do	Merchant	do	do	Brig Union, B. H. Wade,
	Peter Niver	29	do		Martinico	Martinique	
	John Hubbart	54	do	Gentleman	U. States		

Name	Age	Sex	Occupation			Vessel
Jane Hubbard & 2 chil'n	35	female		U. States	Boston	Sloop Anson, John Ross.
Sarah Todd & child	31	do		do	do	
Sarah Mackerell	38	male		do	do	
James Dickson	46	do	Merchant	do	do	
Wm. H. Elliott	24	female	Gentleman	G. Britain	do	
Phebe Robinson	40	do		do	do	
Mary Phillips	20	male	Grocer	do	do	
Thomas Freeman	23	female		do	do	
Mary Ann Freeman	23	do	Servant	do	do	
Elizabeth Stoher	60	do	Merchant	do	do	
Moses Ferguson	23	do	do	Boston	do	
Wm. Combs	40	do	do	do	do	
Benj. Fay	23	do	do	U. States	do	Brig Silkworm, N. Rogers.
Joseph H. Dorr	48	do	do	do	do	Ship Franklin, B. Ring.
Benj. Morgan	38	do	do	do	do	Schr. Gen. Green, J. Bears.
Samuel H. Haws	21	do	do	do	do	
W. S. Shinner	40	do	do	do	do	
Chas. Lawrence	25	do	do	do	do	
C. H. Hammet	29	do	do	do	do	
Pierce Lomargan	40	do	do	Halifax	Halifax	
Wm. Winslow	35	do	do	N. Carolina	N. Carolina	
Wm. P. Filler	30	do	do	Boston	Boston	
Edwd. Stafford	15	do		Salem	Salem	
Mrs. Stafford	60	female		do	do	
Mrs. O'Brien	40	do		Halifax	Halifax	
Judy Dounert	30	do		do	do	
H. Delharty	25	male		do	do	
Jno. Abrahams	35	do	do	U. States	U. States	Brig Swift, Amos Hill.
Chas. Fessenden	25	do	Carpenter	do	do	Schr. Adeline, A. Ellis.
E. Southward	28	do	Trader	Lisbon	do	Brig Despatch, M. Dearing.
John Antonio	35	do		Ireland		
Francis Burk	25	do		Ireland		
Jos. Posannus	30	do	Merchant	U. States	do	Ship Charles, Wm. Pusser.
Thos. Willis	33	do	Shoemaker	Britain	do	
Wm. Scott	20	female	Seaman	do	G. Britain	
Mrs. Brown	42	do		do	do	Schr. Cherub, Wm. Athearn.
Mrs. Loveland	26	do		do	do	
Mrs. Williamson	20	do		do	do	

LIST of Passengers, &c.—Quarter ending September 30, 1820.

Custom House, with the name of the Collector.	Names of Passengers.	Age.	Sex.	Occupation.	Country to which they belong.	Country of which they intend to become inhab's	Ship or Vessel, with the name of the Master or Commander.
BOSTON AND CHARLESTOWN, H. A. S. Dearborn.	Mrs. Sawyer	50	female		U. States	U. States	Schooner Cherub, Wm. Athearn.
	Mrs. Reeding	44	do		do	do	
	Mrs. Emmsley	19	do		do	do	
	Mr. Williamson	29	male	Merchant	G. Britain	do	
	Mr. Messersmith	23	do	do	U. States	do	
	Wm. Bayne	19	do	do	G. Britain	do	
	Alexr. Bayne	22	do	do	do	do	
	John Rich	38	do	Musician	France	France	
	Mrs. Rich	24	female		do	do	
	Stephen Oxnard	45	male	Mariner	U. States	U. States	Ship Concord, Seth Storer.
	Oran House	21	do	do	do	do	Schr. Olive Branch, A. Cooper.
	John B. Davis	31	do	Stud't at Law	do	do	Schr. Miller, A. Brooks.
	Joseph King	37	do	Merchant	do	do	
	Mrs. King	24	female		do	do	
	Chas. Cleland	35	male	Stud't at Law	do	do	
	Ezekiel Tilden	16	do	Shipmaster	do	do	
	Bella Lenistor	14	female		do	do	
	Sister of ditto	39	do		do	do	
	David Putnam	49	male	Merchant	do	do	
	Isaac Hobart	49	do	Farmer	do	do	
	P. B. Hovey	31	do	Trader	do	do	
	J. Allen	26	do	Merchant	do	do	
	Benj. Dodd	36	do	Gentleman	do	do	
	Madame Jessee	26	female		do	do	
	W. L. Williams	36	male	Merchant	do	do	Ship Falcon, Lewis.
	R. Kershaw & 2 chil'n	26	female		G. Britain	do	
	John Slater	22	male		do	do	

Name	Age	Sex	Occupation	Where born	Destination	Vessel
Eliza. Mason & 2 chil.	28	female		G. Britain	U. States	Brig Dingley, William Springer.
Thomas Law	22	male	Carpenter	U. States	do	
David Williams	25	do	Seaman	do	do	
Thomas Jewett	12	do		do	Dist. of Col.	Schooner Victory, S. Barker.
Thomas Brown	31	do	Merchant	Dist. Colum.	Halifax	
Matthew Alman	21	do	do	Halifax	U. States	
William Coen	20	do	Printer	U. States	do	
Samuel Baker	43	do	Butcher	do	do	
Thomas Sloan	21	do	Weaver	Ireland	do	
Ann Sloan & 3 childr.		female		do	do	
John Cammel		male	Sailor	do	do	
William Cammal	40	do	do	do	do	
James Parnake	49	do	Housekeeper	G. Britain	do	Schooner Ranger, R. Freeman.
William Fletcher	22	do	Weaver	do	do	Brig Falcon, J. W. Bingham.
James Bromley	14	do	do	do	do	
Philip Bromley	10	do	do	do	do	
Roger Bromley	22	do	do	Massachu'ts	do	
Hollis Thayer	40	do	do	Ireland	do	Schooner Hope, James Dunn.
Sarah Hurds & 5 chil.	24	female		England	do	
Martha Baker	32	do		U. States	do	
Jones Very	17	male	Shipmaster	St. Johns	do	Brig Ruthy, N. Lindsay.
Cath. Marple & 3 chil.	24	female		do	do	Sloop Milledgeville, G. Knight.
Elizabeth Lufkin	22	do		Boston	Boston	
Elizabeth Sears	26	do		Dominico	N. York	
R. Bloyd and infant	30	do		Boston	Boston	
M. Boland	16	male	Gentleman	U. States	do	
John Stewart	23	do	Mariner	do	U. States	Schooner General Brooks, J. J. Perry.
William White	26	do	do	do	do	
Thomas Barb	13	do	Joiner	St. Johns	do	
John Spear	35	do	Farmer	Boston	do	Schooner Catharine, S. Horton.
Springer	26	do	Carpenter	U. States	do	Schooner Mystic, A. Grove.
Benj. Remar	35	do	Corder	do	do	
John Perry	39	do	do	do	do	
Thomas M. Payne	25	do	Mariner	do	do	Schooner Jane, J. Miller.
George Hobard	30	do	do	do	do	
Edward Doary	35	do	Merchant	do	do	Schooner Albert, J. Schackford.
John Foster	35	do	Mariner	do	do	Schooner Nancy and Mary, J. Sweetzer.
Terence Ferguson	27	do	Laborer	Ireland	do	Schooner Hope, David Patch.

LIST of Passengers, &c.—Quarter ending September 30, 1820.

Custom House, with the name of the Collector.	Names of Passengers.	Age.	Sex.	Occupation.	Country to which they belong.	Country of which they intend to become inhab's	Ship or Vessel, with the name of the Master or Commander.
BOSTON AND CHARLESTOWN, H. A. S. Dearborn.	Edward Logue	23	male	Laborer	Ireland	U. States	Schooner Hope, David Patch.
	John Cassaday	29	do	Brewer	do	do	
	Barney M'Conney	23	do	Laborer	do	do	
	Michael M'Bride	25	do	Carpenter	do	do	
	John Renon	37	do	Laborer	do	do	
	Michael Connor	55	do	do	do	do	
	Patrick Connor	23	do	do	do	do	
	Patrick Pelkington	42	do	do	do	do	
	John Dougherty	25	do	Weaver	do	do	
	Jane Connor & 6 child.	40	female		do	do	
	William Bagot	21	male	Mariner	England	do	Schooner Post Boy, Lemuel Otis.
	Thomas M'Gregor	20	do	do	Scotland	do	
	John Thompson	22	do	do	England	do	
	Joseph Lear	27	do	do	St. Peters	N. Orleans	
	Robert Dawson	30	do	Trader	Halifax	Halifax	Brig Romp, N. Crosby.
	George Sewall	28	do	Tinker	do	do	
	Charles H. J. Lane	18	do	Lieut. of army	England	England	
	Frances Seymour	33	female		Canada	Canada	
	Mrs. Hicks & child	28	do		Demarara	Boston	Schooner Roxana, William Venall.
	Daniel Marple	24	male	Carpenter	U. States	U. States	
	David J. Pollard	27	do	Merchant	do	do	
	Henry B. Bishop	27	do	Watchmaker	do	do	
	Solomon Ingalls	62	do	Schoolmaster	do	do	
	Thomas M. Woodbridge	55	do	Merchant	do	do	Schooner Margaret, E. Bradford.
	Moses Humphrey	41	do	do	do	do	
	David B. Moore	40	do	do	do	do	
	Moses Pond, jun.	21	do	do	do	do	

Name	Age	Sex	Occupation	From	To	Vessel
John McGivin	30	male	Merchant	U. States	U. States	Schooner Galaxy, W. Kimpton.
Mary Findley	38	female	Merchant	do	do	Schooner Enterprize, J. Morton.
Cloutman		male	do	do	do	
Russel Lincoln	26	do	do	do	do	
Jacob Comegys	21	do	do	do	do	
J. Perkins	24	do	Ship carpenter	do	do	
J. Groves	55	do	Stonecutter	do	do	
J. Crotes	24	do		do	do	
N. Sawyer		do	Merchant	do	do	
John Richardson	48	do	Merchant	Halifax	Halifax	Schooner General Greene, J. Bears.
Terence O'Conner	50	do	do	U. States	U. States	
Anthony Gripes	30	do	do	Halifax	Halifax	
Mary Maguire	26	female		do	do	
W. Andrews	15	male	Merchant	do	do	Schooner Cherub, William Athearn.
Mrs. Robertson	48	female	Merchant	do	do	
Mrs. Street and child		do		do	do	
William Bird	20	male	Merchant	G. Britain	G. Britain	
Alexander Mitchell	28	do	Trader	U. States	U. States	Schooner Sally, L. Lawrence.
Leonard Gildert	22	do	do	G. Britain	G. Britain	
John Emmsley	25	do	Baker	do	do	
John Gardner	35	do	Mariner	U. States	U, States	
Thomas Fothege	27	do	Pump & bl. m.			
Edward Walker	28	do	Shipwright			
Thomas Western	38	do	Mariner	U. States	U. States	Brig Economy, E. A. Shaw.
N. W. Skillings	45	do	Merchant	do	do	Brig John Hannah, A. Patterson.
Jos. Traman	26	do	Barber	do	do	
Benjamin Wheelwright	22	do	Merchant	do	do	
John Thomas	30	do	do	do	do	
Joseph Cookayne	25	do	Book keeper	Surinam	Surinam	Brig Oracle, E. Freeman.
Solomon R. Newnes	50	female	Merchant	Liverpool	Liverpool	Schooner Victory, S. Barker.
Susan P. Taylor	45	male	Merchant	do	do	
William P. Taylor	25	do	do	Boston	Boston	
Josiah Nickerson	22	do	Laborer	do	do	
Marks Mackay	38	do	Merchant	New-York	N. York	Schooner Miller, A. Brooks.
W. M. Johnson wife&ch.	52	do	Bishop	Canada	Canada	
John Kelly	37	do				
Abel Sawyer	34	do	Mariner	U. States	U. States	Schooner Laurel, Th. C. Stevens,
William Burns	25	do				

LIST of Passengers, &c.—Quarter ending September 30, 1820.

Custom House, with the name of the Collector.	Names of Passengers.	Age.	Sex.	Occupation.	Country to which they belong.	Country of which they intend to become inhab's	Ship or Vessel, with the name of the Master or Commander.
BOSTON AND CHARLESTOWN, H. A. S. Dearborn.	Nicholas Brohant	23	male	Mariner	Isl. Guernsey	U. States	Schooner Fame, John Wales.
	O. H. Thorpe	21	do	Engraver	U. States	do	Brig Rambler, H. Bishop.
	Ambrose Elliot	47	do	Mariner	do	do	Schooner Juno, Thomas Stoddart.
	David Young	34	do	do	do	do	
	Lazara Morules	35	do	Cameldriver	Spain	Maine	
	Silas Smith	25	do	Merchant	Maine	U. States	Sloop Governor, A. H. Stevens.
	Richard B. Jones	34	do	Late Con. U. S.	U. States	do	Ship Mary, William Smith.
	F. A. Jones & 2 childr.	30	female	Servant			
	John F. Oliver	21	male	Merchant			
	Joseph C. Morgan	36	do	do			
	John H. Nicholas	17	do				Put on board by U. S. Consul at Marseilles.
	Jabez Mann		do				Found secreted on board 3 days after leaving [Marseilles.
	Oliver		do				
DIS. PORTSMOUTH, T. Upham.	James Burroughs	24	do	Merchant	U. States	U. States	Schooner Eliza, Stocker.
	Benjamin Rhodes	40	do	Shipmaster	do	do	
	Wm. M'Cawley	35	do	Laborer	Ireland	do	
	Fanny M'Cawley & 4 ch.	28	female		do	do	
NEW LONDON, T. H. Cushing.	Alexander Gale	55	male	Merchant	U. States	do	Ship Alexander, Griswold, S. Latimer.
	John Wilson	21	do	Seaman	England	do	Ship Martha.
	John Segrave	24	do	Merchant	Ireland	do	Ship Aristobulus.
	Thomas Sauderland	30	do	Cooper	England	do	
PETERSBURG, I. Jones.	Ann Sauderland	28	female		do	do	
	Daniel Downes	30	male	Shoemaker	do	do	
	Han. Downes & 4 child.	25	female		do	do	
	William M'Kee	35	male	Joiner	do	do	Ship Tobacco Plant.
	Martha M'Kee	23	female		do	do	
	John Marsden	20	male	Joiner	do	do	

Name	Age	Sex	Occupation	Country of	Destination	Vessel
KENNEBUNK, James Storer.						
William Chambers	15	male	Seaman	England	U. States	Schooner Beverly, S. Bradley.
John J. Cobleast	34	do	do	N. Orleans	do	
CHARLESTON, James R. Pringle.						
John P. Vallet	27	do	Merchant	Bordeaux	do	Sloop Lady Washington, Waterman.
Francis Sage	42	do	do	U. States	do	
Oliver O. Hara	31	do	do	do	do	
Charles Sully	36	do	do	do	do	
William Travers	30	do	Mariner	do	do	
John Williams	24	do	do	do	do	
Mrs. M'Cauley	20	female	Shoemaker	Spain	St. Augustine	
John Carraras	29	male	do	do	do	
B. Janeworth	20	do	Mariner	do	do	
Captain Walton	26	do	do	G. Britain	do	
Madame Chimenard	28	female	Shopkeeper	France	Charleston	Schooner Mary, Coleman.
John Oates	60	male	do	G. Britain	do	
John Burke	28	do	do	do	do	
Anthony Colingen	27	do	do	France	do	
William Canuet	32	do	do	do	do	
Major Bird	42	do	Officer U. S. ar.	U. States	do	
Lieut. Leigle	20	do	do	do	do	Sloop James, Vincent.
Holmes	19	do	do	do	do	
Humphreys	19	do	do	do	do	
John Barclay	35	do	Merchant	do	Havana	
John Wheeler	33	do	do	France	Charleston	Schooner Comet, N. Forsyth.
William Jerassy	30	do	do	G. Britain	do	
Bottelier	38	do	Mariner	do	U. States	
Ferguson	25	do	do	France	do	Ship Portia, Silliman.
M'Guire	30	do	Merchant	do	do	
Arsdoff	32	do	do	U. States	do	
Le Clair	27	do	Baker	do	do	
Rachait	35	female	Seamstress	do	do	Schooner Jane, Darling.
Niel Campbell	25	male	Merchant	U. States	do	
James Pearson	44	do	Mariner	G. Britain	do	
John Brown	25	do	do	U. States	do	
William Marshall	35	do	do	do	do	
James M. Matthewson	35	do	Gentleman	do	St. Augustine	Ship Arab, Bingham.
Pierce Rowe	26	do	Farmer	G. Britain	do	Brig Christopher, Hayward.
Franklin Gorham	35	do	Merchant	U. States	U. States	Sloop General Washington, Buckley
Joel Dickinson	40	do	do	do	do	Lady Washington, Waterman.

LIST of Passengers, &c.—Quarter ending September 30, 1820.

Custom House, with the name of the Collector.	Names of Passengers.	Age.	Sex.	Occupation.	Country to which they belong.	Country of which they intend to become inh'bs.	Ship or Vessel, with the name of the Master or Commander.
CHARLESTON. Jas. R. Pringle.	John Andrews	30	male	Mariner	U. States	U. States	
	George Delespine	32	do	Merchant	Spain	St Augustine	
	Anthony Tray	28	do	ʚɔ	do	do	
	Joseph Burnet	25	do	Mariner	do	do	
	Francis Saltus	60	do	Merchant	U. States	U. States	Schooner Planter, Osborn.
	Mrs. Saltus	50	female		do	do	
	Francis Yates	19	male		do	do	
	Eliza Burch	40	female		do	do	
	Ruth Righton	30	do		do	do	
	B. Cooper	45	male	Mariner	G. Britain	do	Sloop James, Vincent.
	James Bentham	33	do	Merchant	U. States	do	Schooner Mary Ann, Hilliard.
	Joseph Ciaria	28	do	Mariner	Brazil	do	
	C. Rowman	28	do	do	U. States	do	
	John Henderson	24	do	Merchant	do	N. Orleans	Brig Eliza, Chazell.
	Bazella Gonzales	30	do	do	Spain	U. States	Brig Catharine, Wellsman.
	John Leopez	36	do	do	Portugal	do	
	William Shillbrick	27	do	do	U. States	do	
	William Ward	27	do	do	G. Britain	do	Ship Carolina, Easterby
	Mary Ward & daughter	26	female	Lady	do	do	
	Jack Aikin	30	male	Servant	U. States	do	
	Theodore Sheafe	23	do	Merchant	do	do	Brig Carolinian, M'Intosh.
	Gorham Bassit	32	do	Mariner	do	do	
	Hugh Staples	23	do	do	do	do	
	Rufus S. Kidman	25	do	Gentleman	do	do	Schooner Comet, Forsyth.
	Dr. Kidman	33	do	Physician	do	do	
	James Bowers	34	do	Merchant	do	do	
	Mrs. M. Belcher	3?	female	Lady	do	do	Ship Sybel, Belcher.

NORFOLK AND PORTSMOUTH, James Johnson.

Name	Age	Sex	Occupation	Country	Country	Ship
Mary Reed & 2 children	28	female	Lady	G. Britain	U. States	Ship Octavia, Wilson.
Margaret Haise	19	do	Spinster	do	do	Schooner Alexandria, Smith.
Samuel Cook	35	male	Shopkeeper	U. States	Spain	
Joseph Argotic	25	do	do	Spain	U. States	
Daniel Gaillard	21	do	Gentleman	U. States	do	
William Parker	25	do	do	G. Britain	do	Brig Susan, Pollock.
James Magee	19	do	Farmer	do	do	
Mary M'Guire	18	female	Spinster	do	do	
Lucy Buntin	14	do		do	do	
John F. Walker	23	male	Merchant	do	do	Ship Fame, Barry.
Henry Knust	47	do	do	do	do	
William H. Capers	19	do	Mariner	U. States	do	
Mrs. Smith & 2 children	26	female	Spinster	do	do	
Mitchel	24	male		France	do	
Joseph W. Clark	50	do	Mariner	do	do	Brig Commerce, Messerve.
Bernard Poll	18	do	Clerk	do	do	
— Emills	20	do	do	Holland	do	
F. Monbrun	25	do	do	do	do	
M. Brodat	27	do		London	do	
M. Vankaldrin	38	male	Tailor	do	do	Ship Charles and Henry, Carsdorff.
Mrs. Vankaldrin & child	28	female		do	do	
William Dodd	19	male	Farmer	U. States	do	Brig Pyrenees, N. Clark.
S. Foulton & 4 children	35	do		do	do	
John Allen	20*	male	Servant	England	do	
Elizabeth Allen	23	female	do	Germany	do	
William Robertson	24	male	Mariner	do	do	Schooner Buffaloe, Jno. Ham.
John M. Smith	26	do	Butcher	England	England	
Thomas Wilson	32	do	Mason	U. States	U. States	
Joseph H. Taylor	49	do	Mat. inst. mak.	do	do	Schooner Geo. Washington, J. R. Jackson.
Daniel Schelling	40	do	Coachmaker	England	do	Brig Alonzo, Jno. Caraway.
Ann Schelling	45	female		Germany	do	
Isaac Cox and child	28	male	Merchant	England	do	Schooner Ghent, J. Folger.
William F. Burton	35	do	Mariner	U. States	do	
Ephraim Wentworth	30	do		England	do	
Thomas Sunderland	28	do	Cooper	do	do	Ship Aristides, Jno. Frost.
Ann Sunderland	25	female		do	do	
Samuel Downes	18	male	Shoemaker	do	do	
Ann Downes		female		do	do	

LIST of Passengers, &c.—Quarter ending September 30, 1820.

Custom House, with the name of the Collector.	Names of Passengers.	Age.	Sex.	Occupation.	Country to which they belong.	Country of which they intend to become inhab's	Ship or Vessel, with the name of the Master or Commander.
NORFOLK AND PORTSMOUTH, James Johnson.	James Cummins	32	male	Merchant	Ireland	U. States	Ship Virginia, R. Fisher.
	Maria Cummins & child	25	female		do	do	
	Eliza E. Little & child	20	do		do	do	
	Sally Howell	40	male	Servant	U. States	do	
	Jeremiah Rhodes	30	do	Merchant	England	do	
	William H. Trott	24	female	do	do	do	Schooner Fanny and Mary, Wm. Block.
	Elizabeth Trott	18	male		do	do	
	L. Billerby	40	do	Merchant	U. States	do	Brig Margaret Wright, Thomas Rooke.
	John G. Silva	30	do	Clergyman	Portugal	England	Brig Only Daughter, Wm. Forsyth.
	James D. Tucker	45	do	Merchant	England	U. States	
	Samuel Low	28	do	Clergyman	U. States	do	Schooner Constitution, J. Seward.
	William H. Patterson	16	do	Midshipm.U.S.	England	do	Schooner Decatur, H. Bell.
	Henry Brewer	36	do	Merchant	U. States	do	Brig Philotaxe, T. Corran.
	Richard Gardner	46	female	Mariner	do		Brig Hallan, N. Strong.
	Eliza Gardner	34	male		do		
	John Williams	60	do	do	England	England	Schooner Charles K. Mallary, B. Bissel.
	William Rowland	38	do	do	Ireland	U. States	Schooner Hunter, Geo. Clements.
	John M'Culloch	30	do	Farmer	do	do	
	George Hayward	35	do	do	do	do	
	George Walker	30	do	do	do	do	
	Patrick M'Laughlin	25	do	do	do	do	
	Frank M'Gano	38	female	do	do	do	
	Mary M'Gano & 4 chil.	36	male		do	do	
	Robert Smith	19	female	Farmer	do	do	
	Ann Smith	18	male		do	do	
	Robert Littemore	25	female	Farmer	do	do	
	Mrs. Littemore	30	female		do	do	

Name	Age	Sex	Occupation	Country	Destination	Ship
Elizabeth Littemore	16	female		Ireland	U. States	Ship Astrea, Jno. Wilson
Joseph Littemore	18	male		do	do	
Jane Glenn	18	female	Spinstress	do	do	
Agnes Glenn	16	do	do	do	do	
Charles Murray	25	male	Farmer	do	do	
Daniel Cosgran	22	do	do	do	do	
John Ramsay	30	do	do	Scotland	do	
Thomas Edgar	26	do	do	Ireland	do	
Thomas Harvey	27	do	do	do	do	
Ann Harvey	25	female		do	do	
Lucy Exall	22	do		England	do	
Mrs. Rowland & 2 chil.	48	do		do	do	
William Way	32	male		do	do	
Elizabeth and child	30	female		do	do	
Jane Way	18	do		do	do	
Mrs. Dore and child	27	do		do	do	
Leah Hales	16	do		do	do	
John Hales	22	male	Laborer	do	do	
James Moins	22	do	do	do	do	
Wm. Ricketts	41	do	Weaver	do	do	
Jane Rowland	17	female		do	do	
Michael Lodge	21	male	Mariner	N.Foundland	do	Schooner Triton, James Arey.
John Brown	22	do	Laborer	Ireland	do	Schooner Hancock, Ezra Ryan
Wm. Dudley	55	do	Seaman	U. States	do	
Jno. Martin	27	do	Trader	do	do	Brig Leo, Noble E. Jenkins.
Thomas Mackey	24	do	Farmer	Scotland	do	Sloop Galen, H. Herriman.
Malachi C. Bryan	30	do	Laborer	Ireland	U. Canada	Schooner Abigail, Joseph Elwell.
David Elliot	40	do	Farmer	U. States	U. States	Schooner Packet Eliza, William White.
Phineas Kellum		do	Merchant	do	do	
William Pitcher		do	do	do	do	
William Lunch		do	Farmer	do	do	
Elisha Lewis		do	do	do	do	
John M'Laughlin		do	do	Ireland	do	
Patrick Burns	30	do	do	do	do	
John Burns	23	do	do	do	do	
Miles Cosgrove	43	do	do	do	do	
John Weeks	51	do	do	do	do	
Moses Bunker	22	do	do	U. States	do	

BELFAST,
B. LANE.

LIST of Passengers, &c.—Quarter ending September 30, 1820.

Custom House, with the Name of the Collector.	Names of Passengers.	Age.	Sex.	Occupation.	Country to which they belong.	Country of which they intend to become inhab's.	Ship or Vessel, with the name of the Master or Commander.
BELFAST, D. Lane.	James Barry	17	male	Farmer	U. States	U. States	
	Reuben Kimball	48	do	Joiner	do	do	
	John Green & child	55	do	Stevedore	do	do	
	David Huntoon	36	do	Farmer	do	do	
	Wm. M'Colkell	25	do	do	Ireland	do	
	Hugh Wilson	26	do	do	Scotland	do	
	Jno. R. Brown	25	do	do	England	do	
	Thomas Banister	28	do	House carpt'r	U. States	do	
	George W. Webster	38	do	do	do	do	
	Thomas Bartlett	40	do	Baker	do	do	
	James Wilkins	29	do	House carpt'r	do	do	
	Abner Ford	55	do	Farmer	do	do	
	Jacob Walhern	55	do	do	do	do	
	Joseph Berry	45	do	do	do	do	
	Ebenezer Stratton	29	do	do	do	do	
	Samuel Brown	25	do	do	do	do	
	Wm. Smith	24	do	do	do	do	
	Benjamin Lambert	18	do	do	do	do	
	Judah Stone	21	do	Cordwainer	do	do	
	Thomas Montgomery	52	do	Merchant	France	do	Brig Mermaid, Wm. Pointer.
	John Cazade	28	do	do	Cuba	Cuba.	
	J. F. Morrison	23	do	Farmer	Ireland	U. States	Schr. Dorcas Ann, Samuel Fisher.
	Hugh Donnelly	22	do		do	do	
	Catharine Donnelly	26	female		do	do	
	Susanna Donnelly	24	do		do	do	
	William Groves	26	male	Farmer	do	do	Sloop Betsey, B. Young.
	Charles M'Dermot	25	do	Tailor	do	do	

Name	Age	Sex	Occupation	Nativity	Destination	Ship
Thomas Hanson	32	male	Merchant	U. States	U. States	Brig Mermaid, Wm. Pointer.
Fredk. Leonard	43	do	do	do	do	
E. Nicholson & 2 chil'n	35	female		do	do	
Elizabeth Cain	16	male	Merchant	do	do	Sloop Huntress, Wm. Spencer.
James Russell	28	do	do	Ireland	do	Schr. Independence, E. Haynes.
John M'Kinsey	28	female	Weaver	do	do	
Edward Dill	24	do		do	do	
Elizabeth Dill	23	male	Painter & Glaz.	England	do	Brig H. Clay, Wm. Beall.
Jane Hunter	25	female		do	do	
John Leget	32	male	Sailmaker	do	do	
Hannah Leget	28	female		do	do	
John Alford	25	male	Papermaker	do	do	
Ann Alford	25	female		do	do	
John Elston	25	do		do	do	
Sarah Elston	30	do		do	do	
Han. Jones & 7 child'n	48	male	Mariner	do	do	
Jane Rogers & 7 do	35	female		do	do	
Richard Seamore	50	male	Mariner	do	do	
Eliz. do. & 5 chil'n	50	do	Cabinetmaker	do	do	
Wm. Hardy	30	male		do	do	
John Lauder	34	do		do	do	
Sarah do. & 2 child'n	30	female		do	do	
Louisa Cudliss & 5 do.	38	do		do	do	
Elizabeth Lauder	35	do		do	do	
Michael Labera	35	male	Physician	France	do	Schr. Athenian, Medina.
Flora Langaley	60	female		France	do	
Thos. Medford & child	45	male	Farmer	England	do	Brig Braddock, M'Master.
Chas. Durand	19	do	Merchant	U. States	do	Brig Hannah & Rebecca, Yorke.
Wm. Greenwood	33	do	Engineer	England	do	
Chas. Potier	35	do	Gunsmith	France	do	Brig Sumatra, Smith.
Mrs. Potier & 2 child'n	28	female			do	Brig Hammond.
John Nixon	35	male	Physician	U. States	do	
Anthony Renaud	55	do		Switzerland	do	
A. Chatee	48	do	Merchant	France	Louisiana	Brig Jupiter, Vesser.
John Hayer	23	do	Physician	Bremen	do	
Weazel Brust	40	do	Blacksmith	do	do	
Thos. Kramer	26	do	Carpenter	do		
Conrad Hain	25	do		do		

Mississippi, Beverly Chew,

LIST of Passengers, &c.—Quarter ending September 30, 1820.

Custom House, with the Name of the Collector.	Names of Passengers.	Age.	Sex.	Occupation.	Country to which they belong.	Country of which they intend to become inhab's	Ship or Vessel, with the Name of the Master or Commander.
MISSISSIPPI, B. Chew.	Didier Roselius & child	25	male	Farmer	Hanover	Louisiana	Brig Jupiter, Ves er.
	Fredk. Pitster	22	do	Tailor	do	do	
	John H. Pittster	20	do	Farmer	do	do	
	Cail Kornu	31	do	Butcher	Bremen	do	
	Augustus L. Lossbery	22	do	Baker	do	do	
	Sieviez	27	do	Tinner	Cassel	do	
	John H. Prete	42	do	Cooper	do	do	
	Geo. C. L. Tesse	24	do	Baker	Baden	do	
	G. Passmayer	23	do	Butcher	Oldenburg	do	
	E. Kringer	24	do	Tailor	do	do	
	John H. Teyman	28	do	Mason	Hanover	do	
	C. Heyland	18	female	Hunter	do	do	
	Catharine Sieper	34	do	Farmer	do	do	
	Ernest Valentine	21	male	do	do	do	
	Jno. H. Habbman	16	do	Potmaker	Prussia	do	
	J. B. Raumgartin	59	do	Mariner	do	do	
	C. D. Lainge	27	do	Servant	do	do	
	John D. Hollis	30	do	Tanner	do	do	
	John A. Kremger	38	do	do	do	do	
	Andw. Kermick	23	do	Glazier	Switzerland	do	
	John F. Stammer	26	do	Painter	Bremen	do	
	Fredk. Jang	18	do	Tobacco manuf.	do	do	
	Christian Ticke	32	do	Servant	do	do	
	J. A. W. Muckinheim	25	do	Blacksmith	Brunswick	do	
	Fredk. Erdmann	18	do	do	France	do	
	Barthel Hein	23	do	Farmer	Bremen	do	
	A. H. Lunte	28	do			do	

Name	Age	Sex	Occupation	Country	Destination
Albert Schrader	28	male	Confectioner	Hanover	Louisiana
Ernest Stoesand	28	do	Gardener	do	do
G. E. Bangert	31	do	Bookbinder	do	do
N. Schulke	18	do	Sugarmaker	Switzerland	do
Andrew Lindhest	32	do	Tanner	Russia	do
Frederick W. Battowitz	28	do	Mariner	Hanover	do
W. Martini	35	do	Saddler	Oldenberg	do
Frederick Baumgartin	27	do	Butcher	Prussia	do
Peter E. Fischer	26	do	Cooper	Oldenberg	do
J. H. G. Julss	24	do	Miller	do	do
H. Ripa	32	do	Sailor	Hanover	do
George Knapsten	18	do	Cooper	Prussia	do
John O. Vanhoff	27	do	Servant	Saxony	fe do
Christ. Haiting	26	do	Saddler	Hanover	do
W. Huring	25	do	Shoemaker	Poland	do
J. Anderson	39	do	Sailmaker	Denmark	do
C. L. Hour	23	do	do	Prussia	do
C. F. Haunemaun	22	do	Baker	Wirtemberg	do
Frederick Gehotz	23	do	do	Hanover	do
Conrad Wilgman	20	do	Cooper	do	do
Frederick Stover	33	do	Farmer	Oldenburg	do
C. Warps	31	do	Tanner	do	do
Frederick Lippel	19	do	Clerk	do	do
Verona Wilds	19	do		do	do
A. Leoy	27	do	Watchmaker	do	do
G. Fitcher	33	do	Cloth manuf.	Saxony	do
I. F. Lunker	37	do	Clerk	Hanover	do
Henry Jahunk	22	do	Tailor	do	do
C. Kupur	27	do	Saddler	Saxony	do
Andrew Gayard	20	do	do	Austria	do
J. Koopman	26	do	Tailor	do	do
John Wagener	20	do	Blacksmith	do	do
John F. Kratzer	22	do	Cloth manufac.	Mecklenber.	do
Frederick Ditteloff	18	do	Baker	do	do
Henry Otto	19	do	Cloth manufac.	Hanover	do
Egbert Peterson	35	do	Tailor	do	do
C. H. Ladener	24	do	Surgeon	do	do
Henry Stover	27	do	Tailor	Denmark	do

LIST of Passengers, &c.—*Quarter ending September* 30, 1820.

Custom House, with the name of the Collector.	Names of Passengers.	Age.	Sex.	Occupation.	Country to which they belong.	Country of which they intend to become inhab?	Ship or Vessel, with the Name of the Master or Commander.
Mississippi, Beverly Chew.	F. Myer	19	male	Watchmaker	Denmark	Louisiana	Brig Jupiter, Vesser.
	Edward Haustein	36	do	Saddler	Prussia	do	
	W. Brewure	30	do	Blacksmith	Brunswick	do	
	V. Doormauns	22	do	Shoemaker	Hungary	do	
	Frederick Wetzver	23	do	do	Russia	do	
	Augustus W. Amster	34	do	Clerk	do	do	
	Augustus Schopan	21	do	Baker	Poland	do	
	John Fred. Minguard	32	do	Saddler	do	do	
	John H. Spark	34	do	Farmer	do	do	
	W. Clope	26	do	Baker	Saxony	do	
	John J. Tusser	20	do	Shoemaker	Prussia	do	
	J. F. W. Mark	33	do	Carpenter	Tyrol	do	
	John F. Myer	31	do	Ship carpenter	Hanover	do	
	Jacob Ellilg	21	do	Blacksmith	France	do	
	Frederick Schulze	21	do	Shoemaker	Hanover	do	
	Frederick Plattel	21	do	Joiner	Russia	do	
	Henry K. Muller	45	do	Cooper	do	do	
	C. Vetter	36	do	Cloth manufa.	Mecklenber.	do	
	Christian Witting	26	do	Bricklayer	Bremen	do	
	N. Bekuen	42	do	Translator lan.		do	
	Justus Schur	47	do	Carpenter		do	
	John Schur	21	do	do		do	
	John H. Stock	19	do	Tailor	Hanover	do	
	B. Drus	30	do	Joiner	do	do	
	J. H. Melhop	24	do	Farmer	do	do	
	George Rischoff	25	do	Carpenter		do	
	H. I. Onken	24	do	Tailor	Germany	do	

Name	Age	Sex	Occupation	Country	Louisiana	Ship
Peter Jelle	28	male	Blacksmith	Switzerland	do	Schooner Victoire, Constant
Henry Schnitzer	26	do	Tailor	Hanover	do	Ship Howard, Marshall.
Charles Kochesperger	20	do	Carpenter	France	do	
George Jonnewkell	20	do	Sailor	Hanover	do	
H. W. A. Kinttel	19	do	Tanner	do	do	
M. Louba	50	do	Merchant	U. States	do	
Martin	35	do	Physician	France	do	
William Baincue	24	do		England	do	
Nathan Chandler	27	do		U. States	do	
John Clark	22	do	Mariner	England	do	
Andrew Brown	23	do	do	do	do	Brig Alfred, Liddel.
John Blair	30	do	Engineer	do	do	
Arch. M. Richard	25	do	do	do	do	
William Underwood	30	do	Clerk	do	do	
Madame Mathieu & ch.	30	female		France	do	Sloop Good Intent, Morton.
J. F. P. Palacias	30	male	Spanish officer	Spain	do	
S. Mordella	20	do	do	do	do	
A. Mulinares	23	do	Merchant	do	do	
Julian Mal	32	do	do	do	do	
Gerard Aubert	31	do	do	do	do	
Charles Martousow	28	do	do	do	do	
Samuel Tyler	31	do	Mariner	U. States	do	
P. Rioul	25	do	do	do	do	
C. A. Albert	31	do	Farmer	Gottenburg	do	
J. B. Brochette	58	do	Mariner	U. States	do	
Jean Barieu	32	do	do	do	do	
G. Durand	43	do	do	do	do	
John G. Rap	42	do	Cooper	Germany	do	Ship Maria, Krunstuyver.
Ann Maria & 4 children	30	female		do	do	
Andrew Mugtrup	36	male	Farmer	do	do	
R. M. Mugtrup & 5 chil.	33	female		do	do	
John Bower	46	male	Farmer	do	do	
Barbara Bower & 4 chil.	41	female		do	do	
Conrad Kremer	58	male	Butcher	do	do	
Anna B. Kremer	58	female		do	do	
Rosina Weminer & child	28	do		do	do	
Michael Witman	45	male	Merchant	do	do	
Cornel. Vanderlendine	17	do		Holland	do	

LIST of Passengers, &c.—Quarter ending September 30, 1820.

Custom House, with the name of the Collector.	Names of Passengers.	Age.	Sex.	Occupation.	Country to which they belong.	Country of which they intend to become inhb's.	Ship or Vessel, with the name of the Master or Commander.
MISSISSIPPI, Beverly Chew.	A. Vanderlidst	25	female		Holland	Louisiana	Ship Maria, Kranstuyver.
	Maria T. Staes	40	do		do	do	
	John W. Snover	57	male		Germany	do	
	E. C. Sworver & 4 ch.	38	female	Farmer	do	do	
	Ann B. Sworver	65	do		do	do	
	Godfrey Mourer	50	male		do	do	
	I. Margareta & child	40	female	Farmer	do	do	
	Joseph Hiezel	38	male	Farmer	do	do	
	Barbara Ising & 3 ch.	33	female		do	do	
	J. M. Scheef	30	male	Farmer	do	do	
	Jos. Storick	24	do	do	do	do	
	Catharine Rich	24	female		do	do	
	David Kayzer	42	male	Tailor	do	do	
	Marg. Kayser & 4 ch.	42	female		do	do	
	John George Amen	42	male	Farmer	do	do	
	John F. Kreig	46	do	do	do	do	
	Maria Kreig & 6 ch.	33	female		do	do	
	Catharine Browning	37	do		do	do	
	Christian Cail	13	male		do	do	
	Joseph Horner	40	do	Farmer	do	do	
	Ann M. Horner & 4 ch.	33	female		do	do	
	John Wynard	29	male	Blacksmith	do	do	
	D. Wynard & 6 children	35	female		do	do	
	John G. Gothenburger	51	male	Farmer	do	do	
	M.Gothenburger & 4 ch.	57	female		do	do	
	Jacob Wagner	18	male	Tailor	do	do	
	E. B. Crurton	23	female		do	do	

Name	Age	Sex	Occupation	Country	Destination	Ship
J. M. Pudeleneyer	22	male	Farmer	Germany	Louisiana	
Chas. Mudinge	42	do	do	do	U. States	
Cath. do. & 2 chil'n	40	female		do	do	
Frederick Snabel	40	male	Shoemaker	do	do	
Martin Ebler	34	do	Blacksmith	do	do	
Jacob F. Krak	30	do	Bookbinder	do	do	
Ann B. Krak	28	female		do	do	
Cath. E. do. & 2 chil'n	36	do		do	do	
Jno. C. Buck	16	male		do	do	
Jno. M'Klyn	17	do	Butcher	do	do	
Geo. J. Houzeman	27	do	Shepherd	do	do	
Margaretta do. & child	26	female		do	do	Schr. Theresa, Sarda.
E. C. Schelbanning	22	do		Holland	do	Schr. Brutus, Dumilion.
Anna De Vegel	30	do	Servant	do	do	
Eliza Widecamp	24	do	Shoemaker	Germany	do	
Conrad Scherkked	46	male		do	do	
R. Scherkked & 4 chil'n	40	female		do	do	
Henry Lucke	27	male	Farmer	do	do	
John Keller	50	do	Baker	do	do	
Anna Barbara	32	female		Holland	do	
A. Rumschneeder	25	male	Tailor	do	do	
Peter Conrad	50	do	Farmer	do	do	
Margaretta do. & 3 chil'n	36	female		do	do	
Solomon Kingsbuyer	14	male			do	Ship Beangauze, Oberry.
Johanna Lampi	20	female			do	
Maria Lampi	16	do			do	
H. C. Egemes	19	do			do	
John G. Schol	21	male	Baker		do	
Don Nicolas	27	do	Officer	Germany	Spain	
Julian Canchea	29	do	Mariner	Spain	Louisiana	
Alexr. Etiffal	22	do	do	France	do	
Joseph Solis	18	do	Cigarmaker	do	do	
B. Calamel	50	do	Merchant	do	U. States	
H. L. Sands	35	do	Capt. U. S. army	U. States	do	
Wm. Hugaman	25	do.	Merchant	Brem-n	do	
John Babtiste	50	do	Mariner	Louisiana	do	
James Lynch	25	do	Planter	G. Britain	do	
J. I. Drewe	30	do	Mariner	do	do	Schr. Two Friends, Beauvia.

LIST of Passengers, &c.—Quarter ending September 30, 1820.

Custom House, with the name of the Collector.	Names of Passengers.	Age.	Sex.	Occupation.	Country to which they belong.	Country of which they intend to become inhab's	Ship or Vessel, with the name of the Master or Commander.
MISSISSIPPI, B. Chew.	Wm. Lacoste	28	male	Baker	France	U. States	Schr. Victoire, Constant.
	J. Tanesse	45	do	Engineer	do	do	Schr. Thorn, Fernander.
	Mrs. Tanesse & child	40	female		N. Orleans	do	
	Mrs. Lafond & child	25	do		France	do	
	Peter C. Motino	25	male	Planter	do	do	
	Martin Dubourg	45	do	do	U. States	do	
	J. C. Allen	35	female				
	Tillette Gilbert	35	male	Clerk	Spain	do	
	H. Pedesclaux	23	do	Planter	St. Domingo	do	
	L. Beraud	35	do	Clerk	Spain	do	
	G. Battastel	30	do	do	England	do	
	J. Passett	25	do	Baker	Canada	do	
	Joseph Smith	35	do	Planter	U. States	do	
	—— Lethingham	35	do	Merchant	Spain	do	
	Jose Larinda	55	do	do	U. States	do	
	Jose Frogo	42	do	Clerk	Spain	do	
	—— Par	27	do	Merchant	U. States	do	
	—— Robut	40	female	do	France	do	Brig Rising Sun, Denah.
	Mrs. Robut & child	40	male		do	do	
	—— Bosque	26	do		do	do	
	—— Bosque, jr.	17	female	Chambermaid	do	do	
	Miss Cadele	40	male	Baker	do	do	
	—— Fournieu	26	do		do	do	
	—— Brugur	19	do	do	do	do	
	—— Guillermani	36	female		do	do	
	Mrs. Tukelly	27	male	Merchant	do	do	Ship Virginia, Clements.
	—— Mantel	27					

Name	Age	Sex	Occupation		Destination	Ship
Alexander Dumont	45	male	French officer	France	U. States	Schr. Dos Amicos, Montana.
C. A. Mitchel	45	do	Merchant	do	do	Schr. San Antonio, Bache.
— Langlais	36	do	Servant	do	do	Ship Highlander, Welch.
— Paraguay	35	do		do	do	
Mrs. do. & 2 chil'n	22	female		do	do	
Y. Flore	60	male		do	do	
Jno. B. Le Blank	30	do	Merchant	Louisiana	do	Ship Alexander, Welch.
Francis Gamez	19	do	do	Spain	do	
J. P. V. Dauphin	45	do	do	France	do	
Chas. Dumache	16	do	do	do	do	
Pierre Reaud	15	do	do	do	do	
— Vierzignean	32	do		Bavaria	do	
Chas. Lachute	45	do		N. Orleans	do	
Polexene Seebe & child	26	female	Mason	do	do	
— Totrat	36	male		do	do	Schr. Hope, Galatu.
Mrs. Totrat	30	female		do	do	Schr. Greyhound, Seward.
— Rosseau	28	male	Clerk	Havre	do	
Narcisse Bretele	21	do	Hatter	Louisiana	do	
Mrs. Doisiere	48	female		do	do	
M. N. Lesbois	40	do		do	do	
Mrs. Defossee	50	do		do	do	
Chas. Adams	25	male	Mariner	Flanders	do	Ship Cora, Desberg.
John J. Grenois	25	do	do	Geneva	do	
L. Campanio	30	do	do	Italy	do	
Margaret	23	female	Servant	Louisiana	do	
D. Morant	42	male	Mariner	do	do	
— Lefevre	30	do	Watchmaker	France	do	
F. Soubricaze	32	do	Merchant	do	do	
F. Brunette	37	do	do	do	do	
G. Brun	38	do	do	do	do	
Miguel Estrada	23	do	do	Spain	do	
Jos. Gulierriz	42	do	do	do	do	
F. Fluir	38	do	Clerk	France	do	Ship Adela, Duplessing
Alexis S. Daboraz	19	do	Manufacturer	do	do	
Germain Scheurolly	38	do	Mason	Switzerland	do	
Victor Jacob	16	do		Louisiana	do	
Edward Jacob	14	do		do	do	
Mrs. Roche	63	female		France	do	

LIST of Passengers, &c.—Quarter ending September 30, 1820.

Custom House, with the name of the Collector.	Names of Passengers.	Age.	Sex.	Occupation.	Country to which they belong.	Country of which they intend to become inhab's	Ship or Vessel, with the name of the Master or Commander.
Mississippi, B. Chew.	M. V. Pecket	34	female	Servant	France	Louisiana	Brig Revenge, Rollins.
	A. Benoist	20	male	Supercargo	N. Orleans	do	
	— Brown	22	do	Mariner	do	do	
	— Tisseur	25	do		do	do	
New-York. David Gelston.	J. Leviag		do	Mariner	do	do	
	John Campbell	28	do	Farmer	Scotland	Indiana	Ship Magnet, D. S. Ogden.
	John M. Jackson	45	do	Merchant	G. Britain	Canada	
	Emma Jackson	24	female		do	do	
	Georgiana Jackson	21	do	Merchant	do	do	
	Robert Harwood	22	male	Watchmaker	do	do	
	Thomas Gillon	23	do	Merchant	do	do	
	L. Andrews	28	do	Servant	do	do	
	James Hampton	22	do	Merchant	do	do	
	Mary Harris	24	female		do	do	
	Jas. Sibbald	25	male	Merchant	U. States	do	
	N. Sibbald	21	female		do	do	
	Ira Roony	22	male	Laborer	do	do	
	James Duffee	21	do	do	do	U. States	Brig Apnes, Daniel Furman.
	Stephen Inclin	25	do	Merchant	Spain	do	
	John Walker	24	do	Seaman	U. States	do	Brig Greyhound, T. Benson.
	Adam Richards	23	do	Merchant	do	do	
	Joel F. Eisenhaben	35	do	Farmer	Holland	do	Brig Gamacrau, A. Bales.
	Domingo Paravia	27	do	Merchant	U. States	do	Schr. Eliza Ann, E. B. Smith.
	E. Fernandez	42	do	do	Spain	do	
	Antonio Braggas	23	do	do	do,	do	
	Joseph Garatia	17	do	do	do	do	
	John Mercier		do	do	do,	do	

Name	Age	Sex	Occupation			Ship
James Wall	35	male	Gentleman	England	U. States	Ship Belfast, Wm. Thompson.
Eliza Wall & 4 child'n	34	female		do	do	
Edward Wright	35	male	Farmer	do	do	
Mrs. Wright & 4 child'n	34	female		do	do	
W. Chandler	35	do		do	do	
Ann Morale	55	do		do	do	
Ann Maurice	19	do		do	do	
Ann Haynes	14	do		do	do	
John Thomas	22	male		do	do	
Thomas Lewis	22	do		do	do	
Salome James	26	female		do	do	
John Thompson	55	male		do	do	
Ann Morrisson	51	female		do	do	
& 2 children				do	do	
John Zever	24	male		do	do	
John Day	27	do		do	do	
Wm. Woolley	26	do		do	do	
Geo. Key	35	do		do	do	
J. M'Millen	24	female		do	do	
John Brown	44	male		do	do	
Ann Brown	25	female		do	do	
Mrs. Boulet & child	28	do		U. States	do	Schr. Catharine, D. Hepburn.
Alexr. Fink	25	male	Butcher	do	do	Brig Superb, Dl. Aynear.
James Van Jassel	27	do	do	do	do	
Joseph Antonio	28	do	Gentleman	Portugal	Rio Janeiro	
Alexr. Burton	36	do	Merchant	U. States	U. States	Brig Mary, G. Gore.
Chas. Cunningham	29	do	do	do	do	Brig Boston, N. Knowles.
Wm. Gould	40	do	Shipmaster	do	do	
David Bray	50	do	Seaman	do	do	
Rump Plumber	28	do		do	do	
Samuel M'Arthur	33	do		do	do	
Stephen Harrison	47	do		do	do	
Fredk. Camien	18	do		do	do	
Wm. Gole	21	do		do	do	
Wm. Taite	34	do		do	do	
John Johnson	18	do		do	do	
Thomas Graves	40	do		do	do	
Hugh Scott	42	do		do	do	

LIST of Passengers, &c.—Quarter ending September 30, 1820.

Custom House, with the name of the Collector.	Names of Passengers.	Age.	Sex.	Occupation.	Country to which they belong.	Country of which they intend to become inhab's	Ship or Vessel, with the name of the Master or Commander.
New-York, David Gelston.	John Dixon	29	male	Seaman	U. States	U. States	Brig Boston, N. Knowles.
	D. Rate	33	do	do	do	do	
	James Weeks	23	do	do	do	do	
	James Hughes	57	do	do	do	do	Schooner Abigail, J. Elwell.
	Noah Disbrow	68	do	Merchant	do	do	
	James Hayton	49	do	Ropemaker	do	do	
	Wm. Wheaton & ch.	34	female	Merchant	do	do	
	Elizabeth Clements	45	do		do	do	
	Lydia Conklin	32	do		do	France	
	Peter Decasse	38	male	Merchant	do	U. State	Brig Wilson, V. Corre.
	Theodore S. Hinchen	22	do	do	do	do	Eliza Piggott, R. Waterman.
	Daniel Tucker	26	do	Mariner	do	do	
	John Clayton	38	do	do	do	do	
	Lopez Alonzo	20	do	Merchant	do	do	
	Peter Richard	48	do	Seaman	do	do	Brig Minerva, Melarum.
	Horace Beckworth	26	do		do	do	Brig George, William Kellog.
	H. Stitson	25	do		do	do	
	Alexander Jeard	28	do	Mariner	Florence	dt	Ariadne, Alexander Summers.
	William Freeman	38	do	Merchant	U. States	dt	Schooner Cygnet, N. Kemball.
	Robert Brown	25	do	Ship master	do	do	
	E. Bentham	22	do	Blacksmith	do	do	Schooner Enterprize, S. Lines.
	Charles Lerange	21	do		France	do	
	Pedro Jerago	38	do	Seaman	do	do	
	Sarah Greig & child	20	female		Java	Java	Euno Francit, J. Greig.
	Maria Williams	30	do		do	do	
	John Brown	20	male	Steward	U. States	U. States	Schooner Lady's Delight, E. P. Scribner.
	George W. Farley	24	do	Shipmaster	do	do	

Name	Age	Sex	Occupation	Country	U. Stat	Ship
Niles Williams	26	male	Mariner	U. States	do	Ship Nimrod, J. Center.
Daniel Coffin	31	do	Supercargo	do	do	
Tethio Coffin	37	do	Mariner	do	do	
James C. Swain	25	do	do	do	do	
T. C. O. Reilly	14	do	Traveller	Ireland	do	
Thomas Storrow	29	do		U. States	do	
William F. Elinkley	21	do	Gardener	France	do	
S. Surgemon	12	do	Merchant	U. States	do	
A. Center	22	do		do	do	
Jacob Beneit	20	female	Farmer	Ireland	do	
Jane Mader	24	male	Servant	Russia	do	
V. G. Auman	22	do	Clerk	Switzerland	do	
Joha M. Solisse	27	do	Manufacturer	France	do	
Etienne	25	do	Mathematician	Switzerland	do	
V. Desaunet	26	female	Farmer	France	do	
Jane Connel	43	male	Apothecary	do	do	Ship Packet, S. Weeks.
Louis Acker	44	do	Merchant	England	do	
Abraham Gent	35	do	Mechanic	do	do	
William Hall and child	42	do		do	do	
Jane Hayle & 5 children	24	do	Laborer	Ireland	do	
David Foley	23	female		do	do	
Margaret Foley	42	male		do	do	
John Kelly	24	female		do	do	
Margaret Kelly	32	male	Merchant	G. Britain	do	Ship Hercules, N. Coble.
John B. Jonteuin	30	female		do	do	
Amy Toulmin & 4 chil.	25	do		do	do	
Fanny Leaborough	6	do		do	do	
Elizabeth Knight	47	male	Merchant	do	do	
Francis Platt	27	do	do	do	do	
Daniel Stead	26	do	do	do	do	
James Entwisle	26	do	do	do	do	
Thomas Niley	25	do		do	do	
Edward Holan	19	female		do	do	
Sarah Turner	19	male	Servant	do	do	
Samuel Benton	18	do	do	do	do	
William Cathull	14	female		do	do	
Betsey Cathull	59	male	Weaver	do	do	
Henry Hale					do	

LIST of Passengers, &c.—Quarter ending September 30, 1820.

Custom House, with the name of the Collector.	Names of Passengers.	Age.	Sex.	Occupation.	Country to which they belong.	Country of which they intend to become inhab's	Ship or Vessel with the name of the Master or Commander.
New-York, David Gelston.	Mary Hale and children	42	female		G. Britain	U. States	Ship Hercules, N. Coble.
	John Jones & child	56	male	Farmer	do	do	
	James Brooke	38	do	Weaver	do	do	
	Mary Brooke & 6 ch.	32	female		do	do	
	William Summer	20	male	Farmer	do	do	
	Samuel Brooke	34	do		do	do	
	Eliza. Brooke & 6 ch.	32	female		do	do	
	Ann Whitham & 3 ch.	26	do		do	do	
	Hannah Williams & 5 ch.	34	do		do	do	
	Emanuel Williams	24	male		do	do	
	Mary Williams & 2 ch.	29	female		do	do	
	Ann Bates & 4 children	30	do		do	do	
	O. Blackburn	26	male	Farmer	do	do	
	James Spur	40	do	Mechanic	do	do	
	Daniel Fagan	26	do	Merchant	do	do	
	James Duffee	23	do	Blacksmith	do	do	
	Mary Duffee & child	21	female		do	do	
	John Benton	63	male	Merchant	do	do	
	Hugh Benton	21	do	Weaver	do	do	
	Richard Turner	21	do	Carpenter	do	do	
	James Irving	30	do	Laborer	do	do	
	Henry Duhurst	22	female	Gentleman	St. Croix	England	Ship. S. C. Packet, A. Cartwright.
	Joseph Foster	26	male	do	England	St. Croix	
	George Gosling	30	do	Planter	St. Croix	do	
	John Plasket	22	do	do	England		
	William Plasket	23	do	do	do		
	Edward Thomas	23	do	Servant	New-York	New York	

Name	Age	Sex	Occupation	Country	Destination	Ship
William Sutcliff	50	male	Preacher	England	Quebec	Schooner Washington, F. M. Mouret.
Robert Sutcliff	21	do	Merchant	do	do	
Sarah Sutcliff	50	female		do	do	
P. R. Wyboult	30	male		do	U. States	
John Robertson	36	do	Merchant	do	do	
C. Robertson & 2 child.	31	female		do	do	
John Collins	22	male		do	do	
John Christmas	27	do		do	do	
Henry Franklin	12	do		do	do	
Thomas Pool	48	do	Instrument ma.	do	do	
Elizabeth Coolie	45	female		do	do	
Caroline Pycross	13	do		do	do	
Jane Wren & 4 chil.	35	do		do	do	
Robert Welch	32	male	Weaver	do	do	Ship Circe, T. Humphreys.
John Hugil	49	do	Farmer	do	do	
Eleanor Hugil & 8 chil.	47	female		do	do	
Mary Welch & 9 chil.	37	do		do	do	
John Thomas & son	50	male		do	do	
George Dunn	43	do	Laborer	do	do	
Edward Hatton	18	do	Clerk	do	do	
Joseph Roberts	21	do	Farmer	do	do	
Thomas Briton	30	do	Shoemaker	do	do	
Thomas Cassady	20	do	Clerk	do	do	
Matthew Duff	30	do	do	do	do	
Michael Madden	21	do	Farmer	do	do	
James Baniggro	24	do	Yeoman	do	do	Ship Andes, Charles Selden.
John Smith	22	do.	do	do	do	
John Biodish	25	do.	Laborer	do	do	
S. Smith & 3 children	26	female		England	do	
B. S. David	21	male	Merchant	Germany	do	Schooner Sea Serpent, T. Bunker. Ship Henlopen, Benj. Lord.
E. Lokaway	26	do	Servant	Russia	do	
J. B. M. Boliargu	32	do	Spoonmaker	Holland	do	
Francois Chatlen	21	do	do	do	do	
Jean Schwertzer	36	do	Farmer	do	do	
Han. Schwertzer & ch.	32	female		do	do	
Louis Fadino	32	male	Merchant	Italy	W. Indies	Sloop Sally, Samuel Clark. Ship John Dickerson, J. Baush.
James Bell	26	do		Ireland	U. States	
Mary M'Donald	22	female		do	do	

LIST of Passengers, &c.—Quarter ending September 30, 1820.

Custom House, with the name of the Collector.	Names of Passengers.	Age.	Sex.	Occupation.	Country to which they belong.	Country of which they intend to become inhb's.	Ship or Vessel, with the name of the Master or Commander.
New York, David Gelston.	E. M'Matthews	25	female		Ireland	U. States	Ship John Dickerson, J. Beush.
	Mary Hamilton	10	do		do	do	
	Daniel Phillips	45	male		do	do	
	Margaret Lynn	25	female	Shoemaker	do	do	
	David Henderson	35	male	Farmer	do	do	
	Samuel Alexander	19	do	Saddler	do	do	
	William J. Lowe	21	do	Weaver	do	do	
	Jane Lowe	15	female		do	do	
	James Lowe	10	male		do	do	
	Margaret Trotter & 2 ch.	25	female		do	do	
	James Joyce	22	male		do	do	
	Isabella Lehaggree & ch.	24	female		do	do	
	Martha Gosse	50	do		do	do	
	Catharine Kelly	20	do		do	do	
	Sarah Kelly	16	do		do	do	
	William Pountany	21	male	Painter	do	do	
	Alex. Chambers	42	do	Cooper	do	do	
	Joseph Corbet	10	do		do	do	
	Margaret Corbet	9	female		do	do	
	James Taylor	12	male		do	do	
	Agnes Biggrum	22	female		do	do	
	Isabella Chambers	58	do	Farmer	do	do	
	Henry Chambers	40	male		do	do	
	John Chambers	25	do		do	do	
	James Chambers	19	do		do	do	
	Robert Chambers	22	do		do	do	
	Jane Chambers & 3 ch.	35	female		do	do	

Name	Age	Sex	Occupation	From	To	Ship
Job Palmer	25	male	Merchant	Ireland	U. States	Schooner Diana, S. M. M'Pherson.
Thomas Palmer	21	do	do	do	do	
James Dunford	27	do	Gentleman	do	do	
William Laurie	21	do.	do.	do	do	
W. W. Winans	28	do	do	G. Britain	do	
J. B. Bridge	30	do	do	do	do	
J. R. D. Cordover	40	de	do	do	do	
David Harrison	25	do	do	do	do	
Jack	18	do.	Servant	do	do	
Susan Hersted	22	female	Lady	U. States	do	Schooner Buffaloe, John Hamm.
George B. Peace	21	male	Clerk	do	do	Brig Abellino, J. Moore.
Domingo L. Valvey	26	do	Merchant	France	Spain	Brig William Henry, W. Dugan.
Robert August	50	do	Farmer	England	U. States	Brig Eliza Jane, John M'Farrier.
Mrs. August & 2 child.	38	female		do	do	
David Appleyard	37	male	Weaver	do	do	
Thomas Murgrave	22	do	do	do	do	
Joseph Hepworth	23	do	do	do	do	
James Pearson	27	do	Smith	do	do	
William Snowden	30	do	Farmer	do	do	
Nicholas Connell & 2 ch.	75	do		do	do	
Mary Connell & 2 chil.	39	female		do	do	
George Blincon	22	male	Weaver	do	do	
R. Wilson	36	do	do	do	do	
R. Morris	33	do	do	do	do	
William Gibbon	25	do	Bookbinder	Ireland	do	
T. Gorman	23	do	do	do	do	
E. Fulton	30	do	do	do	do	
Ann Carney & 3 child.	30	female		do	do	
Lawrence Sears	45	male	Preacher	Barbadoes	do	Brig Cameron, S. Turner.
W. Wintingham	34	do.	Merchant	U. States	do	Schooner Nancy, R. Crowell.
Thomas Gibson	37	do	Gentleman	do	do	
James Clark	35	do	Merchant	do	do	
David Adams	40	do	do	do	do	
Abel Banks	25	do	do	do	do	
William Hill	20	do	do	Ireland	do	
James Brit	25	do	Farmer	do	do	
Thomas Murphy	25	do	do	do	do	
John Black	52	do	do	U. States	do	Ship Hector, J. Gillinder.

LIST of Passengers, &c.—Quarter ending September 30, 1820.

Custom House, with the name of the Collector.	Names of Passengers.	Age.	Sex.	Occupation.	Country to which they belong.	Country of which they intend to become inhab's	Ship or Vessel, with the name of the Master or Commander.
New York. David Gelston.	Helen Black	40	female		U. States	U. States	Ship Hector, J. Gillinder.
	Mary Taylor & 4 chil'n	40	do		England	do	
	Elizabeth Bloomilaz	19	do		do	do	
	Ann Carter	22	do		do	do	
	John Agg	36	male	Gentleman	do	do	
	Wm. Maine	22	do	Engraver	do	do	
	John Atkinson	57	do	Farmer	do	do	
	Wm. Atkinson	36	female	do	do	do	
	Sarah Atkinson	54	do		do	do	
	F. Atkinson & 4 child'n	35	do		do	do	
	Thos. Adderton	40	male	Mariner	do	do	
	Wm. Holmes	2	do		do	do	
	Jas. Watson & child	29	do	Farmer	do	do	
	Lucy Watson	28	female		do	do	
	Alexr. Durns	24	male	do	do	do	
	Wm. Cravan	21	do		do	do	
	John White	21	male	Shoemaker	do	do	
	Abraham Bennet	23	do	Maltster	do	do	
	John Watson	41	do	Laborer	do	do	
	B. P. Cruger	50	do	Merchant	U. States	do	Ship Chase, J. Baxter.
	Joseph Ridgway	40	do	Mariner	do	do	
	Samuel Nichols	41	do	Merchant	England	do	
	Catharine Nichols	42	female	Lady	do	do	Schr. Charlotte, J. G. Russell.
	Henry Hardy	24	male	Merchant	do	do	
	Jane Hardy	26	female		do	do	
	Amelia Hanford	26	do		do	do	
	G. J. Wiggins	24	do		do	do	

Name	Age	Sex	Occupation			Ship
David Waterburg	42	male	Merchant	England	U. States	Ship Amity, G. Maxwell.
W. J. Sweet	28	do	do	do	do	
Catharine Singland	25	female		do	do	
Chas. M'Lure	35	male	Carpenter	do	do	
Jane M'Lure	24	female		do	do	
Andrew Kodrick	24	male		do	do	
D. Kodrick	32	do		do	do	
Eliza Crane	34	female		do	do	
Margaret Mills	15	do		do	do	
Joseph Howland	39	male		do	do	
Alexr. Buchanan	23	do	Merchant	Canada	do	
Wm. Hamar	33	do		England	do	
Benj. Nustland	16	do	Merchant	do	do	
Samuel Milford	34	do		do	do	
Elizabeth Milford	32	female	Merchant	do	do	
P. J. Hobson	16	male	Attorney	do	do	
Peter Rice	31	do	Ship master	do	do	
Thomas Gillis	23	do		do	do	
Jane Gillis	19	female		do	do	
Joshua Aikins	35	male	Merchant	do	do	
Jane Aikins & child	23	female		do	do	
Alice Kellsall	20	do		do	do	
James B. Smith	23	male		do	do	
John Mossell	26	do		do	do	
Vincenta Lovell	34	do	Farmer	do	do	
John Robinson	31	do		do	do	
Lydia do. & 2 child'n	30	female		do	do	
John Lancaster	57	male		do	do	
Betty Lancaster	57	female		do	do	
Robert Carr	45	male	Merchant	do	do	Schooner Emerald, E. Rabson.
Sam	40	do	Servant	do	do	
Peter Stanton	29	do	Merchant	U. States	Aux Cayes	
Jane Williams	23	female		do	U. States	
Chas. J. Brooke	35	male	Merchant	do	do	Schr. Venus, G. W. Grice.
Lewis Jacob	20	do	Gentleman	G. Britain	do	Schr. Loire, Isaac Basset.
Chas. Crocker	23	do	Printer	U. States	do	
A. Black	27	do	Merchant	do	do	Schr. Cordelia, R. Augur.
J. Langester	30	do	Laborer	do	do	

32

LIST of Passengers, &c.—Quarter ending September 30, 1820.

Custom House, with the name of the Collector.	Names of Passengers.	Age.	Sex.	Occupation.	Country to which they belong.	Country of which they intend to become inhab's	Ship or Vessel, with the name of the Master or Commander.
New York, David Gelston.	John Gurry	50	male	Merchant	U. States	U. States	Brig Martha, D. P. Halsey.
	John B. Stoddard	23	do.	Blacksmith	do	do	Schr. Genl. Jackson, J. B. Nicholls.
	Henry Gage	25	do	Gentleman	do	do	
	David Thomas	23	do	do	do	do	Brig Reindeer, J. Webray
	Edwd. Clark	50	do.	Mariner	do	do	Schr. Sally Ann, L. B.
	P. Cahanin	45	do	Merchant	do	G. Britain	Schr. Victory, Wm. P. Prescott.
	Samuel Mackey	26	do	Mariner	Bermuda	U. States	Schr. Betsey, Wm. Davis.
	Felix O'Boyle & 3 chil'n	50	do	Mason	U. States	do	
	Patrick Morison	20	female		do	do	
	Ellen Muran	20	do		do	do	
	Christiana Armstrong	30	female		Ireland	do	
	John Montgomery	16	male		do	do	
	Roser M'Genley	30	do		do	do	
	Ellen M'Genley	28	female		do	do	
	Michael Camien	40	male		do	do	
	Ann Camien	40	female		do	do	
	Rose M'Gaghan	30	do		do	do	
	Ed. M'Ginley & 2 chil'n	28	male		do	do	
	Ann Fisher	18	female		do	do	
	John M'Gunigle	40	male		do	do	
	Ann do. & 5 chil'n	35	female		do	do	
	Grace Farron	20	do	Farmer	Benden	do	Ship Golden Grove, N. Thomas.
	M. Denchler	37	male		do	do	
	Catharine do. & 2 chil'n	35	female		do	do	
	Michl. Zink & 4 chil'n	56	male		do	do	
	Philip Heack	38	do		do	do	
	Christiana do. & child	37	female		do	do	

Name	Age	Sex	Occupation		U States
Geo. Jacob Barner	38	male		Benden	U States
Catharine do. & 3 chil'n	27	female		do	do
John Miller	34	male		do	do
Rosina Miller	38	female		do	do
Geo. Kniffer	42	male	Butcher	do	do
Adam Spilling	49	do	Carpenter	do	do
Maria do. & 5 chil'n	46	female		do	do
Chas. W. Knacht	33	male	Farmer	do	do
Catharine do. & 2 chil'n	33	female		do	do
Eliz. Urter & child	25	female		do	do
John Hoffman	28	male		do	do
Eleanor Candles	33	female		U. States	do
Luke Ashburner & son	46	male	Gentleman	England	do
Timothy Jackson	53	do.	do	do	do
John Weatherbee	34	do	Merchant	do	do
Leyen Phillips	36	do	do	do	do
Mary Ewbank & child	26	female		U. States	do
Harriet Wallace	11	do		England	do
Sarah Phelps	17	do		U. States	do
John Snied	43	male	Farmer	England	do
Ruth Snied & child	46	do		do	do
John Chandler	26	do	Wheelwright	do	do
Henry Hyland, jr.	19	male	Farmer	do	do
Hannah Hyland	22	female		do	do
Henry Hyland & son	39	male	do	do	do
John Wright	40	do		do	do
John Edgerly	54	do		do	do
M. A. Howley & 8 chil'n	39	female		do	do
Eliz. Sewall & 4 chil'n	34	do		do	do
Char. Wells & 4 chil'n	35	do		do	do
George Pococke	24	male	do	do	do
Rebecca do. & 2 chil'n	34	female		do	do
John Haywood	21	male		do	do
James Blackburn	25	do		do	do
Wm. Blackburn	19	do		do	do
David Pollock	24	do		do	do
Han. Burne & 2 chil'n	28	female		do	do
Rich'd. W. Knight	26	male		do	do

Ship Venus, S. Chandler.

LIST of Passengers, &c.—Quarter ending September 30, 1820.

Custom House, with the name of the Collector.	Names of Passengers.	Age.	Sex.	Occupation.	Country to which they belong.	Country of which they intend to become inh'bts.	Ship or Vessel, with the Name of the Master or Commander.
New-York, David Gelston.	John Smith	21	male		England	U. States	Ship Venus, S. Chandler.
	Thomas Smith	32	do		do	do	
	Robert S. Bayley	40	do		do	do	
	Sarah Bayley & 2 chil'n	42	female		do	do	
	Thomas Gail	10	male		do	do	
	Robert Holiday	23	do		do	do	
	Jas. Withington	32	do		do	do	
	Thomas Gore	31	do		do	do	
	John Robertson	33	do		do	do	
	Thomas Moore	18	do		do	do	
	John Nicholls	25	do		do	do	
	Robert Grauh	26	do		do	do	
	Simon Alberts	18	do		do	do	
	Richard Whitcham	20	do		do	do	
	Wm. B. Inglis	51	do	Merchant	U. States	do	Schr. Marcello, A. Little.
	Daniel M'Arthur	33	do	Farmer	Scotland	do	
	Margaret Dovenick	19	female	Lady	U. States	do	
	Lavinia Esenkedt	22	do	do	do	do	
	John Marshall	20	male	Merchant	do	do	Schr. Champion, E. Morse.
	Michael Hailes	30	do	Gentlemen	Europe	Europe	
	Harris Hailes	27	do	do	do	do	
	Henry Waterbury	27	do	Merchant	U. States	U. States	Schr. William, A. Hallet.
	Wm. Hall	31	do	Carpenter	do	do	
	J. W. Stewart	32	do	Captain	G. Britain	London	
	Thomas Kitchur	30	do	Preacher	Scotland	U. States	Brig Domestic, P. Barney.
	John Patterson	26	do	Teacher	do	do	
	Robert Fenton	26	do	Farmer	do	do	
	John Mackie	36	do	Mechanic	do	do	

Name	Age	Sex	Occupation		U. States	Ship
mary Fletcher & 2 ch.	38	female		Scotland	do	Schooner Carrier, Thomas Bates.
Grace M'Kinley & 3 ch.	28	do		do	do	
E. Wright & 2 children	25	male		do	do	
William M'Coutley	25	do		U. States	do	
J. W. H. Aymar	21	do	Merchant	England	do	Brig William Howland, A. Southworth.
William Pinte	50	do	do	do	do	Schooner Patty & Sally, T. S. Fitch.
John S. Dabney	22	do	do	U. States	do	
Christiana Gill	30	female	Spinster	do	do	Brig Servt. G. Sanborne.
Janet Barlas	35	do	do	Scotland	do	
Robert Hamilton	28	male	Merchant	do	do	
Colin Campbell	35	do	Farmer	do	do	
Catha. Campbell & 4 ch.	30	female		do	do	
Andrew Monroe	35	male	Farmer	do	do	
Agnes Monroe & 2 chil.	26	female		do	do	
Robert M'Farlan	30	male	Farmer	do	do	
Michael Honeymon	30	do	Artist	do	do	
Christiana M'Farland	16	female	Spinster	do	do	
Peter M'Intire	18	male	Farmer	do	do	
Ann Cuthal	30	female	Spinster	do	do	
Mary Ladowitch & 2 ch.	28	do	do	do	do	
Henry Hirshocks	47	male	Mason	do	do	
Maria Hirshocks & ch.	37	female		do	do	
Johannes Schreder	50	male	Farmer	Unknown	do	
Wife & 7 children	40	female		do	do	
Henry Birle	32	male	do	do	do	
Anna Birle & 2 ch.	30	female		do	do	
Jacob Zetchti	23	male	do	do	do	
Peter Roth	32	do	Barber	do	do	
Nicholas Cock	24	do	Farmer	do	do	
Sebastian Knies	23	do	Baker	do	do	
Peter Kerr	24	do	Carpenter	do	do	
Nicholas Jung	48	do		do	do	
Mrs. Jung & 6 children	46	female		do	do	
Johannes Huthworth	36	male	Farmer	do	do	
John P. Mayer	41	do	Merchant	do	do	
Benjamin Washbaine	30	do	Mariner	U. States	do	Brig Edward, William Blucher.
John Alexander	50	do	Farmer	G. Britain	do	Ship Prince Madoc, J. Watson.
Catharine Alexander	48	female	Spinster	do	do	

LIST of Passengers, &c.—Quarter ending September 30, 1820.

Custom House, with the name of the Collector.	Names of Passengers.	Age.	Sex.	Occupation.	Country to which they belong.	Country of which they intend to become inhab's	Ship or vessel, with the name of the Master or Commander.
New York, David Gelston.	John Willie	23	male	Laborer	G. Britain	U. States	Ship Prince Madoc, J. Watson.
	William Cochran	25	do	do	do	do	
	James Morrison	23	do	do	do	do	
	David Scott	28	do	do	do	do	
	James Hackman	24	do	do	do	do	
	Mary Hackman	25	female	Spinster	do	do	
	Jane Hackman	13	do	do	do	do	
	Margaret Hackman	10	do	do	do	do	
	I. I. Robertson	23	male	Merchant	U. States	Canada	
	Bennet Clark	24	do	Gentleman	G. Britain	U. States	Schooner Content, Charles Baker.
	Robert Thompson	44	do	Shipmaster	U. States	do	Ship Mount Vernon, A. Rawson.
	John Whitham	35	do	Worsted maker	England	do	
	William Whitham	25	do	do	do	do	
	John Dale	67	male	do	do	do	
	Johanna Dale & 2 ch.	46	female		do	do	
	William Otterburn	21	male	Farmer	do	do	
	Hannah Otterburn	18	female		do	do	
	John Bays	25	male	Farmer	do	do	
	William Emmerson	30	do	do	do	do	
	Hannah Emmerson	21	female		do	do	
	John Foster	36	male	Butcher	do	do	
	Elizabeth Foster & child	23	female		do	do	
	Margaret Sayres	19	do		do	do	
	Ann Jones	38	do		do	do	
	Robert Ellingham	27	male	Farmer	do	do	
	E. Matthews & 4 ch.	38	female		do	do	
	Mary Matthews & 3 ch.	35	do		do	d	

Name	Age	Sex	Occupation	Country	U. States	Ship
James Vendane	25	male	Cordwainer	England	do	Ship Atlantic, Wm. Matlock.
George Hathaway	25	do	Merchant	do	do	
H. Jackson	28	do	do	U. States	do	
Rachel Jackson	24	female	Lady	do	do	
Joseph Fowler	30	male	Merchant	England	do	Ship John and Edward, William Webb.
Charlotte Whitehead	20	female	Seamstress	do	do	
William Rowland	36	male	Mariner	do	do	
Robert Green	38	do	Laborer	do	do	
James Walker	38	do	Merchant	do	do	
Thomas A. Null	32	do	Clerk	do	do	
Henry Cosgrove	45	do	Merchant	do	do	
David Poole	40	do	Farmer	do	do	
Mary Walker & 3 chil.	38	female	Seamstress	do	do	
Sarah Sedgewick & ch.	38	do	Farmer	do	do	
John Siran	60	male		do	do	
Margaret Siran	70	female		do	do	
John Lamb	20	male	Clerk	do	do	
Archibald Lamb	22	male	do	do	do	
William Martin	22	do	Servant	do	do	
John Clarke	25	do	Farmer	do	do	
Harriet Clarke	25	female	Seamstress	do	do	
John Rusher	39	male		do	do	
Eliza Rusher & 4 chil.	32	female	do	do	do	
Mary Wilkinson & 4 ch.	32	do	Merchant	do	do	
P. Beaufils	24	male	do	France	do	Ship Jeane Louise, Le Vasseur.
C. Saalacier	45	do		do	do	
C. M. Barry	26	female	Spinster	U. States	do	Ship Hibernia, H. Graham.
E. Kearney	21	do	do		do	
William Guy	7	male			do	
William Barry	23	do			do	
William Boarum	24	do	Officer	U. States	do	Ship Rosalie, H. Murry.
William Chubbs	30	do	Brushmaker	G. Britain	do	
Lydia Chubbs & 3 chil.	30	female		do	do	
Ann Handing & 4 ch.	28	do			do	
A. Oliver	28	male	Seaman	U. States	do	Brig Radius, B. Granger.
George Butterville	30	do	do	Canada	do	
Charles Corcing	45	do	do	U. States	do	
Captain Douglass	30	do	do	do	do	

LIST *of* Passengers, &c.—*Quarter ending September 30, 1820.*

Custom House, with the Name of the Collector.	Names of Passengers.	Age.	Sex.	Occupation.	Country to which they belong.	Country of which they intend to become inhab's	Ship or Vessel, with the name of the Master or Commander.
New York, David Gelston.	Mrs. Williams	25	female		U. States	U. States	Brig Janette Josephine, B. Granger.
	Charles Casey	8	male		do	do	
	James Casey	10	do		do	do	
	William Casey	55	female		do	do	
	Mary Hardy	23	female		do	do	
	Hannah Hardy & 2 ch.	50	male	Grocer	G. Britain	do	Ship William and Jane, Jas. Gill
	W. Humphreys & 2 ch.	24	do	Clerk	do	do	
	Wm. Saunders	23	female		do	do	
	Martha Saunders		male	Merchant	Jamaica	do	
	Thomas F. Kidd		do		U. States	do	Sloop Antelope, J. West
	John Stafford		female		Jamaica	do	
	Mrs. West & 2 sons		male		do	do	
	John Dunster		female		France	do	
	Mrs. Dunster & child		male		do	do	
	Joseph Woolley		male		do	do	
	Raingeard	30	do	do	do	do	Brig Adellio, Laque.
	Benjamin Tennant	47	do	do	Scotland	do	Brig Reuben & Eliza, C. Harris.
	Robert Jackson	26	do	do	England	do	
	Edward Gibson	35	do	do	do	do	
	James Winstunly	18	do	do	do	do	
	William Clark	34	do	Mechanic	Ireland	do	
	Mary Clark	22	female		do	do	
	Wm. D. E. Archaiken	26	male		do	do	
	Rosina Walsh	20	female		do	do	
	Jane Walsh	17	do		do	do	
	Margaret Walsh	16	do		do	do	
	Frances Walsh	14	do		do	do	

Names	Age	Sex	Occupation	Country	U. States	Ship
Juliana Walsh	11	female		Ireland	do	
Thomas Cavenaugh	23	male		do	do	
Margaret Cavenaugh	29	female		do	do	
Felix David	18	male		do	do	
Joseph Brown	11	do		do	do	
Sarah Norman	35	female		do	do	
Ann Norman & 2 ch.	24	do		do	do	
Sarah Bradley & 4 ch.	35	do		do	do	Ship Orison, John Burns.
Robert Hunter	35	male	Mechanic	do	do	
Wm. James & child	50	female	Farmer	do	do	
Mary Thornton & 3 do.	52	do	Spinstress	do	do	
Rosanna M'Fadden	20	male	do	do	do	
James Dauscath	22	do	Farmer	do	do	
Joseph Mayne	40	female	do	do	do	
Nancy Seward & child	30	male	Spinster	do	do	
Peter Tally	23	do	Farmer	do	do	
James Lenox	26	do	do	do	do	
James Smith	18	female	do	do	do	
William May	52	male	do	do	do	
Betty May & 5 chil.	48	do		do	do	
A. S. Le Breton	25	female	Merchant	France	do	Ship Comet, W. Hall.
Ira Cowles & apprentice	42	male	Trader	U. States	do	Schooner Antelope, E. Abeille.
John Sherwin	41	do	Merchant	G. Britain	do	Ship America, E. Rossetter.
John Duscomb & 2 ch.	50	do	do	N.Foundland	do	Brig Greyhound, T. Bedsen.
Ann Hughely	32	female		do	do	
Mrs. A. Boyd & child	40	do		do	do	
Mrs. Patterson & 2 ch.	16	male		do	do	
James Brince	25	female		do	do	
Ellen Murphy	22	male		do	do	
Henry Coit	48	do	do	U. States	do	Schooner Edgar, Robert Johnson.
John Connan	35	female	do	do	do	Ship Trident, J. Watkinson.
S. M. Connan & child	30	male		do	do	
George Gore	25	do	do	do	do	Schooner Sally, John Whitehead.
Jose Gomez	21	do	do	Spain	do	
John De La Port	40	do	do	Italy	do	Ship William, J. Collins.
Daniel Burton	35	do	Farmer	England	do	
Mary Burton & ch.	40	female		do	do	
James Fern	40	male		do	do	

LIST of Passengers, &c.—Quarter ending September 30, 1820.

Custom House, with the name of Collector.	Names of Passengers.	Age.	Sex.	Occupation.	Country to which they belong.	Country of which they intend to become inhab's	Ship or Vessel, with the name of the Master or Commander.
New York. David Gelston.	Sarah Fern & 6 chil'n	44	female		England	U. States	Ship William, J. Collins.
	Zilpha Statty & 7 chil'n	50	male	Farmer	do	do	
	James Harris	24	do	Shoemaker	do	do	
	Catharine Harris	20	female		do	do	
	Mary Winters	17	do		do	do	
	John Rooney	22	male		do	do	
	Thomas Hay	17	do		do	do	
	Nichs. Buckley & child	58	do	Painter	do	do	
	James Watson & child	50	do		do	do	
	John Brig	46	do		do	do	
	John Milney	37	do		do	do	
	Hugh Gill	16	do		Ireland	do	
	Nancy Gill	16	female	Seamstress	do	do	
	Margt. Laden & 2 chil'n	35	do	do	do	do	
	Ann M'Gloire	22	do	Farmer	do	do	
	Saml. Cochrane	60	male		do	do	
	Sarah Cochrane & child	50	female		do	do	
	James Reid	40	male	do	do	do	
	Margt. Reid & 2 chil'n	26	female		do	do	
	Roger Jones	36	male	do	do	do	
	Betty Jones	24	female		do	do	
	John Jones	21	male		do	do	
	Ann Jones	18	female		do	do	
	Ann Lynch	60	do		do	do	
	Bridget Bernan	27	do		do	do	
	Martin Neven	18	male	Laborer	do	do	Ship Ocean, P. Steward.
	Margaret Young	20	female		do	do	

Name	Age	Sex	Occupation	From	To	Ship
Sally Kihaig	20	female		Ireland	U. States	
B. Conaway	28	do		do	do	
Edwd. Boyle	23	male		do	do	
Mary Ivenan	20	female		do	do	
Pat M'Donough	23	male		do	do	
Michael M'Given	23	do		do	do	
Chas. Cavenaugh	23	do		do	do	
N. Killfeather	30	do		do	do	
James Gammell	32	do		do	do	
Ann Leaden	26	female		do	do	
Patty M'Gowan	16	do		do	do	
James Cunningham	21	male	Merchant	do	do	
Mary Jones	11	female		do	do	
Geo. Gillon	26	male	Laborer	do	do	
Owen Gill	22	do	do	do	do	
Brian M'Laughlin	23	do	do	Lisbon	do	Brig L. M. Pelham, R. Schuyler.
Antonio L. F. Gatte	17	do	Gentleman	do	do	Brig Francis, J. Foreman.
John Schaehur	55	do	Merchant	do	do	
John Schaehur, jr.	20	do	do		do	
Simon M'Gregor	21	do	do		do	
John L. Smith	23	do	do		do	
James Smith	35	do	do		do	
Wm. Colrell	56	do	Farmer		do	
Jane Colrell & 3 chil'n	50	female			do	
Gilbert Crawford	30	male	Teacher		do	
Donald Crawford	33	do	Farmer		do	
Peter Crawford	28	do	do		do	
Malcolm M'Farlan	28	do	do		do	
Catharine Crawford	26	female			do	
Sarah Crawford	24	do			do	
Mrs. Wright	40	do			do	
Christian M'Alpin	40	male	Farmer	U. States	do	
Malcom Wright	21	do	do	do	do	
Peter Wright	18	do	do		do	
James Wright	31	do	do		do	
Theophilus Patten	27	do	do		do	
Richd. W. Meade & son	42	do	Merchant		do	Ship Edward, J. Macey.
Samuel Learned	35	do	do		do	

LIST of Passengers, &c.—Quarter ending September 30, 1820.

Custom House, with the Name of the Collector.	Names of Passengers.	Age.	Sex.	Occupation.	Country to which they belong.	Country of which they intend to become inhb'ts.	Ship or Vessel, with the name of the Master or Commander.
New-York, David Gelston.	John Messenger	37	male	Brewer	G. Britain	U. States	Ship Edward, J. Macey.
	Maria do. & child	38	female		do	do	
	H. Christmas & 2 chil'n	27	male		do	do	
	James Bennet	34	male	Surgeon	do	do	
	Mrs. Bennet & 2 chil'n	62	female		do	do	
	Mary Jones & 3 chil'n	29	do		do	do	
	Eleanor Simmons	15	do		do	do	
	John Benson	32	male		do	do	
	John Sands	32	do		do	do	
	Mary Sands & 3 child'n.	26	female		do	do	
	John Reynolds	20	male		do	do	
	Wm. Woodham	23	do		do	do	
	Henry Badger	21	do		do	do	
	Charles Lambell	19	do		do	do	
	John Hutman	45	do		do	do	
	Joseph Atkinson	30	do	Tailor	do	do	Ship Hamlet, J. Dickerson.
	Sarah do and 4 child'n	29	female		do	do	
	Robert Atkinson	22	male		do	do	
	Joseph Aucaw	14	do		do	do	
	Francis Megruff	45	do	Gentleman	Germany	do	Ship Caledonia, Jno. Taubman.
	Christ. Wm. Megruff		do	do	do	do	
	Liliendale	28	do		do	do	
	Christian Saggrott	33	do	Baker	do	do	
	Elias Englandhand	32	do	Painter	do	do	
	John Anderson	20	do	Farmer	U. States	do	Schooner Hope, Elnathan Lewis.
	John Warrener	25	do	Stonecutter	Ireland	do	Brig Hibernia, J. E. Walding.
	Alice Dillon & child	30	female			do	

Name	Age	Sex	Occupation			Ship
Mary Duff	18	female	Lady	Ireland	U. States	
Eliza Martin	18	do	do	do	do	
Michael Longley	11	male		do	do	
Margaret Halligan	9	female		do	do	
James Halligan	22	male		do	do	
John Lynar	27	do		do	do	
Catharine Kearn	19	female		do	do	
Ann Riley	27	do		do	do	
John Clark	22	male		do	do	
Nancy Clark	25	female		do	do	
Pat. Flood	28	male		do	do	
Edward Flood	20	do		do	do	
Thomas Flood	30	do		do	do	
John Watson	28	do		do	do	
Thomas Deane	20	do		do	do	
Pat. Kelly	19	do		do	do	
James Martin	21	female		do	do	
C. Moore	20	do		do	do	
Miss Moore	7	male		do	do	
John Stephens	24	female		do	do	
E. Briggs and child	18	do		do	do	
Mary Martin	19	male		do	do	
W. McCarty	20	do		do	do	
J. Duff	28	do		do	do	
S. Runaghan	21	do		do	do	
Wm. Jackson	27	do	Merchant	do	do	
M. Jackson & child	19	do	do	do	do	
J. Gorham	45	do		do	do	
A. Nugent & 2 chil,	23	do		do	Ireland	
James Berrin	32	do	do	do	do	
William Gibbons	22	do	do	do	U. States	
Charles Gibbons	22	female		do	do	
Miss Rodgers	65	male	Milliner	U. States	do	Schooner Reindeer, E. Crowell,
John Twine	60	do	Merchant	do	do	
Daniel M'Daniel	65	do	do	do	do	
Alexander M'Daniel	50	do	do	do	do	
Copp						
James Hay, jun.	29	do	do	New York	do	Schooner Daniel & James, J. Baxter.

LIST of Passengers, &c.—Quarter ending September 30, 1820.

Custom House, with the Name of the Collector.	Names of Passengers.	Age.	Sex.	Occupation.	Country to which they belong.	Country of which they intend to become inhab's	Ship or Vessel, with the Name of the Master or Commander.
New-York, David Gelston.	Robert Ludlow	18	male	Merchant	New-York	U. States	Schooner Daniel & James, J. Baxter.
	Jane Kingsland	16	female	Lady	St. Johns	do	
	John Adams & 3 ch.	42	male		do	St. Johns	
	Catharine Drake	45	female	Lady	U. States	U. States	
	Nathaniel Hughes	31	male	Merchant	do	do	
	Samuel A. Davenport	21	do	do	do	do	Ship Belle Savage, H. Russell.
	Jonathan Judd	38	do	Clergyman	G. Britain	do	
	William Donaldson	43	do	Hosier	do	do	
	John Brian	25	do	Farmer	do	do	
	William Hoyle & child	46	do	Tailor	do	do	
	Thomas Simpson & ch.	31	do	Farmer	do	do	
	Alexander M'Bean	36	do	do	Ireland	Ireland	Ship Alligator, J. Hart.
	J. Buchanan	22	female	Merchant	U. States	U. States	
	Abraham Saloman	30	male	Merchant	do	do	
	Mr. Coffin	24	do	Painter	do	do	Schooner Logan, Samuel Holmes.
	Vincent Holmes	19	do	Mariner	do	do	
	John Johnson	17	do	do	do	do	
	Thomas Dawson	40	do	Farmer	G. Britain	Canada	
	John Colgan	30	do	Merchant	do	do	Schooner Nancy, R. Crowell.
	Charles O. Fling	35	do	Teacher	Ireland	U. States	
	Hannah Burnes	35	female		G. Britain	Canada	
	Catharine Thorn	40	do		do	do	
	John Campbell	25	male	Farmer	Ireland	U. States	
	Mary Campbell	20	female		do	do	
	Betsey M'Conegen	25	do		do	do	
	William Crawford	25	male	Farmer	G. Britain	do	
	Edward Burgess	35	do	do	do	Canada	

Name	Age	Sex	Occupation	Where born	Destination	Ship
Rachel Burgess	25	female		G. Britain	Canada	
Thomas Bourt	25	male	Farmer	do	do	
Margaret Innis	20	female		do	do	
James Innis	20	male		do	do	
Mary Innis	18	female		do	do	
Benjamin Sprawl	18	male				
Samuel M'Cloud	18	do				
Lettice M'Cloud	18	female				
Henry Herve	35	male	Artist	England	U. States	Brig Venus, William Tarne.
Ebenezer K. Decker	45	do	do	U. States	do	
A. Doolittle	32	do	Teacher	do	do	
John Jones	30	do	Mechanic	do	do	
Benjamin Hinman	24	do	Farmer	do	do	
Richard Redman	31	do	Distiller	England	do	
Albert Dakin	18	do	Baker	U. States	do	
Roquet	40	do	Sea captain	France	France	Schooner Maria Ann, M. Van Horne.
Abraham Lewis	45	do	Merchant	U. States	U. States	Brig Mary, J. M. Noyes.
William Atkerson	26	do	Seaman	do	do	
Sarah Monaham	27	female	Seamstress	Trinidad	do	Schooner Edward, John Carlisle.
George Dickinson	41	male	Clerk	G. Britain	do	Ship Manhattan, D. Frank.
Alice Dickinson	37	female		do	do	
Seth Slack	23	male	Butcher	do	do	
Jane Slack	20	female		do	do	
Felix Quinn	32	male	Laborer	do	do	
Dorothy Quinn & 2 ch.	28	female		do	do	
William Nottingham	36	male	Merchant	do	do	
E. Nottingham & 5 ch.	30	female		do	do	
John M'Arthur	28	male	Laborer	do	do	
William Zerey	37	do	Merchant	do	do	
John Johnson	21	do,	Druggist	do	do	
Stephen Gullet	47	do,	Merchant	U. States	do	Ship James Monroe, J. Rodgers.
N. H. Rutherford	27	do	do	Ireland	Ireland	
Miles Ashforth	21	do	do	G. Britain	G. Britain	
Charles Hayes	35	do		Ireland	Ireland	
Anna M. Hayes	27	female		do	do	
Ellen Smith	16	do		do	do	
John Evans	45	male	Farmer	do	do	
Ann Evans	50	female		do	do	

LIST of Passengers, &c.—Quarter ending September 30, 1820.

Custom House, with the name of the Collector.	Names of Passengers.	Age.	Sex.	Occupation.	Country to which they belong.	Country of which they intend to become inhab's	Ship or Vessel, with the name of the Master or Commander.
New-York, David Gelston.	Elizabeth Hawley	25	female	Servant	Ireland	Ireland	Ship James Monroe, J. Rodgers.
	Sarah Thorp & 2 ch.	24	do		do	do	
	Betty Holden & 4 ch.	40	do		do	do	
	Mary Spraul & 2 ch.	30	do		do	do	
	Mary Moss	27	do		do	do	
	J. Gammel & 2 ch.	20	do		do	St. Domingo	
	Mary Bernard	24	do		France	do	
	George Bexter	30	male	Merchant	England	do	
	Benj. G. Dayton	29	do	Shipmaster	U. States	U. States	
	John M'Donald	25	do	Farmer	do	do	
	Thomas Atkinson	30	do	Upholsterer	England	do	
	John Egan & Son	30	do	Laborer	do	do	
	Thomas Lawson	31	do	Merchant	do	do	
	Fenton Lawson	21	do	do	do	do	
	Emma Lawson & ch.	21	female		do	do	
	Eliz. Hoye & 2 ch.	26	do		do	do	
	Thomas Listre	67	male	Farmer	do	do	
	Martha Listre	60	female		do	do	
	L. Stockwell	13	do		do	do	
	William Leister	35	male		do	do	
	Sarah Leister & ch.	26	female		do	do	
	Mary Wright & ch.	28	do		do	do	
	Thos. Hollings	43	male	Farmer	do	do	
	Mary Hollings & 2 ch.	30	female		do	do	
	John Charlesworth	23	male	Farmer	do	do	
	John Canacle	52	do	do	do	do	
	Thomas Hart	32	do		do	do	

Name	Age	Sex	Occupation	Where from	U. States	Ship
Sarah Wiley	25	female	Gentleman	England Denmark Ireland	do	Ship Solon, C. Smith.
Harman E. Beastress	22	male	Farmer	do	do	Ship Rufus King, Charles Clark
James Campbell	25	do	Laborer	do	do	
Nicholas Scanlan	20	do	do	do	do	
James Neichan	22	do	do	do	do	
Henry Neichan	24	do	do	do	do	
Jane Patterson	22	female	Housewife	do	do	
Mary Patterson	29	do	do	do	do	
Mary Morrow & child	26	do	do	do	do	
James Morrow	19	male	Laborer	do	do	
David Pollock	36	do	Farmer	do	do	
John Loughy	26	do	do	do	do	
Thomas Corcoran	19	do	do	do	do	
James Rankin	24	do	do	do	do	
Edward Dougherty	24	do	do	do	do	
Robert Montgomery	25	do	do	do	do	
James M'Kee	25	do	do	do	do	
Patrick Dickson	30	do	do	do	do	
William Ewing	24	do	do	do	do	
David Smith	30	do	do	do	do	
Nancy Cauthers	20	female	Spinster	do	do	
Elizabeth Hamilton	20	do	do	do	do	
James Miller	20	male	Laborer	do	do	
James Kearney	22	do	do	do	do	
John Gallaugher	40	do	do	do	do	
James Gallaugher	30	do	do	do	do	
Sarah Campbell & 3 chil.	40	female	Housewife	do	do	
George M'Gwine	55	male	Farmer	do	do	
Charles Ban	24	do	do	do	do	
William Davenport	17	do	Clerk	do	do	
James Knox	38	do	do	do	do	
Mary M. Paskey	18	female	Spinster	do	do	
Elizabeth Densmore	21	do	do	do	do	
William Derney	21	male	Clerk	do	do	
Robert Alexander	18	do	do	do	do	
Oliver Campbell	24	do	Farmer	do	do	
Robert Ayers	24	do	do	do	do	
Charles Bonner	40	do	do	do	do	

LIST of Passengers, &c.—Quarter ending September 30, 1820.

Custom House, with the name of the Collector.	Names of Passengers.	Age.	Sex.	Occupation.	Country to which they belong.	Country of which they intend to become inh'bs.	Ship or Vessel, with the name of the Master or Commander.
New York, David Gelston.	Jane Bonner & child	34	female	Housewife	Ireland	U. States	Ship Rufus King, Charles Clark.
	Mary Bonner & 3 chil.	40	do		do	do	
	Mary Walker & 3 chil.	40	do		do	do	
	Joseph Fulton	36	male	Farmer	do	do	
	William White	25	do		do	do	
	James M'Mullen	30	do		do	do	
	Dennis M'Laughlin	22	do		do	do	
	William Donnell	45	do		do	do	
	John Walker	25	do		do	do	
	John M'Crab	20	do		do	do	
	Matthew M'Lane	22	do		do	do	Sloop Jefferson, A. Strout.
	Patrick Trainer	28	do	Farmer	do	do	
	Daniel Dickson	25	do	Merchant	do	do	
	Andrew Nagton	37	do	Mason	do	do	
	Matthew Tarrell	26	do	Laborer	do	do	
	James Tarrell	60	do	Carpenter	U. States	do	Brig Brothers, J. Gardner.
	John Strang	40	do	Cooper	do	do	
	John Mooney	30	do	Merchant	England	do	Brig Sarah Ann, J. Gerandel.
	Bunch and wife	28	do		France	do	
	W. H. Hippe	40	female		do	do	
	D. Lenas and son	22	male		do	do	
	Campagen	38	do		do	do	
	H. Fluon	30	do		do	do	
	W. Raydon	24	do		do	do	
	B. Campbell	22	do		do	do	
	N. Blaine	36	do		do	do	
	E. Brodge	37	female	Spinster	do	do	Schooner Royal Oak, J. Albern.

Name	Age	Sex	Occupation	Country	Dest.	Ship
C. Brodge	17	male	Merchant	France	U. States	Wicker, Richard Burd.
Mary Ann Brodge	19	female	Spinster	do	do	
Mary Garline & child	6	do	Servant	do	do	Schooner George, B. Berry.
George A. Clark	40	male	Merchant	do	do	
Eyre Evans	28	do	Farmer	G. Britain	do	
D. Coffer	25	do	Tailor	do	do	
W. Savage	22	do	Farmer	do	do	
Thomas Doley	29	do	Jeweller	do	do	Schooner Peacock, J. Harden.
Erastus A. Dunkell	25	do	Doctor	U. States	do	
Lawrence Christie	35	do	Nailmaker	do	do	
William Halrage	37	do	Merchant	England	do	Ship Julius Cæsar, C. H. Marshall.
George Oakley	27	do	do	do	do	
A. Marieta	32	do	do	Spain	do	
Thomas Gray	30	do	do	Bermuda	do	Ship James, Robert Blount.
Mrs. Gray & child	24	female		do	do	Brig Ocean, A. C. White.
Servant of Mrs. Gray	25	do		do	do	
Mary Taylor & servant	26	do		do	do	
R. J. Lindsey	34	male		Boston	do	
Mrs. Fitzgerald	51	female		New York	do	
M. Bunnell	38	male		Nantucket	do	
G. Potts	14	do		Bermuda	do	
James Robson	32	do	Farmer	G. Britain	do	Ship Evergreen, J. Rathbone
Ann Robson & 3 chil.	40	female		do	do	
John Croker	27	male	Student	do	do	
Mary Drew	22	female		do	do	
Charles Gauvin	30	male	Laborer	do	do	
Michl. Jenningan	22	do	do	do	do	
Thomas Smith	26	do	do	do	do	
Thomas Moore	18	do	do	do	do	
John M'Carr	28	do	do	do	do	
Phil. Smith	30	do	do	do	do	
Phil. Smith, jr.	20	do	do	do	do	
Andw. Coningan	14	do	do	do	do	
Nicholas Bird	26	do	do	do	do	
Michl. Gaffrey	22	do	do	do	do	
Geo. Burwell	25	do	do	do	do	
Dorothy do. & 7 chil.	50	female	Spinster	do	do	
George Dixon	43	male	Clerk	G. Britain	do	

LIST of Passengers, &c.—Quarter ending September 30, 1820.

Custom House, with the name of the Collector.	Names of Passengers.	Age.	Sex.	Occupation.	Country to which they belong.	Country of which they intend to become inhab's	Ship or Vessel, with the name of the Master or Commander.
NEW YORK, David Gelston.	Margt. Dixon & child	34	female		G. Britain	U. States	Ship Evergreen, J. Rathbone.
	Dorothy Stevens	68	do		do	do	
	Jane Stevens	30	do		do	do	
	Mary Stevens	28	do		do	do	
	Margery Stevens	26	do		do	do	
	Wm. Armstead	48	male	Farmer	do	do	
	John Armstead	41	do	do	do	do	
	Christopher Garnet	9	do		do	do	
	William Shute	16	do	Wheelwright	do	do	
	Cornelius Flood	25	do	Laborer	do	do	
	J. Jones and 6 children	40	female		do	do	
	Ann Owens	20	do		do	do	
	Robert Thomas	30	male	Laborer	do	do	
	Betsey Roberts	25	female		do	do	
	Robert Mickle	35	male	Tailor	do	do	
	Samuel Gunter	23	do	Laborer	do	do	
	Bridget Branan	17	female		do	do	
	Benjamin Jones	34	male	Laborer	do	do	
	Richard D. Popham	52	do	do	do	do	
	John Wilson	30	do	do	do	do	
	Jose Fernandez	35	do	Merchant	Spain	Spain	Schooner Atrevida, Sancho.
	Michael Stevens	33	do	do	U. States	U. States	Ship Radius, T. Deleno.
	Seth Diggs	27	do	Druggist	do	do	Ship Fair Trader, D. Higgins.
	Eliza Diggs & child	17	female		do	do	
	M. Meyer & 3 children	0	do		do	do	
	John Delafield	34	male	Merchant	G. Britain	do	Ship Cossack, S. M. Beth.
	E. A. do & 4 children	25	female		do	do	

Name	Age	Sex	Occupation	G. Britain	U. States
Ann Holland	22	female	Servant	do	do
James Ricketts	28	male	Gentleman	do	do
Ann Ricketts	19	female		do	do
Penelope Creed	52	do		do	do
Johnson Creed	22	male		do	do
Mrs. Banks and child	48	female		do	do
Ann Ridley	60	do		do	do
Jno. B. Hall	34	male		do	do
John Wright	20	do		do	do
Colonel Harriot	34	do		do	do
Granger Watson	48	do	Farmer	do	do
Eliza Watson & 3 chil.	50	female		do	do
Samuel Hunt	32	male		do	do
Lucy Hunt & 6 children	38	female		do	do
Isaac Welsh	36	male		do	do
Ann Welsh	40	female		do	do
Eliza Wood	17	do		do	do
William Phillips	27	male		do	do
Cath. Phillips & 4 chil.	26	female		do	do
William Holland	24	male		do	do
Mary A. Lowe & child	24	female		do	do
Margaret Davidson	42	do		do	do
Clarissa Winters	28	do		do	do
Clarissa Lankman	28	do		do	do
Henry Otten	25	male		do	do
C. Lankman	28	do		do	do
Isaac Halloway	31	do		do	do
John Halloway	25	do		do	do
Russell Halloway	31	do		do	do
Eliza Halloway	25	female		do	do
John Arnold	30	male		do	do
George Stretch	26	do		do	do
John Houghton	28	do		do	do
William Johnston	27	do		do	do
Edward Luhton	24	do		do	do
George Sharp	25	do		do	do
Eliza. Sharp and child	27	female		do	do
Francis Alladay	17	do		do	do

LIST of Passengers, &c.—Quarter ending September 30, 1820.

Custom House, with the name of the Collector.	Names of Passengers.	Age.	Sex.	Occupation.	Country to which they belong.	Country of which they intend to become inhab's	Ship or Vessel, with the name of the Master or Commander.
New York, David Gelston.	Anna Laird	9	female		G. Britain	U. States	Ship Cossack, S. M. Belt.
	Mary Laird	7	do		do	do	
	Jemima Laird	5	do		do	do	
	William Laird	14	male		do	do	
	John Hunt	8	do		do	do	
	James Clark	25	do		do	do	
	Eliza Halloway	38	female		do	do	
	John Gold	23	male	Farmer	U. States	do	Schooner Julia Ann, J. Minot.
	Catharine Gold	26	female		do	do	
	Nicholas Kennedy	29	male	Farmer	Ireland	do	
	Sarah Kennedy & 2 chil.	23	female		do	do	
	Elizabeth Irchey	20	do		do	do	
	Robert Sheppard	43	male	Weaver	England	do	Ship Importer, William Lee.
	Thomas Leach	25	do	Farmer	New-York	do	Schooner Gertrude, F. West.
	Giles Hamilton	45	do	Clergyman	Barbadoes	Barbadoes	Ship Elias Barger, A. Amsby.
	I. H. Orderson	50	do		do	do	
	D. E. Orderson	29	female		do	do	
	J. Wharton	20	do		do	do	
	Mary M. Miller	50	do		do	do	
	Servant	13	do		do	do	
	Servant	50	do		do	do	
	Eliakim Hall	42	male	Butcher	Connecticut	U. States	Brig Hippomenes, L. Bourne.
	Abraham Johnson	60	do	Mariner	Virginia	do	
	Peter Reighot	21	do	Merchant	U. States	do	
	Daniel Peters	34	do	Cabinetmaker	Holland	da	Schooner Sea Serpent, Elisha Adams.
	Adam Lederer	39	do	Merchant	Austria	do	Schooner Franklin, B. Holmes.
	Jauger		do	do	do	do	

Name	Age	Sex	Occupation	Native Country	Destination	Ship
John F. Bailer	21	male	Merchant	Russia	U. States	Brig Helen, H. Patterson.
Frederick Leha	33	do	Saddler	do	do	
Mrs. Leha	33	female	do	do	do	
Christian Auscheropp	33	male	Tailor	Saxony	do	
John A. Wolfer	32	do	Merchant	Ireland	do	
James Doran and son	37	do	do.	do	do	
Peter Gribben	30	do	Laborer	do	do	
Ch. Dowdale	40	do		do	do	
Daniel Karran	17	do		do	do	
Philip Karran	21	do		do	do	
Edward Conyngham	18	do		do	do	
Michl. M. Pailand	22	do		do	do	
Letitia Rodgers & 2 chil.	27	female	Spinster	Denmark	do	Brig Catharine, A. McWeldon.
George Nelthrop	34	male	Merchant	do	do	
Seth S. Barnes & child	22	do	Gentleman	do	do	
George W. Blecker	20	do	do	do	do	
Maria Nelthrop	27	female	Lady	do	do	
Jane Barnes	17	do	do	do	do	
Ann Barnes	22	do	do	do	do	
Mary O. Connell & child	40	do	Servant	do	do	
P. White	30	do	do	do	do	
Deborah Custis	13	do	Planter	do	do	
Cornelle St. Cer	45	male	Planter	Guadaloupe	do	Brig Eliza, Edward R. Grueby.
Madame St. Cer	35	female		do	do	
Sergeant Alliaume	28	male	do	do	do	
Madame Alliaume	19	female		do	do	
Black servant	45	male		do	do	
Black do and infant	36	female		do	do	
William Steward	22	male	Engineer	England	England	Brig Ambuscade, S. Shedmore.
George Herker	38	do	Shopkeeper	U. States	U. States	
Samuel Fernandez	28	do	Mariner	do	do	
Salvadore Felix	38	do	do	do	do	
Antonia Mora	32	do	Merchant	Spain	Spain	
Gregoria Haward	41	female	do	France	France	
P. H. Chatena	22	do	do	do	do	
Oliver Brooks	27	male	do	U. States	U. States	
Jeremiah Melony	40	do	do	do	do	
Stephen Ireland	20	do	do	do	do	

LIST of Passengers, &c.—Quarter ending September 30, 1820.

Custom House, with the name of the Collector.	Names of Passengers.	Age.	Sex.	Occupation.	Country to which they belong.	Country of which they intend to become inhab's	Ship or Vessel, with the name of the Master or Commander.
New York, David Gelston.	James Smith	66	male	Farmer	England	U. States	Schooner Lewis, I. Sears.
	Henry Bar	57	do	do	do	do	
	Mary Cox	17	female		do	do	
	John Car	18	male	Farmer	do	do	
	Mary Mason	25	female		do	do	
	George Bun	16	male	do	do	do	
	George Gilbert	22	do	Merchant	St. Johns	N. Brunsw'k	Schooner Charlotte Corday, J. G. Russel.
	D. J. M. Ciller	28	do	do	do	U. States	
	J. H. Harris & child	26	do	do	do	do	
	Mary Harris	19	female	Lady	do	do	
	G. Cameron	18	male	Merchant	do	do	
	Nancy M'Mullen	22	female	Lady	do	do	
	Daniel Campal	26	male	Farmer	do	do	
	Alexander Gamiel		do			do	
	Alexander Gamiel	22	male		do	do	
	Alexander Guim	26	do		do	do	
	James Bedlow		do		St. Croix	do	Ship Virginia, John Fink.
	Mrs. Bedlow & 5 ch.		female		U. States	do	
	Philip Verplank		male		do	do	
	Daniel M'Carthy		do		do	do	
	Mary Magdalen		female		do	do	
	Alexander Jenkins	45	male	Mariner	Portugal	St. Jago	Schooner Maria, A. J. Martinus.
	Joachim Paulino	47	do	Merchant	Spain	Spain	
	Antonio J. Aloos	32	do	Mariner		do	
	Wm. Moore		do				
	Antonio Pence	12	do		Portugal	St. Jago	

Name	Age	Sex	Occupation			
Thomas Youie						Prisoners taken by the United States ship Cyane, and sent by the Consul at St. Jago.
John Talbot						
Charles Gilson						
Thomas Young						
Thomas Gee						
A. Gauselins						
D. Steel	25	male	Showman	U. States	U. States	Brig Adze, A. Aumington.
Mrs. Steel & child	23	female	do	do	do	
Jane O. Brian	28	do	do	do	do	
A. Graves	50	male	Merchant	do	do	
A. Chapron	30	do	do	do	do	
J. D. Cory	25	do	do	England	do	
Wm. Gilliat	29	do	do	do	do	
Sophia Gilliat	28	female	Merchant	do	do	Ship Courier, J. Eldridge.
James Trimby	22	male	Merchant	do	do	
George Welden	47	do	Captain	do	do	
John S. Henry	24	do	Merchant	do	do	
Augustus Thorndike	22	do	Servant	U. States	do	
J. B. Gevat	42	do	Farmer	France	do	
Charles Phillips	44	do	Minister	U. States	do	
David Williamson	59	do	Merchant	England	do	
Isab. Williamson & 2 ch.	58	female	Merchant	do	do	
Wm. Johnson	19	male		do	do	
John Reid	14	do	Merchant	do	do	
Geo. V. Meyer	44	do	Merchant	New-York	New York	Ship Weser, Wm. G. Pease
Johanna V. do. & 4 ch.	36	female		do	do	
Miss Esselrun	33	do				
Ann Gasulman	17	do				
Francis Gattsbeyer	42	male	Servant	U. States	U. States	Ship Stephania, M. R. Burke.
Theo. C. Wilmerding	27	do	Merchant	do	do	
Charles Mauld	40	do		do	do	
Harriet Mauld & ch.	30	female		do	do	
P. G. Mars	60	male	Planter	do	do	
Francis Maillard	38	do	F. officer	do	do	
Aime Archel	31	do	Traveller	do	do	
Louisa Vignardonne	28	female		do	do	
Richard Smith	37	male	Merchant	do	do	
Joseph Gareau	43	do	do	France	France	

LIST of Passengers, &c.—Quarter ending September 30, 1820.

Custom House, with the Name of the Collector.	Names of Passengers.	Age.	Sex.	Occupation.	Country to which they belong.	Country of which they intend to become inhab's	Ship or Vessel, with the name of the Master or Commander.
New York, David Gelston.	James Nugent	40	male	Merchant	England	France	Ship Stephania, M. R. Burke.
	Camille Marquet	20	do	do	France	do	
	Fran. O. Plator & 5 ch.	32	female		do	do	
	John H. Simplet	12	male				
	Joseph Simplet	10	do				
	Charles Simplet	5	do				
	S. A. Willoughby	20	do		U. States	U. States	Schooner William Allen, Hallet.
	E. R. Belcher	19	do		do	do	
	Jacob Ricketts	28	do	Merchant	do	do	
	David Poore	30	do	do	do	do	Schooner Union, William Leech, jun.
	Arthur N. Vernard	25	do	do	do	do	
	Major Draper	45	do	Mechanic	do	do	
	Lewis B. Sturges	57	do	Merchant	do	do	
	Richard Rodgers	22	do	do	do	do	Ship S. C. Packet, A. J. Cartwright.
	Wm. Billingham	26	do	Mariner	Denmark	England	
	I. I. Lalique	43	do	Clergyman	Jersey in Eur.	Canada	Brig Rebecca Ann, J. Brown.
	J. O. Plessis	57	do	C. bishop	Canada	do	Ship Martha, William Sketchly.
	I. F. Jurgeon	32	do	Clergyman	do	do.	
	Jos. Perant	23	do	Surgeon	do	do.	
	Edmund Molineux	28	do	Merchant	G. Britain	G. Britain	
	John Allen	40	do	do	do	do	
	Frances Allen & ch.	38	female		do	do	
	Ann Valentine	30	do		U. States	do	
	James Edgar	34	male	Merchant	do	do	
	H. M. Edgar	22	female		do	do	
	H. Carnachan & 2 ch.	22	do		do	do	
	Lydia Parker	22	do	Servant	G. Britain	do	

Name	Age	Sex	Occupation			Ship
Ellen Johnson	26	female	Servant	G. Britain	G. Britain	Schooner Loire, J. Basset.
Ellen Jones	30	do	do	W. Indies	do	
Frances Cazot	33	do	do	U. States	Canada	
Stephen Montun	22	male	Merchant	do	U. States	
Richard Montun	40	do	Officer	Canada	do	
James M'Donald	22	do	Merchant	U. States	Canada	
Wm. W. Fowler	27	do	do	Ireland	U. States	Brig Wilmot, Wm. Hathaway.
Wm. J. Bowen	20	do		do	da	
Wm. Wright	21	do	Farmer	do	do	
Jane Wright	21	female		do	do	Ship Imperial, D. Elkins.
Susanna Wright	14	do		do	do	
James Myers	38	male	Farmer	do	do	
John Mullen	22	do	do	do	do	
Ann Myers	25	female		do	do	
Mary Stewart	18	do		do	do	
Stephen Myers	55	male	Farmer	do	do	
William Graham	18	do	Laborer	do	do	
David Dill	50	do	Farmer	do	do	
Margaret Dill	45	female		do	do	
Samuel Dill	28	male	Farmer	do	do	
David Dill	25	do	do	do	do	
Hannah Dill	20	female		do	do	
Nancy Dill	25	do		do	do	
Hannah Campbell	70	female		do	do	
David White	60	male		do	do	
Margaret White & 7 ch.	40	female		do	do	
Mary Brown	12	do		do	do	
Wm. M'Nilands	15	male		do	do	
Elizabeth Campbell	50	female		do	do	
Eliza Campbell	28	do		do	do	
Mary Campbell	34	do		do	do	
Catharine Campbell	26	do.		do	do	
John Ramsay	40	male	Farmer	do	do	
James O. Donnell	18	do		do	do	
Jane M'Keawn	16	female		do	do	
Samuel Floyd	27	male		do	do	
Hannah Fletcher	25	female		do	do	
Wm. Armstrong	24	male		do	do	

LIST of Passengers, &c.—Quarter ending September 30, 1820.

Custom House, with the name of the Collector.	Names of Passengers.	Age.	Sex.	Occupation.	Country to which they belong.	Country of which they intend to become inhab's	Ship or vessel, with the name of the Master or Commander.
New York, David Gelston.	Robert Armstrong	50	male		Ireland	U States	Ship Imperial, D. Elkins,
	Mar. Armstrong & 2 ch.	50	female		do	do	
	Adam Corran	40	male		do	do	
	John Marshall	21	do		do	do	
	Jane S. Parker	27	female		do	do	
	Martha Wallad	7	do		do	do	
	Sarah Wallad	5	do		do	do	
	John Kirkpatrick	25	male		do	do	
	I. M'Donough & 4 ch.	30	female		do	do	
	Michael Conolley	60	male	Shoemaker	do	do	Brig Superb, Wm. Hamilton.
	M. Connolley & 5 ch.	56	female		do	do	
	Owen Gilloon	40	male	Trader	do	do	
	Hugh Gilloon	24	do	do	do	do	
	Biddy Gillespie	18	female		do	do	
	Mary M'Gonegal	19	do	Servant	do	do	
	Patrick Patterson	30	male	Laborer	do	do	
	Geo. M'Ree	25	do	Farmer	do	do	
	Jane M'Ree	20	female		do	do	
	Mary Banks & 2 ch.	30	do		do	do	
	Ann Phehele	18	do		do	do	
	Patrick Whims	12	male		do	do	
	John Todd	19	do	Doctor	do	do	
	M. Jewett	32	do	Merchant	U. States	do	Schooner Diana, S. W. M'Pherson
	Betsey Jewett & ch.	35	female	Lady	do	do	
	Fred. D. Leake	30	male	Gentleman	do	do	
	Peter Guillet	25	do	Planter	do	do	
	E. Tenikin	31	do	Servant	do	do	

Name	Age	Sex	Occupation	G. Britain	U. States	Ship
Job B. Thomas	32	male	Shipmaster	G. Britain	do	Schooner Harmony, Charles Spence.
Isabel. Thomas & 3 ch.	23	female		do	do	
George Craraford	46	male		do	do	
Margaret do. & 6 ch.	40	female		do	do	
William Fisher & son	55	male	Laborer	do	do	
John Graham	25	do	do	do	do	
Margaret do. & ch.	26	female		do	do	
Robert Graham	17	male		do	do	
M. M'Donald & 2 ch.	24	female		da	do	
John Thompson	32	male		do	do	
John Thompson, jun.	28	do		do	do	
James Thompson	22	do		do	do	
George Thompson	20	do		do	do	
Maria Thompson & 2 ch.	24	do		do	do	
John Brown & son	40	male	Laborer	do	do	
John Rodgers	24	do	do	do	do	
Elizabeth Rodgers	30	female		do	do	
James Richardson	25	male		do	do	
Mr. Gomez	45	do	Merchant	N. York	do	Schooner General Jackson, J. B. Nicholls.
Martin Cousoash	22	male	Planter	London	do	
Mr. Seiroof	20	do	Merchant	Charleston	do	Ship Robert Burns, H. Coffin.
James Denny	21	do.	do	G. Britain	do	
Valentine Holmes	22	do.	do	do	do	
Wm. Orr	20	do.	Farmer	do	do	
C. Cunningham	21	female	Spinster	do	do	
Rebecca Bryan	30	male	Shoemaker	do	do	
Samuel Lindsay	26	female	Spinster	do	do	
Biddy Harlowe	18	female	do	do	do	
Rose Dougherty & 2 ch.	24	do	Farmer	do	do	
Alex. Gilmore	38	male		do	do	
Ann Gilmore & 2 ch.	60	female	Doctor	do.	do	
Wm. Shaw	20	male	Shoemaker	U. States	do	
Charles Devine	48	do	Farmer	do	do	
Wm. Rodgers	57	do		do	do	
Han. Rodgers & 3 ch.	55	female	Farmer	do	do	
Andrew M'Ildoney	24	male	do	do	do	
Edward Mullen	20	do	do	do	do	
Joseph Orr	16	do		do	do	

LIST of Passengers, &c.—Quarter ending September 30, 1820.

Custom House, with the name of the Collector.	Names of Passengers.	Age.	Sex.	Occupation.	Country to which they belong.	Country of which they intend to become inh'bts.	Ship or Vessel, with the Name of the Master or Commander.
New-York, David Gelston.	Robt. Orr	28	male	Farmer	U. States	U. States	Ship Robert Burns, H. Coffin.
	William Wiley	28	do	do	do	do	
	James Hoops	28	do	do	do	do	
	Michl. M'Donough	20	do	do	do	do	
	Patrick Dougherty	12	do	do	do	do	
	Jane Lenox	20	female	Servant	do	do	
	Martha Lenox	15	do	do	do	do	
	John Morehead	16	male	do	do	do	
	John Kelly	20	do	Farmer	do	do	
	Henry Kain	25	do	do	do	do	
	Philip Dougherty	24	do	Carpenter	do	do	
	John Black	25	do	Farmer	do	do	
	Edward Dougherty	24	do	Laborer	do	do	
	Mary do and 2 child'n	24	female	Spinster	do	do	
	James Faukner	22	male	Farmer	do	do	
	Robt. M'Williams	50	do	Laborer	do	do	
	Jos. do. and 2 child'n	22	do	do	do	do	
	Mary Band	20	do		do	do	
	M. Jexido	50	do	Mariner	do	do	Brig Victory, H. Sands.
	Thomas Martin	50	do	Merchant	do	do	
	William Cheston	24	do	Carpenter	do	do	Brig Sally and Hope, J. M. Blinn.
	Jose M. Gracia	42	do		Spain	do	
	Philip Cope	25	do	Cooper	U. States	do	
	B. Aikin	40	do		do	do	
	Thomas M'Carthy	30	do	Mason	do	do	
	Samuel Barnes	22	do	Cooper	do	do	
	James Winter	47	do	Dyer	England	do	Ship Maria Caroline, N. Bishop.

Name	Age	Sex	Occupation			Ship
Charles Taylor	16	male.		England	U. States	
Elizabeth Breton	28	female		do	do	
Henry M'Winter	46	male		do	do	
William Blanchard	25	do	Mechanic	do	do	
Frances Blanchard	27	female		do	do	
Jeremiah Chubb	30	male	do	do	do	
Levi Dyre	24	do		do	do	
Keturah Dyre	26	female		do	do	
David Brown	53	male	Farmer	do	do	
Louis Chustenat	55	do	do	do	do	
Joseph Boutard	26	do	Merchant	do	do	Brig Hind, Jno. Boyak.
Laurent Niga	28	do	do	do	do	
Alexander Easson	47	do	Laborer	do	do	
Amelia Wilson	47	female		do	do	
Jane Chisholme	60	do		do	do	
Isabella Chisholme	40	do		do	do	
Margaret Fyfe	22	do	Spinster	do	do	
John Skinner	75	male	Laborer	do	do	
Janet Skinner & child	40	female	Spinster	do	do	
Elizabeth Skinner	30	do	do	do	do	
Lawrence Reilley	24	male		do	do	Brig Hind, Joel Prince.
Antonio Bubio	30	do	Spanish officer	Spain	Spain	
Antonio Meida	21	do	Servant	do	do	
Antonio Leanio	25	do	Merchant	do	do	
John Pettalago	30	do	do	do	do	
I. B. Habert	25	do	do	France	France	Brig Emelie Marie, J. Delamare.
A. Klein	21	do		Germany	U. States	
William Boothe	59.	do	Farmer	G. Britain	do	
Betty Boothe & 5 chil.	59	female		do	do	Ship Mary, R. West,
John Byle	24	male		do	do	
Ellen Byle	22	female		do	do	
Ann Byle	18	do		do	do	
Thomas Long	19	male		do	do	
Thomas Aimet	49	do		do	do	
M. Clough & 3 child'n	37	female		do	do	
Ann Hotham & child	23	do		do	do	
William Collehin	30	male		do	do	
B. M'Lennie	40	do		do	do	

LIST of Passengers, &c.—Quarter ending September 30, 1820.

Custom House, with the Name of the Collector.	Names of Passengers.	Age.	Sex.	Occupation.	Country to which they belong.	Country of which they intend to become inhab's	Ship or Vessel, with the Name of the Master or Commander.
New York, David Gelston.	John Smith	70	male		G. Britain	U. States	Ship Mary, R. West.
	H. Rigby	29	do		do	do	
	Eliz. Rigby and 2 chil.	30	female		do	do	
	John Penn	40	male		do	do	
	Ann Penn and 3 chil.	40	female		do	do	
	G. Jones	26	male		do	do	
	Jane Jones	53	female		do	do	
	Edward Davis	50	male		do	do	
	Marg. Davis & 3 chil.	59	female		do	do	
	John Preston	52	male		do	do	
	Marg. Preston & 5 chil.	59	female		do	do	
	Philip Skein	26	male	Soldier	Holland	do	Sloop Happy Return, E. Wheaton.
	George H. Lensen	26	do	Merchant	Germany	do	Schooner Roseway, George Simmons.
	Bernard Mercello	40	do		England	do	
	Daniel Moran	40	do	Tanner & Cur.	do	do	
	Mary Ann do. & chil.	40	female		Germany	do	Brig Ohio, E. Carman.
	John S. Wolf	35	male	Painter	do	do	
	Jacob rfayer	26	do	Weaver	do	do	
	Christ. J. Bearn	28	do	Butcher	do	do	
	Jasper Shew	52	do	Farmer	do	do	
	B. Summers	30	do	Brewer	do	do	
	Anthony Quampf	22	do	Buttonmaker	do	do	
	David Clardany	40	do	Farmer	do	do	Schooner Nancy, R. Crowley.
	Mary Sullivan	40	female			do	
	Hannah Wilebey	40	do		Bermuda	U. States	Schooner Magnet, B. Waite
	Mary Grant	70	do		do	do	
	Daniel Leon	34	male	Merchant			

Name	Age	Sex	Occupation			Ship
Mrs. Leon and child	28	female		Bermuda	U. States	
Mrs. William do.	26	do		do	do	
Elizabeth Trott	30	do		do	do	
Anthony Atwood, jr.	31	male	Merchant	do	do	
Nathaniel Malony	16	do	Servant	do	do	
Peter Sevier	36	do	Weaver	G. Britain	Canada	Ship Grand Turk, Jno. O'Hara.
John Hodskin	21	do	Stonecutter	do	U. States	Ship Ganges, James Tompkins.
John Smithurst	31	do	Preacher	do	do	
Joseph Calder	45	do	Farmer	do	do	
Edward Tittus	24	do	do	do	do	
Thos. Seddon & 2 chil'n	60	do	do	do	do	
John Brown	38	do	do	do	do	
Eliz. Brown & 6 chil'n	39	female		do	do	
William Lee	17	male	Farmer	do	do	
Richard Baldwin	38	do		do	do	
Ann Baldwin & 6 chil.	34	female		do	do	
Ruth Grayson	20	do		do	do	
William Seadon	23	male	Farmer	do	do	
George Rudford	42	do	do	do	do	
Ann Rudford	36	female		do	do	
William Chaytor	23	male		do	do	
Mary Chaytor	25	female		do	do	
William Walker	33	male		do	do	
James Clark	23	do		do	do	
John Fielding	55	do		do	do	
Elizabeth Smart	35	female		do	do	
Samuel Smith	24	male		do	do	
William Hodgson	25	do		do	do	
Eliz. Hodgson & 3 chil.	26	female		do	do	
James Smith	24	male	Farmer	do	do	
John Wood	21	do		do	do	
John Bullock	21	do		do	do	
Rhodia Bullock	19	female		do	do	
Wm. Winterbotham	25	male		do	do	
Ann do. and 2 chil.	21	female		do	do	
John Winterbotham	23	male		do	do	
William Stone	33	do		do	do	
Jane Stone & 4 children	29	female		do	do	

LIST of Passengers, &c.—Quarter ending September 30, 1820.

Custom House, with the Name of the Collector.	Names of Passengers.	Age.	Sex.	Occupation.	Country to which they belong.	Country of which they intend to become inhb'ts.	Ship or Vessel, with the name of the Master or Commander.
New-York, David Gelston.	Matthew Duffy	35	male		G. Britain	U. States	Ship Ganges, Jas. Tompkins.
	Abraham Smart	49	do		do	do	
	M. Seddon & 7 chil'n	46	female		do	do	
	James Fisher	25	male		do	do	
	Robert Dixon	21	do		do	do	
	Matthew Bradbury	45	do		do	do	
	Alice do. & 3 chil'n	45	female		do	do	
	Joseph Claringham	21	male		do	do	
	Elias Wigley	27	do		do	do	
	Mary Wigley & child	24	female		do	do	
	Samuel Waring	26	male		do	do	
	James Howard	50	do		do	do	
	Richard Clark	21	do		do	do	
	Benj. Hollingsworth	24	female	Seamstress	Ireland	do	Ship Hesperus, A. M'Corkell.
	Isab. Thompson & child	22	male	Flax dresser	do	do	
	H. M'Giverin & 2 chil'n	33	do	Merchant	Baltimore	Baltimore	
	Wm. Smith	30	do	do	do	do	
	Hugh Smith	18	female	Spinster	Ireland	U. States	
	Mary M'Lenaghin	40	male	Farmer	do	do	
	Abraham Hazelton	40	do	do	do	do	
	Sarah do. & 5 chil'n	35	female		do	do	
	Wm. Gilpin	25	male		do	do	
	Joseph Simson	30	do		do	do	
	Sarah do. & 3 chil'n	23	female		do	do	
	John Small	40	male		do	do	
	Nancy Johnson & child	44	female	Cottonspinner	do	do	

Name	Age	Sex	Occupation		U. States	Ship
Ann Gutherell	51	female	Millwright	Ireland	do	
Wm. Lyons	36	male		do	do	
Jane Lyons	33	female		do	do	
John Reid	45	male	Merchant	do	do	
Richard Brown	20	do	do	do	do	
Gilbert Demster	30	do	Farmer	do	do	
Robert Ferguson	13	do		do	do	
Daniel M'Langhlin	24	do	Merchant	do	do	
Jos. M'Creed	11	do		do	do	
Hugh M'Dermot	78	do	Farmer	do	do	Brig Amazot, J. Hatch.
Wm. M'Dermot	24	do	do	do	do	
Elizabeth Peterson	20	female	Spinster	do	do	
R. C. Rutledge	28	male	Gentleman	Germany	do	
Lorenzo Benstern	20	do	Merchant	U. States	do	Ship Pacific, J. Smith.
John Prebble	30	do	do	do	do	Brig Nymph, J. Green.
Jas. Garcin & 3 chil'n	54	do	Cook	France	do	
Valentine Rumley	45	do	Merchant	England	do	
Augustus Gombault	36	do	do	France	do	
Adolphe Crozet	22	do	do	do	do	
J. Frelat and child	36	female		do	do	
A. Lefevre	36	do		do	do	
Peter Lefevre	45	male	Mariner	do	do	
R. Lefevre & 3 chil'n	35	female		do	do	
Robt. Gill & 2 chil'n	48	male	Farmer	England	do	Brig Neptune, H. Diamond.
Crossfield Savage	29	do	Mechanic	U. States	do	
Samuel Fales	28	do	Merchant	do	do	
James Pike	33	do	Cooper	do	do	
Seth Graves	26	do	Jeweller	do	do	
Peter M'Lehlin	23	do	Stonecutter	do	do	
Hezekiah Forth	55	do	Merchant	Bermuda	do	Schr. Lancaster, E. L. B. Lapsco?.
Ann Forth & child	23	female		do	do	
Hezekiah Forth, jr.	28	male	do	do	do	
Thomas L. Smith	18	do	Student	do	do	
Elizabeth Bowles	30	female		do	do	
John Lustre	35	male	Servant	do	do	
John Sheaves	30	do	Mariner	do	do	
Jesse Holbrook	44	do	Supercargo	do	do	
James Musson	60	do	Merchant	G. Britain	do	

LIST of Passengers, &c.—Quarter ending September 30, 1820.

Custom House, with the name of the Collector.	Names of Passengers.	Age.	Sex.	Occupation.	Country to which they belong.	Country of which they intend to become inhab's	Ship or Vessel, with the name of the Master or Commander.
New-York, David Gelston.	Mrs. S. Musson & child	40	female		G. Britain	U. States	Brig Junius, Geo. Dunton.
	Rachel Darnell	18	do	Servant	do	do	
	Miss E. Trott	11	male		do	do	
	Jeremiah Hurst	50	do	Merchant	do	do	
	A. J. Hill	20	do	do	do	do	
	John Q. Aymar	21	do	do	U. States	do	
	John L. Dunton	10	do		G. Britain	do	
	Douglas Par	10	female		Ireland	do	
	Margt. Tully	52	male	Farmer	do	do	
	Patrick Tully	20	do	Currier	do	do	Ship Erin, Wm. Newcomb.
	James O'Neil	22	female		do	do	
	Catharine O'Neil	23	male	Chandler	do	do	
	Michael Whelan	24	female		do	do	
	Alice Whelan	26	do		do	do	
	Margt. M'Kesey	23	do		do	do	
	Alice M'Govern	28	do		do	do	
	Mary Carter	50	male	Farmer	do	do	
	Garret Bryan	22	female		do	do	
	Judy Bryan	28	male	Laborer	do	do	
	Thomas Montgomery	47	female	Spinster	do	do	
	Ann Boyd & child	16	do	do	do	do	
	Julia Beglin	34	male	Farmer	do	do	
	Wm. Vance	25	do	do	do	do	
	Thomas Vance	20	do	do	do	do	
	Peter Morris	25	do	do	do	do	
	P. Donahoe	29	do	Merchant	do	do	
	Joseph Cunningham						

Name	Age	Sex	Occupation	Country	U. States	Ship
Mary Smith	18	female	Dress maker	Ireland	do	Ship Ann Maria, J. Waite.
Thomas Hawkey	29	male	Farmer	do	do	
Martha Griffin	27	female		do	do	
James Brady	22	male	Clerk	do	do	
Peter O. Maher	25	do.	Gentleman	do	do	
Wm. Findley	25	do.	do	G. Britain	do	
Wm. Lindsay & child	47	do.	Merchant	do	do	
Wm. Tait	15	do.	do	do	do	
Thomas Blakely	28	do.	do	do	do	
Wm. North	21	do.	do	do	do	
Edward Wood	24	do.	Gentleman	France	do	
Edward Vernon	28	do.	Merchant	do	do	
Alex. Weddeburn	23	do.	do	G. Britain	do	
Geo. Lund	53	do.		do	do	
E. Johnson	21	do.		do	do	
Jane Johnson	63	female		do	do	
John Bryers	21	male	Farmer	do	do	
James Stark	26	do	Clerk	do	do	
L. Ledgwick	28	do	Shoemaker	do	do	
James Kentworthy	26	do	Merchant	do	do	Ship Ann Rowland, R. Crocker.
M. Turner & 2 child.	24	female		do	do	
R. Tobias & 5 ch.	26	do		do	do	
Jane Graves	20	do		do	do	
Emily Newby & 5 ch.	30	do		do	do	
Mary Barfoot	8	do		do	do	
Betsey Casey	14	do		do	do	
Sarah Casey	3	do.		do	do	
Abraham Runberry	23	male	Merchant	do	do	
Wm. Brady	22	do	do	do	do	
Isaac Phillips	23	do	do	do	do	
Fred. Jonke	33	do	do	do	do	
John Fisher and son	30	do	do	do	do	
Benj. Jones	26	do		do	do	
Abraham Adams	21	do		do	do	
Henry Porter	22	do		do	do	
Ellen O. Hare & 2 ch.	23	female		do	do	
John Stinson	25	male	Farmer	do	do	Ship General Griswold, B. Meador.
Ann Stinson	27	female		do	do	

LIST of Passengers, &c.—Quarter ending September 30, 1820.

Custom House, with the name of Collector.	Names of Passengers.	Age.	Sex.	Occupation.	Country to which they belong.	Country of which they intend to become inhab's	Ship or Vessel, with the name of the Master or Commander.
New York. David Gelston.	Thomas Johnson	33	male	Doctor	G. Britain	U. States	Ship General Griswold, B. Meador.
	John Sugden	42	do	Farmer	do	do	
	Jonas Sugden	39	do		do	do	
	Sarah Sugden & ch.	39	female		do	do	
	Stephen Tatham	27	male		do	do	
	John Tatham	21	do		do	do	
	Catharine Tatham	14	female		do	do	
	C. Tatham & 2 ch.	41	do		do	do	
	A. Moore	35	do		do	do	
	Sarah Moore & 2 ch.	35	do		do	do	
	Benj. Sulcliff	24	male	Farmer	do	do	
	John Ride	30	do	do	do	do	
	Martha Ride & ch.	27	female		do	do	
	John Ride	36	male	Farmer	do	do	
	Thomas Riley	30	do		do	do	
	Mary Riley & 3 ch.	25	female		do	do	
	John Alcock	20	male		do	do	
	Samuel Snowden	27	do		do	do	
	Esther Snowden & 2 ch.	26	female		do	do	
	John Waw	38	male		do	do	
	C. Waw	34	female		do	do	
	H. Holmes & ch.	30	do		do	do	
	Richard Blackwell	23	male		do	do	
	John Burton	24	do		do	do	
	Wm. Mally	20	male		do	do	
	John Hushton	42	do		do	do	
	Marg. Hushton & ch.	39	female		do	do	

Name	Age	Sex	Occupation	G. Britain	U. States	Ship
Luke Tullum	30	male		G. Britain	U. States	Ship Agricola, J. Dunker.
Henry Blower	31	do		do	do	
H. Blower & 4 ch.	30	female		do	do	
Geo. Stemsfield	18	male	Farmer	do	do	
Matthew Fenwick	35	do	do	do	do	
Thomas Fenwick	30	do	do	do	do	
John Jackson	26	do	do	do	do	
Wm. Gill	30	do	Cloth manufa.	England	do	
Bridget Gill	20	female		do	do	
Richard Gunt	31	male		do	do	
R. Wheeler & 2 chil.	43	do		do	do	
Wm. Miller	45	do	Mason	do	do	
Mary Miller	35	female		do	do	
John Garness	48	male	Farmer	do	do	
Susanna Garness	40	female		do	do	
Thomas Goff	26	male		do	do	
Susanna Goff & ch.	21	female		do	do	
Thomas Wainler	24	male		do	do	
H. Snails & 7 chil.	40	female		do	do	
Thomas	32	male		do	do	
Mary do. and child	21	female		do	do	
Thomas Martindale	28	male		do	do	
John Reiley	40	do		do	do	
Thomas Butler	34	do		do	do	
Ann Butler & 2 ch.	34	female		do	do	
Thomas Artingstall	19	male		do	do	
Geo. do. & 5 ch.	29	do		do	do	
Maria Gill	19	female		do	do	
Richard Hoe	40	male	Bricklayer	do	do	
Mary do. & 5 chil.	30	female		do	do	
Geo. Dickinfield	27	male	Tailor	do	do	
Ellen do. & ch.	31	female		do	do	
Erastus Strong	31	male	Merchant	U. States	do	Sloop Chauncy, W. Bulkley.
Samuel Tarries	35	do	do	Portugal	Barbadoes	
Benj. Bausil	33	do	do	England	do	
Nathaniel Strong	26	male	do	do	do	
Paul Twigg	38	do	do	Ireland	Ireland	Brig Edward, James Hunt.
Cornelius Hunt	38	do	do	D. W. Indies	St. Croix	

New Haven, A. Bishop.

LIST of Passengers, &c.—Quarter ending September 30, 1820.

Custom House, with the name of the Collector.	Names of Passengers.	Age.	Sex.	Occupation.	Country to which they belong.	Country of which they intend to become inhab's	Ship or Vessel, with the name of the Master or Commander.
New Haven, A. Bishop.	Geo. Harwell	24	male	Shoemaker	U. States	U. States	Brig Edward, Jas. Hunt.
Plymouth, N. C. Levi Fagan.	John Crow	35	do	Mariner	do	do	Schr. Golden Age, J. Small.
	Charles Morillo	25	do	do	Spain	do	
Marblehead, Jos. Wilson.	James Orot	28	do	Fisherman	Ireland	do	Schr. Hannah.
	John Larger	23	do	do	do	do	
Newbern, N. C. F. Hawks.	Wm. Madison	23	do	Seaman	U. States	do	Schr. Milo, J. Kidmore.
	Julian Essage	40	do	do	do	do	Schr. Hornet, Alexr. M'Kown.
	Levi Sherman	30	do	do	do	do	Brig Columbia, J. Jesselyn.
	John Weaden	38	do	do	do	do	
	Robert Dickson	21	do	do	do	do	
	Geo. W. Slocumb	22	do	do	do	do	
	John M'Cartney	33	do	do	do	do	
	John Merry	35	do	do	do	do	

Number of Passengers arriving in the United States, during the 4th Quarter of the Year 1819, and the three first Quarters of the Year 1820, is 10,247.

INDEX

Burton, Francis W. 189
    Frederick 189
    John 286
    Joseph 183
    Mary 257
    Mary Ann 189
    Richard 188
    Richard 189
    William 189
    William F. 227
Burwell, Dorothy 267
    Geo. 267
Bushmann, H. 40
Busquit, Claude 34
Bussink, Ann Maria 37
    Doltage 36
Butcher, Wm. 202
Butler, Almira 73
    Ann 287
    Anna M. F. 73
    Elizabeth 73
    George 73
    I. 15
    J. 159
    John 15
    John 182
    Norman W. H. 73
    Pat 197
    S. 197
    Thomas 287
Butterfield, Nathl. 131
    Thomas 11
Butters, John 53
Butterville, George 255
Buttrick, Horatio G. 150
Byle, Ann 279
    Ellen 279
    John 279
Byyer, D. 171
Cabaret, J. 105
Cad, Peter 31
Cadele, Miss -- 238
Cadwalader, John 75
    Sarah 75
Caen, Mrs. -- 41
Cahanin, P. 250
Cail, Christian 236
Cailatt, -- 117
Cain, Elizabeth 231
Calamel, B. 237
Calder, Joseph 281
Callacan, Charles 67
Callahan, Patrick 215
Callender, James 100
Calvan, John 99

Calvert, John 208
    Thomas 60
Cambell, Ann 185
    James 185
    John 185
Cambery, Ruth 111
    Thomas 111
Camell, Charles 72
    Margaritta 72
Camerford, Fredk.
    W. 217
Cameron, G. 272
Camett, John 122
Camien, Ann 250
    Fredk. 241
    Michael 250
Cammal, William 221
Cammel, John 221
Campagen, -- 266
Campal, Daniel 272
Campanio, L. 239
Campbell, Mrs. --64
    Agnes 69
    B. 266
    Betsy 9
    Catha. 253
    Catharine 25.
    Catharine 275
    Colin 253
    Eliza 275
    Elizabeth 69
    Elizabeth 275
    Felix 126
    Hannah 275
    Hugh 195
    James 265
    Jane 69
    Jno. 112
    John 68
    John 125
    John 240
    John 262
    Mary 262
    Mary 275
    Nancy 25
    Niel 225
    Oliver 265
    Peter 110
    Samuel 57
    Sarah 265
    William 215
Canalle, John 264
Canchea, Julian 237
Candle, J. 168
Candles, Eleanor 251

Canes, Joaquin A. 8
Cannal, Terence 54
Cannapeau, Guillaume 91
Cannon, John 91
Canon, J. 179
Canovas, Jos. 33
Cant, Wm. 147
Canuet, William 225
Capanell, Lewis 99
Capers, William H. 227
Cappels, James 57
Capper, Wm. 127
Car, John 272
Carey, Dennis 205
Cargill, J. 90
    Wm. 90
Carleron, Jaques 47
Carlisle, Mrs. -- 52
    John 52
Carlos, -- 41
Carmon, C. 111
Carnachan, H. 274
Carnahl, I. I. George 180
Carnes, Miss -- 131
    Mrs. -- 131
    N. G. 54
Carney, Ann 247
    James 73
Caron, -- 33
Carpenter, Caroline 123
    Emily 124
    G. 24
    George 123
    Jane 123
    Joseph 26
    Louisa 123
    Mary Eliza 123
    Sarah 123
Carr, Andrew 141
    John 126
    John 141
    Robert 249
    Sarah 78
Carraras, John 225
Carrier, -- 97
Carrington, Ellen 180
Carroll, Letitia H. 199
    Letitia H. 201
    P. 191
Carse, J. 169
Carson, Frederick 37
    George 73
Carter, Ann 248
    Benj. 129
    John 129

Halloway, Isaac 269
  John 269
  Russell 269
Hallworth, Alfred 59
  Anna 59
Halrage, William 267
Ham, Samuel 183
Hamann, I. 40
Hamar, Wm. 249
Hamegos, Mrs. -- 48
  John 48
Hamilton, A. 85
  C. 107
  Elizabeth 265
  G. 85
  Giles 270
  J. 85
  James 97
  John 196
  L. G. 217
  Mary 11
  Mary 246
  R. 85
  Robert 253
  Sarah 105
  Wm. 61
Hammerton, Ellen 78
  George 78
  James 78
  John 78
  William 78
Hammet, G. H. 219
Hammond, Phebe 8
Hampton, James 240
  Sarah 13
Hancy, William 183
Handing, Ann 255
Handyside, David 115
Hanegan, Catharine 65
  Hugh 65
  Jr., Hugh 65
  Thomas 65
Hanford, Amelia 248
Hanlon, James 134
  Rose 134
Hanlow, E. O. 177
Hann, C. 168
  E. 169
  J. 168
  M. 168
  R. 168
  S. 168
  T. 168
Hanna, Nicholas 211
Hannagan, Catharine 184

Hannagan, Margaret 184
  Nicholas 184
Hannegan, Dennis 149
Hannon, G. 212
Hansbury, John 215
Hanselmann, Catherine 43
  Charles 43
  Earnest F. 43
  Jr., Earnest 43
  Frederica 43
  Gustave 43
  John E. 43
  Louisa 43
  Wilhelm. 43
Hanson, Dominicus 91
  Thomas 231
Hara, Oliver O. 225
Harang, Alexander 47
Harden, Alex. 185
  Eleanor 185
  Harding 186
  Jane 185
  John 185
  Mary 185
  Robert 186
  Sarah 185
  William 185
Hardman, Richard 60
Hardy, Miss -- 131
  Mrs. -- 131
  Hannah 256
  Henry 248
  Jane 248
  Mary 256
  Wm. 231
Hare, Alexander 32
  Ellen O. 285
  Jane 32
  Margaret 32
Hargrave, James 81
Harke, Chris. 125
Harkin, Dennis 198
  Dennis 201
Harlin, J. Van 25
Harlowe, Biddy 277
Harman, Mr. -- 216
  D. 183
Harme, S. L. 170
Harmon, Asa 97
  Asa, Jr. 97
Harnes, S. H. 175
Harnett, Ann 62
  John 62
Harnock, H. Hermanus 37
Harper, James 119

Harper, Robert 31
  Samuel 27
  Thomas P. 99
  William 183
Harrell, P. 159
Harrington, Mary 100
  William 71
Harriot, Colonel -- 269
  Samuel 121
Harris, -- 42
  A. 126
  Catharine 258
  Elizabeth 127
  J. H. 272
  James 258
  Mary 240
  Mary 272
  Samuel 58
  William 187
Harrison, Mrs. -- 68
  David 247
  James 137
  John 68
  John 69
  Joseph 113
  P. 159
  Robert 137
  Samuel 199
  Stephen 241
  Thomas 52
  Wm. 137
Harro, I. O. 79
  I. O., Jr. 79
  Isabel, 79
  M. 79
Harry, Francis 134
  Mary 134
Hart, A. M. D. 217
  Betsey 11
  Betty 130
  Hannah 130
  Thomas 135
  Thomas 264
Harthouse, P. A. 86
Hartigan, J. 158
  M. 158
Hartley, Ann 129
  Enelby 129
  Mary 129
  Sally 129
  Thomas 129
Hartneit, L. 40
Hartnet, Mary 139
Harvey, Ann 229
  Mary 103

Leech, Mary 106
Matilda 106
Wm. J. 106
Leeds, Abbey 5
William R. 21
Leek, Isabella 110
Lees, Mr. -- 200
John 92
Mary 92
Randall 101
Samuel D. 203
Lefevre, -- 239
A. 283
Louis 48
Peter 283
R. 283
Sarah 128
Thomas 128
Wm. 128
Leget, Hannah 231
John 231
Le Grand, Elizabeth 132
Le Grase, Jno. 203
Legross, -- 33
Leha, Mrs. -- 271
Frederick 271
Lehaggee, Isabella 246
Lehman, Johannes H. 37
Leigh, Jane 59
Thomas 119
Leigle, Lieut. -- 225
Leinwold, W. R. 171
Leister, Sarah 264
William 264
Le Lardeaux, Edmund 42
Le Mignon, -- 48
Lemon, Andrew C. 190
Arnisse 85
Elizabeth 190
Thomas 85
Lenas, D. 266
Leney, Martin 103
Lenike, Henry 50
Lenistor, -- 220
Bella 220
Lenniss, J. Van 147
Lenox, Isabella 110
James 257
Jane 278
Martha 278
Nancy 25
Lensen, George H. 280
Leon, Mrs. -- 281
Daniel 280
H. 139

Leonard, Fred'k. 231
G. 47
John 54
Thomas 65
Leopez, John 226
Leopolin, S. 173
Leoy, A. 233
Le Page, F. 93
Lepinoy, V. 78
Leplace, T. 113
Lerange, Charles 242
Le Roy, Mr. -- 200
Leroy, Pre. Riens 52
Lery, James 197
Lesbois, M. N. 239
Leslie, Charles 38
James 142
Lesslace, Jr.,
Theop's.
Lethingham, -- 238
Leunce, I. 161
Leusard, R. 170
Leuston, Jno. L. 217
Levan, George 94
Leven, Antonio 85
Levet, -- 39
Leviag, J. 240
Levillon, Felix 48
Levis, Elizabeth 59
Levy, Mr. -- 200
Chapman 30
Lewis, Abraham 263
Antonio 205
Catharine 111
Elisha 229
Eliza 9
George 61
John 214
Mathew R. 18
Richard 53
Thomas 7
Thomas 9
Thomas 241
William 9
Leyba, Don Jose M. 91
Leyden, Walter 189
Leyer, F. 172
Liberty, M. A. 17
Lick, Thomas 120
Lightburn, Nathl. 98
Liguiffin, -- 84
Liliendale, -- 260
Linch, J. 90
M. 90
Lincoln, Russel 223

Lindhest, Andrew 233
Lindsay, A. 155
Hugh 190
J. 155
M. 155
Mary 93
R. 155
Robert 155
Samuel 277
Wm. 285
Lindsey, R. J. 267
Linet, John 31
Linn, A. de 172
B. De 171
E. De 171
H. De 172
I. De 171
R. De 172
S. De 172
Lino, Lewis 104
Lippel, Frederick 233
Lippers, Elizabeth 35
Listre, Martha 264
Thomas 264
Litchfield, J. 216
Littemore, Mrs. -- 228
Elizabeth 229
Joseph 229
Robert 228
Little, A. 157
Eliza E. 228
I. 161
M. 157
Robert P. 197
Livasor, A. 172
Livingston, Hugh 96
Lloyd, Andrew 105
Mary 105
Robert 105
Samuel 105
Locke, S. T. 143
Lockhart, Robert 104
Lodge, Michael 229
Loefleur, Lapai 94
Logan, Richard 112
Loge, John 198
John 201
Logen, I. 155
M. 155
Logue, Edward 222
Lokaway, E. 245
Lomargan, Pierce 219
Long, Henry 41
James 193
Thomas 279

Siran, Margaret 255
Sirrnitt, John 25
Sirtane, Joseph 109
Skein, Philip 280
Skillings, N. W. 223
Skinner, Elizabeth 279
  Janet 279
  John 279
Skunkraft, J. Michael 37
Slack, Jane 263
  Seth 263
Slaiging, John 112
Slater, James 141
  John 220
Sligman, James 31
Sloan, Ann 221
  Thomas 221
Slocum, Wm. A. 26
Slocumb, Geo. W. 288
Sloer, T. 156
Slossen, James 136
Slotterbeck, J. G. 22
Small, Israel 91
  Jane 13
  John 57
  John 282
Smart, Abraham 282
  Alfred 197
  Elizabeth 281
  Esther 197
Smattes, Valentine 125
Smeton, Archibald 70
Smith, Captain -- 216
  -- 88
  Mr. -- 185
  Mrs. -- 20
  Mrs. -- 134
  Mrs. -- 216
  Mrs. -- 227
  Aaron 195
  Abigail 126
  Aleda 10
  Andrew 77
  Andrew 145
  Ann 228
  Anna 10
  Arthur 135
  Benjamin 149
  Bess 29
  Catharine 135
  Catherine 10
  Charles H. 145
  Daniel 144
  David 265
  Eliza 185

Smith, Elizabeth 10
  Elizabeth 145
  Ellen 263
  Fanny 134
  Frederick A. 145
  G. 154
  George 115
  George 189
  George 213
  George M. 145
  Grace 77
  H. K. 10
  Hannah 127
  Henry 37
  Henry H. 74
  Hugh 282
  I. 154
  I. H. 20
  Isabella 29
  J. 169
  James 26
  James 96
  James 135
  James 185
  James 191
  James 213
  James 257
  James 259
  James 272
  James 281
  James B. 249
  Jane 61
  Jane 77
  Jane 124
  Jane 185
  John 17
  John 35
  John 88
  John 105
  John 106
  John 116
  John 126
  John 134
  John 148
  John 217
  John 245
  John 252
  John 280
  John A. 145
  John L. 259
  John M. 142
  John M. 227
  John S., Jr. 26
  Jno. M. 150
  Jno. 216

Smith, Jos. T. 214
  Joseph 202
  Joseph 238
  Juliet 65
  Margaret 194
  Maria 27
  Maria Ann 202
  Maria C. 61
  Mark A. 92
  Mary 29
  Mary 65
  Mary 285
  Michael C. 145
  Nancy 77
  Parker 15
  Patrick 65
  Peter 150
  Phil. 267
  Phil., Jr. 267
  R. 90
  Rebecca 21
  Rebecca 29
  Richard 273
  Robert 134
  Robert 148
  Robert 185
  Robert 207
  Robert 228
  Rose 65
  Rose 73
  S. 90
  S. 245
  Sally 77
  Samuel 77
  Samuel 213
  Samuel 281
  Sarah 191
  Scott H. 131
  Silas 57
  Silas 224
  Susanna 145
  T. 21
  Thomas 29
  Thomas 58
  Thomas 252
  Thomas 267
  Thomas L. 283
  Thos. 202
  Wilhelmina 61
  William 10
  William 115
  William 214
  William H. 145
  William M. 21
  Wm. 128

Taylor, Thos. 206
William P. 223
Wm. 149
Telfair, Matthew 123
Templeton, Edward 144
Tenikin, E. 276
Tennant, Benjamin 256
Tentason, R. 133
Termpher, J. 167
Tesse, Geo. C. L. 232
Tessinden, Charles 41
Teyman, John H. 232
Thaine, Alexander 135
Thanny, Patrick 218
Thanter, John 53
Thatch, Ann 150
Thaxter, Edwd. 151
Emeline 54
Joshua 53
Mary 53
Mary 54
Sidney 98
William 54
Thayer, Hollis 221
Theband, I. I. 104
Thedan, Wm. 107
Therassen, Lewis 7
Lewis 131
Therby, J. 168
Therr, R. 216
Thirlkill, David W. 55
Thistlewait, Agnes 202
Ann 202
Thitts, Edward 213
Thomas, -- 287
A. 89
David 250
E. 89
Edward 244
I. 15
Isabel. 277
J. 89
Job B. 277
John 51
John 214
John 223
John 241
John 245
M. 155
Mary 287
Robert 268
Stephen 183
Thompson, -- 31
A. 167
A. 179

Thompson, Andrew 205
Christopher 53
Eliza 79
Eliza 187
Francis 135
George 277
Isab. 282
James 212
James 277
John 60
John 147
John 187
John 196
John 222
John 241
John 277
Jr., John 277
M. 167
Maria 277
Mary 29
Ralph 119
Robert 121
Robert 254
Samuel 149
Sarah 187
W. 167
Walter 13
Wm. 191
Wm. D. 13
Wm. H. 79
Thomson, Jane 76
Thorn, Catharine 262
Thornbrook, W. 178
Mrs. -- 178
Thorndike, Augustus 273
Thorner, E. Z. 155
Thornhill, S. 177
Thornton, Mary 257
Thorp, Sarah 264
Thorpe, O. H. 224
Thousley, S. 195
Thomas 195
Thurin, Supply C. 98
Ticke, Christian 232
Tiernan, Jr., L. 89
Tiffer, John M. 35
Tignabe, G. R. 70
M. R. 70
Tilden, Ezekiel 220
Tiley, Francis 25
Tilton, Wm. 111
Timing, Bridget 77
James 77
Tirtrou, Lt. -- 34
Tisseur, -- 240

Titius, Chas.
Henry 53
Tittus, Edward 281
Titus, John 215
Tobias, R. 285
Tobin, B. 159
E. 159
I. 159
John 207
P. 159
Todd, Charlotte 132
John 276
Sarah 219
William 195
Tomlin, William 188
Tompkins, Joseph 146
Tonkapff, B. I. 87
Tontaine, John 149
Topham, C. 199
Robt. 199
Topliff, Samuel 145
Totrat, -- 239
Mrs. -- 239
Toulmin, Amy 243
Tourtelot, A. 205
Towar, Thomas 194
Townsend, Jane 199
Thomas B. 199
Townshend, J. R. 201
James 201
Samuel 111
Thomas B. 201
Toy, John 142
Tracy, Catharine 65
Traddon, James 83
Trainer, Patrick 266
Tram, R. 133
Traman, Jos. 223
Traub, Auguste 42
Charles 42
Mary 42
Travers, William 225
Tray, Anthony 226
Trey, Frederick 49
Trial, Anthony 29
Trier, A. 161
Trimby, James 273
Troding, John P. 180
Trodsham, Samuel 133
Troop, Mathew 13
Trott, Miss E. 284
Elizabeth 228
Elizabeth 281
William H. 228
Trotter, Margaret 246

338

Trugant, James 91
Truitz, M. 170
Trumbull, Mrs. -- 125
  Ann 125
  George 125
  M. 125
Trustrum, Thomas 56
Tryer, A. 161
  E. 161
  I. 161
  M. 161
Tucker, Daniel 242
  James D. 228
Tudor, John 32
Tuill, Hugh 37
Tukelly, Mrs. -- 238
Tull, S. P. 70
Tullum, Luke 287
Tully, Charlotte E. 180
  Margt. 284
  Patrick 284
Tumblin, Catharine 21
  Elora 21
Tupess, C. 63
Tupper, Alfred 53
  Peleg 181
Turnbull, Thos. 141
Turner, Charles 111
  J. 129
  J. H. 64
  M. 285
  R. 115
  Richard 244
  Sarah 243
Turpin, Jos. 35
Turrell, J. 87
Turton, -- 41
Tusser, John J. 234
Tutt, Henry 51
Tuttle, Miss -- 146
Tutton, Joseph 101
Twigg, Paul 287
Twine, John 261
Tyler, Samuel 235
  William H. 213
Tyrell, W. 157
Tyson, Geo. 216
Ultz, John Michael 27
Underwood, Robert 25
  William 235
Upjohn, Aaron 148
  Mary 148
Ure, Andrew 14
  Eliza 102
  John 102

Ure, William 102
Urter, Eliz. 251
Valentine, Ann 274
  Ernest 232
Valhouniver, Chrn.
  G. 36
Vallet, John P. 225
Valloe, Gabriel 6
Valvey, Domingo L. 247
Vance, Margaret 209
  Rebecca 209
  Thomas 284
  Thos. 209
  Wm. 284
Vandenberg, Jasper 115
Vanderlendine, Cor-
  nel. 235.
Vanderlidst, A. 236
Vandston, Charles J. 134
  Edward 134
  J. J. 134
  Wm. J. 134
Vandusky, Gregory 20
Vanhoff, John O. 233
Vankaldrin, Mrs. --227
  M. 227
Vanseigoth, C. 35
Vaquelair, -- 35
Varndell, Martha 62
Vatteau, Gaspard 148
Veal, Ann 182
  Isaac 21
  James 182
  John 182
  Margaret 182
  Mary 21
  Richard 21
  Richard, Jr. 21
  Sarah 182
  Temperance 21
  William 21
Vedal, Sebastian 101
Vegel, Anna De 237
Vendane, James 255
Vendeberg, N. Solo-
  mon 37
Verger, Anter Dounen 36
Vergue, Antonio Cara 34
Vernard, Arthur N. 274
Vernon, Edward 285
Veron, S. 21
Veroni, Carlos de 74
Verplank, Philip 272
Very, Jones 221
Vetter, C. 234

Viall, Benjamin 66
Vickars, E. 168
  G. 168
Victor, -- 181
Viel, Nichodemus 114
Viera, Antonio 25
  Domingo 25
  Manuel 25
Vierzignean, -- 239
Viesch, M. 64
Vignardonne,
  Louisa 273.
Ville, Joseph A. B. 38
Villeneuve, Victor 108
Viller, L. De 171
Villivar, Felix 6
Villoniss, Henry 83
Villouet, Jn. Jn. 35
Vincent, Eliza 103
  Hannah 112
  Jane 103
  Josiah 112
  Michael 10
Violier, -- 49
Vite, Nichols 74
Vives, Gen. Don
  Fra. 101
Viviur, -- 47
Voltyn, Harsog M. 33
Vondamm, I. 40
Vouriot, Claude
  Francois 27
Voyel, Anna 99
  John 99
  John 214
Wachmuth, V. T. 205
Wacker, Frederick 45
  John L. 45
  Magdalen 45
Wade, Catharine 143
  John G. 97
  William 115
Waefer, N. 171
Wagener, C. 41
  John 233
Waggerman, -- 169
Wagner, Jacob 236
Wahrenberg, Jno. H. 51
Wainler, Thomas 287
Wainwright, Miss
  -- 131
  H. 87
  I. 177
  Jno. W. 131
Waldman, John B. 42

www.ingramcontent.com/pod-product-compliance
Lightning Source LLC
Chambersburg PA
CBHW060142280326
41932CB00012B/1603